DILEMMAS OF WEAK STATES

Contemporary Perspectives on Developing Societies

Series Editors
JOHN MUKUM MBAKU
Weber State University, USA
MWANGI S. KIMENYI
The University of Connecticut, USA and The Kenya Institute for Public Policy Research and Analysis, Kenya

The *Contemporary Perspectives on Developing Societies* series was founded to serve as an outlet for policy relevant research. Books published in this series provide rigorous analyses of issues relevant to the peoples of the Third World and their efforts to improve their participation in the global economy.

Also in this series

Akiba, O. (ed.) (2004), *Constitutionalism and Society in Africa.*

Kimenyi, M.S. and Meagher, P. (eds) (2004), *Devolution and Development: Governance Prospects in Decentralizing States.*

Kieh, Jr., G.K. and Agbese, P.O. (2004), *The Military and Politics in Africa: From Engagement to Democratic and Constitutional Control.*

Bangura, A.K. (2004), *Sweden vs Apartheid: Putting Morality Ahead of Profit.*

Kalu, K.A. (ed.) (2004), *Agenda Setting and Public Policy in Africa.*

Kimenyi, M.S., Mbaku, J.M. and Mwaniki, N. (eds) (2003), *Restarting and Sustaining Economic Growth and Development in Africa: The Case of Kenya.*

Darkoh, M.B.K. and Rwomire, A. (eds) (2003), *Human Impact on Environment and Sustainable Development in Africa.*

Mainuddin, R.G. (ed.) (2002), *Religion and Politics in the Developing World: Explosive Interactions.*

Saitoti, G. (2002), *The Challenges of Economic and Institutional Reforms in Africa.*

Mbaku, J.M., Agbese, P.O. and Kimenyi, M.S. (eds) (2001), *Ethnicity and Governance in the Third World.*

Ngoh, V.J. (2001), *Southern Cameroons, 1922-1961: A Constitutional History.*

Udogu, E.I. (ed.) (2001), *The Issue of Political Ethnicity in Africa.*

Magnarella, P.J. (2000), *Justice in Africa: Rwanda's Genocide, its Courts, and the UN Criminal Tribunal.*

Dilemmas of Weak States

Africa and Transnational Terrorism in the Twenty-First Century

TATAH MENTAN
Center for International Studies, Illinois Wesleyan University, USA

Routledge
Taylor & Francis Group
LONDON AND NEW YORK

First published 2004 by Ashgate Publishing

Reissued 2018 by Routledge
2 Park Square, Milton Park, Abingdon, Oxon, OX14 4RN
711 Third Avenue, New York, NY 10017, USA

Routledge is an imprint of the Taylor & Francis Group, an informa business

First issued in paperback 2018

ISBN 13: 978-0-815-38855-5 (hbk)
ISBN 13: 978-1-138-61939-5 (pbk)
ISBN 13: 978-1-351-15992-0 (ebk)

Contents

Preface

Poverty, unemployment and hopelessness create breeding grounds for terrorists (President of the United States, George W. Bush).

In the wake of September 11, the threat of terrorism has given weight to propositions like the one above by President George Bush. The problems of weak or failed nation-states have become an immediacy and importance that transcend their previous humanitarian dimensions. Since the early 1990s, wars in and among weak or failed states have killed about eight million people, most of them civilians, and displaced another four million. The number of those impoverished, malnourished, and deprived of fundamental needs such as security, health care, and education has totaled in the hundreds of millions.

Although the phenomenon of state failure or weakness is not new, it has become much more relevant and worrying than ever before. In less interconnected eras, state weakness could be isolated and kept distant. Failure had fewer implications for peace and security. Now, these states pose dangers not only to themselves and their neighbors but also to peoples around the globe. The reason, which is actually the argument of this work, is that such weak or failed states are prone to capture by special interest groups, like international terrorist networks or cartels. Therefore, preventing states from failing, and resuscitating those that have failed, are thus strategic and moral imperatives today.

The problem of the weak state is not new, either in the 21st century or in the history of mankind. But the post-seventeenth century world and now the post-Cold War world have introduced concepts and objective conditions that serve as turning points, which shape the meaning and the effects of nation-state weakness or failure. The first turning point was The Treaty of Westphalia (1648) that brought to a close the religious wars in Europe. It also marked the beginnings of the modern state, a territorial entity in which the governed and the governing form a compact of reciprocal rights and obligations. In return for individual security—basically freedom from fear, from want, from internal and external conflict, and a varying degree of latitude in their daily endeavors, the governed consent to follow the decrees of the rulers, to support the state structures through the commitment of personal time, energy, fiscal resources, and—in extremis—their lives for the survival of the state. This social contract, in whatever form it assumed, was reinforced in the 19th century by the concept of the 'volk,' in which the governed identify themselves as the state rather than a mere party to an agreement. This psychological fusion of governed with governing and the institutions of governance are called nationalism.

These developments occurred at the same time that Europeans were exploring and then intensively colonizing America, Asia, and Africa, often with no regard for the political structures and historic arrangements of these areas. In the 20th century, from the 1930s to 1991, the great powers were engaged in ideological struggles that strengthened nationalism within opposing nations and gave rise to competition for influence in countries in what was viewed as a zero-sum game for world dominance. These struggles emphasized the political-military arena, with the presumption that the best way to influence political leanings and gain diplomatic support was to provide military hardware and pledges of military support against external foes.

Of course, with the collapse of the Soviet Union in 1991, the zero-sum game in world politics ended, as for the most part did western interest in the southern hemisphere which was left awash in military hardware at the same time that it remained an economic backwater. But it is not the presence of large quantities of arms amassed during the Cold War era that leads to what is termed the weak or failed or failing state. Historically states 'fail' because they cannot prevent conquest by a rival state, a situation that may in fact result from the absence of sufficient quantities of armaments. But in the context of the late 20th century, a weak or failed or failing state is one in which the rulers either break the underlying contract by neglecting or ignoring the fundamental freedoms due their people or, as illustrated most graphically in Rwanda in 1994, actually direct the state apparatus against and encourage one segment of the population to hunt down another segment and massacre.

In either of these contexts, opposition thrives. Unrequited, this opposition is reinforced by armaments either stolen or seized from stocks already within the country or imported from other sources and other, past conflicts. Most often the arms of choice—cheap, plentiful, easily transported and used, low maintenance—are small arms, light weapons, and explosives. And the plentiful supply of such weapons, which continue to be churned out by 50 nations today, is what has earned this class of weaponry the sobriquet of conventional weapons of mass destruction.

From the preceding discussion, it immediately becomes apparent that arms do not weaken or cause states to fail; they do not necessarily even rise to the level of being the proximate catalyst. The root problem, exacerbated by the failure of even rudimentary nationalism to take hold in many artificially created countries, is the lack of responsibility among the governing group to fulfill the state's part of the social contract. But without question, it is the quest for power and availability of foreign arms supplier and trainer which translates the landscape of struggle from the political to the military realm, creating the 'complex emergencies' that involve huge population shifts, long term agricultural insufficiency and general economic collapse, and civil population decimation from disease, starvation, and direct conflict. Such dastardly situations render the state prone to capture by external forces like terrorists in search of recruits and sanctuary.

Weak or failed states are therefore incapable of projecting power and asserting authority within their own borders, leaving their territories governmentally empty. This outcome is troubling to an international system that demands a state's capacity to govern its space. Failed or weak states easily become 'breeding grounds of instability, mass migration, and murder' as well as witting or unwitting reservoirs and exporters of terror. The existence of these kinds of countries, and the instability that they harbor, not only threatens the lives and livelihoods of their own peoples but also endangers world peace.

The reason is that due to their weakness these states have nursed a demographic explosion that has produced a huge bulge of urbanized, unemployed young men and women-the most dangerous social group. The weak states also permit environmental stresses-especially shortages of cropland and fresh water-that have crippled farming in the countryside and forced immense numbers of people into squalid urban slums, where they are easy fodder for fanatics. The impact of these factors is compounded by (1) chronic conflicts that have shattered economies and created vast refugee camps; (2) the corrupt, incompetent and undemocratic African governments; and (3) the international political and economic system that is more concerned about Realpolitik, oil supply, and the interest of global finance than about the well-being of Africans. The receptivity of young

Africans to terror's radical message is enormously increased by this legacy of conflict, social dislocation and poverty in the continent.

Tatah Mentan

Acknowledgments

Whatever originality this study may claim is a matter of building rather than of brick making. Other scholars made most of the bricks for the building. My major task, therefore, has been to fit the bricks together into a coherent structure dictated by contemporary events.

In other words, I have many 'ancestors' on the study of the state in Africa. These are the brick builders. And, I had to review each brick for this new building according to contemporary circumstances dictated by transnational terrorism. This process of reviewing bricks points to one thing: I owe so much to so many people that personal acknowledgments would be either invidious or unduly voluminous.

However, bread-and-butter etiquette compels the giving of thanks to my sponsors, the Lentz Peace Board, for sponsoring my one-year post-doctoral fellowship at the Center for International Studies, University of Missouri-St. Louis. The grant enabled me to work on the first draft. My hearty gratitude also goes to the Director of the Center for International Studies, Professor Joel Glassman, and his staff for their unfailing assistance throughout my stay at the Center.

I am heavily indebted to Professor John Mukum Mbaku whose scholarly weight, critical experience in book publishing and typesetting skills were selflessly deployed to ensure that the manuscript was turned into what it is now worth. I am equally indebted to Godwin Moye Bongyu and Esther Azaa for their unfailing encouragement throughout the research and writing phases.

This heavy debt of gratitude notwithstanding, I take full responsibility for the views expressed in this book.

Acronyms

DARPA	Defense Advanced Research Projects Agency
ECOWAS	Economic Community of West African States
FISA	Foreign Intelligence Service Act
FLN	National Liberation Front (pre-independence liberation movement in Algeria)
GIA	Armed Islamic Group
GII	Global Information Infrastructure
IIRO	International Islamic Relief Organization
IPCI	Islamic Propagation Center International
IPS	International Press Service
IRCC	Iranian Revolutionary Command Council
MDJT	Movement for Democracy and Justice in Chad
MILF	Moro Islamic Liberation Front
MYM	Muslim Youth Movement
NEPAD	New Partnership for African Development
NIF	National Islamic Front
NII	National Information Infrastructure
PCASED	Program of Coordination and Assistance on Security and Development
PIJ	Palestine Islamic Jihad
PIRA	Provisional Irish Republican Army
PNA	Palestinian National Authority
RDD	Radiological Dispersal Device
SOE	Special Operations Executive
UNAMSIL	United Nations Mission in Sierra Leone

This book is dedicated to my dear wife Charity, and to my beloved children, Yiefon, Keleghai, Ntsondeh, Mom, and Berinyuy, who had to live without a husband and father for one year while I was at the University of Missouri-St. Louis completing research for the book.

About the Author

Tatah Mentan is Associate Professor of Politics and Communication. He has a B.A. (Hons.) in Journalism and Mass Communication from the University of Yaoundé, Cameroon, and an M.Sc. and Ph.D. in Political Science from the University of Nigeria, Nsukka. To him, scholarship can, but possibly should not, exist in a social vacuum. He thus, as a Theodore Lentz Peace Fellow, recognizes activism as a valid academic undertaking. He has been working and publishing books in collaboration with research associates and colleagues on a couple of different approaches, mainly in the area of *democratization, civil-military relations, peace and conflict media, as well as ethnicity and the structure of political conflict in Africa.* He is currently researching the impact of ravaging globalization on the state in underdeveloped societies. His belief that learning can and should impinge on the world will be strongly tested in this book where he has offered his reflections on the political realities of the weak state in Africa and its proneness to capture by external forces like marauding transnational terrorist cartels.

1

Introduction

What has Africa got to do with international terrorist cartels, anti-American terrorism, terrorist finance networks, even weapons of mass destruction? Everything! Many young people in Africa who comprise over 60 percent of the population in some countries see their future being sacrificed. Where do they turn? In northern Nigeria, for example, clashes between Muslims and Christians have become increasingly frequent since the 1980s. A confrontation, involving a group of young men who declared themselves followers of al Qaeda, took place in late December 2003 in the state of Yobe, which adopted Sharia law in 2000. The fighting forced more than 10,000 people to leave their homes, according to the Nigerian Emergency Aid Agency of February 20, 2004.

The original riot was caused by a group of religious students called al-Sunna wal-Jamma (Followers of the Prophet) who demand the establishment of an Islamic state. Their leader is called 'Mullah Omar.' They then fled from Nigerian army units, only to regroup in neighboring Niger. These confrontations arouse a profound unease in several of Nigeria's neighbors, like Cameroon, Niger itself and Chad.

Indeed, across the region, there are more and more missionaries from monotheist religions like Pakistanis and bearded Middle Eastern men with a fiery version of Islam, evangelical Christians permanently on 'crusade.' These 'fishers of men' are astute at exploiting misery and deft at enticing the young and unemployed of both sexes into becoming recruits, and occasionally fanatical exponents, of their doctrines.

Similar cases are widespread in much of Africa and in current conditions of political tension, they may provide opportunities for training sites for people in whom religious certainty and hunger mix into a dangerous cocktail. The great majority of African citizens exist in poverty and are locked under corrupt leaders who maintain control through tribalism, fraud, corruption, prebendalism and violence. In this perspective, Africa can be seen as a giant experiment in the genesis of terrorism. The seeds are being sown everywhere.

Africa is the soft underbelly for transnational terrorism. The bombing of U.S. embassies in Kenya and Tanzania in 1998 as well as the Paradise Hotel in Kenya in 2002 demonstrates that anti-American and anti-Israeli terrorism is alive and well in Africa. Al Qaeda and other terrorist cells are active in East, Southern, North and West Africa. These cells plan, finance, train for, and execute terrorist operations in many parts of the continent, not only in Sudan and Somalia. They seek uranium, diamonds, chemical weapons components and tooth-comb the continent from Libya to South Africa in search of renegade nuclear, biological and chemical weapons experts. Indeed, Africa is captive to these networks of terrorists.

Why? Terrorists take advantage of Africa's porous borders, weak law enforcement and security services and nascent and inefficient judicial institutions to move men, weapons and money around the globe. They take advantage of poor, disillusioned populations, often with religious and/or ethnic grievances, to recruit for any jihad against 'infidels' and 'Crusaders.' The bomb attacks on U.S. embassies in Nairobi and Dar-es-Salaam killed 224 people, most of them Africans. And the quotation above therefore clearly points out a few things about the state in Africa: (1) the geographical, religious, etc. ramifications of the power relations between African states and transnational terrorism; (2) terrorism today has become a problem with incalculable dimensions not only for both Africa and America but also for all people of the world; (3) the impotence of the state in Africa when faced with the strikes of terrorist cartels; and (4) conditions in African states that facilitate the realization of terrorist programs.

The U.S. embassy and Paradise Hotel attacks confirmed an emerging trend in terrorism: the infliction of mass, indiscriminate casualties by enigmatic adversaries, striking far beyond terrorism's traditional operational theaters in Europe and the Middle East. By contrast, terrorism in the past was generally practiced by a collection of individuals belonging to an identifiable organization with a clear command and control apparatus, who had a defined set of political, social or economic objectives. Radical leftist organizations such as the Japanese Red Army, Germany's Red Army Faction, Italy's Red Brigades as well as ethno-nationalist terrorist movements like the Abu Nidal organization, the IRA, and the Basque separatist group ETA, reflected this stereotype of the traditional terrorist group. They issued communiqués taking credit for—and explaining—their actions, and however disagreeable or distasteful their aims and motivations were, their ideology and intentions were at least comprehensible. Most significantly, however, these familiar terrorist groups engaged in highly selective and mostly discriminate acts of violence. In order to attract attention to themselves and their causes, they targeted for bombing various symbolic targets representing the source of their animus (e.g., embassies, banks, and national airline carriers) or kidnapped and assassinated specific persons whom they blamed for economic exploitation or political repression.

The terrorist strikes in Kenya and Tanzania radically changed the attitudes of Africans and non-Africans alike toward networked or transnational terrorism in the continent. The extent of the bloodletting shocked the whole world. No one expected the carnage and brutality that attended the strikes. Worse still its perpetrators have shown no remorse. People are asking questions about the capacity of African states to cope with such terrorist networks on African soil.

This study seeks to answer these questions. It suggests that past attempts to answer them failed because they are based on inadequate understanding of the phenomenon of transnational terrorism in Africa. Previous attempts tended to see terrorism everywhere and to conceive it in a self-explanatory manner. They viewed terrorism essentially as a given or vaguely as liberation struggles against one foreign power or another and thus took very little account of its substratum. From this complacent point of view the obvious conclusion is that interests arising from state identities differ from one another because of socio-cultural and economic differences among the relevant states, at times originating from colonial heritage or religious affiliations. Hardly any serious thought is therefore given to what attracts terrorists to penetrate African states, how and why individuals embrace terrorist causes in the first place, and the origin of the group interests in joining terrorist cartels. Thus, the weakness of the African state and its proneness to capture by external forces, especially terrorist network interests is the focus of our study. 'Strong' and/or 'weak' states exist in Africa. And other scholars have examined both.

Review of the literature

Today, the state in Africa is the most demonized social institution. In fact, it is vilified for its weaknesses, its over-extension, its interference with the smooth functioning of the markets, its repressive character, its dependence on foreign powers, its ubiquity, its absence, etc. Indeed, once the cornerstone of development in Africa, the state is now the millstone around efficient markets. It is, according to the numerous epithets, the 'shell state,' the 'rentier state,' the 'overextended state,' the 'parasitical state,' the 'predatory state,' the 'lame leviathan,' the 'patrimonial state,' the 'prebendal state,' the 'crony state,' the 'kleptocratic state,' the 'inverted state,' the 'criminalized state,' the 'captured post-colonial state,' 'sultanic state,' 'praetorian state,' 'overdeveloped state,' and so on.

This inflation of epithets is not a novel phenomenon. It predates Africa's crisis years. Early criticism of the state in Africa came from the neo-Marxists whose own epithets to describe the pathological condition of the African state included the 'petty bourgeois state,' the 'neo-colonial state' and the 'dependent state.' The multiplicity of epithets demonstrates the collapse from grace of the African state. Current arguments contend that the state has become dysfunctional in terms of the management of larger societal issues and also a real nuisance to the citizenry. Evidence of the 'withdrawal' from state-dominated economic and social spaces (Chazan, 1988a; Chazan, 1988b; Rothchild, 1994) has been advanced. Others even conceive of developmental schemes that completely circumvent or marginalize the state as non-governmental organizations, the informal economy, the private sector and local communities proceed almost surreptitiously with addressing issues of poverty and development without the obstruction of the state.

The shift in attitudes is due to the dismal performance of African states during the social and economic crisis as well as a number of ideological, paradigmatic and structural shifts in both the domestic and international spheres. On the ideological level there has been the dramatic ascendancy of neo-liberalism. This is due partly as a result of the rise and political triumph of the neo-conservative movements riding on the discontent with the welfare state and the inflationary impact of Keynesian solutions. Perceptions of welfarism and state interventionism spilled over into the business of aid. Thus, it is not surprising that the aid discourse has embraced some of the anti-statism of neo-liberalism. Furthermore, at the structural level, the process of globalization has forced all African governments to rethink and restructure the state-market relationships in their respective countries and to pay greater homage to 'market forces.' The demonization of the state in Africa is attributable to the fact that it was viewed as 'developmental' from the word go. This developmental conception had two components: one ideological, another structural. It is this ideology-structure nexus that distinguishes developmental states from other forms of states.

The component of ideology holds that such a state is essentially one whose ideological underpinning is 'developmentalist' with its 'mission' being that of ensuring economic development, usually interpreted to mean high rates of accumulation and industrialization. Such a state is legitimized by its ability to promote sustained development. This sustained development is understood to mean 'the steady high rates of economic growth and structural change in the productive system, both domestically and in its relationship to the international economy' (Castells, 1992, p. 55). At this ideational level, the élite must be able to establish an 'ideological hegemony,' so that its developmental project becomes, in a Gramscian sense, a 'hegemonic' project to which key actors in the nation adhere voluntarily.

One recurrent argument often advanced by Africans themselves relates to the lack of an ideology of development anchored in some form of nationalist project. Franz Fanon's (1966 and 1967) outbursts against the ideological numbness of the emergent ruling classes in Africa remain among the most sustained statements of this position. Many other analysts have elaborated on this lacuna. Bade Onimode talks of the 'ideological vacuum' that he attributes to petty bourgeois commitment to their class interests and their fear of 'revolutionary pressures,' to the obscurantism of imperialist powers and to mass illiteracy which imposes a culture of silence and passivity and inhibits popular demand for ideological discourse (1988). Thus, Claude Ake held strongly to the view that the ideology of development was exploited as a means of reproducing political hegemony; it got limited attention and served hardly any purpose as a framework for economic transformation (1996). For some, the lack of ideology is inherent to personal rule under which loyalty is not to some overriding societal goals but to individuals, often holding highly idiosyncratic ideologies that they themselves flout with impunity and with no moral qualms (Jackson and Rosberg, 1982; Sandbrook, 1986).

Consequently, such leaders are said to have no moral basis on which they could demand enthusiastic and internalized compliance to whatever 'national project' they launched. In the more extreme versions the lack of ideology of development is evidence of the cultural rejection of development by African leaders and their followers. Still other analysts (e.g., Mkandawire, 1997) have argued that for most of the first generation of African leaders 'development' was certainly a central preoccupation.

The quest for an ideology to guide the development process inspired African leaders to propound their own idiosyncratic and often incoherent 'ideologies' to 'rally the masses' for national unity and development. If such ideologies are still absent it is definitely not for lack of attempting. For some, such an ideology has essentially served purposes of mystification and obfuscation. Thus Gavin Williams (1997, p. 286), writing about the ruling class in Nigeria, states cynically:

> The Nigerian bourgeoisie lacks the commitment of a religious socialist or nationalist character of the rationalizing, capital accumulating, surplus expropriating classes of Britain, Russia, Germany, or Japan during their period of industrialization. Perhaps it is this, which lies behind the repeated call for a 'national ideology', which seeks to subordinate the energy of the people behind a single national goal. In fact the Nigerian bourgeoisie do have an ideology, in the sense of a theoretical legitimization of the status quo. It is found in the concept of 'development.'

William's cynical view sidesteps the fact that by political commitment and social origins most of the leaders were deeply committed to the eradication of poverty, ignorance and disease, which formed an unholy trinity against which nationalist swords were drawn in the post-colonial era. The first generation of African leaders concentrated their energies on the politics of nation building. Today, there are signs of a new leadership whose focus is on the economics of nation building.

The state-structure component emphasizes the capacity of the state to implement economic policies wisely and effectively. Such a capacity is determined by institutional, technical, administrative and political performance. Undergirding all these is the autonomy of the state from social forces so that it can use these capacities to devise long-term economic policies unencumbered by claims of myopic private interests. It is usually assumed that such a state should, in some sense, be 'strong' and enjoy 'relative autonomy' from key social actors.

The quest for a 'strong state' in the development process was a dominant feature of the 'modernization' literature. Such a state was contrasted to what Myrdal (1968) referred to as the 'soft state' that had neither the administrative capacity nor the political wherewithal to push through its developmental project. And, finally, the state must have some social anchoring that prevents it from using its autonomy in a predatory manner and enables it to gain adhesion of key social actors in order that it could play any role as a 'strong' state or 'developmental state.'

Our appreciation is that this conception of the state as a developmental one runs the risk of being tautological. Evidence that the state is development-oriented is drawn deductively from the performance of the economy. This produces a definition of a state that equates economic success to state strength while measuring the latter by the presumed outcomes of its policies. It has led to myopic concentration of analysis around success to the neglect of the 'trial and error' nature of policy-making. Another risk is that the state is deified into an omnipotent and omniscient leviathan, always getting what it wants. Indeed, the definition must include situations in which exogenous structural dynamic and unforeseen factors can torpedo genuine commitments and efforts made by the state. Such a definition allows for poor performance due to exogenous factors or miscalculations in fending off exogenous forces.

For instance, the spectacular success of the East Asian 'Four Tigers' led to a re-reading of the role of the state in the development process. It also raised the question of replicability of their policies and experiences in other developing countries. The lessons drawn from these experiences were cited as irrefutable evidence of the superiority of essentially laissez-faire policies. More specifically, reliance on market forces and the adoption of market-driven export-oriented development strategies was said to have led to efficient exploitation of the comparative advantage of these countries in cheap labor (Balassa, 1971; Corden, 1971; Little, Scitovsky and Scott, 1970; Little, Cooper, Corden and Rajapatirana, 1993).

The first presentation for African consumption of the lessons from Asia from the neo-liberal perspective was the report issued by the World Bank in 1981, which has been the Holy Bible or definitive document on structural adjustment for some 20 years. There have been amendments, subtractions, additions and refinements of the argument, but as the World Bank's 1994 report on adjustment in Africa clearly suggested, the World Bank was almost congenitally tied to the core argument of the Berg Report with its faith in the market and a minimalist view of the state. The 1994 Report insisted on the dichotomy made in African policy-making between state and market. This dichotomy was said to have vitiated 'development planning' in Africa over the years.

Beautiful as the Berg Report and its recommendations may be, they ignored problems of human capital; possibilities of the state 'crowding in' private investment; market imperfections and failures, industrial policy, etc. The failure of structural adjustment programs has compelled even the most dogmatic institutions to recognize the positive role the state can play in the process of development beyond acting as Africa's 'night watchman.'

It is perhaps because of this failure that Peter Lewis (1996), discussing the repricability of the Asian model, argued that while some aspects of this model (for instance, greater political insulation of economic policy makers) could reasonably be achieved in African countries, the extensive co-coordinated economic interventions of the East Asian states are well beyond the administrative faculties of most African governments. Similar deep feelings are explicitly expressed by Callaghy (1993), who argues that African states lack the capacity to pursue the statist model of Asia since Africa is hemmed in as it tries to navigate between weak states and weak markets and to do so with open political structures.

The result of the incapacity of African states has been: the economic crisis of the 1970s; the demise of the argument for state intervention; the ideological hegemony of neo-conservatism in key funding institutions and donor countries, the failure of development planning in many countries; religious strife, and stagnation. All these point to government failure as more insidious than the market failure that state policies had purportedly been designed to correct. The vacuum left by the disabling of the state in Africa by structural adjustment programs is being filled by marauding terrorists with messianic ideologies.

State failure makes it possible for mineral resources in Africa to fuel some of the world's most brutal wars, sustain the illegal arms trade and those mercenaries and militias who have tortured, detained, sexually exploited, intimidated and enforced the displacement of populations. Poorly enforced arms laws and trade laws and an almost unregulated shipping industry open to abuses bind together minerals, weapons smuggling and war, and keep the business open to criminal cartels in the continent.

In terms of mounting religious feuds, Muslims from Algeria-Morocco to Kenya are apparently increasingly convinced that they will never be allowed to participate fully in national governments, let alone practice their faith freely. A generation of younger, well-educated Muslim leaders, frustrated by political corruption, social decline, and the growing power of Westerners in Africa, are either taking over established Muslim organizations or starting their own. Many keep in close touch with the larger world through satellite TV and the Internet. And, contrary to popular Western assumptions, they generally have little respect for Saudi-style Wahhabi-inspired ideas about Islam.

Yet many of these leaders are outraged at growing repression—and increasingly link that repression to the West, particularly the United States and their national governments. The rhetoric of reform—even among moderate Muslims—has grown more strident and less tolerant. If change won't come peacefully, a mounting number of these new leaders are willing to bring change by force.

These trends have long histories that differ with each nation. But the deeper social and political changes beneath appear to have developed rapidly over the past few years and share growing similarities across African nations. Recent violence in Somalia, Algeria, Egypt, Mauritania, Morocco, Nigeria, Tunisia, Kenya, and Uganda will be just the opening shots of a longer, bloodier series of wars—struggles in which several important African nations may fracture along Muslim/Christian religious lines.

In fact, the disabling of the state in Africa has dashed all the pious hopes and grand designs of the modernization school. The modernization school dominated development studies in the 1950s and 1960s. It was usually assumed that, once colonialism had shaken these underdeveloped countries out of their traditional stupor, they would embark on a process of modernization that would make them traverse certain 'stages,' as spelt out by W.W. Rostow, in his famous *The Stages of Economic Growth: A Non-Communist Manifesto* (1960), towards a full-fledged capitalist system. Considerable empirical work was produced indicating certain historical regularities associated with economic growth. The idea was that 'Traditional society' might set up barriers but these would be overcome by modernizing élites, aid and foreign capital. The first generation of post-colonial 'development plans' were couched in a language that suggested conscious efforts to move economies from one 'stage'—usually the 'pre-take off' stage towards the 'take-off' stage. In all this, the center stage was occupied by 'modernizing élites' guided by the aspirations of nation building and development. The state was seen as not only desirable but possible and able to be facilitated by training programs, aid, and military support (Gendzier, 1985).

By the mid-1970s, this linear and illusionary view of capitalist development began to lose its dominance largely due to the onslaught of the Dependence School that generally denied that capitalism in the periphery could play its historical progressive role in the sense of leading to an increase in the productive forces of social labor and in the socialization of labor.

More significant was the fact that this perspective ruled out the possibility of developmental states in Africa that were either led by a national bourgeoisie or capable of nurturing one. This exclusion, of course, meant that either transnationalization processes had obviated the need for such a national bourgeoisie or the asymmetric nature of center-periphery relations tended to produce class structures that were not conducive to dynamic accumulation and, more specifically, produced a bourgeoisie that was historically condemned to be no more than a 'comprador bourgeoisie' subservient to the interests of foreign capital (Leys, 1975; Nabudere, 1981; Shivji, 1980). Such a ruling class could not produce the 'captains of industry' needed for the mobilization of resources and acquisition of technology as exemplified by the Asian Tigers.

The question that emerged from this analysis was: is the aberration only temporary so that one could envision a set of policies and events that would turn this state into a 'normal bourgeois state,' or was the historical conjecture such that the position of these peripheral African states would remain pathological and that the only solution would be some kind of 'delinking' from the 'world system?' Most of the countries that openly pursued the capitalist path were considered 'neo-colonial' and so beholden to foreign interests that they could not possibly pursue something so eminently 'national' as development. Versions of 'associated dependent development' appeared in literature on Africa to accommodate the high growth rates in such countries as Côte d'Ivoire (Amin, 1967) and Kenya (Leys, 1987). This argument was the more persuasive when informed by the view that the 'revolutionary pressures' were intense and that the revolution was around the corner (Ake, 1978). The actuality of the African revolution, according to Ake, meant that radical change was imminent.

The change has not been imminent because of neo-Weberian accounts of state-society relations or by public choice formulations on how the rational pursuit by individuals of their interests has led rather to lack of autonomy of the state and African malaise due to capture by exogenous societal interests. The neo-Weberian critique has focused on the failure of African states to establish themselves as rational-legal institutions and to rise above the 'patrimonialism' that affects all of them. This failure is irrespective of ideological claims and the moral rectitude of individual leaders.

The neo-Weberian highlights the flawed nature of the performance of the post-independence state, especially in its relationship with a society at large from which it has not been able to distance itself adequately so as to perform efficiently. In these accounts, 'market failure' central to development economics and 'government failure' central to neo-classical economists are replaced by something more debilitating and more recalcitrant. This is 'societal failure' signaled not only by lack of 'social capital,' but also by the disease-like spread of this societal malaise into both market and state structures. Termite-like, Africa's primordial and patrimonial relationship (what Göran Hyden refers to as the 'economy of affection') has eaten into the very core of the edifice of modern administration rendering it both weak and incoherent. In Hyden's (1983, p. 21) words:

> the economy of affection—is an underestimated threat to the macro-economic ambitions of either capitalism or socialism in Africa. Derived from a mode of production in which the structural interdependence of the various production units is minimal or nil it has no provision from a systemic superstructure to keep it together. Instead the economy of affection is a myriad of invisible micro-economic networks which, if allowed to penetrate society, gradually wear down the macro-economic structures, and eventually the whole system. The threat of the affective networks stems from their invisibility and intractability.

Faced with redistributive activities imposed by affective relations, prebendalism or clientelism, the state has not been able to provide the bureaucratic order and predictability that capitalists need if they are to engage in long-term investment.

To the Asian 'autonomous state' is therefore juxtaposed the African 'lame Leviathan' (Callaghy, 1987). The state is thus said to be so porous and 'penetrated' by society, so beholden to particularistic interest groups, so mired in patron-clientelist relationships, and so lacking in 'stateness' that it cannot pursue the collective task of development. And the task of development demands insulation from such redistributive obligations. These relationships constitute what Bayart (1993) terms the 'politics of the belly' that has paralyzed African economies. Of the 'governmentability' (i.e., mode of governance) produced by this 'eating,' Bayart (1993, p. 268) states that 'it has crushed most of the strategies and institutions, in particular the Christian churches, the nationalist parties and the civil services, which have worked for the advent of a modern Africa. The experiences of governments which attempted to break free from their grip have either not lasted a long time or have in their turn been absorbed by its practices' of failure as a 'political shell for capitalism' (Mentan, 1999, p. 161).

By way of summation, the reasons for the weakness of the African state derive from its (1) dependence; (2) lack of a coherent ideology; (3) 'softness;' (4) lack of technical and analytical capacity to comprehend impending consequences of state actions in the current international system; (5) hostile international environment that is impatient with local African needs; and (6) poor record of state performance.

These are the categorizations of the state in Africa that scholars have come up with. But, the works reviewed do not spell out what are the contemporary pressures weakening the African state in the post-Cold War era. Nor do they point out the predatory relationships between weak African states and external forces like transnational terrorism plunging national societies into, and sustaining, wars in the region. The study of the connection between state weakness and its falling prey to being host and victim of terrorist cartels is the gap this work aims at filling.

Objectives

The overall objective for this work is to develop a fundamental understanding and explanation of conditions of weak African states and their proneness to capture by external forces—especially networked terrorism. Ultimately, the work is intended to advance the state of research on state science and to provide scientific information for those making decisions concerning conditions of states and conflict management in permissive environments like Africa. Specific objectives of this multidisciplinary work are:

- To improve understanding of weak state processes by integrating existing and new information into the application, testing, and refinement of theories and models of external penetration and capture of people and environments;
- To fill gaps in present knowledge of state science in Africa through further data collection, and through analyses of spatial and temporal trends in the wake of September 11, 2001;
- To test current methods, and develop new ones, for characterizing state processes in the face of overbearing transnational influence.

With these objectives in mind, this book therefore has as its major argument that there are connections between state weakness and its inability to resist external pressures or penetration. Put differently, the argument of this book is that the state in Africa is weak and incoherent and therefore prone to capture by special interest groups, particularly transnational terrorist organizations. There are two major reasons supporting this argument.

First, these states provide convenient operational bases and safe havens for transnational terrorists. Terrorist organizations take advantage of weak states' porous borders, of their weak or nonexistent law enforcement and security services, and of their ineffective judicial institutions to move men, weapons and money around the globe. They smuggle out precious resources like diamonds and narcotics that help fund their operations. Terrorist organizations may also recruit foot soldiers from local populations, where poor and disillusioned youth often harbor religious or ethnic grievances.

Africa offers several cases in point. Sudan has served as a sanctuary and staging ground for al Qaeda and other global terrorist organizations. It has a radical Islamist government. Somalia, lacking any effective central government, has afforded safe operational space to affiliates of al Qaeda. Al Qaeda and other transnational terrorist organizations have hidden effectively in various African states (including Egypt, Tunisia, Algeria, Kenya, Tanzania, Uganda, South Africa, Côte d'Ivoire, Mauritania, and elsewhere), where they planned, financed, trained for, and successfully executed terrorist operations against American and allied targets.

A second reason is that weak African states often spawn wider regional conflicts, which can substantially weaken security and retard development in their sub-regions. The conflicts in Sierra Leone, Congo, and Sudan, each largely internal in nature, have also directly involved several other states. In some extreme cases, these conflicts have exacerbated conditions in neighboring countries, accelerating, though rarely precipitating, their failure. Examples include the impact of the Sierra Leone conflict on Guinea, and Congo's on Zimbabwe.

This argument concerning the interconnectedness of state weakness and attendant terrorist penetration, capture and use of the porous African environment compels the raising of a few exploratory questions, some even very obvious: Are there any Transnational Terrorist Cartels in Africa? Why is Africa host or victim of this brand of terrorism? Is Africa only victim of circumstances or there is more to its links with this networked variant of terrorism? The task of this work is to seek empirical answers to these questions.

Relevance to political science

Terrorists menaced human beings and states during the latter part of the twentieth century. Some people even believed that 1994 was the beginning of the end of terrorism. There was warrant for such belief. Ilyich Ramirez Sanchez, publicly known all over the world as 'Carlos the Jackal,' was arrested in Sudan (Africa) and handed over to the French police during the summer of that year. The handover was interpreted as a sign of willingness of states to collaborate in ending decades of bloody terrorist activities around the world. This optimism has faded into oblivion.

The capture of Carlos did not put an end to terrorism. Terrorism is still very much alive today. But its forms are changing very rapidly. Its lethal force is also very disquieting to mankind. And, an evaluation of current conditions as well as a prediction of future trends can offer fresh insights to policymakers and citizens in the twenty-first century. Citizens in the twenty-first century even face threats of frightful nuclear terrorism. Such threats were written off decades ago as either too expensive or too delicate for terrorist groups to afford. But, with bomb-grade plutonium finally 'on sale' today, the possibility of networked terrorist groups accumulating enough material for building a bomb is not remote.

Of course, the possibility of building such a bomb in open societies like the United States may be rare. It is even risky. But, it is very easy for such a weapon to be built in a permissive society captured by terrorist agendas. And weak Third World states are very easy targets. This likelihood warranted this study to examine those conditions that attract terrorist leaders of the likes of Osama bin Laden and Carlos the Jackal to seek sanctuary in Africa. Definitely, terrorist ideologies of the extreme left toward fundamentalism of the extreme right still exist. Both types of right or left terror still have a place in international politics. What is not yet clear is the pattern of terrorism in the twenty-first century. Therefore to understand what form terrorism may take in the twenty-first century it is essential to bring out what it has been before and in the twentieth century (the past).

It is, of course, the place of political science to explain and predict actions in this sphere. In response to this disciplinary obligation, our study examined the known facts about the connections between contemporary terrorism and the state in Africa. This examination attempted to answer the essential questions of: what, who, why, and how? Answers to these vital questions enabled prediction of future patterns of state-transnational terrorism relationships to be informed by an understanding of past and present trends in Africa.

Organization of the work

Whatever originality this study claims is a matter of building rather than brickmaking. Most of the bricks for the building were made by other scholars. And my major task was to fit the bricks together into a coherent structure dictated by contemporary terrorist events, particularly in African states. In other words, I have many ancestors on studies of the state in Africa as well as transnational terrorism. These are the brickbuilders. And, I have to review and shape each brick for this new building according to contemporary circumstances; that is, the weak state-networked terrorism nexus.

This book is therefore split into seven chapters. The first chapter is the doorway into the work. As the introductory chapter, it brings out how the work examines the various facets of links between the weak state and contemporary transnational terrorism in order to explain and predict action in the sphere of policy options.

The second chapter threads out the theoretical framework of the book. In other words, it discusses power and weakness of the state in Africa by answering the following questions:

- What is the nature of the power or weakness of an African state in international politics?
- What are the sources and conditions of such power or weakness?
- What are its limits?
- When, how, and why does power change into weakness?
- And, finally, how do special interests like networked terrorism benefit from this weakness to capture the territorial state?

The third chapter gives an overview of the state and terrorism: origins of terrorism, its forms as well as its viral and infectious spread around the world. In chapter four we examine the trajectory, which the state in Africa has traced from crisis to tragic poverty, disease, unemployment, civil strife, etc. creating swamps along its way for the breeding and sustaining of terrorist networks. That is, it highlights swamps which weaken the state thus placing it at the mercy of special interest groups scrambling for 'soft hearts' to capture and use. In other words, the chapter examines economic, historical and political forces that help create and shape a climate conducive to breeding networks of terrorism in Africa.

Chapter Five treats Radical Islamism both as a concept and its institutional growth from the Egyptian Brotherhoods to the present-day unblinking quest ('talibanization') for Islamic theocracies in the continent. The reason for this choice of Islamism is that Transnational Terrorist Cartels identifiable in Africa nowadays are inspired by radical Islamic fundamentalist ideology.

Chapter Six discusses the permissive African environment or swamps conducive for breeding terrorist networks by securing recruits, training, arming and deploying for action. And, finally, chapter seven brings out the established realities connecting networked terrorism and weak African states. It also sums up the links between a disorderly world and transnational terrorism, predicting the trends in the weak state-networked terrorism nexus and suggests some ways of containing both. These range from public diplomacy and targeted strikes to clearing terrorist swamps in weak states.

References

Ake, C. (1978), *Revolutionary Pressures in Africa*, Longman: London.

Ake, C. (1979), 'Ideology and Objective Conditions', in Barkan, J. and Okumu, J. (eds.), *Politics and Public Policy in Kenya and Tanzania*, Heinemann: Nairobi.

Ake, C. (1996), *Democracy and Development in Africa*, The Brookings Institution: Washington, D.C.

Amin, S. (1967), *Le développement du capitalisme en Côte d'Ivoire*, Editions du Minuit: Paris.

Anyang' Nyong'o, P. (1987), 'The Development of Agrarian Capitalist Classes in the Ivory Coast, 1945–1975', in Lubeck, P. (ed.), *The African Bourgeoisie: Capitalist Development in Nigeria, Kenya and the Ivory Coast*, Lynne Rienner: Boulder, CO.

Balassa, B. (1971), *The Structure of Protection in Developing Countries*, Johns Hopkins University Press: Baltimore, MD.

Bates, R. H. (1981), *Markets and States in Tropical Africa*, University of California Press: Berkeley and Los Angeles, CA.

Bates, R. H. and Krueger, A. O. (1993), *Political and Economic Interactions in Economic Policy Reform*, Basil Blackwell: Oxford.

Bayart, J.-F. (1989), *L'état en Afrique*, Fayard: Paris.

Bayart, J.-F. (1993), *The State in Africa: The Politics of the Belly*, Longman: London.

Boone, C. (1994), 'Accumulating Wealth, Consolidating Power: Rentierism in Senegal', in Berman, B. and Leys, C. (eds.), *African Capitalists in African Development*, Lynne Rienner: Boulder, CO.

Callaghy, T. (1987), 'The State as Lame Leviathan: The Patrimonial Administrative State in Africa', in Ergas, Z. (ed.), *The African State in Transition*, Macmillan: London.

Callaghy, T. (1993), 'Political Passions and Economic Interests: Economic Reform and Political Structure in Africa', in Callaghy, T. and Ravenhill, T. (eds.), *Hemmed In: Responses to Africa's Economic Decline*, Columbia University Press: New York.

Castells, M. (1992), 'Four Asian Tigers with a Dragon Head: A Comparative Analysis of the State, Economy and Society in the Asian Pacific Rim', in Henderson, R. and Applebaum, J. (eds.), *State and Development in the Asian Pacific Rim*, Sage Publications: London.

Chazan, N. (1988a), 'Ghana: The Problems of Governance and the Emergence of Civil Society in Africa', in Diamond, L., Linz, J. and Lipset, S. M. (eds.), *Democracy in Developing Countries: Africa*, Lynne Rienner: Boulder, CO.

Chazan, N. (1988b), 'Patterns of State-Society Incorporation and Disengagement', in Chazan, N. and Rothchild, D. (eds.), *The Precarious Balance: State and Society in Africa*, Westview Press: Boulder, CO.

Chege, M. (1992), 'Remembering Africa', *Foreign Affairs*, Vol. 71, No. 1, pp. 146–163.

Corden, W. M. (1971), *The Theory of Protection*, Claredon Press: Oxford.

Ergas, Z. (1986), 'In Search of Development: Some Directions for Further Investigation', *Journal of Modern African Studies*, Vol. 24, No. 2, pp. 303–333.

Evans, P. (1992), 'The State as Problem and Solution: Embedded Autonomy, and Structural Change', in Haggard, S. and Kaufman, R. (eds.), *The Politics of Structural Adjustment: International Constraints, Distributive Conflicts and the State*, Princeton University Press: Princeton, NJ.

Evans, P. (1997), *Transferable Lessons? Re-examining the Institutional Prerequisites of East Asian Economic Policies*, UNCTAD: Geneva.

Fanon, F. (1966), *The Wretched of the Earth*, Grove Press: New York.

Fanon, F. (1967), *Towards the African Revolution*, Grove Press: New York.

Gendzier, I. (1985), *Managing Political Change: Social Scientists and the Third World*, Westview Press: Boulder, CO.

Hyden, G. (1983), *No Shortcuts to Progress: African Development Management in Perspective*, Heinemann: London.

Jackson, R. and Rosberg, C. G. (1982), *Personal Rule in Africa: Prince, Autocrat, Prophet, Tyrant*, University of California Press: Berkeley and Los Angeles.

Krugman, P. (1992), 'Toward a Counter-Counterrevolution in Development Theory', in *Proceedings of the Annual Bank Conference on Development Economics*, World Bank: Washington, D.C.

Krugman, P. (1993), 'International Finance and Development', in Giovannini, A. (ed.), *Finance and Development: Issues and Experience*, Cambridge University Press: Cambridge.

Leys, C. (1975), *Underdevelopment in Kenya: The Political Economy of Neo-colonialism, 1964–71*, Heinemann: London.

Little, I. M. D., Scitovsky, T. and Scott, M. (1970), *Industry and Trade in Some Developing Countries: A Comparative Study*, Oxford University Press: London.

Little, I. M. D., Cooper, R. N., Corden, W. M. and Rajapatirana, S. (1993), *Boom, Crisis and Adjustment: The Macroeconomic Experience of Developing Countries*, Oxford University Press: London.

Mamdani, M., Mkandawire, T. and Wamba-di-Wamba, E. (1988), 'Social Movements, Social Transformation and the Struggle for Democracy', Working Paper No. 1, CODESRIA: Dakar, Senegal.

Marcussen, M. S. and Torp, J. E. (1982), *Internationalization of Capital: Prospects for the Third World*, Zed Books: London.

Marx, K. (1962), *Capital*, Foreign Languages Publishing House: Moscow.

Mentan, T. (1999), 'Globalization, Democratization, Exploitation, and the State in Africa: The Final Conquest?', *Annales de la Faculté des Sciences Juridiques et Politiques*, Vol. (Tome) 3, pp. 161–170.

Mkandawire, T. (1990), 'The Crisis of Economic Development Theory', *Africa Development*, Vol. 15, No. 3, pp. 209–230.

Mkandawire, T. (1994), 'The Political Economy of Privatization in Africa', in Cornia, A. and Helleiner, G. (eds.), *From Adjustment to Development in Africa: Conflict, Controversy, Consensus?*, Macmillan: London.

Myrdal, G. (1968), *Asian Drama: An Inquiry Into the Poverty of Nations*, Pantheon: New York.

Nabudere, D. (1981), *The Political Economy of Imperialism*, Zed Books: London.

Onimode, B. (1988), *The Political Economy of the African Crisis*, Zed Books: London.

Rothchild, D. (1994), 'Structuring State-Society Relations in Africa', in Widner, J. (ed.), *Economic Change and Political Liberalization in sub-Saharan Africa*, John Hopkins University Press: Baltimore, MD.

Rowstow, W. W. (1960), *The Stages of Economic Growth: A Non-Communist Manifesto*, Cambridge University Press: Cambridge.

Sandbrook, R. (1986), 'The State and Economic Stagnation in Tropical Africa', *World Development*, Vol. 14, No. 3, pp. 319–332.

Shivji, I. (1980), 'The State in the Dominated Social Formations of Africa: Some Theoretical Issues', *International Social Science Journal*, Vol. 32, No. 4, pp. 730–742.

Williams, G. (1977), 'Class Relations in a Neo-colony: The Case of Nigeria', in Gutkind, P. and Waterman, P. (eds.), *African Social Studies: A Radical Reader*, Heinemann: London.

World Bank (1981), *Accelerated Development in sub-Saharan Africa: An Agenda for Action*, World Bank: Washington, D.C.

World Bank (1989), *Sub-Saharan Africa: From Crisis to Sustainable Growth*, World Bank: Washington, D.C.

World Bank (1993), *The East Asian Miracle: Economic Growth and Public Policy*, World Bank: Washington, D.C.

World Bank (1994), *Adjustment in Africa: Reforms, Results and the Road Ahead*, World Bank: Washington, D.C.

World Bank (1995), *Bureaucrats in Business: The Economics and Politics of Government Ownership*, World Bank: Washington, D.C.

Yanagihara, T. (1997), 'Economic System Approach and it's Applicability', in Yanagihara, T. and Sambommatsu (eds.), *East Asian Development Experience: Economic System Approach and Its Applicability*, Institute for Developing Economies: Tokyo.

2

Conceptual Framework

Political scientists and others engaged in the study of international affairs may make theory sound grand and complicated. However, they are simply trying to articulate the assumptions underlying different approaches to the examination of political phenomena. In the case of international relations, political scientists therefore seek to organize these assumptions into coherent schools of thought. Theoretical frameworks, of course, are not optional, but are necessary and critical tools utilized to provide rigorous and policy relevant analyses of various political phenomena.

Why weak African states?

Africa, like many poor and underdeveloped regions of the world, is in crisis. For one thing, a significant number of countries in the continent have not been able to maintain peaceful coexistence of their various population groups since independence in the 1960s. As a consequence, ethnic conflict, with some of it deteriorating into civil wars, has become endemic in many of these countries. In recent years, armed intra-state conflicts have become quite prevalent in the continent. For example, out of a total of thirty-three armed conflicts in 2000, fourteen of them took place in Africa (Wallensteen and Sollenberg, 2001, pp. 629–644). Africa is indeed in a crisis, which is manifested by (1) a collapse of most of the continent's domestic economies; (2) marginalization of the continent at the international level, especially in trade and global affairs; (3) increasing political instability, despite the recent adoption of multiparty politics in several countries; and

(4) the growing interest in violent mobilization by ethnic groups that believe they have been marginalized by their national governments. Mobilization by various ethnic nationalities to improve their participation in governance and the economy and minimize further marginalization has resulted in increased domestic political violence, and in certain cases, produced civil wars.

Africa's present crisis is rooted in the weakness of the state. For purposes of this chapter, we shall argue that a weak African state is characterized by (1) lack of societal cohesion and consensus on what organizing principles should determine the contest for state power and how that power should be executed; (2) low capacity and/or low political will of state institutions to provide all citizens with minimum levels of security and well-being; (3) high vulnerability to external economic and political forces; (4) low degree of popular legitimacy accorded to the holders of state power (i.e., state custodians) by portions of the citizenry; and; (5) unskillful flirtations with theopolitics and secularism for purposes of political survival.

Evidence to support the assertion that today's African state is weak is quite plentiful. One need only visit a few African countries to find the following manifestations of the weak state: (1) devastated agricultural and rural sectors; (2) poorly maintained and destroyed infrastructure; (3) over-inflated and worthless currency; (4) absence of well-integrated and viable economies; (5) lack of gainful participation in international trade and global affairs; (6) high rates of unemployment, especially among historically vulnerable groups (e.g., women and youth); (7) high rates of HIV/AIDS that are decimating each country's scarce labor resources; (8) extremely high levels of corruption and public malfeasance; and (9) a general absence of the rule of law. One may also add fear and dislike between societal groups, easy access to guns and other arms, an abundance of unskilled urban youths and soldiers roaming the streets and engaging in criminal activities, no firm lines of political authority, no instruments of law and order (especially in the urban areas), and no legitimate government.

The main argument of this chapter is therefore that this situation renders the African state prone to capture by violent non-state actors such as international terrorist groups in search of wealth, support, recruits, and sanctuary. This instrumentalized African chaos has resulted from the combination of three processes: (1) the collapse of the patrimonial state; (2) the dereliction of political accountability; and (3) the political instrumentalization of disorder. What indeed is this patrimonialism?

Weberian strong state and patrimonialism

To Max Weber (1968, p. 1007), patrimonialism was a type of traditional domination, and this often leads those who try to apply this concept to contemporary non-Western societies right back into the traditional-modern dichotomy. However, the 'traditional' aspect is not what is important in Weber's conceptualization. In his words:

> The roots of patriarchal domination grow out of the Master's authority over his household. Such personal authority has in common with impersonally oriented bureaucratic domination stability and an 'everyday character.' Moreover, both ultimately find their inner support in the subjects' compliance with the norms. But under bureaucratic domination these norms are established rationally, appeal to the sense of abstract legality, and presuppose technical training; under patriarchal domination the norms derive from tradition; the belief in the inviolability of that which has existed from time out of mind (Weber, 1968, p. 1007).

Weber (1968, p. 1013) also talks about patrimonial political structures thus:

> We shall speak of a patrimonial state when the prince organizes his political power over extra-patrimonial areas and political subjects—which is not discretionary and not enforced by physical coercion—just like the exercise of his patriarchal power. The majority of all great continental empires had a fairly strong patrimonial character until and even after the beginning of modern times.

Finally, he distinguishes patrimonialism from the other type of traditional domination, feudalism, when he argues that,

> The structure of feudal relationships can be contrasted with the wide realm of discretion and the related instability of power positions under pure patrimonialism Occidental feudalism (Lehensfeudalitat) is a marginal case of patrimonialism that tends towards stereotyped and fixed relationships between lord and vassal. As the household with its patriarchal domestic communism evolves, in the age of the capitalist bourgeoisie, into the associated enterprise based on contract and specified individual rights, so the large patrimonial estate leads to the

> equally contractual allegiance of the feudatory relationship in the age of knightly militarism (Weber, 1968, p. 1070).

Besides 'discretion' and 'instability,' Weber brings out another important difference between the two forms of traditional domination, which is related to how power is exerted:

> In the association of 'estates,' the lord rules with the aid of an autonomous 'aristocracy' and hence shares its domination with it; the lord who personally administers is supported either by members of his household or by plebeians. These are propertyless strata having no social honor of their own; materially, they are completely chained to him and are not backed up by any competing power of their own. All forms of patriarchal and patrimonial domination, Sultanist despotism, and bureaucratic states belong to this latter type. The bureaucratic state order is especially important; in its most rational development, it is precisely characteristic of the modern state (Weber, 1958, p. 82).

There are a number of theoretical insights that can be drawn from these passages. Let us consider legitimation versus discretion, absolute power versus contract, traditional versus modern patterns of dominance, the problems of rationality, and the possible outgrowths of traditional patrimonialism. Several of these alternative explanatory clues may, and do, overlap. But discussing the concepts will help us to grapple with some very essential questions of contemporary political theory.

Legitimation and discretion

While Weber (1968, p. 1013) speaks of patrimonialism as a form of domination 'which is not discretionary and is not enforced by physical coercion,' he also mentions the 'realm of discretion and the related instability of power positions under pure patrimonialism' (p. 1070). Can one view these as contradictory?

By definition, patrimonial power includes an element of tradition (which makes it a type of traditional domination) and an element of discretion, which has at least two components. First, it may just be part of the tradition that the ruler can rule as he pleases. But, second, what differentiates the feudal from the patrimonial ruler is that the latter exerts unchecked leadership, while the former rules only within the limits defined by the independent powers of the estates, as suggested in Max Weber (1958, p. 82).

Discretion is therefore a necessary component of patrimonialism. Nevertheless, what it means in terms of power instability and the need for physical coercion is an empirical matter that depends on historical circumstances. It might be argued that the difference between the second and the third quotation above has to do with the fact that in the second, Weber is talking about the patrimonial state, while in the third, he is talking about pre-political forms of domination. In the patrimonial state, political power would be exerted upon extra-patrimonial areas, upon subjects who would retain relatively high levels of independence and autonomy.

An element of contract would thus exist between the center of patrimonial power and its political subjects, in a way that is quite similar to the feudal type of political domination. It is difficult to understand how such a political arrangement could still be called 'patrimonial,' if it is essentially based on non-patrimonial relationships. On the other hand, it is reasonably easy to conceive of the existence of large, territorially based political systems with very limited autonomy for political subjects—a truly patrimonial state with great leeway for discretion based on physical coercion or legitimacy. It is precisely the existence of these political systems that makes the reexamination of patrimonialism very instructive.

This does not get us off the hook in that we are faced with, if not a contradiction, at least a serious theoretical difficulty. Two possible developments arise from primitive patrimonialism. Both very easily evolve into 'the associated enterprise based on contract and specified social rights,' that is, capitalism and rational-legal political domination. It may even evolve into traditional patrimonialism, which later breaks into a myriad of feudal relationships, which can in turn evolve into the modern, capitalist state. There is no place, in this perspective, for understanding the origins and social basis of modern, bureaucratic domination. The Weberian concern with the increase and spread of bureaucratic power stemmed from an analysis of the degradation of the rational-legal, 'bourgeois' political regimes. It thus becomes extremely difficult to understand, in this perspective, the modern, bureaucratized political regimes that did not pass through the phases of advanced capitalism and rational-legal political domination.

Pure power versus contract

Weber traces a line of continuity between patrimonial and bureaucratic domination. This line of continuity leads him to speak, sometimes, of 'bureaucratic patrimonialism.' It should be seen in contrast with the similarities between capitalism and feudalism. What the first two have in common is that they are both cases of unquestionable power, even if organized and maintained by entirely different systems of norms and values. The last two are similar at the opposite end of exactly the same dimension: They are both cases of contractual relationships of relatively autonomous units.

Can we say the latter are more 'political' than the former? The assumption is only possible if by 'political' we understand necessarily the presence of independent actors in interplay. In this sense a completely totalitarian and absolutist regime would be 'apolitical,' since it would not have room for a process of political bargaining and conflict. This definition of politics might be useful in some contexts. However, it should never be confused with an empirical theory of state formation, which relates the creation of large, territorially based states with the emergence of contractual or bargaining politics of some kind. This is sometimes the case, but very often it is not.

Traditional and modern patterns

What joins patrimonialism and feudalism at one end, and capitalism and bureaucratic domination at the other, is the dimension of tradition versus modernity. The Weberian notion of tradition can here be kept to a minimum: 'the belief in the everyday routine as an inviolable norm of conduct' (Weber, 1958, p. 82). At the other extreme, modernity is related with norms based on 'the belief in the validity of legal statute and functional "competence" based on the rationally created rules' (Weber, 1958, p. 79). Weber is obviously working with two dimensions, and we may as well categorize them as follows:

Modernity and contract. The Weberian characterization of rational-legal political domination is too well-known to be repeated here. What is important in this context is less its definition than the explanation of its origin. A couple of quotations taken more or less at random from Weber may clarify his perspective:

> Bureaucratic organization has usually come into power on the basis of a leveling of economic and social differences . . . Bureaucracy inevitably accompanies modern mass democracy, in contrast to the self-government of small homogeneous units. This results from its characteristic principle: the abstract regularity of the exercise of authority, which is a result of the demand for 'equality before the law' in the personal and functional sense—hence, of the horror of 'privilege,' and the principled rejection of doing business 'from case to case' (Weber, 1968, p. 983).

Just as the Italians, and after them the English, masterly developed the modern capitalist forms of economic organization, so the Byzantines, later the Italians, then the territorial states of the absolute age, the French revolutionary centralization and finally, surpassing all of them, the Germans perfected the rational, functional and specialized bureaucratic organization of all forms of domination from factory to army and public administration. For the time being, the Germans have been outdone only in the techniques of party organization, specifically by the Americans (Weber, 1968, p. 1400).

The basic question seems to be the following: How essential to the Weberian notion of a modern (that is, a 'rational, functional and specialized') bureaucratic organization is the presence of an underlying social contract? One could continue for a long while to track Weber's ideas on this. Basically, it seems that modern bureaucratic domination emerges as an outcome of two conflicting forces: increasing centralization of power and increasing mass participation in politics. In his analysis of Weber's theories on the emergence of legal rationality, Reinhard Bendix (1962) shows that in Western Europe patrimonial power eventually promoted the formal rationality of law and administration. And, of course, this conflicts with the tendency of patrimonial rulers to promote substantive justice and personal favoritism.

This is explained as, among other things, a consequence of the central government's need to restrain the power pretensions of vassals and officeholders. This was done by establishing a 'centrally-controlled officialdom,' and 'in the struggle against the entrenched position of the state, patrimonial rulers were frequently supported by the rising bourgeoisie' (Weber, 1968, p. 406). Modern rational-legal political domination is thus a child of Western European patrimonialism and an emergent bourgeoisie. It is mostly contractual, efficient, and most suited to modern capitalism.

What about modern, rational domination, without the contractual component? Reference can be made here to the Weberian distinction between formal and substantive rationality. Formal rationality is tantamount to legal rationality, in the sense that a set of rules, or 'laws,' defines what should and should not be done by a bureaucrat in a given circumstance. In a broader sense, these rules are a way of implementing the social contract that limits the arbitrary power of the officeholders: '"Equality before the law" and the demand for legal guarantees against arbitrariness demand a formal and rational "objectivity" of administration, as opposed to the personally free discretion flowing from the "grace" of the old patrimonial domination' (Weber, 1968, p. 220).

So, one opposite of formal rationality is 'free discretion,' which is the old-style patrimonialism; but it has another opposite, which is substantive rationality, a kind of rationality which is concerned with maximizing a given set of goals without any regard for formal rules and regulations. Weber relates the development of this demand for substantive justice to the emergence of public opinion and its instruments, the plebiscitarian democracy so feared by Alexis de Tocqueville. Indeed, the emergence of the 'propertyless masses' in public life can endanger a well-functioning political system based on agreed-upon and strictly defined norms of behavior for the civil servants. There is, however, another determinant of substantive rationality, which is also indicated by Weber: 'raison d'état' as defined by the holders of political power. The combination of a central government only ruled by its 'raison d'état' and a passive and instrumental 'propertyless' mass is the definition of a modern, patrimonial-bureaucratic regime. The combination of the same normless political power with an active and mobilized 'propertyless' periphery is what later became known as fascism.

Bendix (1962) in effect stresses that Weber was as concerned as de Tocqueville about the totalitarian possibilities of mass democracy and universal bureaucratization, and he could conceive of a future society in which the social contract, as defined by the 'right-granting laws,' would cease to exist. As Bendix writes, 'In such a situation, the entire body of norms consists exclusively of regulations . . . All private interests enjoy protection . . . only as the obverse aspect of the effectiveness of these regulations . . . All forms of law become absorbed within "administration" and become part and parcel of "government"' (Weber, 1968, p. 463).

As rational-legal domination can degenerate into bureaucratic totalitarianism, so is it possible for this type of bureaucracy to subsist with its 'rational,' but not necessarily its 'legal,' component. This is, in a word, the theoretical link that is missing, the basis for rationality in the absence of contractualism. Bendix, for instance, does not think that it is possible since he argues that:

> An ideally functioning bureaucracy in [Weber's] sense is the most efficient method of solving large-scale organizational tasks. But this is true only if these tasks involve more or less stable norms and hence the effort to maintain the rule of law and achieve an equitable administration of affairs. These conditions are absent where the tasks are assigned by an omnipotent and revolutionary authority (Bendix, quoted in Weber, 1968, p. 467).

In other words, the predominance of substantive over formal rationality would tend to lead from rational-legal to charismatic domination, which is inherently changing and unstable. We shall see that one could argue with Bendix about the necessity of this reversal to charismatic leadership, as well as the limits of rationality and governmental efficiency and stability in a context of absolute authority. What is certain, however, is that we are not facing a return to traditional power relationships. In this sense, the use of the term 'patrimonialism' as applied to modern societies can be very misleading. Indeed, bureaucratic domination seems to be the modern version of traditional, large-scale patrimonialism and this is where the political problems of contemporary developed and underdeveloped countries meet.

Patrimonialism: processes. There is already an important theoretical point to begin with. It is simply that the problems and issues of a modern, underdeveloped, 'patrimonialistic' regime should be considered in terms of its system of bureaucratic domination, rather than in terms of some eventually surviving traditional patterns of behavior and values. One may even feel more comfortable to consider that thinking in terms of patrimonialism and bureaucratic domination does not simply lead to identifying a given structure and its set of problems and alternatives; it should also lead to the explanation of historical processes, an explanation that should be better than those provided by the 'modern-traditional' continuum, if it is to stand.

The basic issue in the analysis of the historical socio-economic formation and development of patrimonial states is the relationships between central power and the centrifugal tendency of officeholders and private entrepreneurs. Richard M. Morse, who in 1961 was already using the concept of patrimonialism to understand Latin American politics, gives a good summary of the problems a ruler has to cope with in this type of regime:

> The patrimonial ruler is ever alert to forestall the growth of an independent landed aristocracy enjoying inherited privileges. He awards benefices, or prebends, as a remuneration for services; income accruing from benefices is an attribute of the office, not of the incumbent as a person. Characteristic ways for maintaining the ruler's authority intact are: limiting the tenure of royal officials, forbidding officials to acquire family and economic ties in their jurisdictions, using inspectors and spies (Morse, 1961, p. 157).

This general problem of patrimonial power acquires very precise contours as one looks into a specific context. For instance, in the case of Brazil, it is possible to think of the relationships between the central, patrimonial-bureaucratic regime and the other areas of the country exactly in those terms (Schwartzman, 1973, 1975). What comes out of this analysis is not the simple description of a patrimonial power, but propositions about the relationships between the political center, Rio, and the economic and military 'peripheries' (São Paulo and Rio Grande do Sul), and a line of analysis that is proving much more fruitful for the understanding of Brazilian political history than the usual modernization framework could.

Patrimonialism and political participation

Here again, it is important to look back to Weber and his distinction between class and status groups. 'Class' is used to refer to people who share the same 'typical chance for a supply of goods, external living conditions and personal life experiences,' in terms of their economic power. 'Class situation' is, in this sense, ultimately a reference to the 'market situation.' And, later on:

> In contrast to the purely economically determined 'class situation' we wish to designate as 'status situation' every typical component of the life fate of men that is determined by a specific, positive or negative, social estimation of honor . . . Stratification by status goes hand in hand with a monopolization of ideal and material goods or opportunities (Weber, 1968, pp. 180–195).

Both class and status situations, often lead to political participation, which tends to be organized as political parties. Parties are based on class or status situations, or both. One central issue of contemporary political analysis is the determination of how much of the political action of individuals and parties is determined by status and class situations, and still more important, how much they are aimed at consolidating or destroying the forced inequalities of the market or tine privileges of status. The bourgeois political revolution is a movement that breaks the monopolies of goods and opportunities based on ascribed status and puts into its place a stratification system, which refers directly to the market. The system of political participation is characterized by the unabashed use of power to acquire better market positions and to consolidate them into political 'rights' (that is, rights that are enjoyed independently from the market).

In general, there is a sociological axiom that says that positions of privilege, once acquired, tend to be subtracted from the market and transformed into ascribed, status based monopolies, while there is always a tendency to take underprivileged positions out of the status system and put them into the market. A version of this axiom, which is at first glance unrelated to Weber, is Schattschneider's (1960, pp. 1–3) proposition that 'the most important strategy of politics is concerned with tine scope of conflict.' The tendency of the underdog is to widen the scope of political conflict, bring more actors into the arena, and thus change the power relationships. The top dog, on the contrary, tends to monopolize the arena for those already enfranchised to participate in the conflict. The struggle of monopoly versus open market has to do with both the functional quality of the participants and their sheer number. In the extreme market situation, issues are never kept within functional or professional boundaries, and there is universal enfranchisement. Politics is territorially based; specific issues are translated into broad political questions; and each gets his share according to his economic power and capacity for political maneuvering. At the other extreme, monopoly prevails; power positions are so established that there is little room for conflict; and when conflict occurs, it tends to be circumscribed and privatized by functional groups. This is the typical corporative mode of political organization and participation.

There are thus two ways by which a monopolistic, status based corporatist system can be established. One is through the development of self-sufficient, strongly organized professional groups that are able to impose themselves and their own rules of trade and privilege upon the rest of society. This is the type of corporation one thinks of when one considers the medieval guilds or, today, some particularly strong professional groups.

The other way is through grants of social and economic rights and monopolies by the state. Both systems can have the same ideological frame of reference, in terms of an organic integration of functional groups but it makes a big difference whether this integration results from several entrenched status positions or from a powerful and (sometimes) benevolent central state.

Contemporary corporatism tends to be of the second type, and this has had a series of important consequences. First, no contemporary state was really able to develop a full-fledged corporatist system that could take the place of traditional class or interest-group politics in the Western-liberal regimes. I have suggested in another place the term 'political co-optation' to describe the dominant side of the system of political participation created in Brazil since the Second World War (Schwartzman, 1970, pp. 9–14). The Labor party and the bureaucratic structures of the Ministry of Labor and Social Welfare represented one type of political co-optation in Brazil. One could consider this a type of corporatism, since it linked a whole section of society to the state and granted special social and economic rights to the workers, outside the market. But this system was controlled from above and had little participation from below. Co-optation systems lie midway between corporatism and open, interest-group politics. When they are effective, they tend to reduce political conflict to undisputed monopolies of privilege. By the same token, this type of political structure lacks internal consistency and strength. Second, and related to the above, is the fact that political life tends to be very dependent upon the state and its central figure. Morse (1961, pp. 173–176) stated this idea very succinctly in two of his five propositions about Latin American political life:

> The Latin American peoples still appear willing to alienate, rather than delegate, power to their chosen or accepted leaders. Society is perceived in Latin America as composed of parts which relate through a patrimonial and symbolic center rather than directly to one another.

These are not unique traits of the Latin American political culture (and as such forever established and impossible to change). It is noteworthy that Bendix (1956) had made exactly the same point about czarist Russia and communist Germany several years before. 'Stateless' England and the United States allowed for open, competitive, and self-regulating class conflict and politics (see, e.g., Nettl, 1968, pp. 559–592). In contrast, countries with a strong, centralized, patrimonially based structure tend to inhibit the emergence of autonomous political groups, not to allow for established patterns of political conflict through direct bargaining, but, on the contrary, to stimulate bilateral relationships between the central state and social groups of dependency, subordination, and the search for grants of privilege.

Third, corporatism does emerge in contemporary centralized states, but not quite where one would expect it. The absence of an arena of political participation, that is, of an open political 'market,' leads to widespread search for status privileges throughout society. Corporations are not to be found among privileged economic groups or organized as ostensive political institutions. Rather, corporatist tendencies are to be looked for in the educational system, the multiplication of formally defined professional privileges and prerogatives, and self-serving sections of the civilian and military public bureaucracy. Another quotation from Max Weber could enlighten the relationship between education and professionalism:

> The development of the diploma from universities, and business and engineering colleges, and the universal clamor for the creation of educational certificates in all fields make for the formation of a privileged stratum in bureaus and in offices. Such certificates support their holder's claims for . . . a 'respectable' remuneration rather than remuneration for work done, claims for assured advancement and old-age insurance, and, above all, claims to monopolize socially and economically advantageous positions (Weber, 1968, p. 241).

Democracy, rationality, and bureaucratic patrimonialism

It may be safe to conclude with the scenario of the supposedly emerging bureaucratic, patrimonialistic, and corporatist society. Society is sharply divided into well-defined status groups based on functional differentiations, educational credentials, or monopolistic control of property. These status groups tend to be strongly organized along corporatist lines that define their own internal rules of behavior and access, and are structured according to the legal-bureaucratic model. Government belongs to one or two corporations of this kind, the military and the 'technocrats.' Political activities outside the well-defined rules of inter-corporation behavior are minimal or nonexistent. Is this scenario likely to occur?

One can only say that it is well within the range of possibility. Weber himself was very concerned with this problem. As Bendix (quoted in Weber, 1968, p. 459) says,

> Universal bureaucratization was for Weber the symbol of a cultural transformation that would affect all phases, of modern society. If this, development ran its, full course it would result in a new despotism more rigid even than the ancient Egyptian dynasties because it would have a technically efficient administration at its disposal.

This scenario of a bureaucratic and corporatist nightmare haunts contemporary political science, and it is almost certain that any ingenious suggestion to avoid it would be fallacious. Ending this discussion, however, with a few perspectives on the relationship between this scenario and the ideals of freedom, democracy, and rationality may be refreshing.

One of the most important conceptual clues to this question is provided by Albert O. Hiirschman's (1970) *Exit, Voice and Loyalty*. He establishes a link between the freedom of members to influence the behavior of an organization and the level of efficiency on which it operates. There are two ways of acquiring influence: exit, the typical market mechanism by which a customer (or employee, or supporter of a political party) changes allegiance; and voice, the political mechanism of influence and protest. The relationships between voice and exit are complex and are elegantly spelled out by Hiirschman. What is important here is that voice is more likely to be used and is more effective when there is no possibility of exit; for example, in situations of economic or organizational monopoly. Without exit or voice—that is, without freedom—centralized bureaucracy cannot work efficiently in the long run and must resort to systems of double government (the administration and the party, or the administration and the security apparatus) or to the expediency of recurring cultural revolutions and declarations of national emergency in order to recover from systematic stagnation and routine.

The alternative to these systems of double government and constant mobilization is the establishment of new forms of self-government and internal democracy in corporations and within the new patrimonial bureaucratic state. It may just be that, in the long run, Weber was right, in that a system of large-scale political domination is inherently unstable if it does not have an underlying contract, right-granting laws, and, accordingly, freedom to participate and to influence and the feelings of dignity and self-respect that accompany the effective exercise of opinion, the right of association, and the achievement of the intended goals.

Thus, the theoretical challenge is to give up the traditional modes of political organization which are apparently limited to an already old fashioned Western European tradition, without giving up the ideals of freedom and individual rights, and in doing so, to combine political concern with theoretical relevance; to help draw a new social contract based on a proper consideration of the political reality of the times, and not on its rejection. This is Weber's conception of patrimonialism in a strong capitalist state. In sum, and according to Weber, the defining properties of the state include the following: (1) unchallenged control of the territory within the defined boundaries under its control; (2) monopolization of the legitimate use of force within the borders of the state; and (3) reliance upon impersonal rules in the governance of its citizens and subjects. However, the situation in the underdeveloped state is certainly not identical.

The weak African patrimonial state

In Africa there is very little to be celebrated about mutually agreed rules for the contest for power, and a renunciation of violence as a method for resolving political conflicts. As such, this situation enlarges the number of possible outcomes beyond losing power or winning it. A democratic system allows one group of power contenders to win state power, while other groups or parties remain safe and sound. This is far from being the case in Africa today. The dilemma is that power contenders view politics as a zero-sum game. This perception forces the contest for power to take the form of a do-or-die fight for state power not as a common resource that offers protection and sustainable life conditions for all but as a private possession. The internecine struggle for state power therefore weakens the state itself. In other words, the weakness of African states derives from (1) the collapse of the patrimonial state; (2) the dereliction of political accountability; and (3) the political instrumentalisation of disorder (see, e.g., Chabal and Daloz, 1999).

Collapse of the patrimonial state

The demise of the weak patrimonial African state derives from a legitimacy gap. Legitimacy in strong states rests on a kind of social contract between key actors in society (state, civil society, market, etc.). This contract has at least the following three criteria: (1) the use of violence by the state is predictable and limited; (2) the state contributes to or guarantees minimum levels of socioeconomic well-being and physical security of the citizens; and (3) citizens have a measure of control over the polity, how power is exercised and by whom (Wallensteen, 1994, pp. 63–64).

The collapse of the patrimonial state refers to the economic causes of the African crisis. The political systems put in place at independence by withdrawing European colonialists were similar to those of the metropolitan countries. However, the reality of strength or weakness of post-colonial Africa is that, whatever the constitutional niceties of the newly independent countries, politics was very rapidly organized around the practices of patrimonialism—that is, the establishment of patron/client networks fed by resources from the state. Overwhelmed by the problems of development, the African state abandoned the task of building more unity within the society, constructing national identities and creating legitimacy by providing security and other services. It rather resorted to predatory and kleptocratic practices, which tended to exacerbate social tensions between groups in society. Indeed, since the very legitimacy of post-colonial regimes hinged on the extent to which the political patrons were able to fulfill their obligations to their clients, regimes tended to adopt policies that promoted the utilization of scarce resources for military equipment and manpower, stifling opposition groups demanding greater participation as well as regarding as dangerous any movements that promoted alternative identifications and loyalties (Callaghy, 1984, pp. 141–232).

The reasons are obvious. The first is that the African people participated in the patrimonial state system through their involvement in a web of patronage and clientship. Survival at the bottom of the hierarchy required powerful patrons. Survival at the top depended on establishing a network of clients large enough to neutralize potential rivals. Secondly, the notion of mutual obligation never existed. Essentially, those at the top governed while those at the bottom existed to be governed. The relationship between those with power and those over whom that power was exercised flowed in only one direction. The result, of course, was that power became an end in itself. Those with authority sought to become more powerful while having absolutely no obligation to better the lives of those upon whom their authority had been established. And thus the African state was caught in a vicious circle. That is, everything it did to enhance its ability to develop into a strong and viable state actually perpetuated its weakness (Kalevi, 1996, p. 117).

That this happened is not altogether surprising since such patrimonial-clientelist relations were very precisely those that had characterized pre-colonial societies in Africa. So, in a very real sense, the development of the patrimonial state was nothing other than the Africanization of the colonial legacy. The patrimonial state could not, of course, be a system of economic management, which is conducive to development, although in economically propitious circumstances it can create the conditions for stable polities. This is because its prime economic logic is to display the ostentation and feed the patron/client networks required for holding power rather than to accumulate in order to invest productively, which is the foundation of capitalism.

In addition, patrimonial systems of the ilk being discussed here are exclusive. The lack of both will and resources makes it impossible for leaders to co-opt all segments of the population into the system. The fact that the system excludes others from access to power, wealth, and influence makes it conflict-prone and undemocratic.

Furthermore, patrimonial systems of the type we have in Africa today tend to reward loyalty and obedience. There is thus cynical disregard for efficiency and creativity. And productivity and resource development are obvious victims of the system. The employment of unacceptable forms and degrees of corruption negate the goal of development.

The economic circumstances of the last thirty years, however, have been such as to prevent any virtuous transition from patrimonialism to a more productive system. Many African countries were not economically viable at independence, but even those that were—and some achieved respectable economic growth in the sixties—could not cope with the economic crisis triggered by the rise in oil prices in the seventies. In the absence of substantial wealth creation, African patrimonial states were simply unable to continue to feed the networks, which linked those in power with the rest of the population.

In the face of dwindling resources, African politicians sought to borrow resources from abroad in order to seek to maintain the patrimonial structure on which their political legitimacy depended. Soon, debt spiraled out of control and the means of state largesse declined. Bereft of resources, the holders of state power resorted increasingly to coercion, with the result that they both lost support and undermined the very legitimacy of the political system in place (Rotberg, 2002). Once the patrimonial state had collapsed, the exercise of power became much more nakedly violent and, inevitably, opposition to the state itself took on an increasingly violent hue—a spiral of force of which Sierra Leone is only one of the most extreme cases. In some terminal cases, such as Zaire (Democratic Republic of Congo) and Somalia the nation-state ceased to exist (see, e.g., Gould, 1985; Gould and Mukendi, 1989; Mbaku, 1994; MacGaffey, 1983).

Dereliction of political accountability

The main reason why the patrimonial system spanned out of control is because of the lack of political accountability in post-colonial Africa. The transfer of power that followed decolonization established formal institutions of political accountability. Parliament, trade unions, the press, and other institutions existed but with no historical roots in the traditions of the continent. The democratic political framework was an artificial construct, hastily put in place by the retreating colonial powers and readily embraced by the nationalists because it was the price to pay to be entrusted with control over the post-colonial state.

Of course, wherever and whenever parliamentary democracy works it does provide an efficient system of political accountability. However, it was naïve to assume that the hurried establishment of parliamentary democracy in former colonies with no actual experience of such a form of government would result in a functioning system of democratic political accountability.

The experience of post-colonial Africa is varied and complex. But, by and large, it is one in which rulers have been able to flout the constitutional mechanisms of political accountability put in place at independence. The checkered political history of Nigeria and Ghana amply demonstrates this fact. They inherited the colonial state, a highly bureaucratic and coercive institution bereft of democratic tradition, and with it the machinery of force. Their legitimacy originally stemmed from their success as nationalists, not from their democratic credentials. As time passed, nationalism became increasingly irrelevant, the patrimonial state weakened and its legitimacy faded. The failures of government led to increasing demands for more accountability (Sklar, 1986, pp. 135–144).

Political accountability, insofar as it existed under the patrimonial state, took the form of a certain redistribution of state resources by those in power to their national, regional or local clients—a form of accountability considered legitimate in pre-colonial Africa. Where there were sufficient resources to lubricate the system of patronage, clients and their dependents accepted the politics of the authoritarian one-party state as reasonably accountable. As the economic crisis grew more severe and resources dwindled, patron-client relations began to dissolve. In the absence of any other form of political accountability, rulers sought to keep power by force. The recourse to coercion invalidated the legitimacy of the fragile edifice of post-colonial political accountability. The predicament of post-colonial Africa from the 1970s was thus severe: how could Africans generate new forms of political accountability in an environment marked by the collapse of the patrimonial state, the abuse of power, a growing economic crisis, and a wide legitimacy gap? They did not (Sklar, 1986).

Legitimacy is critical to any meaningful explanation of the strength and weaknesses of states (Kalevi, 1996, pp. 82–98). We are dealing here with two dimensions of legitimacy: the vertical as well as the horizontal. Vertical legitimacy establishes the 'right to rule' between society and political institutions and regimes. This connection strengthens the belief in the citizens that the state and its authority have a right to rule them. It is here that any ruler seeks to justify his claim to rule. However, where legitimacy claims and popular expectations overlap or coincide, the state gains strength since its rule is based on the consent of the people. In terms of social turmoil and rapidly changing ideas, the bases of legitimacy seldom, if at all, last. This has been the case in Africa with the state gaining significant weakness.

Horizontal legitimacy entails the creation of a political community for its members. That is, the state stands as the incarnation of the attitudes and practices of individuals and groups towards each other. If the individuals and groups within a state accept and tolerate each other, then horizontal legitimacy is high. This legitimacy diminishes when one group seeks either to systematically dominate, oppress, exclude or threaten the very existence of other groups or communities within the state. Those excluded, threatened with extinction, or oppressed, are always at pains to extend loyalty to a state or other groups within it (Kalevi, 1996, pp. 106–107).

In sum, vertical legitimacy is about responsible authority and voluntary subordination. Horizontal legitimacy is about mutual acceptance and tolerance at elite and mass levels. Lack of horizontal legitimacy paves the way for the withdrawal of loyalty to the state and its institutions. Dubious or ambiguous vertical legitimacy could create, nurse, maintain, and exacerbate horizontal legitimacy since both interact. The difference between the expectations of security, participation, and distribution by citizens and the ability of the state to fulfill them creates a legitimacy gap. And the wider the legitimacy gap the greater the risk of igniting intra-state violence (Kalevi, 1996, p. 90).

Political instrumentalization of disorder

The paradigm for this section of the analysis is the political instrumentalization of disorder. In brief, it refers to the process by which political actors in Africa seek to maximize their returns on the state of disorder and uncertainty, which characterizes most African polities. Although there obviously are vast differences between countries in this respect, all African nation-states share a generalized system of patrimonialism (however destitute) and an acute degree of apparent disorder, as evidenced by a high degree of governmental and administrative inefficiency, a lack of instrumental institutionalization, a general disregard for the rules of the formal political and economic sectors, and a universal resort to personal(ized) solutions to societal problems (Chabal and Daloz, 1999, p. 14).

To understand politics in such a context is to understand the ways in which individuals, groups, communities and societies seek to instrumentalize the resources, which they command within this general moral economy of disorder. To speak of disorder is not, of course, to speak of irrationality. There is, however, logic to disorder, or perhaps even chaos, even if that logic is, at first sight, incomprehensible to the outside observer. In an ordered, regulated polity, political opportunities and resources are defined explicitly and codified by legislation or precedent. Order is secured by functioning institutions in the Weberian sense. In a world of disorder, however, there is necessarily a premium both on the personal (as opposed to institutional) relations through which the 'business' of politics can be conducted and on access to the means of maximizing the returns, which the 'domestication' of such disorder demands. To give an example, if the permeability of borders is arbitrary, personal access to those who control trade flows through those borders is a requisite for those who want to maximize their returns on the disorder generated by such apparent arbitrariness (Chabal and Daloz, 1999).

The notion of disorder should not merely be construed, as it normally is in classical political analysis, as a state of non-performance. It should be seen instead as a condition, which offers opportunities for those who know how to play that system (as is obvious, for example, in the criminalization of the Russian economy today). Whether such a situation is conducive to development, as it is normally understood in Western societies, however, is a totally different question. The concern here is with knowing how such a state of generalized disorder is instrumentalized politically.

Disorder also incorporates the notion of uncertainty, a concept with which economists are familiar. Again, uncertainty is both a cost and an opportunity, against which there is a premium. In a polity of disorder, the ability to hedge uncertainty is a valuable resource. The greater the uncertainty, the more valuable the hedge is—hence, for instance, the perennial significance which witchcraft retains as an almighty hedge in

Africa. Knowledge and the control of information are important in all polities but they are critical in disordered societies, where they impinge even more directly on the management of uncertainty. Whether, for example, the ruler is unwell, or prey to new influences, will be of substantially greater significance in Africa than it would be in Europe, for it could unleash a wholesale change in the patrimonial networks extant and radically reshape the existing moral economy of disorder (Chabal and Daloz, 1999, p. 14).

Disorder in African states should not be viewed as a state of failure or neglect. In fact, disorder should rather be seen as a condition that offers opportunities for those who are adept or skilled at playing the system. Certainly, the failure of the African state to be emancipated from society has limited the scope for governance and sustainable economic growth. However, its weakness and inefficiency have paid handsome dividends to local political elites, foreign economic actors, and even violent non-state actors like international terrorists.

Essentially, the clientelist networks within the formal political apparatus have created opportunities for elites to raise the resources necessary for providing protection and services to local constituents in exchange for the recognition of their political and social status. The instrumentalization of political disorder therefore functions as a disincentive to the establishment of well structured Weberian system of strong state for implementing a liberal democratic system. After all, 'Why should the African political elites dismantle a political system which serves them so well?' (Chabal and Daloz, 1999, p. 14).

Captured African state

As the old European empires were disappearing and giving birth to dozens of young new nations in Africa, the societies had to develop from tradition to modernity, from isolation to communication, from reduced to expanded political participation, from political underdevelopment to political maturity, from national isolationism to international integration (see Tipps, 1973; Bendix, 1967, pp. 318–346).

After inheriting power from withdrawing colonial powers, African leaders embarked on transforming the political landscape of their respective states, dissolving parliaments or building up what has come to be referred to as a 'kept press' (i.e., one that is muzzled, tamed, and reduced to regurgitating government pronouncements instead of investigating and reporting the news), fusing political parties, and militarizing personal safety within their countries. This huge and authoritarian system of personal rule yielded rich new insights into their characters, their reign, politics and religion, foreign policy and finance, the importance of parliaments, and the process of government without them.

In the seventies it was as if all this had started to crumble: democracies were giving way to dictatorships, participation to repression, economic development to stagnation, and integration to new forms of isolation on religious, ethnic or class lines. As democratic regimes fell one after another throughout Africa, so did the theories of continuous progress and well-being that were used to explain and predict the future of these countries. It is important to notice that these theories had certainly been challenged all along by counter theories, which denied the idea of a continuous and well-integrated process of progress and change. But both evolutionary and revolutionary theorists shared optimism, a belief in historical progress and the future well-being of mankind and every one of its nations. Revolutionary theorists, of course, would deny the notion of political development as a progressive increase in political institutionalization; instead, they would think in terms of increasing class awareness and class conflict. For a while, the failure of the democratic regimes in Africa seemed to give credibility to the theories of conflictive and revolutionary development. But slowly it became clear that the new authoritarian regimes were more stable than expected, and that the closing of the political arena usually meant, not a corresponding increase in political conflict and radicalization, but an overall reduction of political participation and political concern (Geertz, 1963).

In short, the new problem faced by social and political theorists is the failure of the new African countries to comply with the evolutionary pattern of Western Europe, either by attaining their type of bargaining democracy or creating the socialist and revolutionary regimes that one would 'naturally' have expected in Europe if the growing demands of the working class had not been met. This is, of course, an old question—How and in what sense is Africa different from Europe and the United States?

Corporatism and patrimonialism, sometimes apart and sometimes together, seem to be good, old, solid answers to this old question. When properly used, these terms can help to free the political analyzes of Africa from the bias produced by the Western European and North American experience, and at the same time lead to the recovery of a well-established tradition of historical analysis overshadowed for some time by the liberal and revolutionary optimistic tradition. Improperly used, however, they can have precisely the opposite effect: to increase ethnocentrism and bias and bring us back to the same mistakes and misunderstandings which helped to put these concepts in the limbo of social thought for so long.

Essentially, the difference between the proper and the improper use of these concepts lies in whether they are applied to a structural feature of these societies and its process or, on the contrary, to a more or less fixed cultural or historical trait or character and its permanence. A common criticism of modernization theories is that they tended to imply a very simplified model of unidirectional change, from tradition to modernity, or a dichotomous view of societies, according to the classic distinction between 'community' and 'society.' Valid as this criticism may be, one should notice that the use of concepts like 'patrimonialism' or 'corporatism' could mean the substitution of a continuum or a dichotomy, that is, a variable, for a single and static concept, that is, a constant.

Returning to a founding father of the social sciences such as Max Weber has great advantages and some pitfalls. The main advantages are probably that it helps us to recover a broad conceptual frame in which our discussion belongs, or should belong, and also that it links us with a solid and well-proved intellectual tradition. The main danger is that it can lead us very rapidly into an endless debate about the 'proper' understanding and interpretation of the author's concepts and ideas, which may turn a concern with theoretical relevance into a task of literary exegesis.

However, 'corporatist theory,' or the corporatist's prescription for the organization of society or 'corporatist ideology' (Malloy, 1974) is insufficient to explain the phenomenon of sate weakness in Africa. The picture that emerges from 'corporatist ideology' is the ideal of a harmonious well-regulated, non-conflictive society, based on moral principles and well-defined norms, which are issued and maintained by the public authority, the state. According to this ideology, there should be some intra-group autonomy and self-regulation, but the very existence of groups and their relationships with each other are granted and regulated by the state.

A corporatist state can be more or less authoritarian in the sense that these grants of autonomy and the regulation of inter- and intra-group activities can be more or less strict; but it is the state that legitimates and enfranchises group and individual participation in public affairs. This is exactly the opposite of the ideology that stems from the Western European tradition, in which society and its groups legitimate the power of the state. It is equally the opposite of what obtained in post-colonial Africa, in which the chief of state used his personal power to legitimate the power of the state. Indeed, this was a strange alternative source of legitimation for the exercise of political power and political participation.

Since Max Weber, at least, we have known that the source of legitimation of a power relationship is very important when one is interested in the motivations, values, ideologies, organizational projects, and everything else related to this basic normative component. However, it is reasonable to assume that a given type of legitimation does not happen by chance, but tends to emerge in relatively well-defined contexts and historical circumstances. Consideration of these structural contexts and historical circumstances allows us to understand more from the phenomenology of political ideology to theories that try to establish causal relationships of some kind. There is thus an empirical proposition that gives the foundation and explains the different types of legitimation of political activities in the two contexts. Broadly, this proposition says that in corporatist regimes, the state is stronger than civil society; while in North American and Western European, non-corporative regimes, civil society is stronger than the state (Swartzman, 1979, pp. 89–106).

To say that the state is 'stronger than society' is to say that the group which controls the state apparatus is able to impose its will upon other, private sectors of society, thanks to its control of extractive resources, military manpower, or communication networks. This strength is bound to have consequences at several levels: first, in the allocation of scarce resources; second, in the decisions about who can and cannot participate in political decisions; and finally, in the very ideology which gives the central government the right to grant legitimacy to actors in the political arena.

The type of corporatism we have been discussing does not encompass all the possible connotations of the term, which often implies the notion of autonomous, self-contained, and strongly institutionalized professional groups, the 'corporations.' The relative autonomy of the corporations is certainly one of the central issues in understanding this kind of regime. However, it is important to remember that, as Malloy (1974) puts it, in the corporatist scheme the principle is that groups are to be relatively antonymous in intra-group decisions but the groups exist by virtue of recognition and to that extent are dependent on the state. If they have semi-sovereign qualities in their spheres, it is because the state confers them and then assumes the role of regulating inter-group relations (Malloy, 1974, p. 58; also Schmitter, 1974, pp. 85–131).

When this relationship of superordination is established in principle, we are talking about an ideology, a 'scheme' or a 'theory' in the sense of an ideal type. What is more important, however, is to establish if and to what extent this is an empirical fact in a given context, and then try to see if it has the consequences that one would expect from the conceptual model. If we assume that this is the case for a great number of African countries, the next problem is to determine whether the distinction between 'the state' and 'civil society' really has any meaning, and to evaluate whether the state is really 'stronger' than society. This is where the concept of patrimonialism enters the picture.

In sum, there are four important components in the concept of corporatism: (1) the rights of association and public action performed by the corporations tend to be granted by the state; (2) corporations tend to enjoy a fairly high degree of autonomy in internal matters; (3) the boundaries between corporations tend to be sharply defined and difficult to cross; and (4) corporations tend to be defined in terms of functional (professional) status dimensions, rather than according to geographical or ethnic dimensions. Empirically, contemporary corporatist systems tend to emerge in contexts of strong, centralized politically dominant state structures, of a bureaucratic-patrimonial kind. These structures are in themselves organized along corporatist lines, which use the state apparatus as their property, their patrimony.

But all this does not explain the emergence and permanence of personal rule as a system of political participation and its relationship with the better-known class-like or interest-group systems. This is where consideration of the concept of personal rule and the discussion related to its weaknesses becomes central. Cabral (1973, p. 84) once said that 'The problem of the nature of the state created after independence is perhaps the secret failure of African independence.' The failure is no longer a 'secret.' The failure lies in the inability of the state to control the dialectic of oppression generated by personal rule as well as the active exacerbation of the very vicious elements of the dialectic of oppression by instruments of preservation and nurture of personal rule.

Success as a personal or patrimonial ruler depended on an extensive network of clients who exercise power in the ruler's favor. He manages vulnerability with new non-bureaucratic strategies of rule through manipulating market opportunities, even where actual sources of accumulation may not be under his direct control. Individual military units and commercial syndicates forage on their own, signaling what appears to be the dissolution of the state. Different factions jealously guard useful territory and opportunity from rival entrepreneurs. But competition among these groups reduces chances of mutiny or coordinated attack on the patrimonial ruler. Individual strongmen appeal to him for protection against local rivals even as they consolidate virtually autonomous fiefdoms organized around commerce (a hidden economy), religion, etc. This benefits the personal ruler insofar as it forestalls resistance and contains challenges amidst collapsing patron-client networks. The best chance for survival of personal rule lies thus in using opposition among factions of his patronage network to neutralize the network's threat to him.

Personal rulers in Africa used this method because it did not require a command hierarchy that could acquire interests of its own and it obstructed attempts by rivals to build their own organizations. The existence of multiple centers of accumulation facilitated this radical decentralization of politics. With time, collapsing infrastructure encourages the ruler's associates to exploit local opportunities rather than joining others to mutiny. In this context ownership of air cargo firms highlight contours of political competition or alliances better than do formal agreements or individuals' titles. Competition at these centers of accumulation for control over trade is what leaves a political space for him to manage crises. Sovereignty, then, becomes important only as a license to make deals with essentially private allies (cf. Schatzberg, 1988, p. 53).

Globalization and state failure

The state in Africa is withering before the advance of globalization. With the rise of globalization, the circuits of money, commodity, and productive capital have become internationalized under the dominance of finance capital. But during the last twenty to twenty-five years there has been a substantial increase in the degree of integration of the world economy, in particular in the integration of internationally dispersed production activities depriving the patrimonial ruler of an archipelago of resources to use for recruiting and maintaining clientelist networks.

This 'functional integration' turns on tightly woven production and trade networks and is facilitated by global financial markets, new production and transport technologies, and leaps in 'real-time communications' capabilities. This greater ability to break down, scatter, and link production processes and serve different markets, to diversify production worldwide, and to seek out 'least-cost' locations for specific products and exploit comparative regional advantages—this ability to undertake a kind of 'global scan' in pursuit of the most profitable deployment and redeployment of capital—is a trend of qualitative significance.

More so than ever, the capitalist labor process is being integrated, cheapened, and transformed on a global scale. One measure of what is happening is that changes in the international division of labor are resulting in a shift of the center of gravity for production activities of some global industries toward the poor and oppressed nations. For instance, São Paulo is today the second most important center for production by German transnational corporations. Only a generation ago, most of the global shifting of manufacturing activity was in apparel and consumer electronics. Now a much wider spectrum of manufacturing, agricultural, and service activities is globalized. U.S. car companies, for example, can attain the same levels of productivity and quality at their Mexican plants today as in their U.S. operations (while paying Mexican auto workers one-seventh of what workers are paid in the United States). Globalization has accelerated in the wake of the Soviet collapse and has been promoted through treaties, agreements, and policies. There is a global push toward deregulation and liberalization. There is the 'intellectual property rights' juggernaut, with monopoly making its 'proprietary' claims over everything in sight—technology, agricultural inputs and seed varieties, pharmaceuticals, and now genetic material (Douglas and Sharpe, 1985).

There are three elements of the globalization process: intensified globalization of production, which is the key element; intensified globalization of finance; and globalization of 'macroeconomic policy' in the impoverished and oppressed nations (the virtual takeover of the national management of Third World economies by the IMF and the World Bank and the imposition of neoliberal policies and restructuring). *Globalization* is a more recent development than *internationalization*. But it does not represent a new stage of capitalist development (as imperialism did for capitalism). It is not obliterating rivalry between monopolistic firms or between national-imperialist states, or the division of the world into oppressor and oppressed nations. Rather, globalization represents the heightening of some of the most essential features of imperialism.

The fact is that humanity has been living in a global economy for over 100 years and the results and costs of that globalization are well known: the subjugation of entire nations, the wars, the crises, the famines, and the exploitation of billions of people. Globalization is therefore both an active process of corporate expansion across borders and a structure of cross-border facilities and economic linkages that has been steadily growing and changing as the process gathers steam. Like its conceptual partner 'free trade,' globalization is also an ideology, whose function is to reduce any resistance to the process by making it seem both highly beneficent and unstoppable. This intolerance of attempts to stop the deleterious effects of globalization is what accounts for the weakness and/or failure of the African state and its attendant proneness to capture by actors in the international system.

Weak African states can no longer cope with the demands of globalization (Scholte, 1997, pp. 427–253). For instance, feeble states could control internationalization, which is the process of greater degrees of interaction between different parts of the world. Here, the geographical positioning of things is important. But globalization renders territoriality irrelevant and weak states tend to fail because they cannot cope with it. That is, first, non-state actors, especially multi-national corporations (MNCs), as well as violent non-state actors like transnational terrorism seeking sanctuary and wealth; second, volatile speculative markets which could be very destructive to fragile economies like those of most African states; third, there is the vast arms trade from light weapons to the threat of trade in nuclear weapons ('dirty bombs'); and, finally, advances in the electronic transfer of funds, particularly those of multinationals. The weak state cannot afford the means to bring under its control the illegal activities of various transnational criminal organizations, including terrorists, international crime syndicates, drug dealers, arms traffickers, and other cross-border criminals.

In sum, the fragile or weak state in Africa is bound to collapse in this current global era because of powerful non-state actors capable of bribing their way to political influence; of speculative markets since they lack even rudimentary institutions for trying to cope with high degrees of uncertainty; of rampant arms trade facilitating the rise of warlordism, protracted and fatal conflicts, and violent overthrow of governments; and of tax evasions which make it very difficult for any weak African state to provide collective goods.

References

Bendix, R. (1956), *Work and Authority in Industry: Ideologies of Management in the Course of Industrialization*, John Wiley & Sons: New York.

Bendix, R. (1962), *Max Weber: An Intellectual Portrait*, Doubleday: New York.

Bendix, R. (1967), 'Tradition and Modernity Reconsidered', *Comparative Studies in Society and History*, Vol. 9, No. 3, pp. 292–346.

Cabral, A. (1973), *Return to the Source: Selected Speeches*, Monthly Review Press: New York.

Callaghy, T. (1984), *The State-Society Struggle: Zaire in Comparative Perspective*, Columbia University Press: New York.
Chabal, P. and Daloz, J.-P. (1999), *Africa Works: Disorder as a Political Instrument*, James Currey: Oxford.
Douglas, B. and Sharpe, K. (eds.) (1985), *Transnational Corporations versus the State: The Political Economy of the Mexican Auto Industry*, Princeton University Press: Princeton, NJ.
Geertz, C. (ed.) (1963), *Old Societies and New States: The Quest for Modernity in Asia and Africa*, Free Press of Glencoe: New York.
Gould, D. J. (1980), *Bureaucratic Corruption and Underdevelopment in the Third World: The Case of Zaire*, Pergamon Press: New York.
Gould, D. J. and Mukendi, T. B. (1989), 'Bureaucratic Corruption in Africa: Causes, Consequences and Remedies', *International Journal of Public Administration*, Vol. 12, No. 3, pp. 427–457.
Hiirschman, A. O. (1970), *Exit, Voice and Loyalty*, Harvard University Press: Cambridge, MA.
Kalevi, H. (1996), *The State, War, and the State of War*, Cambridge University Press: Cambridge.
MacGaffey, J. (1983), 'How to Survive and Become Rich Amidst Devastation: The Second Economy of Zaire', *African Affairs*, Vol. 82, No. 328, pp. 351–366.
Malloy, J. M. (1974), 'Authoritarianism, Corporatism and Mobilization in Peru', in Pike, F. B. and Stritch, T. (eds.), *The New Corporatism Social-Political Structures in the Iberian World*, University of Notre Dame Press: Notre Dame.
Mbaku, J. M. (1994), 'Bureaucratic Corruption and Policy Reform in Africa', *Journal of Social, Political and Economic Studies*, Vol. 19, No. 2, pp. 149–170.
Morse, R. M. (1961), 'The Heritage of Latin America', in Hartz, L. (ed.), *The Founding of New Societies*, Harcourt, Brace & World, Inc.: New York.
Nettl, J. P. (1968), 'The State as a Conceptual Variable', *World Politics*, Vol. 20, No. 4, pp. 559–592.
Rotberg, R. (2002), 'Failed States in a World of Terror', *Foreign Affairs*, Vol. 81, No. 4, pp. 127–140.
Schattschneider, E. E. (1960), *The Semi-sovereign People*, Holt, Rinehart and Winston: New York.
Schatzberg, M. (1988), *Dialectics of Oppression in Zaire*, Indiana University Press: Bloomington, IN.
Schmitter, P. C. (1974), 'Still the Century of Corporatism?', in Pike, F. B. and Stritch, T. (eds.), *The New Corporatism Social-Political Structures in the Iberian World*, University of Notre Dame Press: Notre Dame.
Scholte, J. A. (1997), 'Local Capitalism and the State', *International Affairs,* Vol. 3, No. 3, pp. 427–253.
Schwartzman, S. (1970), 'Representação e cooptação política no Brasil', *Dados*, Vol. 7, pp. 9–41.
Schwartzman, S. (1973), 'Regional Contrasts Within a Continental Scale Nation: Brazil', in Eisenstadt, S. N. and Rokkan, S. (eds.), *Building States and Nations*, Sage Publications: Beverly Hills, CA.
Schwartzman, S. (1975), *São Paulo e o Estado Nacional*, Difusão Européia do Livro: São Paulo.

Sklar, R. L. (1986), 'Reds and Rights', in Ronen, D. (ed.), *Democracy and Pluralism in Africa*, Lynne Rienner: Boulder, CO.

Tipps, D. C. (1973), 'Modernization Theory as the Study of National Societies: A Critical Perspective', *Comparative Studies in Society and History*, Vol. 15, No. 2 (March), pp. 199–226.

Wallensteen, P. (1994), 'Conflict Resolution in Larger Southeast Asia: Trends and Challenges', Paper presented at the Conference on Conflict Resolution, Human Rights and Development, Penang, Malaysia.

Wallensteen, P. and Sollenberg, M. (2001), 'Armed Conflicts, 1989–2000', *Journal of Peace Research*, Vol. 38, No. 5, pp. 629–644.

Weber, M. (1958), 'Politics as a Vocation', in Gerth, H. H. and Mills, C. W. (eds.), *From Max Weber: Essays in Sociology*, Oxford University Press: New York.

Weber, M. (1968), *Economy and Society*, Bedminster Press: New York.

3

State and Terrorism: A Global Overview

In a global context, successive regimes have tried to address and root out the evil of terrorism. The latest efforts spearheaded by the United States show that many who engage with the problematic of terrorism do not really know what they are dealing with, or the implications of what they are doing to address it. Fighting terrorism has become the facetious culture of a seemingly bi-polar world. In this bi-polar world, one is either with terrorists or against them. However, rhetoric and action that claim to root out terrorism often disguises the vacuity of anti-terrorism's greatest exponents, who, like weathervanes in a storm, like to self-importantly spin and rattle largely in a world of their own imagination. And this is a world where the causes of terrorism are ignored in the battle against its manifestations, where arrogant self-interests define the borderlines of conflict, and where the difference between an ally and an enemy is judged by the degree of subservience to a soi-disant coalition against terror.

While we think of terrorism as being both a political and irrational act (especially suicide terrorism), terrorism can also be thought of as a rational act conducted specifically because of the impact it will have—fear, confusion, submission, etc. Today, terrorism must be viewed within the context of the modern nation-state. Indeed, it was the rise of a bureaucratic state, which could not be destroyed by the death of one leader that forced terrorists to widen their scope of targets in order to create a public atmosphere of anxiety and undermine confidence in government. This reality is at the heart of the ever more violent terrorism of the last 100 years.

Following the tragic events of September 11, 2001, fighting terrorism became a worldwide priority for the obvious reason that hundreds of millions of people were suddenly at risk. The issue of confronting and preventing terrorism, up to now, the mission of a select few, became overnight, a top international priority. A strong demand for anti-terrorist educational tools and information resources has emerged for organizations, local governments, corporations, and citizens throughout the world and in particular the United States.

However, terrorism is not a novel phenomenon in world politics. Indeed, it is a method of violence with ancient historical roots. For instance, anarchists and other revolutionaries used terrorist methods in the nineteenth century. In fact, World War I was triggered partly by an act of terror. The assassination of Franz Ferdinand, Archduke (1863–1914) and heir to the imperial throne of the Austro-Hungarian Empire on June 28, 1914, provided the spark that ignited World War I.

What is new about terrorism at the close of the twentieth, and beginning of the twenty-first centuries is therefore that technology has been put into the hands of destructive groups and individuals. The destructive capabilities of technology, once reserved for governments, are now at the reach of many, even the most elusive enemies of mankind. Thus technology has rendered modern societies very vulnerable to large-scale attacks. And, this vulnerability of modern society accounts for why transnational terrorism has become very important today. The September 11, 2001 terrorist attack on the United States and the global reverberations it triggered made it categorically clear that even Americans are not safe anymore. Besides pointing up the United States' vulnerability, it left historical landmarks.

First, it was apparently the worst crime in American history. And it has triggered the greatest dragnet ever known. The investigation into the atrocities of September 11 has involved police forces across the United States and around the world. From Michigan to Malaysia, from San Diego to Ciudad del Este, Paraguay, law-enforcement agencies have been trying to figure out how the terrorists carried out their attacks, who helped them, and what they might do next. Along the way, the world has been introduced to a confusing mass of names and faces and has learned of more links between them than any but the most nimble fingered could ever untangle. Indeed, there is much that we know about the global terrorist network that goes by the name of al Qaeda. But there is an awful lot that is still hunch.

Any simple investigation into al Qaeda's structure reveals that it is as global in its range as it is ruthless in its ideology.

Second, September 11 rendered the conception of national geographical space thoroughly obsolete. Of course, geographical space was already anachronistic with respect to thermonuclear war. It had already been called to question by earlier acts of transnational informal violence like piracy. But this globalized informal violence or transnational terrorism carried out by non-state actors has altered the assumptions of foreign policy in a fundamental way (Keohane, 2002, p. 80). For example, Afghanistan was never a foreign policy concern in the United States until the Soviet Union's invasion in 1979 and the latter's collapse in 1991. On traditional grounds of U.S. national interest, Afghanistan became critical after September 11 and eventually a theater of war—a demonstration that threats to U.S. homeland security can come from anywhere in the global era.

Third, the transnationalization of informal violence defined by commitments rather than by territory brought to the fore the fact that all mainstream theories of world politics have been basically secular with respect to motivation. They ignore religion despite the fact that many earth-shaking movements have often been motivated by religious fervor. Though human desires either to dominate or hate have been very strong in human history as well as in classical realist thought, most theoreticians erroneously assume that 'rational and unheroic' members of the bourgeoisie run the world (Schumpeter, 1950, p. 137).

Fourth, September 11 took terrorism to entirely new levels of destructiveness. It was not the terrorism of the powerful against the weak, as in the case of the Ku Klux Klan violence against underprivileged blacks in the United States. September 11, 2001, was terrorism against the most powerful in the world. The Pentagon is the symbol of America's military might, and the World Trade Center a symbol of its economic might. Criminal and cruel as the action stands, the accused al Qaeda cave-dwellers picked on the super-rich and the mightiest military power in the world to challenge.

Finally, after September 11, 'belief' as a motivation for terrorism must be taken into account. Religious motivations in world politics are rarely highlighted in theoretical considerations. But, when Osama bin Laden declares that terrorism against 'infidels' will assure one 'a supreme place in heaven' (*New York Times*, October 8, 2001, p. B7), theopolitics should neither be ignored nor given casual attention. These historical and theoretical landmarks can be ignored only at man's peril. After all, are human activities across regions and continents not being increasingly linked together through technological and social change? And, has globalism as a state of affairs not been defined as 'a state of the world involving networks of interdependence at multicontinental distances, linked through flows of capital and goods, information and ideas, people and force, as well as environmentally relevant substances?' (Keohane and Nye, 2001, p. 229).

Technological and social change have dwarfed distances as well as rendered mankind very vulnerable. The World Trade Center bombing of February 26, 1993 and the Oklahoma bombing that followed some years later had already brought the United States within the circle of vulnerable states. The Middle East, Europe, Asia, Africa, and Latin America were already at the center of the waves of terrorist attacks from the late 1960s onwards. What then is terrorism, which has humbled people and nations as never before?

Terrorism: An elusive concept

On April 8, 2002, Mushahid Hussein filed a news story to the International Press Service (IPS). The report stated that:

> [d]espite being the driving force and the principal buzzword in international politics after September 11, political interests still define who is a terrorist or what constitutes an act of terrorism. Nowhere is this dichotomy more apparent than the United States-led 'war on terrorism' that is focused on those perceived as inimical to American interests, but looks the other way when 'state terrorism' of Israel is involved or those combating such 'state terrorism' as the Palestinians are concerned.

Conversely, a similar dilemma confronts the Muslim world, resulting in a divide on the definition of terrorism. This was apparent during the Conference of Islamic Foreign Ministers in Kuala Lumpur, Malaysia, which ended without a unanimous view on this all-important but contentious issue. That conference was convened in a changed international context post-September 11, one where the United States treats 'terrorism' as the number one priority in foreign and domestic policy.

Meantime, the 'intifadah' in Palestine since the full-fledged Israeli invasion of the Palestinian Authority after March 29, 2003 had cost 200 Palestinian lives. There is the perception among Muslims that their religion and religious brethren are being singled out, while their governments remain reluctant to defend them. Given this context, the Kuala Lumpur meeting was aimed at achieving three goals.

First, it aimed to give reassurance and a sense of hope to Muslims that their governments are capable of protecting their rights and promoting Islam as a religion that rejects terrorism and violence. Second, it was held to counter the American policy that ends up tarring all terrorism with the same brush, which has an undercurrent of religious coloring—as if only Muslims are responsible for terrorism, given the policies toward Palestine, Kashmir, Chechnya or the operations against the Abu Sayyaf guerrillas in the Philippines. Third, it aimed to present a consensual, Islamic definition of terrorism that could then form the basis of building a global consensus given the current international focus on this issue.

However, the conference got bogged down over the issue of Palestinian suicide bombers, whom the host, Malaysian Prime Minister Mahathir Mohamad, denounced as 'terrorists.' The Arab delegates rejected this notion, viewing Palestinian attacks as legitimate resistance to Israeli state terrorism.

This disagreement over definitions of the phenomenon of terrorism only confirms three things: one, that terrorism is an ever-present threat to modern society; two, that it is prevalent; and, three, that terrorism is an elusive concept. However, 'Terrorism' might be an accurate term for the September 11 attacks, but it becomes dangerously simplistic and self-serving when used by interested parties to characterize all forms of conflict, violence, and resistance to oppression. For that reason Amnesty International does not use the term, but speaks instead of 'attacks against civilians.'

The indiscriminate use of the term 'terrorist' allows strong parties—especially states—to define who is or is not a 'terrorist,' what is 'legitimate' use of power and what isn't, who is 'with us' and who is not. This approach to viewing terrorism risks stigmatizing whole populations or religions. The by-products of such an approach—ever-escalating conflict in which the 'nuclear option' has been mentioned, rising levels of personal insecurity, global xenophobia, and the setting aside of human rights in favor of ethnic 'profiling' and other discriminatory practices—certainly outweigh the emotional satisfaction of taking revenge. And, in the end, it is almost a truism that combating what is essentially a political problem by military means is futile and self-defeating. But, in order to find effective counter-measures for terrorism, one must first understand its meaning, history, modern tactics and underlying principles. Only then can effective counter-terrorism policies be developed.

Does the fact that one side's 'terrorist' is usually another's 'freedom fighter' mean that there is no possibility of agreeing on ethical norms applicable to armed conflicts between governments and their opponents? There are no easy answers to this question. We cannot simply condemn all violence against established governments; surely, the Jews of the Warsaw ghetto were right to defend themselves. Nor can we accept the cynical view that ethical judgments are irrelevant, that violence is justified when it succeeds, and that 'might makes right.' This view is morally repugnant and impractical. In practice, we must make judgments before we know which actions will succeed and which will fail according to definitions of actions called terrorist ones.

Terror is a condition or state of mind induced by the power of the unknown, unknowable, or unpredictable acts (or omissions) of nature or of man. According to Webster's *Third New International Dictionary* (p. 2361), the origin of the word can be traced to the Sanskrit 'trasati,' meaning 'he trembles, is afraid' and to the Greek 'trein,' to 'flee from fear, be afraid.'

Since September 11, 2001, acts committed by terrorists have become increasingly very destructive. Natural forces—volcanoes, hurricanes, earthquakes, disease—while remaining untamed and powerful, are no longer quite as unpredictable or untreatable as in the past. Less predictable are the acts of terror instigated by human beings. These are called terrorism. As stated in the *Joint Publication 1-02, Department of Defense Dictionary of Military and Associated Terms*, of April 12, 2001 (p. 435), terrorism is 'the calculated use of unlawful violence or threat of unlawful violence to inculcate fear; intended to coerce or to intimidate governments or societies in pursuit of goals that are generally political, religious, or ideological.'

Terror or terrorism seems to be a staple of human relations. It can be inflicted either on its own terms or be associated with more general warfare. From World War I through the Iran-Iraq War (1980–1988), the use of gas induced added terror among soldiers and civilians. Air raids on cities during World War II using incendiary munitions were another instance of terror within the larger war, as were the V-1 and V-2 rockets aimed at cities by the Nazis. In the nuclear era, the term 'balance of terror' became a common alternative to mutual assured destruction (MAD).

International conventions on terrorism

Terrorism as a subject of concern for the international community as a whole is relatively recent. Chapter VII of the United Nations Charter addresses the existence of 'any threat to the peace, breach of the peace, or act of aggression' and the 'inherent right of individual and collective self-defense if an armed attack occurs against a member' state. But the intent of the charter was to preclude state-to-state violence, not violence by sub-national organizations.

On September 14, 1963, in Tokyo, the United Nations sponsored the initial international agreement on terrorism connected with aircraft: the Convention on Offences and Certain Other Acts Committed on Board Aircraft was opened for signature. The convention entered into force on December 4, 1969, and currently has 41 signatories and 172 contracting states. Charter IV deals with unlawful seizure of an aircraft.

The Convention for the Suppression of Unlawful Seizure of Aircraft, signed December 16, 1970 at The Hague, entered into force October 14, 1971 (now with 77 signatories and 174 ratifications/accessions); and the Convention for the Suppression of Unlawful Acts Against the Safety of Civil Aviation, signed September 23, 1971 at Montreal, entered into force Jan. 26, 1973 (now with 60 signatories and 175 ratifications/accessions). A supplementary convention to the latter was signed in Montreal on February 24, 1988.

Other anti-terrorism conventions of the 1980s and early 1990s dealt with hostage-taking, oil platforms, ships, nuclear materials, and plastic explosives. But the word 'terrorist' did not specifically appear in the titles of agreements until the mid-1990s. In 1994, the General Assembly adopted the Declaration on Measures to Eliminate International Terrorism, supplementing it in 1996. On December 15, 1997, the U.N. General Assembly adopted the Convention on the Suppression of Terrorist Bombings, which went into force May 23, 2001 (with 58 signatories and 29 ratifications/accessions—Afghanistan, Pakistan, Iran, Iraq, Syria, North Korea, China, and Saudi Arabia were not party to the treaty. Russia and all NATO countries are all signatories). And on December 9, 1999 the Assembly adopted the Convention for the Suppression of the Financing of Terrorism. With 54 signatories and 4 contracting states, the 1999 convention is not yet in force—it needs 22 ratifications/accessions.

Also in 1999, the U.N. Security Council passed two resolutions—1267 and 1269 concerning terrorism. While 1269 'unequivocally condemned all acts of terrorism as criminal and unjustifiable,' 1267 was more directly focused, demanding Afghanistan surrender Osama bin Laden 'to appropriate authorities so that he can be brought to justice.' Resolution 1333, passed in 2000, called on the 'Taliban to close' terrorist training camps in Afghanistan.

In an accident of timing, the 56th session of the U.N. General Assembly opened September 12, 2001. In one of its first actions, the assembly condemned the attacks of the previous day. Between September 11 and the end of that month, seven of 16 press announcements concerning the General Assembly dealt with terrorism. On September 12, the Security Council passed resolution 1368 (2001), which 'condemned in the strongest terms the terrorist attack against the United States and called on all states to work together urgently to bring the perpetrators to justice.' And on September 28, the Security Council passed resolution 13773 (2001) which called for suppressing terrorist financing and improving international cooperation on stopping the movement of funds for terrorists.

Finally, there are seven anti-terrorist conventions that are regionally based: the Organization of American States (1971), the Council of Europe (1977), the South Asian Association for Regional Cooperation (1987), the Arab League (1998), the Islamic Conference (1999), the Commonwealth of Independent States (1999), and the Organization of African Unity (1999).

With post-Cold War globalization supposedly breaking down barriers and uniting peoples, why does terrorism seem to be so difficult to define but flourishing and becoming more virulent despite the numerous recent conventions and resolutions calling on nations to act against terror?

The plethora of definitions as seen above teaches us one important lesson: That defining terrorism therefore poses a multiplicity of problems. The first problem is that the term itself is subjective in nature. Terrorism is disturbing. It disturbs not just emotionally and morally but also intellectually. And commentaries on terrorism, more than on other subjects, seem liable to be swayed by wishful thinking, to base themselves on unwarranted or flawed assumptions, and to draw from these assumptions irrational inferences. This is the case with the ideas on terrorism expressed muzzily above.

Like 'fanaticism,' 'guerilla warfare,' 'fundamentalism,' 'extremism,' and 'rebels,' terrorism is a preconditioned political term. And it is generally applied in a manner that satisfies the needs of the person using it. This application makes the term elusive. This elusiveness gives credence to the adage that 'One man's terrorist is another man's freedom fighter.' Nevertheless, today the term 'terrorism' has come to mean something negative, whereas terms such 'guerilla fighters,' and 'freedom fighters,' often carry a positive connotation. Unfortunately, these concepts cannot be utilized interchangeably.

The second problem is that of the limited scope in which terrorism is defined. Numerous history books and studies fail to recognize the application of terrorism prior to the French Revolution. According to many historians (e.g., Lefebvre, 1965), the French Revolution marked the beginning of terrorism. In fact, the word terrorism was first used in 1795, a grim spawn of the heady period that brought the American War of Independence and the French Revolution. The word was born with the Reign of Terror, the use of the guillotine by the French revolutionaries to consolidate their regime by killing their enemies and intimidating the potential opposition. However, the concept and application of terrorism existed prior to man's first recordings. To classify terrorism as a current phenomenon fails to recognize its role throughout human history (Walker, 2001).

A third problem with defining terrorism, especially today, is that it is often associated with an 'extreme form of violence.' However, terrorism can take place in forms other than violence-psychological or economic terrorism. Nowadays the face of terrorism is rapidly changing. From passive resistance to technological and economic terrorism, terrorism no longer necessarily implies spilling of blood to be effective (Rapoport, 1984).

A fourth and final problem with defining terrorism is that it is not a catch-all phrase. It can be divided into two distinct categories. One category involves terrorism of the state and another is terrorism of the individual. The tactics utilized by both are distinctly different in that: (1) Terrorism of the individual is normally focused on disrupting a government to the point that individual liberties are gradually rescinded and a more authoritarian regime is put into place, which as history has shown, is more vulnerable to uprising and will assist the terrorist in achieving his desired objective of stirring up a revolution. Terrorism of the individual also aims at drawing international attention to its plight, and to diverting resources of the state until the latter can no longer adequately cope with demands and thus becomes weaker. (2) Terrorism of the state, in contrast, seeks to quiet the masses and harshly suppress any rebellion. Its supreme goal is unchecked authoritarian power.

These distinctions notwithstanding, international opinion has deplored terrorism in all forms, regardless of political motives, yet the international community has never agreed on what exactly constitutes terrorism. As a result, international law has instead chosen to address specific forms of terrorism, such as hijackings and abduction of foreign dignitaries, and to introduce measures to ensure international cooperation to combat and investigate terrorist incidents. For example, four UN conventions address aircraft and airport seizure or sabotage (1963, 1970, 1971, 1988), and a recent resolution issued by the UN Security Council requests UN-member states to report on their counter terrorism measures within 90 days (Resolution 1373, issued September 28, 2001).

No one definition of terrorism has already gained universal acceptance. However, many in the international community would like to see one definition and law supplant the dozen-odd conventions and protocols governing hijackings, use of nuclear materials, hostage seizure, and other manifestations of terrorism. Without a law defining terrorism, there can be no enforcement of the would-be law. For the purposes of this study, however, we have chosen the definition of terrorism contained in Title 22 of the United States Code, Section 2656f(d). That statute contains the following definitions:

- The term 'terrorism' means premeditated, politically motivated violence perpetrated against noncombatant targets by subnational groups or clandestine agents, usually intended to influence an audience.
- The term 'international terrorism' means terrorism involving citizens or the territory of more than one country.
- The term 'terrorist group' means any group practicing, or that has significant subgroups that practice, international terrorism. The U.S. government has employed this definition of terrorism for statistical and analytical purposes since 1983.

On terrorism, more than on other subjects, commentary seems therefore liable to be swayed by wishful thinking. It is also liable to base itself on unwarranted or flawed assumptions. And, commentary is even likely to draw from these assumptions irrational inferences that may be muzzily expressed. We shall therefore not go into any sterile polemics on the definition of terrorism. However, we shall use four crucial elements to define acts of terrorism. That is, an act of terrorism: (1) is an act of violence; (2) has a political motive or goal; (3) is perpetrated against innocent persons; and (4) is staged for an audience whose reaction of fear and terror is the desired result.

Historical background

For the nearest historical parallel, the war against piracy in the nineteenth century was an important element in the expansion of colonialism. It could be that a new form of colony, the Western-administered former terrorist state, is only just over the horizon. The colonial expansion of the major imperialist powers, above all the British Empire, was claimed to be bringing a halt to piracy. In fact, imperialist conquest in the nineteenth century had nothing to do with 'piracy.' It was rather the outcome of a struggle by the major capitalist powers to enhance their position in the global competition for profits, markets and resources. Is today's war against 'terrorism' being pursued for the same aims? Or, is it a war to rid the international as well as national communities of destructive irritants?

Until well into the twentieth century, terror usually meant state terror. The tactics of the French revolutionaries were copied by the Cheka secret police founded by Vladimir Lenin in 1918 to ensure the Bolshevik grip on power and later by Nazi Germany's Gestapo in the 1930s and 1940s. Incidentally, it was the Nazi occupiers of Europe during the World War II who characterized the work of the French, Czech, Polish, and other resistance movements that were supplied and fomented by Britain's Special Operations (SOE) Executive, as 'terrorism' (Mackenzie, 2002).

For the resistance movements, and for their British backers in SOE who had been ordered by Prime Minister Winston Churchill to 'set Europe ablaze,' they were not terrorists but freedom fighters. Their clandestine work of sabotage and ambush—destroying bridges and railroads and assassinating German officials and their local collaborators—was a wholly justifiable tactic of a war of national liberation. That was precisely the justification used after the war by a series of anticolonial movements. British and American forces pitted against the Japanese had supplied some justifications, like the Viet Minh against French rule in Vietnam. After 1945, the Viet Minh used the wartime tactics of resistance to attack the returning French with the classic weapons of terrorism, raiding remote plantations to kill French overseers, random shootings and bombs in crowded cafes, all designed to destroy the morale of the French civilians. Similar tactics were used against the British in Palestine by Israeli freedom fighters (or 'terrorists' as the British called them at that time), including the future Israeli Prime Ministers Menachem Begin and Yitzhak Shamir. The Irgun and Stern Gang blew up civilians in hotels, assassinated British troops, and ambushed British patrols, all in the name of the national liberation of Israel.

Learning from these examples of terror, the National Liberation Front (FLN) of Algeria fought French rule with a ruthless terror campaign, using Arab women dressed as fashionable young Frenchwomen, to place bombs in cafes, dancehalls, and cinemas. The French fought back ferociously, and in the battle of Algiers, General Jacques Massu's battalion of paratroopers broke the FLN terrorist networks in the *casbah*, or Arab quarter, with ruthless interrogations and the widespread use of torture. The Battle of Algiers was a military victory, but a political defeat. The victory was horrifying to public opinion in France and elsewhere, toppling French governments, and eroding the French national will to maintain the struggle against the FLN. France suffered a political collapse that returned the wartime hero General Charles de Gaulle to power. Charles de Gaulle, of course, eventually launched negotiations that led to Algerian independence in 1962.

These were the lessons that inspired contemporary terrorism, a phenomenon that emerged from the twin roots of the Arab-Israeli Six Day War of 1967 and the worldwide student movements of 1968. The devastating Arab defeat and the Israeli occupation of the West Bank and Gaza Strip inspired the Palestine Liberation Organization to adopt terrorist tactics since it was too weak to fight an orthodox struggle. Other pro-Palestine groups imposed their demands on a global audience by hijacking airliners and kidnapping and killing Israeli athletes at the 1972 Olympic Games in Munich (Hoffman, 1999).

Phenomenon of terrorism today

The world today is different because the context and the fundamentals are different. Globally, the world is living through an increase in population and change in other arenas that are exponential—growing at rates never before seen in human history. In very real terms this is a systems problem—different parts of the system are rapidly shifting at the same time and in the process the behavior of the whole system is necessarily changing. Poverty and religious differences continue as they have in the past, operating within economic and governmental systems that largely have no fundamental incentives built into them for ultimately eliminating, let alone dealing effectively in the short term with the basic problems. The structure and even philosophy is the product of the past—a time when all of this change was not in place.

The structure and philosophy of the past are on their dying throes. Today, people are living in a time when the rich are getting richer faster than any time in history, when extraordinary population increases are producing multitudes of poor people who have access to television—and unlike only fifty years ago, are aware of how the rich live (*New York Times*, September 9, 1998; *The Economist*, April 28, 2001, pp. 72–74, 80). This rapidly growing technology is an amplifier of the economic and theological differences that people feel and these perspectives are only likely to become more acute in the coming decade as the have/have-not divide broadens. Reactions to these changes vary from passive resistance to violent opposition. It is this violent opposition that becomes terror, depending on who views it.

The terrorism which prevailed in Europe and Latin America during the 1970s and 1980s tended to be an outgrowth of national liberation struggles, or of anti-capitalist movements, and frequently had state-backing, most notably from the Soviet Union directly, or indirectly from Soviet Bloc countries such as East Germany, Cuba, and so on as alleged at that time. It was therefore often possible to observe the ideological steps through which the players passed in their conversion from political activism to terrorism. Generally, this transformation would include several of the following elements: (1) opposition to the state or to perceived injustice, expressed through democratic means; (2) a lack of response, or an inappropriate response, by authority; (3) extreme, but not necessarily violent, opposition to the authority; (4) repression by that authority; (5) terrorism against a specific target seen as a symbol of that authority; and (6) further repression.

This process has as its objective to de-legitimize the terrorist's target. Indeed, the common factor in all types of terrorism today is an observable process of demonstrating that the target is not conforming to recognized principles or accepted rules and standards. That is the process of 'de-legitimization' of the target by the terrorist or the terrorist group (Sprinzak, 2000, pp. 9–12). There are universal criteria by which the process of de-legitimization can be observed and measured for the sake of scientific research. First of all, there is the 'crisis of confidence,' which may be the product of anger and might lead to extra-parliamentary action. But the anger may not yet amount to the total rejection of the target's legitimacy. Secondly, there is the 'conflict of legitimacy itself,' which is similar to the foregoing. But here the opponent's legitimacy is rejected although there may still be a gap between the intention and the capability of the 'embryonic' terrorist. Finally, there is the 'action,' which is a consequence of closing the gap between the words (or protests) and the deed.

The most important indicators of the monitoring process suggested by Sprinzak (2000) are: (1) previous involvement of the organization and/or its leaders in violence; (2) conviction within the group that they can get away with violence; (3) the presence, or absence, of charismatic, and sometimes paranoiac leaders who promote violence; (4) a sense of looming disaster (e.g., an influx of foreign workers coinciding with an increase in unemployment); and (5) recent humiliation and an urge for revenge.

Terrorism today still bears some features of the pre-1990 terrorism. But, the most marked difference is that the new characteristics of contemporary terrorism make it much more difficult to monitor and prevent despite the availability of modern technology. Terrorism of the 1990s and that of today includes some elements of the aforementioned pre-1990 type; but new ones also characterize it. By way of explanation, two types of terrorism are now predominant; that is to say, in the United States and Europe: (1) 'new' far right terrorism; and, (2) religious terrorism. The new far right is often not distinguished by membership in visible and well-organized groups with hierarchical structures. The most overt features of the traditional far right are public manifestations, such as marching in uniform or rioting against immigrants like in France, and an open adherence to Nazi or fascist ideology. The new ideology is influenced by concepts such as 'leaderless resistance' and 'lone-wolf' or 'individual' acts of terrorism. The ideological mentors are not Hitler and Mussolini, or other far right ideologues of the 1930s and 1940s (although they play an influential part).

Examples are not in limited supply. The American white supremacists William Pierce, Louis Beam, and others readily come to mind here. William Pierce, a former member of both the John Birch Society and the American Nazi Party, has been leading the National Alliance. In his fictional writing (using the nom de plume of Andrew Macdonald) he promotes the concept of a 'white race war' and the violent overthrow of the federal government. Beam, a former Ku Klux Klan instructor in guerrilla warfare, and now a leader in Aryan Nations, promotes the ideology of 'leaderless resistance' (Macdonald, 1978; Beam, 1992).

The second type is religious terrorism. Religious terrorism promotes a stark and uncompromising world-view dictated by the belief that a specific religion has the sole key to a 'messianic' age. This brand of terrorism rejects all other paths to that messianic age. It uses religion as a cloak for its revolutionary and violent theology. It may be anti-Western and anti-modernist, as in Islamism, or it may have developed as a reactionary response, as with Jewish and Hindu ultra-nationalists (e.g., Kahane-Chai,

Rashtriya Swayamsevak Sangh, Bajrang Dal). The new terrorism is mostly played out on the domestic scene.

Domestic terrorism

Domestic terrorism is probably a more widespread phenomenon than international terrorism. In other parts of the world, species of domestic terrorists tend to be systemic; in the United States, they are cyclic. Domestic terrorism can involve right-wing, left-wing, anti-government, pro-government, anti-tax, paramilitary, anti-abortion, anti-religious, anti-ethnic, and militia groups. The United States has it all, but for the most part, much of the domestic counter terrorism in the United States is militia-watching. In dealing with right-wing domestic terrorism, often a good counterstrategy is simply to watch, and let them know you are watching (Laqueur, 1999). This keeps the terrorists underground, and deprives them of publicity and a wider audience. It is often said that journalists are terrorists' best friends. Depriving terrorists of publicity acts as a deterrent. The best counter terrorism strategy, however, involves advanced computer technology and informants.

U.S. domestic terrorism was at one time a left-wing phenomenon with groups such as the Weathermen and Black Panthers active in the 1960s and 1970s. Before that, it was anti-Catholic during the nineteenth century, and then became anti-black and anti-Semitic in the twentieth century. It has now evolved into diverse and divided right-wing extremism consisting of white supremacists, tax rebels, militia patriots, Christian patriots, Christian reconstructionists, anti-abortionists, and neo-Nazis. Such extremism has not been confined to the United States—it exists worldwide in places like Germany and Italy. Israel even has right-wing terrorism. It embraces all the exotic forms of terror—cyber- (groups operate over 200 websites at last count), eco- (they hate the 'tree huggers' but share a common vision), and weapons of mass destruction—WMD (groups have been caught preparing biological weapons). The extreme right does not have a well-delineated party line, and is best seen as a breeding ground for terrorism since there is no command-and-control structure. They take leaderless resistance to new levels with self-made 'phantom' cells, which ensure the movement's survival even if everyone else in the group is eliminated or compromised. The one thing they have in common is hate.

Recent evidence suggests that acts of international terrorism now only account for 10 percent of all terrorist attacks (Gunaratna, 2001, p. 47). This applies even to Islamist terrorism, with the exception of the international unaffiliated *jihadist mujahideen* organizations who operate worldwide with impunity. In the United States, domestic terrorist bombings or attempted bombings (i.e., carried out by U.S. nationals) increased by 52 percent from 1990 (2,098 incidents) to 1994 (3,199 incidents), even before the Oklahoma City bombing in 1995. In the same period international terrorist attacks declined by 24 percent, from 437 to 332 incidents. In the following four years they declined even further, by 46 percent, to 174 incidents (U.S. State Department, 1996).

A second difference between 'new' and 'old' terrorism is that new terrorism tends to adopt a networked and less hierarchical form. Both the anti-capitalist and the national liberation terrorist groups of the 1970s and 1980s mostly had hierarchical forms and chains of command. Some even had identifiable operational leaders (e.g., Andreas Baader and Ulrike Meinhof of the German extreme left Rote Armed Faction; Ahmed Jibril of the Popular Front for the Liberation of Palestine—General Command; Abimael Guzman, of the Peruvian Sendero Luminoso).

Moreover, new terrorism tends to be diffused. In defining 'leaderless resistance,' Louis Beam, suggested that hierarchy be downplayed in favor of a network of elusive or 'phantom cells.' These cells would communicate covertly. But there must be allowance for offensive flexibility while protecting the security of the organization as a whole. In fact, Beam (1992, p. 4) argues that

> utilizing the leaderless resistance concept, all individuals in groups operate independently of each other, and never report to a central headquarters or single leader for directional instruction . . . participants in a program of leaderless resistance through phantom cell or individual action, must know exactly what they are doing and exactly how to do it . . . all members of phantom cells or individuals, will tend to react to objective events in the same way through usual tactics of resistance. Organs of information distribution, such as newspapers, leaflets, computers, etc which are widely available to all, keep each person informed of events allowing for a planned response that will take many variations. No one need issue an order to anyone.

The U.S. State Department notes that the greatest terrorist threat comes from the Middle East and Southeast Asia (with Afghanistan and Pakistan serving as the primary hosts and the source of most recruits). Here terrorism is almost completely Islamist. Islamist terrorists have also adopted the network form, with disparate actors coming together to commit a terrorist act. The GIA bombings in France in the early 1990s were carried out by a networked organization with its command and control center in London, safe-housing in Belgium and targets in France. Likewise the American Jihad group of Shaykh Omar Abdurrahman was composed of members from disparate backgrounds, as is the al Qaeda group of Osama bin Laden. And the group arrested by police in January 2001 in Germany, Italy and the United Kingdom alleged to have been plotting to blow up Strasbourg Cathedral also operates as a network (U.S. State Department, 2001).

Islamists have successfully demonstrated that geographical dispersion provides the security that a rigid hierarchy does not. Hamas constitutes yet another example of the network format, compared with, for instance, the hierarchical format of Arafat's al-Fatah. Hamas has separated its political and military wings, and its leadership is divided between Gaza, Jordan and Syria. Yet, some of its political direction and most of its fund-raising has been carried out in the United States while its publications are partly produced in the United Kingdom. (*Filistin al Muslima*, the main Hamas newspaper is published in London, as is *Palestine Times*, the editorial line of which is pro-Hamas.)

It is noteworthy that Islamists have been more effective in their coordination and networking than have the far right. The far right, particularly in the United States and Germany, have been unable to follow through with their stated goals, and currently pose no effective terrorist challenge to the state. Because the far right has been so individualistic and random, it has taken on a self-destructive and nihilistic character. Islamists, even without state backing, have coordinated terrorism transnationally in pursuit of pre-determined goals. Criminal activity by Algerian Islamists in Canada and the United Kingdom to finance terrorism in a second country, while retaining command and control in a third country, indicates a sophisticated level of networking which the far right has been unable to achieve so far.

Third, the networked form is assisted by the growing use of information and communication technologies (ICTs). ICTs enable extremists to communicate covertly and to bridge distances and the far right was the first to understand its potential. ICTs allow the publication of material, which in hard copy format would be illegal. They also allow encryption, thus frustrating the efforts of law enforcement agencies to investigate their plans. Islamists have also seized on the advantages offered by ICTs, which allow advanced communications within the Diaspora and between the military and religious leadership and their followers. In contrast to the heavily surveilled, oppressive atmosphere within most Middle Eastern countries, terrorist leaders who have relocated in the West face no difficulties in acquiring state-of-the-art communications technology. They have spread throughout the West to make use of ever more advanced modes of communication—audio tapes, video tapes, fax machines, and now the Internet (Barsky, 1996, pp. 3–9). In the early 1990s Hamas was able to collect and analyze field reports from Gaza in Chicago and send the resultant operational orders back to Gaza.[1]

Fourth, the new terrorist frequently does not claim responsibility for the action and may even deny it. It is the act that is important and not the claim to it, exemplified in the 1998 East African bombings. The terrorism of the 1970s and 1980s was often marked by the issuing of post-factum communiqués. And indeed with the Provisional Irish Republican Army (PIRA) and other terrorist groups, what is en vogue is the issuing of co-warnings beforehand. The new terrorist intends to strike, and to go on striking without publicity for himself or his cause, until he is caught. He does not need to claim responsibility perhaps because he acknowledges only God as his master, and God has seen his action. No one else matters.

Fifth, many of the new terrorists are amateurs or operate on a part-time basis. The terrorism of the 1970s and 1980s was characterized by professionalism in the sense that many of its actors had dropped out of society to concentrate on this activity. European anti-capitalist groups, particularly, were frequently composed of people living in communes. Therefore, law enforcers only had to infiltrate the commune to find out what their plans were. With the lone terrorist or small cell, this is now impossible. It has been noted that law enforcement and security agencies now complain that while the new terrorists may have religious or quasi-religious motives they are not linked to any organization, have no base, raise their own funds and attack soft targets, leaving no trace. This has been described as 'a more amorphous, enigmatic, form of terrorism' (Norton-Taylor and Walker, 1995).

Sixth, the new terrorism, especially religiously-impelled terrorism, does not confine itself to any boundaries and possesses a terrifying lethality. When terrorism was backed by states, there were limits to the extent to which the perpetrators would go. These inhibitions no longer apply. Frequently the old terrorism sought out representative targets and made its point by one or two surgical strikes. The new terrorism tends to go for the highest possible body count, (e.g., the Oklahoma City bombing, 1995; the World Trade Center bombing, 1993; the Tokyo sarin gas attack, 1995; and the World Trade Center bombing of 2001). Exceptions to this pattern do exist such as in recent cases of covert state-sponsored terrorism, e.g., the downing of Pan Am 103 over Lockerbie in December 1988, and the UTA flight over Chad in August 1989, both perpetrated by Libya; the bombing of the AMIA building in Buenos Aires in 1994, where Iran is regarded as culpable.

It is to be understood that not only Islamists are driven by religious motives. The influence of Christian 'identity' ideology is vital to our understanding of modern far right terrorism. Christian 'identity' adherents believe that the white Anglo-Saxon Protestant is the true descendant of the lost tribes of Israel and that the Jews are impostors. The Jews and the 'mud' people (African-Americans and Asians), the Christian identity believers argue, are polluting the United States and/or Europe, and their influence must be stopped. The threat from the 'religiously impelled' American far right and Islamists will likely continue as long as their only strategic agenda is to wage Jihad in order to reconstitute the 'Muslim community' (umma) beyond the national and ethnic divides; hence their support for the various jihad at the periphery of the Muslim world: Kashmir, the Philippines, Chechnya, Uzbekistan, Bosnia and so forth. In this sense, they are genuinely global and recruit among uprooted cosmopolite, 'de-territorialized' militants, themselves a sociological product of globalization: many migrated in order to find employment or education opportunities, they easily travel and change their citizenship. In their use of English, computers, satellite phones and other technology, they are an authentic product of the modern, globalized world. Their battlefield is the whole world from New Jersey to the Philippines.

State-sponsored (international) terrorism

Terrorism is a modus operandi through which targeted violence is used against citizens, in order to achieve political objectives or even strategic goals. Terrorist organizations are the organizations that carry out acts of terror as a means to promote their goals. For many years, terrorism was perceived as a contest between two sides: on the one hand, a group of people or an organization, and on the other, a sovereign state. However, during the course of the second half of the twentieth century, various countries began to use terrorist organizations to promote state interests in the international domain. In some cases, states have established 'puppet' terrorist organizations, whose purpose is to act on behalf of the sponsoring state, to further the interests of the state, and to represent its positions in domestic or regional fronts. In other cases, states sponsor existing organizations, on the basis of mutual interests.

The patron state provides its beneficiary terrorist organization with political support, financial assistance, logistics, and the sponsorship necessary to maintain and expand its struggle. The patron uses the beneficiary to perpetrate acts of terrorism as a means of spreading the former's ideology throughout the word, or in some cases, the patron ultimately expects the beneficiary to gain control of the state in which it resides or impart its ideology to broad sections of the general public. State sponsored terrorism can only achieve strategic ends where the use of conventional armed forces is not practical or effective. The high costs of modern warfare, and concern about non-conventional escalation, as well as the danger of defeat and the unwillingness to appear as the aggressor, have turned terrorism into an efficient, convenient, and generally discrete weapon for attaining state interests in the international realm.

Countries that sponsor terrorism are those that use terrorism and terrorist organizations as instruments to advance their objectives, host terror organizations and provide them shelter and support. The involvement of these countries is liable to manifest in various ways, beginning with different levels of indirect aid to terrorists or terrorist organizations, escalate to initiation and marshaling of terrorist attacks by terrorist organizations, and end with directly carrying out acts of terror through the state-run apparatuses of the country.

Iran, Iraq, Syria, Libya, Cuba, North Korea, and Sudan continue to be the seven governments that the United States has designated as state sponsors of international terrorism, while Iran remained the most active state sponsor of terrorism in 2000. Iran provided increasing support to numerous terrorist groups, including the Lebanese Hizballah, Hamas, and the Palestine Islamic Jihad (PIJ), which seek to undermine the Middle East peace negotiations through the use of terrorism. Iraq under Saddam Hussein provided safe haven and support to a variety of Palestinian rejectionist groups, as well as bases, weapons, and protection to the Mujahedin-e-Khalq (MEK), an Iranian terrorist group that opposes the current Iranian regime. Syria continued to provide safe haven and support to several terrorist groups, some of which oppose the Middle East peace negotiations. Libya at the end of 2000 was attempting to mend its international image following its surrender in 1999 of two Libyan suspects for trial in the Pan Am 103 bombing. In early 2001, one of the suspects was convicted of murder. The judges in the case found that he acted 'in furtherance of the purposes of . . . Libyan Intelligence Services' (U.S. State Department, 2000). Cuba continued to provide safe haven to several terrorists and U.S. fugitives and maintained ties to state sponsors and Latin American insurgents. North Korea harbored several hijackers of a Japanese Airlines flight to North Korea in the 1970s and maintained links to other terrorist groups. Finally, Sudan continued to serve as a safe haven for members of al Qaeda, the Lebanese Hizballah, al-Gama'a al-Islamiyya, Egyptian Islamic Jihad, the PIJ, and Hamas, but it has been engaged in a counterterrorism dialogue with the United States since mid-2000 (U.S. State Department, 2000).

State sponsorship has decreased over the past several decades. As it decreases, it becomes increasingly important for all countries to adopt 'zero tolerance' for terrorist activity within their borders. Terrorists will seek safe haven in those areas where they are able to avoid the rule of law and to travel, prepare, raise funds, and operate. The United States continues actively researching and gathering intelligence on other states that will be considered for designation as state sponsors. If the United States deems a country to 'repeatedly provide support for acts of international terrorism,' the U.S. government is required by law to add such a country to the list (U.S. State Department, 2000).

In South Asia, the United States has been increasingly concerned about reports of Pakistani support to terrorist groups and elements active in Kashmir, as well as Pakistani support, especially military support, to the Taliban, which continues to harbor terrorist groups, including al Qaeda, the Egyptian Islamic Jihad, al-Gama'a al-Islamiyya, and the Islamic Movement of Uzbekistan. In the Middle East, the United States was concerned that a variety of terrorist groups operated and trained inside Lebanon, although Lebanon has acted against some of those groups. Lebanon also has been unresponsive to U.S. requests to bring to justice terrorists who conducted attacks against U.S. citizens and property in Lebanon in previous years.

The designation of state sponsors of terrorism by the United States—and the imposition of sanctions—is a mechanism for isolating nations that use terrorism as a means of political expression. U.S. policy seeks to pressure and isolate state sponsors so they will renounce the use of terrorism, end support to terrorists, and bring terrorists to justice for past crimes. The United States is committed to holding terrorists and those who harbor them accountable for past attacks, regardless of when the acts occurred. The U.S. government has a long memory and is not ready to simply expunge a terrorist's record because time has passed. The states that choose to harbor terrorists are deemed accomplices who provide shelter for criminals, liable to be held accountable for the actions of their 'guests.'

Iran's involvement in terrorist-related activities remained focused on support for groups opposed to Israel and peace between Israel and its neighbors. Statements by Iran's leaders demonstrated Iran's unrelenting hostility to Israel. Supreme Leader Khamenei continued to refer to Israel as a 'cancerous tumor' that must be removed; President Khatami, labeling Israel an 'illegal entity,' called for sanctions against Israel during the intifadah; and Expediency Council Secretary Rezai said, 'Iran will continue its campaign against Zionism until Israel is completely eradicated.' Iran has long provided Lebanese Hizballah and the Palestinian rejectionist groups—notably Hamas, the Palestine Islamic Jihad, and Ahmad Jibril's PFLP-GC—with varying amounts of funding, safe haven, training, and weapons. This activity continued at its already high levels following the Israeli withdrawal from southern Lebanon in May and during the intifadah in the fall. Iran continued to encourage Hizballah and the Palestinian groups to coordinate their planning and to escalate their activities against Israel. Iran also provided a lower level of support—including funding, training, and logistics assistance—to extremist groups in the Gulf, Africa, Turkey, and Central Asia (Cordesman and Hashim, 1997).

Although the Iranian government has taken no direct action to date to implement Ayatollah Khomeini's *fatwa* against Salman Rushdie, the decree has not been revoked, and the $2.8 million bounty for his assassination has not been withdrawn. Moreover, hard line Iranians continued to stress that the decree is irrevocable. On the anniversary of the *fatwa* in February, the IRGC released a statement that the decree remains in force, and Ayatollah Yazdi, a member of the Council of Guardians, reiterated that 'the decree is irrevocable and, God willing, will be carried out.' Iran also was a victim of Mujahedin-e-Khalq (MEK)-sponsored terrorism. The Islamic Republic presented a letter to the UN Secretary General in October citing seven acts of sabotage by the MEK against Iran between January and August 2000. The United States has designated the MEK as a foreign terrorist organization.

Saddam's Iraq is viewed by the U.S. State Department as having planned and sponsored international terrorism in 2000. Although Baghdad focused on anti-dissident activity overseas, the regime continued to support various terrorist groups. The regime has not attempted an anti-Western terrorist attack since its failed plot to assassinate former President Bush in 1993 in Kuwait.

Czech police continued to provide protection to the Prague office of the U.S. government-funded Radio Free Europe/Radio Liberty (RFE/RL), which produces Radio Free Iraq programs and employs expatriate journalists. The police presence was augmented in 1999, following reports that the Iraqi Intelligence Service (IIS) might retaliate against RFE/RL for broadcasts critical of the Iraqi regime.

To intimidate or silence Iraqi opponents of the regime living overseas, the IIS reportedly opened several new stations in foreign capitals during 2000. Various opposition groups joined in warning Iraqi dissidents abroad against newly established 'expatriate' associations, which, they asserted, are IIS front organizations. Opposition leaders in London contended that the IIS had dispatched women agents to infiltrate their ranks and was targeting dissidents for assassination. In Germany, an Iraqi opposition figure denounced the IIS for murdering his son, who had recently left Iraq to join him abroad. Dr. Ayad 'Allawi, Secretary General of the Iraqi National Accord, an opposition group, stated that relatives of dissidents living abroad are often arrested and jailed to intimidate activists overseas (Amnesty International, 2001).

In northern Iraq, Iraqi agents reportedly killed a locally well-known religious personality who declined to echo the regime line. The regional security director in As Sulaymaniyah stated that Iraqi operatives were responsible for the car-bomb explosion that injured a score of passersby. Officials of the Iraqi Communist Party asserted that an attack on a provincial party headquarters had been thwarted when party security officers shot and wounded a terrorist employed by the IIS.

Baghdad continued to denounce and de-legitimize UN personnel working in Iraq, particularly UN de-mining teams, in the wake of the killing in 1999 of an expatriate UN de-mining worker in northern Iraq under circumstances suggesting regime involvement. An Iraqi who opened fire at the UN Food and Agriculture Organization (FAO) office in Baghdad, killing two persons and wounding six, was permitted to hold a heavily publicized press conference at which he contended that his action had been motivated by the harshness of UN sanctions, which the regime regularly excoriates.

The Iraqi regime rebuffed a request from Riyadh for the extradition of two Saudis who had hijacked a Saudi Arabian Airlines flight to Baghdad, but did return promptly the passengers and the aircraft. Disregarding its obligations under international law, the regime granted political asylum to the hijackers and gave them ample opportunity to ventilate in the Iraqi government-controlled and international media their criticisms of alleged abuses by the Saudi Arabian government, echoing an Iraqi propaganda theme.

While the origins of the FAO attack and the hijacking were unclear, the Iraqi regime readily exploited these terrorist acts to further its policy objectives.

Several expatriate terrorist groups continued to maintain offices in Baghdad, including the Arab Liberation Front, the inactive 15 May Organization, the Palestine Liberation Front (PLF), and the Abu Nidal organization (ANO). PLF leader Abu Abbas appeared on state-controlled television to praise Iraq's leadership under Saddam Hussein in rallying Arab opposition to Israeli violence against Palestinians. The ANO threatened to attack Austrian interests unless several million dollars in a frozen ANO account in a Vienna bank were turned over to the group.

The Iraq-supported Iranian terrorist group, Mujahedin-e Khalq (MEK), regularly claimed responsibility for armed incursions into Iran that targeted police and military outposts, as well as for mortar and bomb attacks on security organization headquarters in various Iranian cities. MEK publicists reported that in March group members killed an Iranian colonel having intelligence responsibilities. An MEK claim to have wounded a general was denied by the Iranian government. The Iraqi regime deployed MEK forces against its domestic opponents.

In 2000, Libya continued efforts to mend its international image in the wake of its surrender in 1999 of two Libyans accused of the bombing of Pan Am flight 103 over Lockerbie, Scotland, in 1988. Trial proceedings for the two defendants began in the Netherlands in May and were ongoing at year's end. The court issued its verdict on January 31, 2001. It found Abdel Basset al-Megrahi guilty of murder, concluding that he caused an explosive device to detonate on board the airplane resulting in the murder of the flight's 259 passengers and crew as well as 11 residents of Lockerbie, Scotland. The judges found that he acted 'in furtherance of the purposes of . . . Libyan Intelligence Services.' Concerning the other defendant, Al-Amin Kalifa Fahima, the court concluded that the Crown failed to present sufficient evidence to satisfy the high standard of 'proof beyond reasonable doubt' that is necessary in criminal cases (ICJ, 1998).

In 1999, Libya paid compensation for the death of a British policewoman, a move that preceded the reopening of the British Embassy. Libya also paid damages to the families of victims in the bombing of UTA Flight 772. Six Libyans were convicted in absentia in that case, and the French judicial system is considering further indictments against other Libyan officials, including Libyan leader Muammar Qadhafi.

In April 1984, a British policewoman was killed and 11 demonstrators were wounded when gunmen in the Libyan People's Bureau in London fired on a peaceful anti-Qadhafi demonstration outside their building.

Libya played a high-profile role in negotiating the release of a group of foreign hostages seized in the Philippines by the Abu Sayyaf Group, reportedly in exchange for a ransom payment. The hostages included citizens of France, Germany, Malaysia, South Africa, Finland, the Philippines, and Lebanon. The payment of ransom to kidnappers only encourages additional hostage taking, and the Abu Sayyaf Group, emboldened by its success, did seize additional hostages—including a U.S. citizen—later in the year. Libya's behavior and that of other parties involved in the alleged ransom arrangement served only to encourage further terrorism and to make that region far more dangerous for residents and travelers.

Libya also remained the primary suspect in several other past terrorist operations, including the Labelle discotheque bombing in Berlin in 1986 that killed two U.S. servicemen and one Turkish civilian and wounded more than 200 persons. The trial in Germany of five suspects in the bombing, which began in November 1997, continued in 2000. Although Libya expelled the Abu Nidal organization and distanced itself from the Palestinian rejectionists in 1999, it continued to have contact with groups that use violence to oppose the Middle East Peace Process, including the Palestine Islamic Jihad and the Popular Front for the Liberation of Palestine-General Command.

In 2000 the Democratic People's Republic of Korea (DPRK) engaged in three rounds of terrorism talks that culminated in a joint DPRK-U.S. statement wherein the DPRK reiterated its opposition to terrorism and agreed to support international actions against such activity. The DPRK, however, continued to provide safe haven to the Japanese Communist League-Red Army Faction members who participated in the hijacking of a Japanese Airlines flight to North Korea in 1970. Some evidence also suggests the DPRK may have sold weapons directly or indirectly to terrorist groups during the year; Philippine officials publicly declared that the Moro Islamic Liberation Front had purchased weapons from North Korea with funds provided by Middle East sources.

The United States and Sudan in mid-2000 entered into a dialogue to discuss U.S. counterterrorism concerns. The talks, which were ongoing at the end of the year, were constructive and obtained some positive results. By the end of the year Sudan had signed all twelve international conventions for combating terrorism and had taken several other positive counterterrorism steps, including closing down the Popular Arab and Islamic Conference, which served as a forum for terrorists.

Sudan, however, continued to be used as a safe haven by members of various groups, including associates of Osama bin Laden's al Qaeda organization, Egyptian al-Gama'a al-Islamiyya, Egyptian Islamic Jihad, the Palestine Islamic Jihad, and Hamas. Most groups used Sudan primarily as a secure base for assisting compatriots elsewhere.

Khartoum also still had not complied fully with UN Security Council Resolutions 1044, 1054, and 1070, passed in 1996—which demand that Sudan end all support to terrorists. They also require Khartoum to hand over three Egyptian Gama'a fugitives linked to the assassination attempt in 1995 against Egyptian President Hosni Mubarak in Ethiopia. Sudanese officials continued to deny that they had a role in the attack (U.S. State Department, 2000).

Syria continued to provide safe haven and support to several terrorist groups, some of which maintained training camps or other facilities on Syrian territory. Ahmad Jibril's Popular Front for the Liberation of Palestine-General Command (PFLP-GC), the Palestine Islamic Jihad (PIJ), Abu Musa's Fatah-the-Intifada, and George Habash's Popular Front for the Liberation of Palestine (PFLP) maintained their headquarters in Damascus. The Syrian government allowed Hamas to open a new main office in Damascus in March, although the arrangement may be temporary while Hamas continues to seek permission to reestablish its headquarters in Jordan. In addition, Syria granted a variety of terrorist groups—including Hamas, the PFLP-GC, and the PIJ—basing privileges or refuge in areas of Lebanon's Bekaa Valley under Syrian control. Damascus generally upheld its agreement with Ankara not to support the Kurdish PKK (U.S. State Department, 2000).

The designation of the United States as a state sponsor of terrorism is based on the following activities (Mannoni, 2000; also see Blum, 2003):

- 1946: The United States opens School of the Americas in Panama. Now located in Fort Benning, Georgia, the 'School of the Assassins' has taught over 60,000 personnel from some of the world's most brutal regimes how to subvert the truth, to muzzle union leaders, activist clergy, and journalists, and to make war on their own people.
- 1951: The U.S. Central Intelligence Agency (CIA) is involved in a coup to overthrow nationalist prime minister, Dr. Muhammed Mossadeq in Iran. Supports Iranian military in massacre of Mossadeq supporters and returns the Shah to power. In 1976, Amnesty

International concluded that the Shah's CIA-trained security force, SAVAK, had the worst human rights record on the planet, and that the number and variety of torture techniques the CIA had taught SAVAK were 'beyond belief.'

- 1951: CIA involved in terror campaign against democratically elected Jacobo Arbenz in Guatemala. After Arbenz government is overthrown, CIA backed regimes murder more than 100,000 Guatemalans over the next 40 years.
- 1961: The CIA recruits 1500 Cuban exiles to invade Cuba and overthrow the Castro regime. The Bay of Pigs invasion would be a disaster, however the CIA would continue with more than two-dozen attempts to kill Castro.
- 1963: The CIA had South Vietnamese president Ngo Dinh Diem overthrown and assassinated for supporting negotiations with the north. After 20 years of covert war the United States turns to direct military invasion, in a war that costs tens of thousands of Vietnamese, Cambodian and U.S. lives.
- 1963: The CIA recruits the Iraqi Baath Party (including a young Saddam Hussein) to assassinate the new leader, Abdul-Karim Kassem. After the coup, the CIA gave the Baath a long list of communists and others to liquidate. During the 1980s the CIA would go on to help provide weapons to both Iraq and Iran in a war that would kill over one million people.
- 1965: The CIA provokes a coup that leads to the overthrow of Indonesian leader Sukarno, who is replaced by General Suharto. In the following weeks between 500,000 and one million people are murdered by death squads using lists provided by U.S. State Department.
- 1973: After interfering in Chilean elections in 1958 and 1964, the CIA begins a campaign of sabotage and terror after leftist Salvadore Allende is elected president in 1970. In 1973, a CIA supported coup overthrew and assassinated Allende and installed fascist General Pinochet, resulting in thousands of murders over the next two decades. This year in France, former U.S. secretary of state, Henry Kissinger was served a (mostly symbolic) warrant for arrest as a war criminal for his role in the coup.
- 1979: After Nicaraguan dictator Samosa is overthrown in 1979, the CIA helps to train Samosa's National Guard into death squads known as the Contras. The Contras are used to terrorize rural Nicaragua while the U.S. military blockades Nicaragua's harbors with mines. In 1989,

after 10,000 deaths, the United States is successful in ousting the Sandanista government.

- 1989: The United States invades Panama to overthrow and 'arrest' Manuel Noriega, who has been on the CIA payroll since 1966 and supported through decades of drug running, political assassination and corrupt elections. After the invasion, which included the fire bombing of an entire urban ghetto, human rights observers uncover mass graves and estimate that over 4,000 died during the invasion.
- 1991: The United States and allies (mostly Britain) invade Iraq after U.S./CIA supported Saddam Hussein invades Kuwait. 200,000 Iraqis are killed, including over 400 civilians killed by two U.S. missiles in the Al-Amerya air shelter. Over the next 10 years another 400 tons of explosives will be dropped on Iraq killing another 300 civilians, and hundreds of thousands more starved through U.S. imposed sanctions. The United States forces Saudi Arabia to allow thousands of U.S. military to remain indefinitely within its boarders.
- 1998: Al Shifa pharmaceutical plant in Khartoum, Sudan is bombed without warning by 13 U.S. cruise missiles killing a janitor. The attack deprives Sudan of desperately needed medical drugs and potentially killing tens of thousands of people. The CIA later admits that information linking the plant to Osama bin Laden was probably 'incorrect.'
- The atomic bombing of 200,000 civilians in Nagasaki and Hiroshima, the numerous other U.S. invasions south of the Rio Grande, the invasion of Grenada, the 19th century war of terror against U.S. indigenous peoples or the 200 years of slave trade, though not mentioned, fall within state-sponsored terrorism.

Other acts of terrorism

International terrorism has many manifestations and many sources. The multilateral efforts aimed at developing international cooperation to counter terrorism have a relatively long history. The League of Nations attempted to confront the challenge of individual or group terrorism by means of the 1937 Geneva Convention for the Prevention and Punishment of Terrorism. Unfortunately, this Convention never entered into force. But the dealings of the international community with the terrorist menace have, in the subsequent decades, given rise to a certain crystallization of the main policy elements for combating terrorism. And of course, these counter-measures have formed a set of applicable principles and rules of international law.

Progressive development of international law is important. Thus, by virtue of their human rights guarantees, the Universal Declaration of Human rights and the two International Covenants from 1966 are, in essence, also anti-terrorism legal instruments in themselves. Furthermore, specific legal documents relating to the prevention and suppression of specific terrorist acts have been adopted. The existing conventions deal in particular with terrorist acts directed against civil aviation and maritime navigation and against internationally protected persons, as well as hostage taking and the use of certain substances or devices for terrorist purposes.

This abundant legislation notwithstanding, in recent years terrorism has become one of the most important and serious threats to individuals and governments in many parts of the world. Since terrorist acts often, albeit not always, take place on an international scale, terrorism cannot effectively be combated by the isolated action of individual states.

According to the U.S. State Department's *Patterns of Global Terrorism, 1995* (U.S. State Department, 1995), the total number of international terrorist acts rose from 322 in 1994 to 420 in 1995, but the increase was largely due to a rise in nonlethal attacks in Germany. The 1995 total, while higher than the previous year, is close to the average annual number of incidents from 1989 to 1994 (356)—and that five-year average is considerably lower than the annual average from 1980 to 1988 (562).

The following is a listing of some incidents in which U.S. citizens are known to have been killed by Middle East-based terrorists (Rubin and Rubin, 2002; also see Schweitzer and Dorsch, 1998):

- February 23, 1970: Halhoul, West Bank. Palestinian Liberation Organization terrorists open fire on a busload of pilgrims killing Barbara Ertle of Michigan and wounding two other Americans.
- March 28–29, 1970: Beirut, Lebanon. The Popular Front for the Liberation of Palestine (PFLP) fired seven rockets at the U.S. embassy, the American Insurance Company, Bank of America and the John F. Kennedy library.
- September 14, 1970: En route to Amman, Jordan. The PFLP hijacked a TWA flight from Zurich, Switzerland and forced it to land in Amman. Four American citizens were injured.
- May 30, 1972: Ben Gurion Airport, Israel. Three members of the Japanese Red Army, acting on the PFLP's behalf, carried out a

machine-gun and grenade attack at Israel's main airport, killing twenty-six and wounding seventy-eight people. Many of the casualties were American citizens, mostly from Puerto Rico.

- September 5, 1972: Munich, Germany. During the Olympic Games in Munich, Black September, a front for Fatah, took hostage 11 members of the Israeli Olympic team. Nine athletes were killed including weightlifter David Berger, an American-Israeli from Cleveland, Ohio.
- March 2, 1973: Khartoum, Sudan. Cleo A. Noel, Jr., U.S. ambassador to Sudan, and George C. Moore, also a U.S. diplomat, were held hostage and then killed by terrorists at the U.S. embassy in Khartoum. It seems likely that Fatah was responsible for the attack.
- June 29, 1975: Beirut, Lebanon. The PFLP kidnapped the U.S. military attaché to Lebanon, Ernest Morgan, and demanded food, clothing and building materials for indigent residents living near Beirut harbor. The American diplomat was released after an anonymous benefactor provided food to the neighborhood.
- November 14, 1975: Jerusalem, Israel. Lola Nunberg, 53, of New York, was injured during a bombing attack in downtown Jerusalem. Fatah claimed responsibility for the bombing, which killed six people and wounded 38.
- November 21: 1975, Ramat Hamagshimim, Israel. Michael Nadler, an American-Israeli from Miami Beach, Florida, was killed when axe-wielding terrorists from the Democrat Front for the Liberation of Palestine, a PLO faction, attacked students in the Golan Heights.
- August 11, 1976: Istanbul, Turkey. The PFLP launched an attack on the terminal of Israel's major airline, El Al, at the Istanbul airport. Four civilians, including Harold Rosenthal of Philadelphia, Pennsylvania, were killed and 20 injured.
- January 1, 1977: Beirut, Lebanon. Frances E. Meloy, U.S. ambassador to Lebanon, and Robert O. Waring, the U.S. economic counselor, were kidnapped by PFLP members as they crossed a militia checkpoint separating the Christian from the Muslim parts of Beirut. They were later shot to death.
- March 11, 1978: Tel Aviv, Israel. Gail Rubin, niece of U.S. Senator Abraham Ribicoff, was among 38 people shot to death by PLO terrorists on an Israeli beach.
- June 2, 1978: Jerusalem, Israel. Richard Fishman, a medical student from Maryland, was among six killed in a PLO bus bombing in Jerusalem. Chava Sprecher, another American citizen from Seattle, Washington, was injured.

- May 4, 1979: Tiberias, Israel. Haim Mark and his wife, Haya, of New Haven, Connecticut were injured in a PLO bombing attack in northern Israel.
- November 4, 1979: Teheran, Iran. After President Carter agreed to admit the Shah of Iran into the United States, Iranian radicals seized the U.S. embassy in Tehran and took 66 American diplomats hostage. Thirteen hostages were soon freed, but the remaining fifty-three were held until their release on January 20, 1981.
- May 2, 1980: Hebron, West Bank. Eli Haze'ev, an American-Israeli from Alexandria, Virginia, was killed in a PLO attack on Jewish worshippers walking home from a synagogue in Hebron.
- July 19, 1982: Beirut, Lebanon. Hizballah members kidnapped David Dodge, acting president of the American University in Beirut. After a year in captivity, Dodge was released. Rifat Assad, head of Syrian Intelligence, helped in the negotiation with the terrorists.
- August 19, 1982: Paris, France. Two American citizens, Anne Van Zanten and Grace Cutler, were killed when the PLO bombed a Jewish restaurant in Paris.
- March 16, 1983: Beirut, Lebanon. Five American Marines were wounded in a hand grenade attack while on patrol north of Beirut International Airport. The Islamic Jihad and Al-Amal, a Shi'ite militia, claimed responsibility for the attack.
- April 18, 1983: Beirut, Lebanon. A truck-bomb detonated by a remote control exploded in front of the U.S. Embassy in Beirut, killing 63 employees, including the CIA's Middle East director, and wounding 120. Hizballah, with financial backing from Iran, was responsible for the attack.
- July 1, 1983: Hebron, Israel. Aharon Gross, 19, an American-Israeli from New York, was stabbed to death by PLO terrorists in the Hebron marketplace.
- September 29, 1983: Beirut, Lebanon. Two American marines were kidnapped by Amal members. They were released after intervention by a Lebanese army officer.
- October 23, 1983: Beirut, Lebanon. A truck loaded with a bomb crashed into the lobby of the U.S. Marines headquarters in Beirut, killing 241 soldiers and wounding eighty-one. The attack was carried out by Hizballah with the help of Syrian intelligence and financed by Iran.

- December 19, 1983: Jerusalem, Israel. Serena Sussman, a 60-year-old tourist from Anderson, South Carolina, died from injuries from the PLO bombing of a bus in Jerusalem 13 days earlier.
- January 18, 1984: Beirut, Lebanon. Malcolm Kerr, a Lebanese born American who was president of the American University of Beirut, was killed by two gunmen outside his office. Hizballah said the assassination was part of the organization's plan to 'drive all Americans out from Lebanon.'
- March 7, 1984: Beirut, Lebanon. Hizballah members kidnapped Jeremy Levin, Beirut bureau chief of Cable News Network (CNN). Levin managed to escape and reach Syrian army barracks. He was later transferred to American hands.
- March 8, 1984: Beirut, Lebanon. Three Hizballah members kidnapped Reverend Benjamin T. Weir, while he was walking with his wife in Beirut's Manara neighborhood. Weir was released after 16 months of captivity with Syrian and Iranian assistance.
- March 16, 1984: Beirut, Lebanon. Hizballah kidnapped William Buckley, a political officer at the U.S. embassy in Beirut. Buckley was supposed to be exchanged for prisoners. However when the transaction failed to take place, he was reportedly transported to Iran. Although his body was never found, the U.S. administration declared the American diplomat dead.
- April 12, 1984: Torrejon, Spain. Hizballah bombed a restaurant near an U.S. Air Force base in Torrejon, Spain, wounding 83 people.
- September 20, 1984: Beirut, Lebanon. A suicide bomb attack on the U.S. embassy in East Beirut killed 23 people and injured 21. The American and British ambassadors were slightly injured in the attack, attributed to the Iranian backed Hizballah group.
- September 20, 1984: Aukar, Lebanon. Islamic Jihad detonate a van full of explosives 30 feet in front of the U.S. embassy annex severely damaging the building, killing two U.S. servicemen and seven Lebanese employees, as well as 5 to 15 non-employees. Twenty Americans were injured, including U.S. Ambassador Reginald Bartholomew and visiting British Ambassador David Miers. An estimated 40 to 50 Lebanese were hurt. The attack came in response to the U.S. veto September 6 of a U.N. Security Council resolution.
- December 4, 1984: Tehran, Iran. Hizballah terrorists hijacked a Kuwait Airlines plane en route from Dubai, United Emirates, to Karachi, Pakistan. They demanded the release from Kuwaiti jails of members of Da'Wa, a group of Shiite extremists serving sentences for attacks on

French and American targets on Kuwaiti territory. The terrorists forced the pilot to fly to Tehran where the terrorists murdered two passengers—U.S. Agency for International Development employees, Charles Hegna and William Stanford. Although an Iranian special unit ended the incident by storming the plane and arresting the terrorists, the Iranian government might also have been involved in the hijacking.

- June 14, 1985: Between Athens and Rome. Two Hizballah members hijacked a TWA flight en route to Rome from Athens and forced the pilot to fly to Beirut. The terrorists, believed to belong to Hizballah, asked for the release of members of the group Kuwait 17 and 700 Shi'ite prisoners held in Israeli and South Lebanese prisons. The eight crewmembers and 145 passengers were held for 17 days during which one of the hostages, Robert Stethem, a U.S. Navy diver, was murdered. After being flown twice to Algiers, the aircraft returned to Beirut and the hostages were released. Later on, four Hizballah members were secretly indicted. One of them, the Hizballah senior officer Imad Mughniyah, was indicted in absentia.
- October 7, 1985: Between Alexandria, Egypt and Haifa, Israel. A four-member PFLP squad took over the Italian cruise ship Achille Lauro, as it was sailing from Alexandria, Egypt, to Israel. The squad murdered a disabled U.S. citizen, Leon Klinghoffer, by throwing him in the ocean. The rest of the passengers were held hostage for two days and later released after the terrorists turned themselves in to Egyptian authorities in return for safe passage. But U.S. Navy fighters intercepted the Egyptian aircraft flying the terrorists to Tunis and forced it to land at the NATO airbase in Italy, where the terrorists were arrested. Two of the terrorists were tried in Italy and sentenced to prison. The Italian authorities however let the two others escape on diplomatic passports. Abu Abbas, who masterminded the hijacking, was later convicted to life imprisonment in absentia.
- December 27, 1985: Rome, Italy. Four terrorists from Abu Nidal's organization attacked El Al offices at the Leonardo di Vinci Airport in Rome. Thirteen people, including five Americans, were killed and 74 wounded, among them two Americans. The terrorists had come from Damascus and were supported by the Syrian regime.
- March 30, 1986: Athens, Greece. A bomb exploded on a TWA flight from Rome as it approached Athens airport. The attack killed four U.S. citizens who were sucked through a hole made by the blast, although the plane safely landed. The bombing was attributed to the Fatah

Special Operations Group's intelligence and security apparatus, headed by Abdullah Abd al-Hamid Labib, alias Colonel Hawari.

- April 5, 1986: West Berlin, Germany. An explosion at the 'La Belle' nightclub in Berlin, frequented by American soldiers, killed three—2 U.S. soldiers and a Turkish woman-and wounded 191 including 41 U.S. soldiers. Given evidence of Libyan involvement, the U.S. Air Force made a retaliatory attack against Libyan targets on April 17. Libya refused to hand over to Germany five suspects believed to be there. Others, however, were tried including Yassir Shraidi and Musbah Eter, arrested in Rome in August 1997 and extradited; and also Ali Chanaa, his wife, Verena Chanaa, and her sister, Andrea Haeusler. Shraidi, accused of masterminding the attack, was sentenced to 14 years in jail. The Libyan diplomat Musbah Eter and Ali Chanaa were both sentenced to 12 years in jail. Verena Chanaa was sentenced to 14 years in prison. Andrea Haeusler was acquitted.
- September 5, 1986: Karachi, Pakistan. Abu Nidal members hijacked a Pan Am flight leaving Karachi, Pakistan bound for Frankfurt, Germany and New York with 379 passengers, including 89 Americans. The terrorists forced the plane to land in Larnaca, Cyprus, where they demanded the release of two Palestinians and a Briton jailed for the murder of three Israelis there in 1985. The terrorists killed 22 of the passengers, including two American citizens and wounded many others. They were caught and indicted by a Washington grand jury in 1991.
- September 9, 1986: Beirut, Lebanon. Continuing its anti-American attacks, Hizballah kidnapped Frank Reed, director of the American University in Beirut, whom they accused of being 'a CIA agent.' He was released 44 months later. September 12, 1986, Beirut, Lebanon. Hizballah kidnapped Joseph Cicippio, the acting comptroller at the American University in Beirut. Cicippio was released five years later on December 1991.
- October 15, 1986: Jerusalem, Israel. Gali Klein, an American citizen, was killed in a grenade attack by Fatah at the Western Wall in Jerusalem.
- October 21, 1986: Beirut, Lebanon. Hizballah kidnapped Edward A. Tracy, an American citizen in Beirut. He was released five years later, on August 1991.
- February 17, 1988: Ras-Al-Ein Tyre, Lebanon. Col. William Higgins, the American chief of the United Nations Truce Supervisory Organization, was abducted by Hizballah while driving from Tyre to

Nakura. The hostages demanded the withdrawal of Israeli forces from Lebanon and the release of all Palestinian and Lebanese held prisoners in Israel. The U.S. government refused to answer the request. Hizballah later claimed they killed Higgins.

- December 21, 1988: Lockerbie, Scotland. Pan Am Flight 103 departing from Frankfurt to New York was blown up in midair, killing all 259 passengers and another 11 people on the ground in Scotland. Two Libyan agents were found responsible for planting a sophisticated suitcase bomb onboard the plane. On November 14, 1991, arrest warrants were issued for Al-Amin Khalifa Fahima and Abdel Baset Ali Mohamed al-Megrahi. After Libya refused to extradite the suspects to stand trial, the United Nations leveled sanctions against the country in April 1992, including the freezing of Libyan assets abroad. In 1999, Libyan leader Muammar Gadhafi agreed to hand over the two suspects, but only if their trial was held in a neutral country and presided over by a Scottish judge. With the help of Saudi Arabia's King Fahd and Crown Prince Abdullah, Al-Megrahi and Fahima were finally extradited and tried in Camp Zeist in the Netherlands. Megrahi was found guilty and jailed for life, while Fahima was acquitted due to a 'lack of evidence' of his involvement. After the extradition, UN sanctions against Libya were automatically lifted.
- January 27, 1989: Istanbul and Ankara, Turkey. Three simultaneous bombings were carried out against U.S. business targets—the Turkish American Businessmen Association and the Economic Development Foundation in Istanbul, and the Metal Employees Union in Ankara. The Dev Sol (Revolutionary Left) was held responsible for the attacks.
- March 6, 1989: Cairo, Egypt. Two explosive devices were safely removed from the grounds of the American and British Cultural centers in Cairo. Three organizations were believed to be responsible for the attack: The January 15 organization, which had sent a letter bomb to the Israeli ambassador to London in January; the Egyptian Revolutionary Organization that from 1984 to 1986 carried out attacks against U.S. and Israeli targets; and the Nasserite Organization, which had attacked British and American targets in 1988.
- June 12, 1989: Bosphorus Straits, Turkey. A bomb exploded aboard an unoccupied boat used by U.S. consular staff. The explosion caused extensive damage but no casualties. An organization previously unknown, the Warriors of the June 16th Movement, claimed responsibility for the attack.

- October 11, 1989: Izmir, Turkey. An explosive charge went off outside a U.S. military PX. Dev Sol was held responsible for the attack.
- February 7, 1991: Incirlik Air Base, Turkey. Dev Sol members shot and killed a U.S. civilian contractor as he was getting into his car at the Incirlik Air Base in Adana, Turkey.
- February 28, 1991: Izmir, Turkey. Two Dev Sol gunmen shot and wounded a U.S. Air Force officer as he entered his residence in Izmir.
- March 28, 1991: Jubial, Saudi Arabia. Three U.S. marines were shot at and injured by an unknown terrorist while driving near Camp Three, Jubial. No organization claimed responsibility for the attack.
- October 28, 1991: Ankara, Turkey. Victor Marwick, an American soldier serving at the Turkish-American base, Tuslog, was killed and his wife wounded in a car bomb attack. The Turkish Islamic Jihad claimed responsibility for the attack.
- October 28, 1991: Istanbul, Turkey. Two car bombings killed a U.S. Air Force sergeant and severely wounded an Egyptian diplomat in Istanbul. Turkish Islamic Jihad claimed responsibility.
- November 8, 1991: Beirut, Lebanon. A 100-kg car bomb destroyed the administration building of the American University in Beirut, killing one person and wounding at least a dozen.
- October 12, 1992: Umm Qasr, Iraq. A U.S. soldier serving with the United Nations was stabbed and wounded near the port of Umm Qasr. No organization claimed responsibility for the attack.
- January 25, 1993: Virginia, United States. A Pakistani gunman opened fire on Central Intelligence Agency (CIA) employees standing outside of the building. Two agents, Frank Darling and Bennett Lansing, were killed and three others wounded. The assailant was never caught and reportedly fled to Pakistan.
- February 26, 1993: Cairo, Egypt. A bomb exploded inside a café in downtown Cairo killing three. Among the 18 wounded were two U.S. citizens. No one claimed responsibility for the attack.
- February 26, 1993: New York. A massive van bomb exploded in an underground parking garage below the World Trade Center in New York City, killing six and wounding 1,042. Four Islamist activists were responsible for the attack. Ramzi Ahmed Yousef, the operation's alleged mastermind, escaped but was later arrested in Pakistan and extradited to the United States. Abd al-Hakim Murad, another suspected conspirator, was arrested by local authorities in the Philippines and handed over to the United States. The two, along with two other terrorists, were tried in the U.S. and sentenced to 240 years.

- April 14, 1993: Kuwait. The Iraqi intelligence service attempted to assassinate former U.S. President George Bush during a visit to Kuwait. In retaliation, the U.S. launched a cruise missile attack two months later on the Iraqi capital, Baghdad.
- July 5, 1993: Southeast Turkey. In eight separate incidents, the Kurdistan Workers' Party (PKK) kidnapped a total of 19 Western tourists traveling in southeastern Turkey. The hostages, including U.S. citizen Colin Patrick Starger, were released unharmed after spending several weeks in captivity.
- December 1, 1993: north of Jerusalem, West Bank. Yitzhak Weinstock, 19, whose family came from Los Angeles, was killed in a drive-by shooting. Hamas took responsibility for the attack.
- Sometime in 1994: Near Atzmona, Gaza. U.S. citizen Mrs. Sheila Deutsch of Brooklyn, NY was injured in a shooting attack.
- October 9, 1994: Nachshon Wachsman, 19, whose family came from New York, was kidnapped and then murdered by Hamas.
- October 9, 1994: Jerusalem, Israel. Shooting attack on cafe-goers in Jerusalem. U.S. citizens Scot Doberstein and Eric Goldberg were injured.
- March 8, 1995: Karachi, Pakistan. Two unidentified gunmen armed with AK-47 assault rifles opened fire on a U.S. Consulate van in Karachi, killing two U.S. diplomats, Jacqueline Keys Van Landingham and Gary C. Durell, and wounding a third, Mark McCloy.
- April 9, 1995: Kfar Darom and Netzarim, Gaza Strip. Two suicide attacks were carried out within a few hours of each other in Jewish settlements in the Gaza Strip. In the first attack a suicide bomber crashed an explosive-rigged van into an Israeli bus in Netzarim, killing eight including U.S. citizen Alisa Flatow, 20, of West Orange, NJ. Over 30 others were injured. In the second attack, a suicide bomber detonated a car bomb in the midst of a convoy of cars in Kfar Darom, injuring 12. The Palestine Islamic Jihad (PIJ)-Shaqaqi Faction claimed responsibility for the attacks. U.S. citizens Chava Levine and Seth Klein were injured.
- June 15, 1995: Jerusalem. U.S. citizen Howard Tavens of Cleveland, OH was injured in a stabbing attack.
- July 4, 1995: Kashmir, India. In Kashmir, a previously unknown militant group, Al-Faran, with suspected links to a Kashmiri separatist group in Pakistan, took hostage six tourists, including two U.S. citizens. They demanded the release of Muslim militants held in Indian prisons. One of the U.S. citizens escaped on July 8, while on August 13

the decapitated body of the Norwegian hostage was found along with a note stating that the other hostages also would be killed if the group's demands were not met. The Indian government refused. Both Indian and American authorities believe the rest of the hostages were most likely killed in 1996 by their jailers.

- August 1995: Istanbul, Turkey. A bombing of Istanbul's popular Taksim Square injured two U.S. citizens. This attack was part of a three-year-old attempt by the PKK to drive foreign tourists away from Turkey by striking at tourist sites.
- August 21, 1995: Jerusalem. A bus bombing in Jerusalem by the Islamic Resistance Movement killed four, including American Joan Davenny of New Haven, CT, and wounded more than 100. U.S. citizens including Chanoch Bleier, Judith Shulewitz, and Bernard Batta.
- September 9, 1995: Ma'ale Michmash. American killed: Unborn child of Mrs. Mara Frey of Chicago. Mara Frey was injured.
- November 9, 1995: Algiers, Algeria. Islamic extremists set fire to a warehouse belonging to the U.S. embassy, threatened the Algerian security guard because he was working for the United States, and demanded to know whether any U.S. citizens were present. The Armed Islamic Group (GIA) probably carried out the attacks. The group had threatened to strike other foreign targets and especially U.S. objectives in Algeria, and the attack's style was similar to past GIA operations against foreign facilities.
- November 13, 1995: Riyadh, Saudi Arabia. A car bomb exploded in the parking lot outside of the Riyadh headquarters of the Office of the Program Manager/Saudi Arabian National Guard, killing seven persons, five of them U.S. citizens, and wounding 42. The blast severely damaged the three-story building, which houses a U.S. military advisory group, and several neighboring office buildings. Three groups—the Islamic Movement for Change, the Tigers of the Gulf, and the Combatant Partisans of God—claimed responsibility for the attack.
- February 25, 1996: Jerusalem. A suicide bomber blew up a commuter bus in Jerusalem, killing 26, including three U.S. citizens, and injuring 80 others, among them another two U.S. citizens. Hamas claimed responsibility for the bombing. U.S. citizens killed: Sara Duker, of Teaneck, NJ, Matthew Eisenfeld of West Hartford, CT, Ira Weinstein of Bronx, NY. U.S. citizens injured: Beatrice Kramer, Steven Lapides.
- March 4, 1996: Tel Aviv, Israel. A suicide bomber detonated an explosive device outside the Dizengoff Center, Tel Aviv's largest

shopping mall, killing 20 persons and injuring 75 others, including two U.S. citizens. Both Hamas and the Islamic Jihad claimed responsibility for the bombing. U.S. citizens injured included Julie K. Negrin of Seattle, WA.

- May 13, 1996: Beit-El, West Bank. Arab gunmen opened fire on a hitchhiking stand near Beit El, wounding three Israelis and killing David Boim, 17, an American-Israeli from New York. No one claimed responsibility for the attack, although either the Islamic Jihad or Hamas are suspected. U.S. citizens injured: Moshe Greenbaum, 17.
- June 9, 1996: Zekharya, West Bank. Yaron Ungar, an American-Israeli, and his Israeli wife were killed in a drive-by shooting near their West Bank home. The PFLP is suspected.
- June 25, 1996: Dhahran, Saudi Arabia. A fuel truck carrying a bomb exploded outside the U.S. military's Khobar Towers housing facility in Dhahran, killing 19 U.S. military personnel and wounding 515 persons, including 240 U.S. personnel. Several groups claimed responsibility for the attack. In June 2001, a U.S. District Court in Alexandria, Virginia, identified Saudi Hizballah as the party responsible for the attack. The court indicated that the members of the organization, banned from Saudi Arabia, 'frequently met and were trained in Lebanon, Syria, or Iran' with Libyan help.
- August 17, 1996: Mapourdit, Sudan. Sudan People's Liberation Army (SPLA) rebels kidnapped six missionaries in Mapourdit, including a U.S citizen. The SPLA released the hostages on August 28.
- November 1, 1996: Sudan. A breakaway group of the Sudanese People's Liberation Army (SPLA) kidnapped three workers of the International Committee of the Red Cross (ICRC), including one U.S citizen. The rebels released the hostages on December 9 in exchange for ICRC supplies and a health survey of their camp.
- December 3, 1996: Paris, France. A bomb exploded aboard a Paris subway train, killing four and injuring 86 persons, including a U.S. citizen. No one claimed responsibility for the attack, but Algerian extremists are suspected.
- January 2, 1997: Major cities worldwide, United States. A series of letter bombs with Alexandria, Egypt postmarks were discovered at Al-Hayat newspaper bureaus in Washington, D.C., New York, London, and Riyadh. Three similar devices, also postmarked in Egypt, were found at a prison facility in Leavenworth, Kansas. Bomb disposal experts defused all the devices, but one detonated at the Al-Hayat

newspaper office in London, injuring two security guards and causing minor damage.

- February 23, 1997: New York. A Palestinian gunman opened fire on tourists at an observation deck atop the Empire State building in New York, killing a Danish national and wounding visitors from the United States, Argentina, Switzerland and France before turning the gun on himself. A handwritten note carried by the gunman claimed this was a punishment attack against the 'enemies of Palestine.'
- July 30, 1997: Jerusalem. Two bombs detonated in Jerusalem's Mahane Yehuda market, killing 15 persons, including a U.S. citizen and wounding 168 others, among them two U.S. citizens. The Izz-el-Din al-Qassam Brigades, Hamas' military wing, claimed responsibility for the attack. U.S. citizens killed: Mrs. Leah Stern of Passaic, NJ. U.S. citizens injured: Dov Dalin.
- September 4, 1997: Jerusalem. Bombing on Ben-Yehuda Street, Jerusalem. U.S. citizens killed: Yael Botwin, 14, of Los Angeles and Jerusalem. U.S. citizens injured: Diana Campuzano of New York, Abraham Mendelson of Los Angeles, Greg Salzman of New Jersey, Stuart E. Hersh of Kiryat Arba, Israel, Michael Alzer, Abraham Elias, David Keinan, Daniel Miller of Boca Raton, FL, Noam Rozenman of Jerusalem, Jenny (Yocheved) Rubin of Los Angeles. Hamas claimed responsibility for the attack.
- October 30, 1997: Sanaa, Yemen. Al-Sha'if tribesmen kidnapped a U.S. businessman near Sanaa. The tribesmen sought the release of two fellow tribesmen who were arrested on smuggling charges and several public works projects they claim the government promised them. The hostage was released on November 27.
- November 12, 1997: Karachi, Pakistan. Two unidentified gunmen shot to death four U.S. auditors from Union Texas Petroleum and their Pakistani driver as they drove away from the Sheraton Hotel in Karachi. Two groups claimed responsibility—the Islamic Inqilabi Council, or Islamic Revolutionary Council and the Aimal Secret Committee, also known as the Aimal Khufia Action Committee.
- November 25, 1997: Aden, Yemen. Yemenite tribesmen kidnapped a U.S citizen, two Italians, and two unspecified Westerners near Aden to protest the eviction of a tribe member from his home. The kidnappers released the five hostages on November 27.
- April 19, 1998: Maon, Israel. Dov Driben, a twenty-eight-year-old American-Israeli farmer was killed by terrorists near the West Bank town of Maon. One of his assailants, Issa Debavseh, a member of Fatah

Tanzim, was killed on November 7, 2001, by the IDF after being on their wanted list for the murder.

- June 21, 1998: Beirut, Lebanon. Two hand-grenades were thrown at the U.S. embassy in Beirut. No casualties were reported.
- June 21, 1998: Beirut, Lebanon. Three rocket-propelled grenades attached to a crude detonator exploded near the U.S. embassy compound in Beirut, causing no casualties and little damage.
- August 7, 1998, Nairobi, Kenya. A car bomb exploded at the rear entrance of the U.S. embassy in Nairobi. The attack killed a total of 292, including 12 U.S. citizens, and injured over 5,000, among them six Americans. The perpetrators belonged to al Qaeda, Osama bin Laden's network.
- August 7, 1998: Dar es Sala'am, Tanzania. A car bomb exploded outside the U.S. Embassy in Dar es Sala'am, killing 11 and injuring 86. Osama bin Laden's organization al Qaeda claimed responsibility for the attack. Two suspects were arrested.
- November 21, 1998: Teheran, Iran. Members of Fedayeen Islam, shouting anti-American slogans and wielding stones and iron rods, attacked a group of American tourists in Tehran. Some of the tourists suffered minor injuries from flying glass.
- December 28, 1998: Mawdiyah, Yemen. Sixteen tourists—12 Britons, two Americans and two Australians—were taken hostage in the largest kidnapping in Yemen's recent history. The tourists were seized in the Abyan province (some 175 miles south of Sanaa the capital). One Briton and a Yemeni guide escaped, while the rest were taken to the city of Mawdiyah. Four hostages were killed when troops closed in and two were wounded, including an American woman. The kidnappers, members of the Islamic Army of Aden-Abyan, an offshoot of Al-Jihad, had demanded the release from jail of their leader, Saleh Haidara al-Atwi.
- October 31, 1999: Nantucket, Massachusetts. EgyptAir Flight 990 crashed off the U.S. coast killing all 217 people on board, including 100 Americans. Although it is not precisely clear what happened, evidence indicated that an Egyptian pilot crashed the plane for personal or political reasons.
- November 4, 1999: Athens, Greece. A group protesting President Clinton's visit to Greece hid a gas bomb at an American car dealership in Athens. Two cars were destroyed and several others damaged. Anti-State Action claimed responsibility for the attack, but the November 17 group was also suspected.

- November 12, 1999: Islamabad, Pakistan. Six rockets were fired at the U.S. Information Services cultural center and United Nations offices in Islamabad, injuring a Pakistani guard.
- September 29, 2000: Near Jerusalem. Attack on motorists. U.S. citizens injured: Avi Herman of Teaneck, NJ, Naomi Herman of Teaneck, NJ.
- September 29, 2000: Jerusalem. Attack on taxi passengers. U.S. citizens injured: Tuvia Grossman of Chicago, Todd Pollack of Norfolk, VA, Andrew Feibusch of New York.
- October 4, 2000: Near Bethlehem, West Bank. U.S. citizens injured: An unidentified American tourist.
- October 5, 2000: Near Jerusalem. Attack on a motorist. U.S. citizens injured: Rabbi Chaim Brovender of Brooklyn.
- October 8, 2000: Nablus, West Bank. The bullet-ridden body of Rabbi Hillel Lieberman, a U.S. citizen from Brooklyn living in the Jewish settlement of Elon Moreh, was found at the entrance to the West Bank town of Nablus. Lieberman had headed there after hearing that Palestinians had desecrated the religious site, Joseph's Tomb. No organization claimed responsibility for the murder.
- October 12, 2000: Aden Harbor, Yemen. A suicide squad rammed the warship U.S.S. Cole with an explosives-laden boat killing 13 American sailors and injuring 33. The attack was likely by Osama bin Laden's al Qaeda organization.
- October 30, 2000: Jerusalem. Gunmen killed Eish Kodesh Gilmor, a twenty-five-year-old American-Israeli on duty as a security guard at the National Insurance Institute in Jerusalem. The 'Martyrs of the Al-Aqsa Intifada,' a group linked to Fatah, claimed responsibility for the attack. Gilmor's family filed a suit in the U.S. District Court in Washington against the Palestinian Authority, the PLO, Chairman Yasser Arafat and members of Force 17, as being responsible for the attack.
- December 31, 2000: Ofra, Israel. Rabbi Binyamin Kahane, 34, and his wife, Talia Hertzlich Kahane, both formerly of Brooklyn, NY were killed in a drive-by shooting. Their children, Yehudit Leah Kahane, Bitya Kahane, Tzivya Kahane, Rivka Kahane, and Shlomtsion Kahane, were injured in the attack.
- March 28, 2001: Neve Yamin. Bombing at bus stop. U.S. citizens injured: Netanel Herskovitz, 15, formerly of Hempstead, NY.
- May 9, 2001: Tekoa, West Bank. Kobi Mandell, 13, of Silver Spring, MD, an American-Israeli, was found stoned to death along with a friend in a cave near the Jewish settlement of Tekoa. Two

organizations, the Islamic Jihad and Hizballah-Palestine, claimed responsibility for the attack.

- May 29, 2001: Gush Etzion, West Bank. The Fatah Tanzim claimed responsibility for a drive-by shooting of six in the West Bank that killed two American-Israeli citizens, Samuel Berg, and his mother, Sarah Blaustein. U.S. citizens injured: Norman Blaustein of Lawrence, NY.
- July 19, 2001: Hebron, West Bank. Shooting attack. U.S. citizens injured: An unidentified woman from Brooklyn, NY.
- August 9, 2001: Jerusalem. A suicide bombing at Sbarro's, a pizzeria situated in one of the busiest areas of downtown Jerusalem, killed 15 people and wounded more than 90. Hamas claimed responsibility for the attack. U.S. citizens killed: Judith L. Greenbaum, 31, of New Jersey and California, Malka Roth, 15, whose family was from New York. U.S. citizens injured: David Danzig, 21, of Wynnewood, PA, Matthew P. Gordon, 25, of New York, Joanne (Chana) Nachenberg, 31, Sara Shifra Nachenberg, 2.
- August 18, 2001: Jerusalem. Shooting at a bus. U.S. citizen injured: Andrew Feibusch of New York.
- August 27, 2001: Near Roglit, Israel. Shooting attack. U.S. citizen injured: Ben Dansker.
- September 11, 2001: New York, Washington D.C., and Pennsylvania, United States.
- November 4, 2001: Jerusalem, Israel. Shoshana Ben-Yishai, 16, of Queens, NY was killed in a shooting at a bus station. U.S. citizen injured: Shlomo Kaye.
- December 2, 2001: Jerusalem, Israel. Bombing on Ben-Yehuda Street, Jerusalem. U.S. citizens injured: Ziv Brill, 17, of West Hempstead, Long Island, NY, Temima Spetner, 19, of St. Louis, MI, Jason Kirshenbaum of New Rochelle, NY, Israel Hirschfield, 18, Joseph Leifer, 29, of Borough Park (Brooklyn), NY.
- December 18, 2001: Shooting on the Jerusalem-Shilo road. U.S. citizens injured: David Rubin, 44, of Brooklyn, NY, Asher 'Ruby' Rubin, 3.
- January 15, 2002: Bethlehem, West Bank. Avraham Boaz, 71, of New York, a dual Israeli-American citizen, was kidnapped at a PA security checkpoint in Beit Jala and murdered.
- January 18, 2002: Shooting in Hadera. U.S. citizen killed: Aaron Elis, 32, son of Chicago family.

- January 22, 2002: Shooting in Jerusalem, Israel. U.S. citizen injured: Shayna Gould, 19, of Chicago, IL.
- January 27, 2002: Jerusalem. A Palestinian woman triggered a massive explosion in downtown Jerusalem killing one elderly Israeli and injuring more than 150, including American Mark Sokolow, his wife, and 16 and twelve-year-old daughters. Sokolow had earlier survived the September 11 attack on the World Trade Center, escaping from his law office on the 38th floor of the South Tower before it collapsed.
- February 15, 2002, near Ramallah, West Bank. Lee Akunis was shot to death.
- February 16, 2002: Bombing in Karnei Shomron. U.S. citizens killed: Keren Shatsky, 14, of Brooklyn, NY and Maine, Rachel Thaler, 16, of Baltimore, MD. U.S. citizens injured: Lior Thaler, 14, of Baltimore, MD, Hillel Trattner of Chicago, IL, Ronit Yucht Trattner of Chicago, IL, Chani Friedman of New York.
- February 19, 2002: Shooting near Neve Dekalim. U.S. citizens injured: Moshe Saperstein of New York.
- February 25, 2002: Jerusalem. Moran Amit, 25, was stabbed to death in Abu Tor Peace Forest in Jerusalem.
- March 7, 2002, Eshel Hashomron Hotel, Ariel, Israel. A Christian tourist from Arkansas lost her right eye in an attack by a suicide bomber.
- March 27, 2002: Netanya, Israel. U.S. citizen Hannah Rogen, 90, was killed in a suicide attack at a Passover Seder.
- June 18, 2002: Jerusalem. Moshe Gottlieb, 70, of Los Angeles, CA was killed in a bus bombing in Jerusalem.
- June 19, 2002: Jerusalem. Gila Sara Kessler, 19, whose family came from New York, was killed in a bombing at a bus stop.
- July 30, 2002: Hebrew University, Jerusalem, Israel. Nine people were killed when a bomb exploded in the main cafeteria at the Hebrew University's Mount Scopus campus in Jerusalem. Five were U.S. citizens: Janis Ruth Coulter, 36, of MA; Marla Bennet, 24, of San Diego, CA; David Gritz (also a French citizen), 24, of Peru, MA; Benjamin Blutstein, 25, of Susquehanna Township, PA; and Dina Carter, 37, of NC. Israelis David Ladovsky, 29, and Levina Shapira, 53 also died in the bombing. U.S. citizens injured: Spencer Dew, 26, of Owensboro, Kentucky; Zeev Spencer; Harris Gershon. Hamas claimed responsibility for the attack.

September 11, 2001 casualties

During a carefully coordinated attack, 19 Islamist extremists hijacked four U.S. jetliners and forced them to crash into the World Trade Center and the Pentagon. In all, 266 people perished in the four planes, and more than 3,000 people were killed on the ground. Indeed, the whole world was affected. According to information from the U.S. State Department (2001), the following countries and territories suffered losses from the September 11, 2001 attacks: Antigua and Barbuda, Argentina, Australia, Austria, Bangladesh, Barbados, Belarus, Belgium, Belize, Bolivia, Brazil, Canada, Chile, China, Colombia, Czech Republic, Dominica, Dominican Republic, Ecuador, Egypt, El Salvador, Ethiopia, France, The Gambia, Germany, Ghana, Greece, Grenada, Guatemala, Guyana, Haiti, Honduras, Hong Kong, India, Indonesia, Ireland, Israel, Italy, Jamaica, Japan, Jordan, Kazakhstan, Kenya, Lesotho, Liberia, Lithuania, Malaysia, Mexico, The Netherlands, New Zealand, Nicaragua, Nigeria, Pakistan, Panama, Paraguay, Peru, Philippines, Poland, Romania, Russian Federation, South Africa, South Korea, Spain, Sri Lanka, St. Kitts & Nevis, St. Lucia, St. Vincent & the Grenadines, Sweden, Switzerland, Taiwan, Thailand, Togo, Trinidad & Tobago, Turkey, Ukraine, United Kingdom, United States, Uruguay, Uzbekistan, Venezuela, Yemen, Yugoslavia, Zimbabwe (also see Moyers, 2001; Dwyer, 2001).

U.S. investigators have determined, based on extensive evidence, that Osama bin Laden's al Qaeda group was responsible for the September 11 attacks. The first plane, American Airlines Flight 11 en route from Boston to Los Angeles, crashed into the World Trade Center's north tower at 8:48 a.m. Eighteen minutes later, United Airlines Flight 175, also headed from Boston to Los Angeles, smashed into the World Trade Center's south tower. At 9:40 a.m., a third airplane, an American Airlines Boeing 757, that left Washington's Dulles International Airport for Los Angeles, crashed into the western part of the Pentagon where 24,000 people worked. The fourth plane, a United Airlines Flight 93 flying from Newark to San Francisco, crashed near Pittsburgh, Pennsylvania, most likely before it could hit its target. Hundreds of firefighters, police officers and other rescue workers who arrived in the site after the first plane crash were killed or injured.

Transnational or networked terrorist groups

Terrorists are nothing if not adaptable. International terrorists have shifted tactics and targets many times over the years in response to changing circumstances. Shifting political fortunes and new antiterrorism measures will continue to force existing terrorist groups to reinvent themselves and new groups to find new methods. Terrorism experts (see, e.g., Pillar, 2001; Miller, 2001; Simon, 2001; Sprinzak, 2000) generally agree that the role of states in promoting terrorism is in sharp decline. Unfortunately, that alone is not guaranteed to reduce terrorists' activity given their likely ability to find other means of attaining the needed funds, weapons, and technology. In addition, state-sponsored terrorism may rebound over the next few years if adversarial nations conclude that terrorism—rather than direct warfare—is their most viable means of attack against the United States.

Increasingly, terrorists are organized into ad hoc groups. Such groups are fluid organizationally and tend to coalesce into task forces for specific missions. Alexander (2002, p. 36) has called the new mode of operation 'well organized disorganization.' As a result, terrorist groups are harder to track and penetrate, and their targets are harder to predict. These groups are increasing numerically as the years pass. Below, we present a non-exhaustive list of international terrorist organizations considered by the U.S. State Department (2002) to be active (also see Alexander, 1995):

Al Qaeda

Led by Osama bin Laden and aided by his lieutenant, Dr. Ayman Al-Zawahari, and with religious leadership provided by Mullah Mohammed Omar of Afghanistan, al Qaeda's main objective is to overthrow and/or destroy the governments of countries that are currently not following Osama bin Laden's and Mullah Mohammed Omar's interpretation of Islamic law. Al Qaeda has acknowledged the bombing of U.S. and Israeli embassies, as well as attacks on various commercial aircraft. It supports and trains terrorists with various interests and from various countries. Its supporters currently number in the thousands; it has hundreds of active operators, organized in cells or serving as part of smaller networks. A typical al Qaeda terrorist is young, radical, and a member of the Shia Muslim sect. Most of its active members can be found in Afghanistan, Pakistan, Lebanon, Syria, and Egypt (without the consent of the government). There may be sleeping or active cells in the United States, Canada, France, the United Kingdom, and Germany. Al Qaeda, has in the past, conducted training exercises in Lebanon's Bekka Valley and in the deserts of Sudan.

The Islamic Jihad

The Islamic Jihad is also known by various other names, including, Islamic Group, the Egyptian Islamic Jihad, Al-Hidad, Al-Gama'a al-Islamiyya. Its leader is Dr. Aymna Al-Zawahari and the group's main objective is to overthrow the government of current Egyptian president Mohammed Hosni Mubarak who has ruled the country since October 14, 1981 and institute what they claim to be 'true Islamic' law to Egypt. The group also provides various forms of support to other terrorist groups, including al Qaeda. The Islamic Jihad has thousands of supporters and maintains a list of hundreds of active terrorists. It maintains a presence in Pakistan, Afghanistan, Syria, and without the consent of the government, in Egypt.

Hezbollah

Also known as Al-'Asifa, Revolutionary Justice Organization, Organization of the Oppressed on Earth, Islamic Jihad for the Liberation of Palestine, Hezbollah is closely tied to and often directed by elements within Iran, including members of the government and clergy. Hezbollah's main goal is to destroy all individuals and organizations (including governments) that oppose the establishment of a Palestinian homeland. In its activities, the organization has placed emphasis on the destruction of Israel as a way to ensure the establishment of a Palestinian homeland. It has admitted responsibility for the bombing of the U.S. Marine barracks in Lebanon in 1983, the hijacking of TWA 847 in 1985, and the bombing of the Israeli embassy in Buenos Aires in 1992. The organization currently has between 6,000 and 8,000 members, with a little over 500 active terrorists. Its main operators can be found in Lebanon (Al Biqa'—Bekka Valley), Syria, the Sudan and without the consent of the various governments, in Jordan, Saudi Arabia, and Egypt. Hezbollah has established cells in various European countries, Africa, South America, the United States, and Canada. Significant Hezbollah activities and presence have been found in Germany, France, and Great Britain. It is known to have held training or participated in training in the Bekka Valley, as well as in the deserts of Sudan.

Al-Fatah

Also known as the Palestinian Liberation Front (PLO), Al-Fatah, is the best known of the several groups that are fighting for the establishment of a Palestinian homeland. Its leader is Yassar Arafat. Its main objective is to destroy all those who oppose (or stand in the way of) the establishment of a Palestinian state. In the last few years, Al-Fatah is said to have disavowed terrorism in order to participate in the Oslo accords. Unfortunately, in recent years, its leadership has been unable to stop terrorist acts committed against Israel by its members. Al-Fatah has thousands of members and supporters, most of whom are located throughout the region surrounding the state of Israel.

Democratic Front for the Liberation of Palestine (DFLP)

The DFLP is led by Nayif Hawatmah and has been violently opposed to the various Middle East peace initiatives sponsored by the United States and several European countries. It opposed the accords at Oslo and the Declaration of Principles and Arafat's disavowing terrorism, resulting in its eventual split from Al-Fatah. The DFLP is known to support Al Gama and al Qaeda with recruits and weapons in exchange for training. Although its membership is quite modest, it is an extremely violent organization with great potential to do a lot of harm. It maintains a presence in Syria, Lebanon, and the Israeli occupied territories. Important funding sources for the DFLP include Syria and Libya. It is speculated that it may have held training sessions in Lebanon, Afghanistan (with Osama bin Laden's support) and the deserts of Sudan and Libya.

Harkat ul-Mujahedeen (HUA)

The HUA is led by Fazlur Rehman Khalil and targets Indian troops and civilians, primarily in Kashmir. Its supporters can be found in Pakistan and Afghanistan (in training camps linked to Osama bin Laden's al Qaeda).

Islamic Movement of Uzbekistan (IMU)

IMU's main objective is to overthrow of the government of Uzbekistan and create an Islamic state in the country. Its supporters can be found in Pakistan and Afghanistan. Some cells operate in Kazakhstan and Uzbekistan without the consent of the governments of these countries.

Abu Sayyaf Group (ASG)

The main objective of the ASG is to overthrow the current Philippine government and found an Islamic state. It has an active membership of about 50–100 'soldiers' who operate in the Philippines without the permission of the government. Osama bin Laden's al Qaeda has provided the ASG with a significant amount of its training.

Armed Islamic Group (AIG)

The AIG is determined to overthrow the present Algerian government. It has, through the years, developed a strong hatred of the government of France. It currently operates in Algeria without the consent of the government. Its members have received al Qaeda training at camps run by Osama bin Laden in Afghanistan and have also participated in training activities with Bosnian Muslims.

Salafist Group for Call and Combat

The Salafist Group for Call and Combat is a splinter group from the Armed Islamic Group. Resources for operations have been obtained through racketeering, smuggling, real estate investments, and money laundering in Algeria.

Asbat Al Ansar

Asbat Al Ansar is an extremist anti-Israel, pro-Palestine group prone to violence in the occupied territories. Some of the funds collected by this group have made their way to other radical groups, including Hezbollah and Al-Fatah. Members can be found in Lebanon and the territories now occupied by Israel.

Islamic Army of Aden

The Islamic Army of Aden has one overriding objective: to overthrow secular governments in Yemen and surrounding states and establish Islamic rule and law in each of them. Although it is relatively small, it has proven to be very dangerous. Its members can be found primarily in Yemen and surrounding countries.

Islamic Army for the Liberation of Holy Sites

Led by Muhammad Atif, the Islamic Army for the Liberation of Holy Sites is dedicated the removal of Israelis from Muslim holy grounds. In the past, the group has attacked Israeli targets and those of its supporters, such as the United States. Its membership can be found primarily in the occupied territories and North Africa.

Al-Rashid Trust

The Al-Rashid Trust was founded as a nongovernmental charitable group in Pakistan whose primary objective was to supply subsidized baked goods to the poor and offer financial and home support to the Taliban government in Afghanistan. However, it is considered by most Western governments as a terrorist group with links to other radical anti-West organizations. Most of its members are located in Pakistan and Afghanistan.

Al-Taqwa

Al-Taqwa is led by Youssef M. Nada, a Tunisian born Egyptian citizen, and Ali Himmat, a Syrian born Swiss citizen. The organization is primarily a major 'hawalas' or money exchange used worldwide by many people who do not trust banks or understand them. However, many Western observers now believe that Al-Taqwa has involved into a conduit used by transnational terrorist groups to channel funds to their operators worldwide. It has a large number of worldwide money transfer stations that allow for the easy and effective transfer of funds globally.

Other hawalas

The following are major 'hawalas' or money exchange, located in the United States, Canada, the Bahamas, and Western Europe. There are considered important structures used by transnational terrorist groups to transfer money to their operators worldwide (The Muslim Brotherhood Worldwide is reputed to engage in money raising activities from which it obtains funds to assist terrorists in their activities): *Aaran Money Wire Service, Inc.* (Minneapolis); *Al-Barakaat Wiring Service* (Minneapolis); *Barakaat Boston* (Dorchester, MA); *Barakaat North America Inc.* (Dorchester, MA and Ottawa, Canada); *Barakat Wire Transfer Company of Seattle*; *Global Service International of Seattle*; *Somali International Relief*

Organization of Minneapolis; *Youssef M. Nada and Company* (Switzerland); *Al Taqwa Management Company* (Switzerland); *Al Taqwa Bank* (Bahamas); and *Muslim Brotherhood Worldwide*.

These organizations have been listed by the U.S. State Department as targets of anti-terrorist financial sanctions by the U.S. government as directed by Presidential Executive Order on September 27, 2001 (*San Jose Mercury News*, September, 2001).

Terrorist weapons and tactics

However radical their political ideology, most terrorists remain conservative in their choice of weapons and tactics, preferring the tried and familiar—bombs and bullets—to more exotic methods. As noted by Bruce (1994), bombings have accounted for nearly half of all international terrorist attacks over the last twenty-five years.

But significant changes have recently occurred—bigger and more powerful bombs, more car and truck bombs, the use of two closely placed bombs timed to go off a few minutes apart, and the use of photoelectric cells as triggering devices.

When airliners were prime targets, terrorists seemed to compete to make bombs more ingeniously compact and harder to detect. As public buildings have become prime targets, bombs have become larger. The World Trade Center bomb had the explosive power of about 2,000 pounds of TNT. The bomb that destroyed the Murrah Federal Building in Oklahoma City had the power of about 4,800 pounds of TNT. The truck bomb that destroyed the Al Khobar Towers building near Dhahran, Saudi Arabia, has been estimated to have been equivalent to between 20,000 and 30,000 pounds of TNT. This bomb was actually larger than the Oklahoma City explosive and surprised U.S. security personnel with its size and power.

Ironically, security measures that push protective perimeters further away from otherwise vulnerable buildings may well cause terrorists to turn to still larger bombs (now typically car and truck bombs) meant to kill as many people as possible.

Another tactic, especially aimed at security personnel, is the use of two devices placed close to each other, with the second device timed to go off a few minutes after the first. The first explosion is intended to attract security personnel to the scene; the second is intended to kill and injure them. This tactic has been used by Islamic terrorists in Israel and by the Provisional

Irish Republican Army (PIRA) in Northern Ireland and the United Kingdom. It was used for the first time in the United States in January 1997 at an Atlanta abortion clinic bombing. More troubling still is that terrorists, both international and domestic, have access to a wider range of weapons and explosives than at any time in the past. These include chemical, biological, and nuclear devices.

Chemical and biological

Since at least the mid-1980s, many terrorism experts (e.g., Smithson, 2000; Tu, 2000) have believed that the first successful use of chemical weapons by terrorists would significantly lower the threshold of restraint on their use by other terrorist groups and increase the risk of subsequent use. That successful first use, and a second (as well as three subsequent unsuccessful attempts), occurred in Japan.

A threshold has been breached. The possibility that other terrorists will copy these attacks is a source of real concern, especially in light of the apparent easy availability of chemical ingredients and expertise on how to use these materials.

U.S. officials believe the threat is real and have said that it is no longer a question of 'if' but 'when' the next such attack will occur. The post-September 11 environment in the United States renewed these fears of terrorist attacks, and activities of rogue states have prompted increased levels of military spending. Since space systems are growing in importance in conducting theater warfare and tracking the activities of terrorists and rogue states, further developments and spending for next-generation satellites will ensue in coming years. The United States specifically will lead the globe in deploying military payloads in space. Indeed, the U.S. next generation of spy satellites under the Future Imagery Architecture (FIA) program are currently being built and are planned to be launched in 2005. The National Reconnaissance Office (NRO) plans to deploy a dozen or more new satellites that are smaller and smarter to replace the current generation. The twenty-year program is estimated to cost $25 billion, making it the most expensive military space program ever mounted by the United States. What has ignited this fear is that international terrorist groups have relatively easy access to the raw materials (many of which have industrial applications) and to knowledge of how to combine them to produce lethal chemical agents and biological weapons (Tu, 2000; Smithson, 2000).

The raw materials for both chemical and biological weapons can be easily purchased on open, gray, or black markets. Moreover, terrorist groups either have technically trained members with sufficient knowledge of chemistry and laboratory procedures to manufacture such weapons or the money to hire them. Some terrorist groups have state sponsors, such as Iran and Syria that have used terrorism as an instrument of policy and may well do so again. These sponsors have active chemical and biological weapons that could be turned to terrorist groups to attack nations seen as enemies.

In the case of the Tokyo gas attacks, Aum Shinrikyo cult members manufactured the nerve agent *sarin* and used it on two separate occasions (June 1994 and March 1995) to kill a total of 19 people, injure 5,500, and terrorize tens of thousands more. Aum Shinrikyo used various business enterprises as fronts for acquiring the necessary raw materials, and numbered among its members individuals with advanced training in organic chemistry and related technical disciplines from some of Japan's best universities (Tu, 2000).

Aum Shinrikyo built a large sophisticated laboratory, stockpiled tons of chemicals, and acquired computers and commercial software to help it produce chemical weapons and investigate methods for producing biological weapons. The first attack occurred only one year after the leader, Shoko Asahara, ordered his followers to develop the agent. The precedent is significant. As was the case with Soviet atomic bomb-builders after the July 16, 1945, Trinity test at Almagordo, New Mexico, any doubts that other terrorists might have had about whether it could be done have now been removed.

Although the Japanese have the dubious distinction of experiencing the first actual terrorist chemical weapon attack, it is not so much a new turn as a culmination of an idea that has been inching its way forward on the terrorist fringes. In 1985, U.S. law enforcement agencies raided the north Arkansas compound of a right-wing, white supremacist, anti-Semitic group called the Covenant, Sword, and Arm of the Lord. Among other things, federal agents found a drum containing 35 gallons of a cyanide compound, apparently intended for poisoning the water supply of Washington, D.C., or New York. There is also some evidence that the World Trade Center bombers added sodium cyanide to the bomb that blew up in the parking garage under that building, apparently in the hope of killing more people. Some terrorists have turned to more exotic, biologically based poisons. In May 1995, four Minnesota men affiliated with a domestic terrorist group called the Patriots' Council were convicted for a 1992 plot to kill federal officials with *ricin*, a deadly toxin extracted from castor beans.

The materials and instructions on how to make the toxin were obtained from public sources, according to testimony by Robert Blitzer, chief domestic terrorism section, FBI, who spoke before a U.S. House of Representatives National Security subcommittee. Their plan was to mix the ricin with DMSO, a solvent that passes easily through the skin, and put the mixture on doorknobs and steering wheels where the victims would be sure to come in contact with it. The 0.7 grams of ricin produced by these men would have been sufficient to kill more than 100 people.

Disease-causing biological agents are also available. In May 1995, a man with ties to right-wing groups purchased three vials of yersina pestis, the micro-organism that causes bubonic plague, from a biological culture lab in Maryland. The purchaser had used a fraudulent government agency authorization number to place the order. It is not clear what he intended to do with the material, but the laboratory became suspicious and called the police. The man was apprehended and imprisoned before he could do any harm (*Jerusalem Cloakroom*, August 8, 2001; see also http://www.acpr.org.il/cloakrm/index.html).

Nuclear

The possibility that terrorists might somehow buy, steal, or build a nuclear explosive device has worried analysts for twenty years or more, although others believe the risk has been overstated. Buying one is probably the easier route. That may be why, according to one Russian newspaper, one of Russia's nuclear weapon research centers (Arzamas 16) received a faxed letter, purportedly from an Egyptian Islamic terrorist group, offering to buy a nuclear weapon in 1991.

Terrorists could simply decide to wrap radioactive material of some kind around a core of conventional explosives and use the resulting radiological dispersal device (RDD) to contaminate a large area. CIA Director John Deutch (1996) made precisely that point in March 1996 Senate testimony. A terrorist organization, he noted, does not necessarily need fissile material that is more difficult to acquire for its purposes. But, nonfissile radioactive materials dispersed by conventional explosive or even released accidentally could cause damage to property and the environment, and cause social, political, and economic disruption.

Two recent developments have increased anxieties about the possibility of such attacks: the large but uncertain quantities of poorly secured weapons-usable and other nuclear materials in the former Soviet Union, and the 1995 incident in which Chechen terrorists planted a radioactive substance designed to create fear of contamination and radiation sickness in a Moscow park. The basic facts about Russian nuclear materials are not encouraging. First, the Russians simply do not know precisely how much nuclear material they have or where it is all located. Estimates by *Janes Intelligence Review* place the Russian stockpile of weapons-grade material at more than 1,200 tons of highly enriched uranium and 150 tons of plutonium. These materials are believed to be spread around some 100 different locations, including some 50 tons at nonmilitary sites. Whatever the actual number, nuclear warheads being dismantled under arms control agreements present a temptation for insiders, professional criminals, and terrorists (see 'Special Report: Iran's Nuclear Ambitions,' *Jane's Intelligence Review*, June 1, 1995).

State sponsorship: Implications

Designating countries that repeatedly support international terrorism (i.e., placing a country on the 'terrorism list') imposes four main sets of U.S. government sanctions:

- A ban on arms-related exports and sales;
- Controls over exports of dual use items, requiring 30-day congressional notification for goods or services that could significantly enhance the listed country's military capability or ability to support terrorism;
- Prohibitions on economic assistance; and
- Imposition of miscellaneous financial and other restrictions, including

    - Requiring the United States to oppose loans by the World Bank and other international financial institutions;
    - Lifting the diplomatic immunity to allow families of terrorist victims to file civil lawsuits in US courts;
    - Denying companies and individuals tax credits for income earned in terrorist list countries;
    - Denial of duty-free treatment for goods exported to the United States;
    - Authority to prohibit any US person from engaging in a financial transaction with terrorism list government without a Treasury Department license;
    - Prohibition of Defense Department contracts above $100,000 with companies controlled by terrorist list states.

The African connection to terrorism

What have all the alarming terrorist destructions and mass killings as well as definitional confusions got to do with the state in Africa? Africa, potentially the most vulnerable part of the globe, did not feel intimately the international character and the destructive power of terrorism until the bombings of the U.S. embassies in Kenya and Tanzania in August 1998. Of course, Africa was used to some forms of terrorism driven largely by ideology or nationalism, state terrorism or home-grown cults. This was a stage in the historical growth of a transnational force.

Africa[2] includes a large number of states, most of them 'artificial' in that they result from vertical colonial partition. The boundaries of these states generally were drawn by the Europeans to suit their own purposes and typically divide indigenous cultural communities. Even 'traditional,' (precolonial states) underwent major surgery at the hands of Europe. Morocco lost huge chunks of territory to the French in Algeria and to the Spanish in Western Sahara. In contrast, Rwanda nearly doubled its size under German and Belgian rule.

Most of Africa's states are weak, in terms of their relations with domestic society and external threats. A few have collapsed—notably Somalia, Sierra Leone, and the Democratic Republic of Congo. Conflict is widespread. A number of African governments face major insurgencies (Angola, Rwanda, Sudan, Burundi), sometimes coupled with foreign intervention. However, despite the weakness of today's African states and the permissiveness and arbitrariness of their borders, the African state system generally has been accepted by the leaders and the populations of the continent. While the number of ethno-cultural conflicts is quite high, cases of outright irredentism and secessionism are few and far apart.

There is a major zone of conflict in the 'Sahel' or southern shore of the Sahara, where Arab North Africa shades into sub-Saharan or 'black' Africa: Mauritania, Mali, Niger, Chad, and—most tragically—Sudan. In these countries, the Muslim Arab peoples of the north have often fought with the black peoples of the south, many of whom are non-Muslim. In Mauritania and Sudan, incidents of slavery are not uncommon to this day. Discrimination and repression against black Christians and 'animists' in the south by the Arab-dominated Sudanese government have varied in severity during the nearly fifty years of that country's independence, with civil wars raging periodically for greater southern autonomy or independence. The repression by Khartoum's extremist Islamic military government in recent years has been particularly severe, and pro-independence rebel groups control much of the southern part of the country. The death toll in Sudan from war and war-related shortages of food and medicine has reached the hundreds of thousands.

Muslim-Christian dimension

While the frontier between Arab and non-Arab largely coincides with the frontier between Muslim and non-Muslim in Sudan, this case is exceptional. West African states such as Senegal and Mali have few Arabic speakers but are overwhelmingly Muslim. Along the West African coast, from Côte d'Ivoire to Cameroon, there is a belt of states in which the coastal peoples are predominantly Christian while the land-locked northerners are predominantly Muslim. Along the Indian Ocean coast, from Kenya south to Mozambique, the situation is reversed, since the coastal peoples are Muslim while those of the interior tend to be Christian.

Religious pluralism itself does not lead to conflict. Some of these situations are much more explosive than others. In West Africa, Côte d'Ivoire and Nigeria stand out as particular examples. Nigeria, scene of one of Africa's bloodiest self-determination struggles, the Biafra war of 1967-1970, again appears in crisis. One dimension involves a rivalry between the Muslim North and the Christian South, aggravated by the adoption of Sharia (Islamic law) by a number of the northern states. In the Southeast, a new Biafran movement has appeared, but to date it does not enjoy the support of the elite of the Igbo (Ibo) ethnic community. Perhaps the most serious problem facing Nigeria pits the oil-producing states of the southeast, including the Igbo states, against the central government, in a struggle over the division of oil revenues. At the mass level, this problem takes the form of clashes between ethnic militias and between the federal army and militias. In Côte d'Ivoire, the rise of a xenophobic nationalism known as *ivoirité* (ivorianness) led to ethno-regional violence.

This xenophobic ideology defines the country as belonging not just to its citizens but to southerners in particular. Victims of the violence include Muslims, foreigners from Burkina Faso and Mali but also Muslims from northern Côte d'Ivoire. Some of the grievances expressed by this ideology are economic, but the form the dispute takes is a claim regarding membership in the national community. In this sense, the Ivorian conflict echoes those in the Great Lakes region (Rwanda-Burundi-Democratic Congo).

Along the East African coast, the most explosive situation is found in Tanzania. The semi-autonomous islands of Zanzibar have been the theater of violent clashes between security forces and supporters of an opposition party, leading many Zanzibaris to flee to Kenya. Here again, the problem is not religious or cultural pluralism as such, even though Zanzibar is almost 100 percent Muslim whereas the mainland is predominantly Christian. Rather, the problem centers on the pace of democratization and the degree of autonomy accorded to the islands. The fact that Zanzibar was a separate territory under colonial rule (like Somaliland or Eritrea) means that there is a greater potential for separatism than in other conflict zones.

In 1960, trumpeted as the 'Year of Africa,' and as late as the 1970s, one might have distinguished a front line separating independent, black-ruled states, to the north, from white-ruled southern Africa. With the transition to majority rule in South Africa, in the early 1990s, the concept of the 'front line' disappeared from usage. Yet it is clear that the former settler-ruled territories of Zimbabwe, Namibia, and South Africa still constitute a distinct subset of African states, ones in which the question of land ownership poses special problems.

Blood minerals

The African continent is characterized by both weak states and widespread poverty. In this context, struggles to control precious minerals are common, and civilian casualties are numerous. Even in the absence of open warfare, there are serious problems with the distribution of the proceeds of mineral wealth between central governments and the wealth-producing regions.

The most worrisome trend in African politics is the emergence of multi-state conflict zones defined by interlocking civil wars. In West Africa, the Sierra Leonean civil war has spilled over into Liberia and Guinea-Conakry. Another, far larger conflict zone stretches from the Horn of Africa (Somalia, Eritrea, Ethiopia, Sudan) diagonally across the continent to Angola and Namibia. The epicenters of the two zones are the mineral-rich collapsed states of Sierra Leone and Democratic Republic of Congo (formerly called Zaire).

The importance of minerals in fueling such conflicts has led some to exaggerate their role. As Paul Collier (2000a) observes 'Diamonds are the guerrilla's best friend . . . Civil wars are far more likely to be caused by economic opportunities than by grievance.' Rebels fighting civil conflicts around the world are more often motivated by greedy pursuit of lucrative commodities, like diamonds and drugs, than by political, ethnic, or religious goals as Collier (2000b, p. 4) argues, based on his study of 47 civil wars that took place from Afghanistan to Zimbabwe between 1960 and 1999. He stated that the single biggest risk factor for the outbreak of war was a nation's economic dependence on commodities. Eagerness to profit from coffee, narcotics, diamonds, and other gemstones prompted outbreaks of violence and determined their strength over time. African examples cited include the Biafra secession in the 1960s and the ongoing civil war in Sierra Leone.

Rebels typically claim that they are fighting their governments to right religious, ethnic, and political wrongs but those are often either coincidental or after-the-fact justifications for war. In a paper on ethnic conflict, Lipschutz and Crawford (1995) argue that such conflict is not caused by ethnic diversity or ancient grievances but by the breakdown of the social contract. Written or unwritten, the social contract sets the terms of citizenship and inclusion in and/or exclusion, from a country's political community, the political relationship between the central government and the regions, and the distribution of material resources within the country. Economic liberalization and democratization put pressure on social contracts, in Africa as elsewhere. In such situations, ethnic, religious, and class identities become points of conflict as ethnic entrepreneurs mobilize their constituencies in support of struggles with other elites for political power, social status, and economic resources (Collier, 2000b).

The weak states of the continent and at the same time, highly centralized and personalized power make the populations of various regions, poor regions as well as wealth-producing ones, feel no greater stake in the management of their affairs. Such a broken social contract causes disaffection, which can be exploited by domestic and external forces. This disaffection explains why: 'Terrorism will remain a major transnational problem, driven by continued ethnic, religious, nationalist, separatist, political, and economic motivations' (Hughes, 1997, pp. 5–6).

Hughes' thinking helps explain why the linkage between terrorism and African societies can be traced back to the anti-colonial struggle. The Mau Mau uprisings in Kenya and the atrocities associated with it were generally characterized by the British authorities as acts of terrorism carried out by what was then perceived to be a predominately Kikuyu movement. The other instance of political violence that received the name terrorism was the Algerian uprising against French rule. This bloody uprising led to the death of thousands of Algerians and Frenchmen. Yet, until the Tricontinental Conference of 1966 in Havana, Cuba, sub-Saharan Africa did not witness any major forms of political violence one can retrospectively call transnational terrorism. Up until the Havana conference, which declared the violence in waging wars of national liberation justifiable, most of the

African liberation movements took the path of non-violence to fight for political independence. The change of rhetoric and tactics in the prosecution of the national wars in former Portuguese territories and in the former settler states of South Africa and Southern Rhodesia, would create the precedents for the employment of low level terrorism in these parts of the African continent. Although many system challengers of that period would now claim their acts to be those of the freedom fighters against oppressive regimes, their acts were perceived in most Western circles as violent acts of terrorism. These sentiments greatly affected the policies and decisions of the U.S. government until the collapse of apartheid and the rise to power of the African National Congress.

It is indeed against this background that we now turn to the rise and menace of Islamic radicalism in Africa. But, before we go into any serious analysis of the threat of Islamic radicalism, we must first identify the factors and forces responsible for the development of Islamic militancy in Africa. Prior to the collapse of the colonial order in Africa, African Muslims were becoming increasingly secularized. This process of secularization was a global phenomenon and scholars like American social scientist Daniel Lerner (1958) saw it as 'the passing of traditional society.' This transition from a traditional society dominated by Islam to another on the verge of modernization, was widely celebrated by the champions of African and Arab nationalism. This thus marked the heyday of African and Arab nationalism on the one hand and African and Arab socialism on the other.

Taking place within the framework of the Cold War, this secularization process put Islam as a religion generally on the defensive. In the special case of Africa, the only defenders of Islam were the traditional conservative members of the Ulema (learned scholars) and the sufi orders committed to Islamic mysticism (tassawuf). Because the young people were sold on the ideas of development and modernization Islam continued to be observed ritually but its political potency remained either underestimated or ignored completely by the political class. Some global and regional African developments changed the course of African and world history. The present state of Islamic militancy and terrorism in Africa and the world could be traced back to these changes in the international system.

The first development was the export into Africa of the political troubles of the Middle East. The Middle East of the Cold War era was different from all other regions of the world because of the trinity of conflicts raging within its borders, which consisted of (1) the bipolar Cold War between the United States and her Allies and the Soviet Union and her

Eastern Bloc allies; (2) the Arab-Israeli conflict; and (3) the Arab Cold War. To understand the present state of affairs regarding Islamic militancy in Africa and the potential for terrorism in Muslim lands and among Muslim minorities in African societies, one must first examine how the African Muslims became involved in the theater of conflicts in the Middle East.

The trinity of conflicts from the Middle East came into Africa because of the Arab-Israeli conflict on the one hand and the Arab Cold War on the other. Because of Gamal Abdul Nasser's campaign against Israel and Zionism, African states became the target of both Arab and Israeli propaganda. The Arabs capitalized on both Islam and Pan-Africanism to ingratiate themselves with the Africans. On the other hand, the Israelis played on the fact that both blacks and Jews have historically suffered at the hands of other human groups. This idea of a community of shared suffering was an important card in the hand of the Israelis. Although in retrospect, one can now argue that this ideological game of the Middle Eastern states resulted in a mixed bag of Arab and Israeli victories, the fact remains that these two struggles imported into Africa set the stage for the revitalization of Islam in the continent. To put it another way, one could say that political Islam in contemporary sub-Saharan Africa owed a great debt to the activities of secular Egypt under Nasser, and the Arab-Israeli conflict. These are unintended consequences because although Nasser gave thousands of scholarships to young Muslims to study and receive training at Egyptian centers of higher learning, he could not predict the fact that many of these young men and women would later return home to replicate politically what he himself tried hard to prevent the Islamic Brotherhood from doing in Egypt. This post colonial phenomenon of revitalized militant Islam, was a reversal of the colonial process of secularization that came with the advancing armies of the newly installed colonial powers.

The second factor responsible for the revivification of militant Islam in Africa was the Arab Cold War. Saudi Arabia played a crucial role and ironically the Western powers who were totally preoccupied with the Cold War willingly or unwillingly supported this venture. Because Nasser and the Baathist forces in the Arab World were suspected to be collaborators with the Soviet Bloc, this Saudi attempt to use Islam for political and strategic ends in Africa received some encouragement. Because of these political uses of Islam in Africa, the Saudi brand of Wahabism soon gained some attention in sub-Saharan Africa. This was most evident after the 1973 War between Israel and Arab states and the oil embargo and its aftermath. It should be noted here that the sharp rise in oil prices in the mid-1970s catapulted Saudi Arabia to the plateau of economic success, and this new state of affairs in Arab and world politics enhanced Saudi prestige in Muslim circles. Because of this development, thousands of young Muslims from various African lands went to study in Saudi Arabia. Saudi literature and Saudi financed missionaries spread across the African continent. This process of radical Islamization became more intense in Africa after the Iranian revolution, when it became evident to Saudi leaders that their brand of Islam could be threatened by the Shiite revolutionary state next door. The Iran-Iraq War was just one consequence of this struggle between the two major sects of the Islamic world. But, how has Islamic radicalism become a problem in Africa? The relevance of this question lies in the ability of Islamist terrorist organizations (e.g., al Qaeda) to seek sanctuary in African countries where they could count on some degree of local support. Present Somalia is such a place. It is a failed state whose lawless anarchy would permit terrorists to operate relatively freely. The al Qaeda network operated there in the past and has longstanding ties to a small minority of Somali Islamists. The Islamists are using a patient incremental strategy that involves the long-term infiltration of regional institutions, promotion of fundamentalist Islamic education institutions, and decentralized work within clans to avoid unnecessary clashes with traditional clan leaders.

Transnational terrorism: The al Qaeda factor

September 11, 2001 catapulted terrorism onto an entirely new level of strategic importance. Catastrophic or mass-casualty terrorism, once a theory, had now become a reality. But the larger issue revolved around the nature of terrorism itself and its emerging modus operandi. Whether the September 11 attacks in the United States were the delayed manifestation of Oplan Bojinka, as some believe, or whether they were an isolated plan, it is clear that terrorism—and particularly that form of terrorism practiced by al Qaeda—has fundamentally changed.[3]

The September 11 attacks on the United States were a bold, calculated transnational or networked attack by an organization that has established and maintained a multinational presence in more than fifty countries, directed by a base located—at least until recently—in Afghanistan. Like many multinational corporations, al Qaeda is both the product and beneficiary of globalization. The organization took advantage of the fruits of globalization and modernization—including satellite technology, accessible air travel, fax machines, the Internet, and other modern conveniences—to advance its political agenda. No longer geographically constrained within a particular territory, or financially tied to a particular state, al Qaeda emerged as the ultimate transnational terror organization, relying on an array of legitimate and illicit sources of cash, including international charities that were often based in the West.

In the weeks following the attacks, many politicians, journalists, and pundits pointed to a 'massive intelligence failure' that facilitated or allowed the attacks (Blanche, 2002, pp. 27–28). Some attributed this failure to the lack of human intelligence operations within Afghanistan. However, some experts have argued that the greatest intelligence failure of the September 11 attacks was the inability on the part of intelligence and law enforcement agencies to grasp and understand that al Qaeda represented a different type of terrorism, one less anchored to specific geographic locations or political constituencies and one capable of achieving transglobal strategic reach in its operations (Blanche, 2001a, pp. 16–17; Mintz and Jackman, 2002, p. A01).

The September 11 attacks also exposed fundamental weaknesses of modern Western states, including vulnerable borders, inadequate immigration controls, and insufficient internal antiterrorism surveillance. Indeed, investigations conducted following the terror attacks on the United States revealed an uncomfortable truth about al Qaeda and its affiliate groups. Probably their most important bases of operation—from a financial and logistical perspective—were located not in Afghanistan or Sudan, but rather in Western Europe and North America, including the United States itself.[4]

The al Qaeda multi-cellular terror model

Al Qaeda (Arabic for 'the base') traces its roots to Afghanistan and the pan-Islamic resistance to the invasion of that country by the Soviet Union in 1979. In 1982, Osama bin Laden, then a young Saudi Arabian national, joined the anti-Soviet jihad. He traveled to Afghanistan where, after just a few years, he established his own military camps from which anti-Soviet assaults could be launched. In 1988, Osama bin Laden and others established al Qaeda, not as a terrorist organization, but rather as a reporting infrastructure so that relatives of foreign soldiers who had come to Afghanistan to join the resistance could be properly tracked.[5] Al Qaeda reportedly had the additional function of funneling money to the Afghan resistance (Bergen, 2001, p. 79).

In 1989, the year the Soviets withdrew their last troops from Afghanistan, Osama bin Laden returned to Saudi Arabia, where he began delivering public lectures about topics that were sensitive to the government, including predictions that Kuwait would soon be invaded by Iraq. When his prediction came true, he became frustrated when the Saudi government ignored his advice (including offers of military assistance), and instead turned to the United States for military help. Increasingly unhappy with Osama bin Laden's public activities and his militant views, the Saudi government placed him under house arrest. Through his family connections, Osama bin Laden was nevertheless able to secure permission for a business trip to Pakistan. Once in Pakistan, he traveled to Afghanistan and stayed a few months. But soon after, he left for the Sudan where he was welcomed by the National Islamic Front (NIF) leader, Hassan al-Turabi (Bergen, 2001, p. 85). Osama bin Laden's time in Sudan is probably the most important in terms of al Qaeda's development. During this period, al Qaeda forged alliances with militant groups from Egypt, Pakistan, Algeria, and Tunisia, as well as with Palestinian Jihad and Hamas (Bergen, 2001, p. 86). Also while in the Sudan, al Qaeda began to develop its signature transnational modus operandi by engaging in a range of international operations, such as deploying fighters to Chechnya and Tajikistan, establishing satellite offices in Baku, Azerbaijan, and funding affiliates based in Jordan and Eritrea.[6] Under pressure from the United States, however, the Sudan forced Osama bin Laden to leave in 1996. He and other members of al Qaeda relocated their operations to Afghanistan.

Al Qaeda has traditionally operated with an informal horizontal structure, comprising more than twenty-four constituent terrorist organizations, combined with a formal vertical structure. Below Osama bin Laden was the 'majlis al shura,' a consultative council that directed the four key committees (military, religious, finance, and media), members of which were handpicked by its senior leadership. The majlis al shura discussed and approved major operations, including terrorist attacks (Bergen, 2001, p. 93). Osama bin Laden and his two cohorts, Ayman-al-Zawahiri and Mohammed Atef, set general policies and approved large-scale actions. Until the U.S. intervention in Afghanistan, al Qaeda acted in a manner somewhat resembling a large charity organization that funded terrorist projects to be conducted by preexisting or affiliate terrorist groups.

The United States emerged as a central enemy to al Qaeda almost from the beginning of the organization's existence for a variety of reasons, including al Qaeda's unhappiness with U.S. operations in the 1990–1991 Gulf War and the 1992–1993 Operation Restore Hope in Somalia. Al Qaeda's overarching complaint against the United States has centered on its continued military presence in Saudi Arabia and throughout the Arabian peninsula.

To publicize its disdain for the United States, al Qaeda issued various 'fatwas' (verdicts based on Islamic law) urging that U.S. forces should be attacked. In 1992 and 1993, the group issued specific fatwas urging that American forces in Somalia should be attacked. In 1996, the group issued a 'Declaration of Jihad on the Americans Occupying the Country of the Two Sacred Places,' which urged the expulsion of American forces from the Arabian peninsula (Bergen, 2001, p. 94). This was followed by a media interview in 1997 in which Osama bin Laden called for attacks on U.S. soldiers (Bergen, 2001, p. 95).

The anti-American rhetoric emanating from al Qaeda hit a high pitch in 1998 when the organization essentially fused with Egypt's two main terrorist organizations, al Jihad (Islamic Jihad) and al Gamaa al Islamiya (Islamic Group), both of which were linked to the assassination of former Egyptian President Anwar Sadat. The new campaign would be known as the World Islamic Front for Jihad Against the Jews and the Crusaders, and would also include co-signatories from Pakistan and Bangladesh. Contained in the text that announces the World Islamic Front are calls to attack not only U.S. soldiers, but also U.S. civilians. The proclamation demands that Muslims everywhere should 'abide by Allah's order by killing Americans and stealing their money anywhere, anytime, and whenever possible' (Bergen, 2001, p. 96).

To understand al Qaeda's evolution, it is especially critical to recognize the importance of Egyptian influence on Osama bin Laden, which dates back to his time in Afghanistan. Currently most of al Qaeda's membership is drawn from these two Egyptian groups. Moreover, one Egyptian in particular, Ayman al-Zawahiri—a former key figure in al Jihad—has had a tremendous intellectual influence on Osama bin Laden and is considered by many to be a candidate to succeed him (Blanche, 2001b, pp. 19–21). As indicated above, al Qaeda's model has been to establish bases with indigenous groups throughout the world. Early in its existence, al Qaeda developed the ability to penetrate Islamic nongovernmental organizations (NGOs) to the point that it was 'inseparably enmeshed with the religious, social, and economic fabric of Muslim communities worldwide' (Hirschkorn, Gunaratna, Blanche and Leader, 2001, pp. 42–45). In some cases, al Qaeda pursued a virtual 'hands off' policy with its affiliated group.

It may have guided or directed the group's operations, but at the same time required it to raise its own funds. Ahmed Ressam, who was intercepted entering the United States in December 1999 as part of the infamous 'Millennium Plot,' was part of a cell in Montreal, Canada, that survived by engaging in petty theft, including passport theft, and other crimes. However, for certain operations, such as the September 11 attacks in the United States, al Qaeda was much more willing to provide substantial and direct financial support.

Al Qaeda's strength lay in its reliance on a multi-cellular structure, spanning the entire globe, which gave the organization agility and cover. One French terrorism expert recently lamented, 'If you have good knowledge of the [al Qaeda] network today, it's not operational tomorrow' (Erlanger and Hedges, 2001, p. 1). He compared its networks to a constantly changing virus that is impossible to totally grasp or destroy. Al Qaeda's multi-cellular international structure provided an ironic backdrop to President George Bush's proclamation that the United States would find terrorists wherever they were located and would consider attacking any nation that harbored terrorists. The uncomfortable reality is that many states, including those allied with the United States, harbored al Qaeda cells, but did nothing to neutralize them, either because they did not know of their presence (or the precise danger they posed) or were unwilling, for political or security reasons, to disrupt their operations. Certain German investigators, for instance, ruefully admit that their lack of aggressive intervention, despite full awareness of al Qaeda's activities in many of its main cities, probably contributed to the September 11 tragedy.

As a truly transnational terrorist organization, al Qaeda has sought to expand beyond the traditional venue of the Middle East, Western Europe, North America, and South Asia. Increasingly the organization has pursued Southeast Asia as a key basing and staging region. Al Qaeda has long cultivated links with groups such as the Philippine-based Abu Sayyaf and Moro Islamic Liberation Front (MILF) and the Indonesian group Laskar Jihad. Al Qaeda is also linked to region-wide organizations, such as Jemaah Islamiah, the mastermind of plots against the U.S. embassy in Singapore and other critical American and Western targets. In late September 2001, the Philippine military's chief of staff confirmed speculation that al Qaeda was seeking to support the Abu Sayyaf Group with 'material, leadership, and training support.'[7]

Similar trends have been detected in Indonesia, where officials suspect growing linkages between al Qaeda and indigenous groups such as Laskar Jihad. In December 2001, the head of Indonesia's intelligence services,

Abdullah Hendropriyono, asserted that al Qaeda and other international terrorist organizations were attempting to sow unrest on the Indonesian island of Sulawesi by promoting inter-ethnic violence between Muslims and Christians. He also confirmed that al Qaeda and other international groups had used the territory as a base and training site for international terrorist operations (Unidjaja, 2001).

Al Qaeda has also established links in Africa and South America. In South America, the 'triple border' area (where Brazil, Argentina, and Paraguay meet) is viewed as a base for such Middle Eastern terrorist organizations as Hezbollah, al Gamaa al Islamiya, and Hamas, all al Qaeda constituent or affiliate groups. A 1999 Argentine intelligence report stated that al Qaeda was operating in the region in an attempt to forge links with Hezbollah supporters (Montoya, 2001, pp. 12–15). The region, and other locations in Brazil, appear to have played a significant role in the planning of the September 11 attacks (Daly, 2001, p. 13). Al Qaeda also has established links in various African countries, including Somalia, Sudan, and South Africa.[8] Al Qaeda reportedly has considered moving to Somalia following U.S. military operations in Afghanistan, a possibility that prompted a U.S. naval blockade of the entire Somali coastline.

Al Qaeda has flourished in an environment of weak or quasi-states that are undergoing disruptive political or social change. Vast swaths of political instability in many parts of the world, and particularly in Africa and Asia, have provided a breeding ground for al Qaeda and its analogues. As one French analyst stated, wide expanses of anarchic territory 'need no longer be considered a regrettable feature of the postmodern world, but rather a strategic challenge that should be addressed urgently' (Delpech, 2002, p. 31). Such areas are not only hospitable to terrorists, they may also attract transnational crime groups, drug traffickers, and maritime pirates. Despite their isolation, paradoxically, these areas constitute an acute threat to global security.

Global impact of transnational terrorism

There are two main impacts, beyond the toll of death and devastation: economic and psychological. Nations are sorely tempted to spend more fighting homeland terror than international terror. Doing both exceeds the capacities of most deficit spending wartime budgets. Following September 11, the U.S. Congress allocated $60 billion to counterterrorism, roughly five times the latter's budget for previous years. Homeland security is expected to average $150 billion a year over the next decade, approximately half of the U.S military's $345 million budget (Barletta, 2002). The money is expected to be spent on things like protecting nuclear power plants to building up federal vaccine stockpiles. The nation is most concerned about protecting its critical infrastructure from disruption and destruction. The eight critical infrastructures of the U.S. include the electric power system, gas and oil (storage and transportation), telecommunications, banking and finance, transportation, water supply systems, emergency services (including medical, police, fire and rescue), and continuity of government services. Threats to these infrastructures fall into two categories: physical threats to tangible property ('physical threats'), and threats of electronic, radio-frequency, or computer-based attacks on the information or communications components that control critical infrastructures ('cyber threats').

The psychological impact involves short-term and long-term trauma, especially in children, who are most vulnerable to WMD attacks, and nothing exposes the weaknesses and vulnerabilities of a national healthcare system like a campaign of domestic terrorism. Emergency rooms become overworked, vaccines run out, and decontamination teams are found in short supply. Stress and incident-related counseling becomes of paramount importance.

By far, however, the greatest threat of a war on terrorism is the loss of civil liberties. Wartime powers often erode them to the point where they cannot be regained. Protection against intrusive surveillance measures are difficult to win back because technology is put into place. Loosening of the rules of evidence is difficult to overcome because the legal system operates slowly by precedent. Now is the time to carefully scrutinize anything in the name of anti-terrorism. The United States, has, in the past, been able to reconcile the requirements of security with the demands of liberty, and it is important to have faith, but it is also important to have a healthy dose of skepticism.

Abandonment of civil liberties is another price to be paid by a society attacked by terrorists. For instance, in November 2002, the top-secret Foreign Intelligence Surveillance Court handed the government broad new authority to wiretap phone calls, intercept mail and spy on the Internet use of ordinary Americans. The FISA (Foreign Intelligence Surveillance Act), as amended by the Patriot Act, now supports cooperation between intelligence and law enforcement agencies in establishing probable cause for the issuance of wiretaps against any U.S. citizen suspected of aiding, abetting, or conspiring with others in international terrorism. In the past, restrictions had prevented criminal investigators and intelligence agents from sharing information.

It is much easier now for authorities to justify secret wiretaps and surveillance since probable cause under FISA represents a lower threshold of evidence based on a record of automatic approval for most warrant applications. Agents in the FBI's National Security Law Unit can now also use an electronic system to draft surveillance applications instantly. Citizens may never know who might be accessing their personal and business e-mails, their Internet usage, their medical and financial records, or their cordless and cellular telephone conversations.

Prototype computer monitoring systems such as those being developed at Defense Advanced Research Projects Agency (DARPA) would search for terrorists by probing through networked databases of 'transactional' information. Such data mining projects make programs like Carnivore seem antiquated. They proactively search the Internet for terrorist plots in progress. They flag for instance, certain steps a terrorist might take—cruising government websites on Monday, for example, followed by foreign e-mails on Tuesday, followed by looking up how to make explosives on Wednesday, and so on.

In conclusion, under the banner of the global fight against terrorism the world's leading powers, led by the United States, are preparing nothing less than the reorganization of the world through the imposition of military power. This has immediate political consequences. Militarization of international relations inevitably implies militarization of politics at home: militarism is incompatible with democratic forms of rule.

Definitions of terrorism must therefore tread warily between restricting the freedoms of the individual with legal provisions required to guard against the contingencies and imperatives confronting the state and the primary necessity to protect democratic processes without excessive intrusion into the private domain of the individuals. Maintaining the democratic process, which is the ultimate guarantor of individual liberties and human rights, must be uppermost in any definition of terrorism. A single definition of terrorism then, cannot account for all possible uses of the term.

Furthermore, the 'glory days' of British imperialism led to the carve-up of the world in the latter part of the nineteenth century and the first part of the twentieth century. Did this bring peace and prosperity? Rather, it led to two inter-imperialist wars, resulting in hundreds of millions of deaths as the major capitalist powers—the United States, Britain, Germany, France, and Japan—inevitably came into conflict with each other in the global struggle for resources, markets and spheres of influence. In fact, these wars were fought for looting rights.

Terrorism is unconventional warfare. There are no fronts, no armies, and no battlefields. The solutions therefore cannot come strictly from militaries, which are largely designed for fighting other armed forces. The solutions will come from new approaches that address the whole person, not just the political and economic components. This is about individual people, their values and aspirations—and cultures, some of which have not changed much over centuries. Different people and groups will require different approaches. The new solutions will be complex and sophisticated and necessarily not look like the past.

Notes

1. In the Matter of the Ex tradition of Moussa Abu Marzuk, U.S. District Court, Southern District of New York, Affirmation 95, Cr. Misc 1, October 5, 1995, statement of Bassam Musa, February 17, 1993, p. 12.
2. Many Africans, including those on the offshore islands, identify strongly with the continent as a whole. The Organization of African Unity was continental in scope and included predominantly Arab North Africa. The newly formed African Union (AU) continues this tradition. I will refer to Africa in general, in this chapter, but defer to others the issue of self-determination in North Africa.
3. This specific phrase was uttered by U.S. Senator Richard Shelby on the CBS News Show, *Face the Nation*, on September 16, 2001.
4. A biography of Osama bin Laden, background article for PBS documentary series *Frontline*, retrieved on March 24, 2002 from: www.pbs.org/wgbh/pages/frontline/shows/binladen/who/bio.html.
5. 'Osama bin Laden: A Chronology of His Political Life', background article for PBS documentary series Frontline, retrieved on March 24, 2002 from: www.pbs.org/wgbh/pages/frontline/shows/binladen/etc/cron.html.
6. Indictment of Zacarias Moussaoui, United States District Court for the Eastern District of Virginia, Alexandria Division (December 2001).
7. 'Abu Sayyaf Gets Arms, Training from Bin Laden: Philippine Military', *Agence France Presse*, September 28, 2001.
8. See testimony of Dr. J. Stephen Morrison before the House International Relations Committee, Subcommittee on Africa, Hearing on 'Africa and the War on Global Terrorism', Federal Document Clearing House Congressional Testimony, November 15, 2001.

References

Alexander, Y. (1995), 'Terrorism and Resistance', in Alexander, Y. (ed.), *Middle East Terrorism: Current Threats and Future Prospects*, McGraw-Hill: New York.

Alexander, Y. (2002), *Palestinian Religious Terrorism: Hamas and Islamic Jihad*, Transnational Publishers: Ardsley, NY.

Amnesty International (2001), *Amnesty International Report on Iraq, 2001*, Amnesty International: London.

Barletta, M. (ed.) (2002), *After 9/11: Preventing Mass-Destruction Terrorism and Weapons Proliferation*, Occasional Papers 8, Center for Nonproliferation Studies: Monterey, CA.

Barsky, Y. (1996), 'Terror by Remote Control', *Middle East Quarterly*, Vol. 3, No. 2, pp. 3–9.

Beam, L. (1992), 'Leaderless Resistance', *The Seditionist*, Vol. 12 (February).

Bergen, P. L. (2001), *Holy War: Inside The Secret World of Osama bin Laden*, Free Press: New York.

Blanche, Ed (2001a), 'What the Investigation Reveals', *Jane's Intelligence Review*, Vol. 13 (November), pp. 16–17.

Blanche, Ed (2001b), 'The Egyptians around Bin Laden', *Jane's Intelligence Review*, Vol. 13 (December), pp. 19–21.

Blanche, Ed (2002), 'Al Qaeda Recruitment', *Jane's Intelligence Review*, Vol. 14, pp. 27–28.

Blum, W. (2003), *Killing Hope: U.S. Military and CIA Interventions Since World War II*, Zed Books: London.

Collier, P. (2000a), *Economic Causes of Civil Conflict and their Implications for Policy*, World Bank: Washington, D.C.

Collier, P. (2000b), 'Doing Well Out of War: An Economic Perspective', in Berdal, M. and Malone, D. (eds.), *Greed and Grievance: Economic Agendas in Civil Wars*, Lynne Rienner: Boulder, CO.

Cordesman, A. H. and Hashim, A. S. (1997), *Iran: Dilemmas of Dual Containment*, Westview Press: Boulder, CO.

Daly, J.C.K. (2001), 'Moroccan Has "Much to Tell"', *Jane's Intelligence Review*, Vol. 13 (December), p. 13.

Delpech, T. (2002), 'The Imbalance of Terror', *Washington, Quarterly*, Vol. 25, No. 1, pp. 31–40.

Deutch, J. M. (1996), *Brief to the Senate Select Committee on Intelligence on the Worldwide Threat Assessment*, U.S. Senate: Washington, D.C.

Dwyer, J. (2001), 'The Memorial that Vanished', *New York Times Magazine*, September 23, p. 81.

Erlanger, S. and Hedges, C. (2001), 'Terror Cells Slip Through Europe's Grasp', *New York Times*, December 28, 2001, p. A1.

Gunaratna, R. (2001), 'Terrorist Trends Suggest Shift of Focus to National Activities', *Jane's Intelligence Review* (June), p. 47.

Gurr, T. (1979), 'Some Characteristics of Political Terrorism in the 1960s', in Stohl, M. (ed.), *The Politics of Terrorism*, Marcel Dekker: New York.

Hirschkorn, P. (2001), 'Convictions Mark the First Step in Breaking up al Qaeda Network', *Janes Intelligence Review*.

Hirschkorn, P., Gunaratna, T. Blanche, Ed., and Leader, S. (2001), 'Blowback', *Jane's Intelligence Review*, Vol. 13 (August), pp. 42–45.

Hoffman, B. (1999), *Inside Terrorism*, New York: Columbia University Press.

Hughes, P. M. (1997), 'Global Threats and Challenges to the United States and its Interests Abroad', U.S. Director, Defense Intelligence Agency, February 5–6, Washington, D.C.

ICJ (International Court of Justice) (1998), *Case Concerning Questions of Interpretation and Application of the 1971 Montreal Convention Arising from the Aerial Incident at Lockerbie (Libyan Arab Jamahiriya v. United Kingdom): Summary of the Judgment of 27 February 1998*, ICJ: The Hague.

Keohane, R. O. (2002), 'The Globalization of Informal Violence, Theories of World Politics, and "the Liberalism of Fear"', in Calhoun, C. J., Price, P. and Timmer, A. S. (eds.), *Understanding September 11*, New Press: New York.

Keohane, R. O. and Nye, J. S. (2001), *Power and Interdependence*, 3rd edition, Addison Wesley Longman: New York.

Laqueur, W. (1999), *The New Terrorism: Fanaticism and the Arms of Mass Destruction*, Oxford University Press: New York.

Lefebvre, H. (1965), *La proclamation de la commune, 26 mars 1871*, Gallimard: Paris.

Lerner, D. (1958), *The Passing of Traditional Society: Modernizing the Middle East*, The Free Press: New York.

Lipschutz, R. and Crawford, B. (1995), 'Ethnic Conflict Isn't', *Institute on Global Conflict and Cooperation Brief* (University of California), Vol. 2, p. 4.

MacDonald, A. (1978), *The Turner Diaries*, National Vanguard Books: Hillsboro, WV.

Mackenzie, W. (2002), *The Secret History of SOE: Special Operations Executive 1940–1945*, St. Ermin's Press: London.

Mannoni, J. (2000), 'The U.S.: A Party to Murder?', *The Jakarta Post* (Editorial and Opinion), January 13 and 14.

Miller, M. (2001), *Terrorism Factbook: Our Nation at War*, Bollix Books: Peoria, IL.

Mintz, J. and Jackman, R. (2002), 'Finances Prompted Raids on Muslims',

Montoya, M. D. (2001), 'War on Terrorism Reaches Paraguay's Triple Border', *Jane's Intelligence Review*, Vol. 13, pp. 12–15.

Moyers, B. (2001), 'Which America will we be Now?', *The Nation*, November 19, pp. 11–14.

Norton-Taylor, R. and Walker, M. (1995), 'Blast Alerts West to Elusive Threat', *The Guardian*, April 21.

Pillar, P. R. (2001), *Terrorism and U.S. Foreign Policy*, Brookings Institution Press: Washington, D.C.

Rapoport, D. C. (1984), 'Fear and Trembling: Terrorism in Three Religious Traditions', *American Political Science Review*, Vol. 78, No. 3, pp. 668–672.

Rubin, B. and Rubin, J. C. (2002), *Anti-American Terrorism and the Middle East: Understanding the Violence*, Oxford University Press: New York.

Schumpeter, J. (1950), *Capitalism, Socialism and Democracy*, Harper and Row: New York.

Schweitzer, G. and Dorsch, C. (1998), *Super Terrorism: Assassins, Mobsters and Weapons of Mass Destruction*, Plenum Press: London.

Simon, J. D. (2001), *Terrorist Trap: America's Experience with Terrorism*, Indiana University Press: Bloomington, IN.

Smithson, A. E. (2000), 'Rethinking the Lessons of Tokyo', in Smithson, A. E. and Levy, L. A. (eds.), *Ataxia: The Chemical and Biological Terrorism Threat and the U.S. Response*, The Henry L. Stimson Center: Washington, D.C.

Sprinzak, E. (2000), 'From Ideology to Terrorism: The Case of the Extreme Right', Paper presented at the conference on Extremism and Antisemitism in the Face of the New Millennium, Tel Aviv University/Anti-Defamation League, New York, January 9–12.

Tu, A. T. (2000), 'Overview of Sarin Terrorist Attacks in Japan', in *Natural and Selected Synthetic Toxins: Biological Implications*, American Chemical Society Symposium Series No. 745: Washington, D.C.

Unidjaja, F. D. (2001), 'International Terrorists Train in Poso', *Jakarta Post*, December 13.

U.S. State Department (1995), *Patterns of Global Terrorism*, Office of the Coordinator for Counterterrorism: Washington, D.C.

U.S. State Department (1996), *Patterns of Global Terrorism*, Office of the Coordinator for Counterterrorism: Washington, D.C.

U.S. State Department (2000), *Patterns of Global Terrorism*, Office of the Coordinator for Counterterrorism: Washington, D.C.

U.S. State Department (2001), *Patterns of Global Terrorism*, Office of the Coordinator for Counterterrorism: Washington, D.C.

U.S. State Department (2002), *Patterns of Global Terrorism*, Office of the Coordinator for Counterterrorism: Washington, D.C.

Walker, M. (2001), 'A Brief History of Terrorism', *Europe: Magazine of the European Union*, No. 410 (October), pp. 26.

4

The State, Africa's Tragic Anarchy, and Terrorism

Most conflicts in Africa today are anarchic, internal, and tragic. Often and increasingly these conflicts center on access to arable land, water resources and mining, oil or diamond resources due to the crisis-prone and chaotic situation of the African states. Dictatorships, oppression and corruption further aggravate conflicts in Africa. However, the analysis of recent conflicts in Africa has sometimes distorted issues of ethnicity, race, religion and ideology, depicting them as the sole causes of conflict and disregarding political manipulation of religious and ethnic differences. Continuous drought, floods and the debt burden compound the grim economic situation of countries resulting in further causes for conflict. This gruesome situation thus renders the state too weak to handle the attendant crisis and tragedies facing Africa. The consequence is that wars are fought over scarce resources; and war itself becomes continuous with crime, as armed bands of stateless marauding terrorists seek refuge and recruits among the disaffected Africans.

In the context of Africa therefore, terrorism cannot be tackled without addressing its domestic and international causes. The tactics of terror and murder cannot, and should certainly not, be tolerated by any state or government. The strictest action should be taken efficiently and expeditiously, against all movements and individuals participating in or condoning terrorism as a political strategy. But the causes that have generated such movements must be addressed. There are rational political, social and economic aspirations of peoples which, when frustrated continuously, give rise to full blown terrorism. These aspirations must be sifted out of the process of terrorist actions and looked at separately. This is an approach that has not thus far been lucidly articulated though, in Africa, the frustrating conditions that fertilize the soil for the nurturing and growth of networked terrorism are in abundance.

Is Africa's natural wealth a curse?

The abundant natural resources within the continent have become a curse, indeed, ripe targets for unscrupulous exploitation, including terrorist organizations seeking financial gains by bartering arms for minerals like diamonds. The article 'Mineral Wealth Fuels Africa's Most Protracted Wars' in *Agence France Presse* of November 27, 2002, is indicative. Africa produces more than sixty metal and mineral products and is a major producer of several of the world's most important minerals and metals including gold, primary platinum group elements (PGEs), diamonds, uranium, manganese, chromium, nickel, bauxite and cobalt. It is interesting to note that Africa's contribution to the world's major metals (copper, lead and zinc) is less than 7 percent. As a result silver production is low (less than 3 percent of the world's production) due to the fact that most silver is produced as a by-product of lead—zinc and copper mining. Although underexplored, Africa hosts about 30 percent of the planet's mineral reserves, including 40 percent of gold, 60 percent cobalt and 90 percent of the world's platinum group mineral (PGM) reserves—making it a truly strategic producer of these precious metals (UNU, 1997, C5).

Some of the largest and richest mineral deposits in the world have been found in Africa. For much of the last half of the twentieth century little mineral exploration and development work was done in Africa, except for southern Africa, even though there is significant potential for the discovery of new deposits. By the mid-1990s modern exploration started to spread across much of Africa and many new deposits have been discovered and developed and some of the old major deposits are being renovated. The potential in Africa for the discovery and development of mineral resources is therefore quite immense since minerals are present throughout the continent in virtually all the countries (see http://www.africaminerals.com/mineral_resources.htm).

But, in spite of its mineral wealth, as contained in the Africa Mineral Resource Specialists (AMRS), Inc. report, the continent is home to the world's most impoverished and abused people. Of the forty-one sub-

Saharan African nations, only a few (Senegal, South Africa, Ghana, Nigeria, Benin, Botswana, and Mauritius) allow their people the right to vote and choose their own leaders. Only two (Botswana and Senegal) permit freedom of expression and criticism of government policies. In countries like Uganda, Rwanda, Burundi, Mozambique, Sudan, Chad and others, ethnic genocide has taken the lives of untold millions of innocent civilians. Slavery is still practiced in the Sudan and Mauritania. Escalating inter-and intra-state conflict, xenophobic attitudes and micro-nationalism emerging from conflicts in East and Central Africa, coupled with the poor socio-economic conditions of the people, is resulting in growing polarization of the communities and the different states of the region.

Despite this bleak and tragic[1] situation, the struggle for power and mineral wealth has fueled fratricidal wars raising the refugee toll to 9.5 million in Africa. Ironically, one time Director of the International Monetary Fund (IMF), Michel Camdessus, and his colleagues and others at the World Bank (i.e., the Bretton Woods Institutions) claimed: 'Africa is on the move' (*International Herald Tribune*, December 21–22, 1997). Global growth is creating a 'rational dynamism'[2] and for the first time in a generation there are encouraging signs of progress.[3] 'Hope and real success are transforming the continent . . . The changes we are witnessing, building foundations for prosperity and welfare, are creating a new sense of hope in the future.' This flawed perception of African realities is not new. The highly respected magazine, *The Economist* is guilty of presenting such contrasting images of Africa. On the cover page of its May 13–19, 2000 edition, the magazine declared Africa to be the continent without hope. This was just three years after claiming that sub-Saharan Africa was in a better shape than it had been in a generation.

These contrasting images of rich-poor and prosperous-stagnating Africa compel one to question the scientific nature of the methodology used in acquiring the evidence from which the conclusions are drawn (Barongo, 1983). One defining characteristic of science as distinct from *belles lettres*, criticism, propaganda and philosophic speculation is the accumulation of knowledge in the form of more or less verifiable propositions about the world. In the conventional view of science, propositions are verified deductively when they are inferred indisputably from an axiom system and verified empirically when they have survived repeated attempts at falsification. However, in practice, scientific propositions are typically neither so theoretically indisputable nor so empirically unfalsifiable as the conventional view may suggest. Rather, most tests of propositions involve either discrediting a theory or successful falsification. This study does not concern itself with any of these. Our concern is simply to explain the African crisis, which has been transformed into a tragic situation over the years, exposing the entire continent to capture and abuse by terrorist networks.

The issues

Africa is facing a tragedy of enormous proportions. While the world looks on, its people and their cultures are literally disappearing. Sub-Saharan Africa is one of the poorest regions of the world, and produces only 1 percent of the world's gross domestic product despite being home to 10 percent of its population. In Basil Davidson's (1990, p. 591) dramatic words:

> Isn't Africa, after all, a primitive continent? Although stubbornly backward, great hopes of development and progress flared brilliantly when the continent shook itself free of European colonial rule, but since then, one after another, these hopes have been confounded in crisis and despair. Most of Africa today is in deep trouble. Few of its governments seem able to win the popular support required to face their problems and resolve them. Some of these governments are military or bureaucratic tyrannies feared by their people. Others are honest administrations that wrestle with adversities too baleful for their strength. Still others are popular regimes beset by externally directed banditry and armed subversion.

Agreeing or disagreeing with Basil Davidson is beside the point. The root causes of the crisis and tragedy are that in Africa 'Men [have taken] over into private property the values and riches of the land, whereas they should have possessed them in common' (Meslier, 1864, p. 210). The consequences are evident in that equality disappeared, property was introduced, labor became a necessity. And, vast forests have been turned into riant fields, which are being watered with human sweat and where slavery and poverty have now been sown and where they grow together with the harvest.

Only history can best serve as a compass into the genesis and evolution of such a cynical situation of both doom and gloom in Africa. This chapter argues therefore that the trajectory traced by Africa from crisis to tragedy has historical antecedents and cannot be explained fully by either 'internalist' or 'externalist' analytical stopping points (Arrighi, 2002). Rather, it should better be explained in terms of the historical forces that have shaped African realities, giving the continent faces perceived by some as one of smiles and still by others as one of snarls, from the time the continent was inserted into the world capitalist system.

Historical perspectives

To understand the political economy of African societies, we must study first the internal dynamics of the free-market system, better known as the 'capitalist system.' In sum, the world economy today is a multidimensional system within which factors of production (capital and labor) move according to decisions that are made by transnational agents (transnational corporations) operating in oligopolistic markets. Trade flows, capital movements, inward and outward foreign direct investment, technology flows, and labor movements are all regulated by transnational agents operating in these oligopolistic markets.

The world economy therefore joins industrialized societies and less developed and underdeveloped societies in a web built by the main agents dominating these oligopolistic markets where in less developed societies like Africa the relationships between external and internal forces form a complicated whole whose structural links are not based on mere external forms of exploitation and coercion, but are rooted in coincidences of interests between local dominant classes and international ones, and, on the other side, are challenged by local dominated groups (like terrorist cartels) and classes.

Historically, the installation of capitalism in Africa from the colonial era required the creation of certain socio-political structures to ensure the reorganization of indigenous economies for European accumulation of wealth. This precipitated the violent extension of the colonial state into the hinterland of Africa. The concept 'colonial state' here denotes its characteristic difference from the state as it emerged in the context of European capitalism and celebrated in the Treaty of Westphalia in 1648. The state in the colonies was imposed from above and it supervised a captive population and economy, which together were 'protected' for expatriate metropolitan capitalism, and was largely responsible to the metropolitan state.

Colonial capitalism was a 'bastard' form of capitalism (Dumett, 1998, pp. xviii, 396) as the state's presence was over-arching and also denied indigenous capitalist entrepreneurs from any substantial participation in the economy. The colonial state did this within Africa through legislation, which undercut locals and favored expatriate capital and allowed the latter considerable freedom of operation. The colonial state underwrote the process of expatriate capital accumulation by encouraging labor recruitment (many times forcefully, especially brutal in French, Portuguese and Belgian colonies) and the payment of low wages and by restricting labor unionization. Agricultural producers were denied direct access to markets except through expatriate merchant houses, which manipulated prices. Control of the colonial economy affected the process of class formation as the colonial state encouraged differential participation in the economy by various regions and communities among the colonized population.

Trade had existed between African communities and Europeans before colonization. In this pre-colonial pattern of trade, relatively equal partners had exchanged their goods without the need for domination. Colonization introduced the domination of one partner by making sure that European capital wrested the control of trade and resources from the hands of local traders and reduced them to cash crop producers, wage earners or both. This militarized domination of the colonial state ensured a constant production of commodities for export, which did not depend upon the goodwill of indigenous rulers. Thus, the colonial state was a vampire state feeding on the blood of its colony.

Africa's journey towards underdevelopment and state terrorism therefore dates from the eighteenth century. Imperialism and colonialism distorted and abrogated the essence of African cultural norms and institutions. The systematic approach that the European invaders utilized to usurp land in Africa has contributed greatly to the disunity and dysfunction of indigenous Africans; coups take place in Africa not because Africans cannot govern themselves, but because African leaders have inherited a colonial legacy that tends to pit African against African, or brother against brother. This schism can be traced directly to the different types of colonial masters that held sway on the continent. Each colonized African, for the most part, took on the psycho-social and cultural milieu of his colonizer. Each colonial power pursued a cultural policy, which it believed would give it efficacious results of dominance and exploitation, and a policy that was in tune with his philosophy of colonial administration.

Most of the problems that haunt Africa had their origins in a diplomatic, agreed-upon meeting known as the Berlin Conference in which fourteen western nations attended the three-month session. It was a chaotic, and haphazard process that threatened on several occasions to plunge the

Europeans into war. German Chancellor Otto Von Bismarck, who at one time had no interest in African colonies, wanted to ensure Germany a piece of the spoils; he decided it was time to lay down some ground rules. His French and British counterparts, who were his main competitors in Africa, unanimously agreed with the rules that would eventually despoil most of the African continent.

Another reason for Bismarck's decision was the pressure of commercial interests involved in Africa and the political arguments of the colonial nations convinced him that colonies were indeed an economic necessity to Germany. Thus the ascension of the colonialism/imperialism ideology was based on the belief that colonies were an essential attribute of any great nation. Whether the reason was economic, political, or diplomatic, the quest for overseas possessions was of paramount concern for European nations. Another important aspect of colonialism is that immediately following the abolition of the slave trade, the desire and quest for more scientific knowledge about Africa intensified. Thus more explorations took place, and these events took on a new meaning. In the decade preceding the Berlin Conference of 1884–1885, African Associations emerged all over Europe.

Besides the ones that existed in England and France, there were the German Association for the Exploration of Africa, the Italian Association for the Exploration and Civilization of Africa, King Leopold's (Belgium) International African Association, the Hungarian African Association, the Swiss Committee for the Exploration of Central Africa, and the African Association of Rotterdam. The interest in scientific knowledge started to decline as each nation sought to establish its colonial dominance over occupied and unoccupied lands in Africa; hence, the Berlin Conference was (is) considered to be the crux of European colonialism. Europeans needed to satisfy the material necessities of Europe; therefore, the dream of an African empire developed as an avenue for the investment of surplus capital, and as a boost to national prestige. In essence, the Berlin Conference was very important in African history because of the way it sought to minimize competition among the European colonial powers in their haste to acquire mineral rich lands in Africa (Onimode, 1982, pp. 95–113).

For example, fired by the desire for personal wealth and British nationalism, Cecil Rhodes stated frankly: 'I contend that we are the first race in the world, and that, the more of the world we inhabit the better it is for the human race' (Wilhelm and vanZyl, 1981, pp. 36–46). From the time that Cecil Rhodes became the prime minister of the Cape Colony in 1890, his actions conveyed his belief in British superiority. As a 'zealous and compulsive empire builder,' Rhodes' convictions were manifested in his desire for the British to control Africa from 'Cairo to Capetown' (Boyles, 1988, p. 188). Rhodes used every means possible to further his cause while also benefiting himself. He 'legally' used his political power in the expansion of the railroad system across Africa. He was also a conniving politician when planning and implementing the Jameson Raid and was a major contributor in spurring the Boer War of 1899.

One of the ways Rhodes believed he could accomplish his goal of 'Cairo to Capetown' control was by building a railroad and telegraph line connecting the two cities (Marquard, 1969, pp. 200–201). He could use his power as Prime Minister of Cape Colony and his personal fortune from the De Beers Mining Company diamond-mines to show Britain's power. His ambition was that success in the railroad and telegraph line completion would establish British control and weaken other countries in their colonial enterprises. Other countries would have to rely on the British owned railways whenever crossing Africa from north to south or east to west. This was the ringing and untiring ambition of Cecil Rhodes. The railroad would also enhance Rhodes' ability to move diamonds more easily to Europe for his financial benefit (Wilhelm and vanZyl, 1981, p. 38).

Rhodes' plan for British railroad domination ran into problems when the leaders of the Transvaal Republic, a region held by the Dutch, began to see railroads as their way to be independent of the British Empire. If they could build a line from their gold mines in the Transvaal Republic to the Delgoa Bay, they would be able to escape the need to rely on the British government-owned Cape Line (Wheatcroft, 1985, p. 78). During this time, Rhodes was looking to expand his power into the Transvaal region. While the Delgoa Bay Line had been completed in 1894, the Cape Line had crossed the Transvaal two years earlier. The new line had dropped the price of transportation to about a third of that of the British line. This hurt the business on the British-owned line and created a tense situation between the two regions. By 1895, Rhodes was so infuriated that he requested the British Secretary of State for the Colonies to get involved, and the two issued an ultimatum to the Transvaal Republic to raise their price of transportation. The Transvaal had no option other than to give in to Rhodes' request because of British military superiority.

Rhodes' nationalistic feelings led him to plan to unite all of South Africa under the British Empire through any means necessary. As early as 1894, Rhodes had begun to prepare to conquer the Transvaal Republic. Rhodes' first attempt to economically control the gold mining region of the

Transvaal failed when the Transvaal President, Paul Kruger, supported Dutch and opposed British rule of the land. Rhodes decided to drastically change his approach to conquering the Transvaal Republic when he realized that Kruger would not allow him to have control. Rhodes's plan was to instigate an uprising in Johannesburg, the capital of the Transvaal Republic. The uprising would be secretly financed by Rhodes and would consist primarily of his personal friends and business partners from the area. An army also financed by Rhodes and led by Dr. Leander Starr Jameson would pretend to quell this uprising. The hope was that the people of the Transvaal Republic would instead take up arms against the government and only with the help of a British mediator become satisfied. The people would ask to be a part of the Cape Colony and under Rhodes' power (Flint, 1974, pp. 50–207).

The plan failed and was the direct cause of Rhodes' downfall. The 'secret' coup d'état was a conspiracy full of dishonesty. Rhodes' dishonesty led to little support in Johannesburg for the uprising, not enough weaponry for the military, and a lack of surprise when the plan was leaked to the public. Though Rhodes owned two of the major newspapers of South Africa, the *Johannesburg Star* and the *Cape Times*, he was not able to keep the Transvaal Republic from finding out about the raid. Even with these obvious failures in the plan, Rhodes never had Jameson pull his army out. Rhodes had financed the endeavor and had been given ample time to send a telegram as Prime Minster of the colony to stop the invasion. Instead, on December 29, 1895, Jameson and his army of five hundred men crossed the border. On January 2, 1896, only four days later, Jameson and his men were forced to surrender. Though Rhodes was never found responsible for his role in instigating the raid, he was censured, paid the fines of the four officers found guilty of treason, and resigned from his position in the government. Cecil Rhodes' imperialistic motives had caused his own downfall.

Although Rhodes was no longer in office, he still had enough power to influence the British during major political events. After the Jameson Raid, the tension between the Dutch (Boers) and the British (Anglos) would never be the same. The tension had subsided until 1897 when the people in the Transvaal began to bear arms. Efforts were made by both sides to avoid war, but war broke out on October 11, 1898 ('Boer War'). Once again, this war had been created for economic reasons. Much like the Jameson Raid, which had been used to 'open the Transvaal to [Rhode's] corporate mining interests,' the Anglo-Boer war was the result of capitalist interests and imperialist motives.

Many historians now trace those capitalist and imperialist attitudes that led to the war back to Rhodes. Although Rhodes was forced out of office, he and a few business partners still owned the two leading South African newspapers that informed Britain of the events in their new colonies. These papers held the power to influence public opinion in Britain and the African colonies. J.A. Hobson, an economist and journalist, contends that although Rhodes had not created nationalism and the use of propaganda, the British will to fight in the Boer War of 1899 could be traced to him. Along with British nationalism, the Jameson Raid and the tension brought on between the Boers and the Anglos could be traced to Rhodes.

During the Boer War, Rhodes concentrated on securing his economic ventures versus spreading British control. Rhodes set out to protect the mining city of Kimberly in Rhodesia, a northern colony that had been named in his honor. Rhodesia became Cecil Rhodes' private enterprise where he hoped to develop the region into another economically profitable area. His enthusiasm to save Rhodesia from the Boers led to Rhodes taking part in hand-to-hand combat. Rhodes was even known to say, 'You should kill all you can' after coming back from a battle. He was no longer the prime minister of Cape Colony, and had been asked to step down from the British South African Board, a company he had created earlier in the Transvaal, and his sole purpose was now to protect Rhodesia. He seemed to do anything if it might further his expansionist capitalist motives.[4]

Rhodes never saw the end of the war. He died in Cape Town on March 26, 1902, from a severe cold he had caught while at sea. By this time, Rhodes' desire of the Transvaal Republic being under British control existed. Rhodesia had also been protected from the Boers and was under British control. But the formal end of the war did not come until the peace treaty was signed on May 31, 1902. Cecil Rhodes was a man who forever shaped South Africa. By using his power to expand the British control of the railroad system, through trying to gain power over Johannesburg in the Jameson Raid, and by playing a major role in the Boer War of 1899, Rhodes showed nationalist and economic motives. They all show his deep desire for Britain's empire to expand across Africa economically and politically while also giving Rhodes political and economic power. Rhodes will never be forgotten for spreading British nationalism, imperialism and capitalism throughout Africa.

In confirmation British historian, Basil Davidson, admitted with disarming frankness (Davidson, 1974, pp. 100–154) that the Europeans came and assumed command of African history, and the solutions they found were solutions for themselves, not for Africans. The Africa of a century ago consisted of a large number of independent states. Some of these states were large and powerful; others were smaller and weaker. When the Europeans finished drawing their lines of partition, these states had been condensed into about fifty pieces of territory all of which came under European colonial rule. The systematic, indiscriminate partition (scramble) brought different ethnic groups (tribes) under one or more colonial powers (Chamberlain, 1999).

This situation disrupted the political development of these social groups. Furthermore, ethnic groups were cleaved into fragments (MacKenzie, 1983). For example, Nigeria under colonial rule brought more than a hundred ethnic groups into the British colonial sphere. This colonial sphere included the theocracies of Northern Nigeria, the Chiefdoms of the Yoruba, Edo, and Itskiri, in the South, and the Igbo and Ibibio, in the East. In the then Tanganyika (Tanzania), former President Julius Nyerere demonstrated that the territory under German, and later British rule consisted of more than a hundred ethnic groups. The atomization of one or more ethnic groups among two or more colonial powers created a situation very akin to slavery. Families were forcibly separated into two or more groups; each group under a colonial power spoke a different European language. Obviously, this kind of situation laid the foundation for present ethnic (tribal) disputes, or at least contributed to the problem (Asiwaju, 1984).

In addition, Africa had become so atomized into smaller, conflicting groups that people readily identified themselves by tribe, ideology, profession, religion, and economic class, as does most victims of European colonialism, racism, and slavery. As a consequence of this ethnic fragmentation, groups such as the Hausas and Fulanis exist in British Nigeria, German (later French/British) Cameroons, French Niger and Chad. The Arabs of North Africa were (are) scattered in French, Spanish and Italian colonies. The Mandingo were (are) in French and British colonies such as Senegal, Guinea, Mali, Ivory Coast, Gambia and Sierra Leone. There were (are) the Fang in different French colonies of Cameroon and Gabon in Equatorial Africa and in Spanish Equatorial Guinea, the Mende in Liberia and Sierra Leone, and the Ewe in British Gold Coast (Ghana), French Togoland, and Dahomey (Benin). The result of the arbitrary partitioning, most people now agree, is that disparate units forced to be together are constantly at war. Prior to the attainment of independence from the 1950s, there were many bloody revolts against colonial oppression and racism.

What is important to note is that King Leopold of Belgium initiated the partitioning process by hiring the explorer Henry Stanley to acquire territory in the rich Congo basin (Hochschild, 1998). In the period 1879–1880, Stanley gained the title to over 900,000 square miles (over seventy-six times the entire area of Belgium) from local chiefs who could not comprehend the true meaning of the scraps of paper they were signing in return for worthless items such as cases of rum and gin, and brightly colored clothes, and trinkets. The notion or reality of selling the title to tribal lands would be as ludicrous to these chiefs as it would be for an American governor to sell the title to his house, or state. Yet this was the case all over Africa. Not only did Stanley do it for Belgium, but it was also done by Count De Brazza for France (north of the Congo), by Dr. Karl Peters for Germany (East Africa), and by other adventurers in the service of other colonial powers.

It is quite apparent that the overall effect of colonialism on Africa was (is) immensely deleterious. The European powers desired and needed slaves, ivory, ports, raw materials, new markets for European finished products, and equally important, as in the case of Kenya, a dumping ground for some of its semi-literate and unskilled citizens. To avoid the drain on treasuries in Europe, the colonialists introduced cash-crop economies: cocoa was planted in Ghana, peanuts in Senegal and Gambia, tobacco in Malawi, coffee and tea in Kenya, cotton in Angola, etc., leading inexorably to a situation of economic extraversion and domestic anarchy.

These were export crops and they subjected Africa to total dependence on Europe. Thus Africa was cast into independence without an industrial base. Each African economy was based on one-crop harvests that were irrelevant to Africa and were subjected to wild price fluctuations on the world market. The above points demand elaboration simply because they address an obviously fragile subject, and that is economic stagnation in Africa. The colonial rulers encouraged the production of only a few materials in each colony at the expense of stimulating the growth of diverse industries and crops needed to sustain Europe. The colonial rulers employed a very pragmatic program. It essentially followed this line of logic: once each colony was a part of a European nation, why should each colony be self-sufficient? If Senegal was the best peanut producer in French Africa, or if cotton from the Sudan was the most useful export as far as the British were concerned, then Senegal would grow peanuts and the Sudan cotton.

The result of pushing the best crop at the expense of all the rest was to make each colony totally dependent on the world price of its single export.

Thus if the world supply of copper were to double because of new deposits in Brazil or Chile, the boom in Katanga and Zambia would quickly come to an end. Similarly, the prosperity or poverty of Ghanaian farmers depended directly on the price of cocoa on the world market. The other type of subjugation that emerged in Africa, which was in effect an economic extension of colonialism, was settlerism. It has been established by a number of historians and political theorists that white settlers in Africa, or in other areas for that matter, took land for themselves, and in the process exacted political control over its indigenous inhabitants, exemplified by cases like South Africa and Northern Rhodesia (now Zimbabwe).

Settler communities ignored and opposed all pleas for African education, promotion of Africans to responsible jobs, or the exercise of political rights such as the freedom to express political ideas or form political organizations. However, the logic of settler dominance was extended to its extreme in the racist doctrine of apartheid. The settlers still ruled directly and indirectly. The first settlers in the era of European colonial expansion were the Dutch and the British at the Cape. In 1652 colonialists from Holland, France and Britain came in small, but steady numbers to the southern tip of Africa. In 1840 several thousand Frenchmen settled in Algeria. By 1900 more than half a million had arrived and occupied most of the narrow belt of fertile land along the coast (Horne, 1998, pp. 21–25).

In other parts of Africa, settlers came later and in smaller numbers. Until the late nineteenth century the hinterland of the two former Portuguese colonies, Angola and Mozambique were ruled by settlers who held large tracts of lands. However, it was not until the establishment of companies, and the coming of soldiers did Portugal completely subdue the Africans and entrench their settlement. In fact, this scenario held true for all of the colonial settler communities (Brunschwig, 1971, pp. 139–141).

The indigenous population was displaced, forced to work for meager wages, and forced to pay taxes imposed by the colonial authorities. East Indians and Arabs (usually Lebanese) were the non-European immigrants in East and West Africa and in the Natal province of South Africa. They came as indentured laborers on the Uganda railroad and the sugar plantations of Natal, or as trading agents for the East India Company. The Arabs came as merchants and traders. Both groups gained control over local commerce in the respective areas in which they settled. In other words, they dominated the export trade of East, West, and Southern Africa.

The discovery of diamonds and gold in South Africa's Transvaal region and in other areas during the end of the nineteenth century led to more problems. The mindset and abuse of the native people as an expendable workforce, the horrible environmental impact, and the conflicts, mainly the Boer Wars, that erupted as a result of this newfound mineral wealth are just some of the many problems that developed. These issues and more have left a rather ugly scar on the parts of Africa lucky enough to be 'blessed' with gold and diamonds. To consolidate their gains, European rulers set up pass laws that restricted native landholding and movement much like the American Indian Reservation system (Farah, 1994, p. 60). This heralded the beginning of apartheid, a system of government-sanctioned race segregation in South Africa that lasted until only a few years ago (Farah, 1994. p. 67).

The mining practices used in South Africa to extract the gold and diamonds have utterly destroyed large portions of land in the Transvaal and other regions. Practically every mine staked out during the turn of the 19th century was an open pit mine. Aside from the increased efficiency in production that came of this, huge environmental problems were the main result. Open pit mining, more commonly known as strip mining, leaves the mined area completely non-arable as all the top soil is removed in the process (Ripley, Redman, Crowder and Ariano, 1996, pp. 70–74). Due to the large amount of strip mining along with South Africa's naturally dry climate, there is very little arable land to grow crops on anymore. As a result, South Africa currently imports most of its food. The destruction of land through open pit mining is just one of the environmental problems caused by the discovery of mineral lucre in the Transvaal.

Diamond mining is a simple enough process of sifting diamonds out of sand. Gold, however, needs to be chemically extracted and separated from the other mineral deposits in the earth. In loose deposits, gold panning and sluicing are used to extract the gold (nuggets and fine gold). One of the side effects of separating the fine gold is the use of liquid mercury, which can remain in the environment (Pronk, 2000). Mercury has a rather nasty effect upon animal and human life. Creatures that are in contact with a quantity of mercury either through tactile absorption or consumption of mercury tainted water run the risk of developing what was referred to as Mad Hatter's Syndrome. This was a reference to the insanity common amongst hatters who used mercury-shined hats, causing the absorption of mercury salts into their brains (Ripley, Redman, Crowder and Ariano, 1996, p. 213). This has a devastating effect on local wildlife and even human populations as prolonged contact with the mercury salts can lead to permanent mental retardation. The complete disregard for environmental contamination led to an increase in disease and cancer amongst the people living near these mines.

South Africa was rife with conflict after the discovery of diamonds in the Transvaal. Before then, the British, who controlled Cape Colony, a major port, and the Dutch Boers, who controlled the Transvaal, lived in peace as neither side thought it could gain much from the other (Kagan, 1995, p. 958). The Boers were content to herd sheep while the British were content to trade with them. There was slight tension earlier when the Cape Colony expanded, forcing many Boer settlers to go on the Great Trek and officially settle the Transvaal region along with Natal and the Orange Free State (Kagan, 1995, p. 959). When diamonds were discovered in the Boer territory, the British saw they could gain quite a lot from the relatively weak Boers. After some initial successes, the tide was quickly turned against the Boers as the British expanded their army to 500,000 men; a huge army compared to the Boers' 88,000 men (Farah, 1994, p. 58). Except for some small pockets of guerrilla resistance, the Boers were defeated. After the war and the signing of the Treaty of Verneegiging, the Boer territories were turned into British colonies (Kagan, 1995, p. 969). Thus began the subjugation of the Boers who would later be called Afrikaners. The wars, fighting, strife, and resentment amongst Africans in mineral-rich Democratic Republic of Congo, Sierra Leone, and Angola demonstrate how these gems can lead people into being overrun by greed.

The period under review (1884–1960) was when African colonies had no say in the determination of their own fate, no control over their own resources, and were obliged to live with whatever political institutions their political masters in Europe imposed. The worst aspect came up when there was war in Europe. Africans were drafted to fight without knowing exactly what it was they were fighting or dying for. And, when in the 1960s, most African countries began gradually to achieve their independence, they inherited severely depleted natural resources and monetarized economies that were contrived almost entirely for the benefit of the former colonial masters (Hopkins, 1993, p. 489).

In terms of political legacy, colonial norms of governance varied according to the racial hue of colonial subjects and whether those subjects had been conquered or 'protected' by the former colonial powers. The white settler colonies, or dominions—Canada, Australia, New Zealand, and South Africa—had a long tradition of internal representative government for the white settler population; the 'yellow' colonial subjects like the Indians were more respected than the black African who was at the bottom of the heap. Traditional rulers in the British Empire like the chiefs of the

Ngwato of Bechuanaland (now Botswana) and the sultans of the Malay states who were allowed to rule their people had limited exposure to the authoritarian and arbitrary display of power typical in the black African colony. In the hierarchy of colonial powers, the British were better than the French who surpassed the Belgians who salved their consciences with the thought that their subjects were not under Portugese rule. The Amharics of Ethiopia and the Americo-Liberians of Liberia were also colonizers of African people. The era of so-called independence in Africa was to be one of a change of rulers, but not of the colonial political regime in which, unfortunately, the members of the poorest least-educated and least commercialized tribes were soldiers of the colonial army. The predictable consequences of this explanation are: (1) rulers who had received little preparation for ruling modern states would rule in the tyrannical manner of the former colonial masters and in a distinctly incompetent manner; (2) the rulers of colonies with a long tradition of internal rule would take responsibility for their countries and do a decent job—Malaysia and Botswana; (3) leaders who had been exposed to the best education and political traditions of liberal democracy of the colonial powers would adhere to them as rulers of independent countries—Senghor of Senegal, Sir Seretse Khama of Botswana, Lee Kuan Yew of Singapore, Jawaharlal Nehru of India; (4) South Africa was unlikely to go the way of the rest of Africa because its citizens inherited the norms of internal representative government which white South Africans considered an exclusive birth right.

Building thunderstorms

The thunderstorms of Africa's economic crisis had its roots deeply sunk into the ground during the colonial era and cemented by those who inherited power from retreating colonialists. State enterprises inherited from colonial powers were national airlines, public utilities, large-scale agricultural products, and financial institutions. These enterprises also regulated the sale and price of many commodities. The presence of the government in the economy was substantial and in socialist-oriented countries, these enterprises were hostile to private investment. These governments were subject to political influence and pressures (Almond and Verba, 1965; Pye and Verba, 1965) and when these enterprises failed to operate efficiently, they became a financial drain on the government and were replaced with a new group of leaders.

African leaders who replaced the withdrawing colonial powers attempted to develop their respective states by first personalizing and monopolizing state power (Chabal, 1992; Sklar, 1986). National economic resources and policies became a political battleground. Political leaders sought to enhance national pride, but more so, their own. Government agencies became sources of employment of supporters of the party in power and selected and located investment projects on political rather than economic grounds. In many countries, politicians created lavish lifestyles (Mazrui and Tidy, 1984) financed by public resources. This also allowed and possibly persuaded lower level public officials into corruption in order to supplement their inadequate incomes.

Another increasingly prominent factor in African politics was the military (Sparks, 1990) and its demands. The military was often motivated by a desire to improve its own circumstances. Enlarging arsenals, modernizing equipment, and raising salaries were top priorities. In 1970, African countries spent $175 million on importing arms; by 1979, these estimates had skyrocketed to $2.3 billion. All these arms were borrowed and the attendant swelling debt dragged the continent squarely into the vicious international lending cycles. This lending cycle had succinctly been underscored and prophetically explained by Frank Taussig long ago. His explanation is that loans from the creditor country, far from being granted at an equal annual rate, begin in modest amounts, then increase, and reach a crescendo. Usually they are granted in exceptionally large sums when a culminating phase of activity and speculative fever approaches, and during this phase they become larger from month to month for as long as the upswing continues. With the emergence of the crisis, loans suddenly fall off or even cease altogether. Payment of interest on old loans is not any more compensated by the granting of new ones; interest becomes the net burden for the debtor country. A sudden reversal takes place in the balance of payments of the debtor country; it feels the consequence suddenly in the form of immediate need to make remittances in favor of the creditor country, pressure on its banks, in a high discount rate, in falling commodity prices. And this sequence may occur not only once, but two or three times in a row. After the first crisis and recovery, it is possible that the debtor country will manage to get on its feet. After several years the loans from the creditor country will start flowing again, another period of activity and speculative investment takes place, the old round gets repeated, until finally another crisis comes and another sudden reversal in the debtor country's balance of payments (Taussig, 1915).

This explanation given in 1915 is as valid today in the case of Africa as it was then. In general, international lending had expanded in the 1920s and stopped almost completely during the economic depression of the 1930s. This stoppage saved mankind from its defaults. But, international lending occurred in the 1970s and 1980s despite the universally available knowledge and experience of inter-war speculation and tragedy. Moreover, it was in some leading international financial agencies that a doctrine of 'debt-led growth' was proclaimed in the late 1970s, in pursuit of a broader view that markets could make no mistake and that commercial banks knew what they were doing. And, into this 'debt-led growth' Africa fell.

Table 4.1 Net financial transfers on long-term lending 1972–1990, U.S. $ billion

Year	*All developing countries*	*Major borrowers* (a)	*Year*	*All developing countries*	*Major borrowers* (a)
1972	7.1	n.a.	1982	20.1	11.1
1973	10.8	8.1	1983	3.7	-6.3
1974	16.7	10.5	1984	-10.2	-14.3
1975	n.a	n.a.	1985	-20.5	-21.2
1976	21.5	n.a.	1986	-23.6	-20.0
1977	21.0	n.a.	1987	-34.0	-17.1
1978	33.2	17.2	1988	-35.2	-26.0
1979	31.2	18.8	1989	-29.6	-21.2
1980	29.5	15.1	1990 (b)	-21.7	-13.7
1981	35.9	24.8	1991 (c)	-23.4	-19.4

Notes: (a) From 1978, 'severely indebted countries', (b) Revised, (c) Projected.
Sources: World Bank (1983), *World Debt Tables, 1982–83*, First Supplement, for 1972, 1976 and 1977; World Bank (1984), *World Debt Tables, 1983–84*, for 1973 and 1979; World Bank (1985), *World Debt Tables, 1984–85*, for 1974 and 1978; World Bank (1991), *World Debt Tables, 1990–91*, for 1980–89; and World Bank (1992), *World Debt Tables 1991–92*, for 1990 and 1991. The World Bank is in Washington, D.C.

For instance, lending commitments to developing countries by the international capital market, mainly commercial banks, reached a peak of U.S. $51 billion in 1981, on the eve of the eruption of the debt crisis in August 1992 when Mexico stopped paying. The market collapsed quickly thereafter. Table 4.1 sets forth the data on net transfer of funds (loan receipts minus debt service): the funds moved to developing countries until early 1980s and from developing countries to their creditors thereafter.

The data refer to disbursements. The latter normally lag behind commitments and therefore it took some time for the collapse of lending to be fully felt. The peak reverse flow of resources was recorded in 1988.

The collapse of capital inflow affected not only the countries which were experiencing debt servicing difficulties, but also others. According to an African Development Bank memorandum of 1988, in Africa 'in particular, suppliers have become increasingly concerned about sovereign risk factors, especially the ability of governments and their central banks to make foreign exchange available to importers to meet their obligations. Furthermore, the world debt problem, associated mainly with Latin American countries, has caused the major international banks as a matter of policy, to sharply reduce their total cross border balance sheet exposure. This sharp reduction by commercial banks has hit Africa most. In several cases (e.g., Zimbabwe and Côte d'Ivoire), banks have cut credit lines, which they were willing to extend previously, even though these lines were properly serviced' (Collier, 1991).

Transfer cost was prohibitively high. The mechanism through which reverse transfers have been extracted has frequently included devaluation of debtor country currencies significantly in excess of domestic inflation. The resulting greater profitability of export industries has led to export volume expansion and to a declining tendency for dollar export prices. Export sales have been maintained in the face of heavy competition, insufficient foreign demand, particularly for primary products, and frequent trade obstacles; a large number of primary producing countries have devalued their currencies one after another in order to be able to compete at low world prices; as demand is frequently depressed and does not respond to price cuts, the main result of devaluations in these cases has been to reduce real wages all around and further depress world prices.

During the propagated great debate concerning payment of German reparations in the inter-war period, Keynes was of the devious view that debtors face the double burden: paying the debt service (budget burden) and experiencing a deterioration in their terms of trade-transfer burden.[5] This view was vindicated in the present debt crisis: the inelastic demand of the debtors for foreign exchange confronted the inelastic demand for the debtors' primary products, and the terms of trade gave in. The effect was a significant transfer of income of primary producers, which was additional to that reflected in the monetary amounts of debt service payments which they were making.

The experience of the 1980s with the transfer problem confirmed bitter earlier experiences. When credits are no longer extended to the same degree as before, cash-hungry debtors begin to liquidate inventories. Prices of many commodities begin to fall, a phenomenon long described by economists. The fall in prices makes life much harder for the debtors, because the value of the dollars owed, in terms of those commodities they are producing, is rising. It may even happen, as Irving Fischer so magnificently put it in an article published in the first quarter *Econometrica* of 1933, that 'the liquidation of debts cannot keep up with the fall in prices which it causes. In that case, the liquidation defeats itself. While it diminishes the numbers of dollars owed, it may not do so as fast as it increases the value of each dollar owed . . . Then we have the great paradox which, I submit, is the chief secret of most, if not all, great depressions: *the more debtors pay, the more they owe*' (italics in original; Fabra, 1983, p. 11).

The depression in Latin America and Africa, the two main debtor regions, and in debtor countries elsewhere during the 1980s, was not due exclusively to the debt problem or that the entire fall in commodity prices can be attributed to the transfer problem. There were other factors at work. But the collapse of international credit, the debt problem and the terms of trade deterioration did play a major role. The United Nations Secretariat confirmed that 'if commodity prices, including oil, had remained at their 1980 levels throughout the decade, it is likely that the debt crisis would have been averted.'[6] The World Bank index of real commodity prices other than oil declined by 41 percent and oil also declined by 50 percent, between 1980 and 1990.

Historical factors cannot thus be discounted in understanding and analyzing the contemporary African political and economic condition (Nkrumah, 1964; Senghor, 1964). The fact that the colonial political community resulted from conquest provides a rich insight into its character and structure. It was an ensemble of diverse ethnic and cultural African groupings, which the colonial overlords welded into political communities. As a subjugated people they were more or less held together by force and to the extent that they accepted their subjugated status, the colonial overlords were willing to reach an accommodation with them. This accommodation explains why cooperation with a colonial regime was dictated largely by political expediency. The appeal of the colonizers to a 'civilizing mission' (Cohen and Middleton, 1970) was by no means legitimating and the colonized did not buy into it. The colonial administrators were accountable only to their imperial governments; in other words, the colonial state was set up by the colonizer for subjugating and exploiting the colonized.

Though nationalist agitation ultimately contributed to the decolonization process, the colonizers dictated both the pace and outcome of the postcolonial political order in the majority of cases. From the above, one should question the view held by most nationalists that the advent of independence was a rupture with the colonial past and the dawn of a new political era with former colonial political communities now firmly mastering their own fate.

Postcolonial communities were indeed bequeathed with European democratic constitutions and representative institutions. African nationalist leaders quickly replaced the colonial administrators as rulers in the new political dispensation. Apart from such changes, little else had changed. The postcolonial state was in many respects not very different from its predecessor, the colonial state. But this time the state was shaped to create in general an 'administrative' organization by which those in the government (civil servants) worked in partnership with the non-African wealthy class to exploit the rest of the population through business transactions with various transnational corporations. The process of decolonization, after defeating nationalistic attempts in the 1960s, organized the African economy in such a way that a wealthy white minority in alliance with a wealthy native civil servant minority, both in partnership with transnational capital 'neo-colonized' the African continent.

Thus, the failure of democracy and economic development in Africa are due in a large part to the scramble for wealth by predator elites who have dominated African politics since independence. They tended to see the state as a source of personal wealth accumulation. There is high premium on the control of the state, which is the biggest and most easily accessible source of wealth accumulation. The people in power and those who seek power use all means to attain their goal. This includes fostering ethnic sectarianism and political repression. Competition for control of the state, whether between the military and civilian classes or between civilian political parties, is invariably ferocious and generates instability. Many of the apparently senseless civil conflicts in Africa, including those in Sierra Leone, Democratic Republic of Congo, Liberia, Rwanda, Uganda, and Somalia, are due to the battle for the spoils of power or 'rent-seeking behavior' (Mbaku, 1994a, pp. 241–284).

Franz Fanon in his book, *The Wretched of the Earth*, published in 1961, fittingly described the character of the class that inherited power from the colonialists. It is a sort of little greedy caste, avid and voracious, with the mind of a huckster, only too glad to accept the dividends that the former colonial power hands out. This get-rich-quick middle class shows itself incapable of great ideas or of inventiveness. It remembers what it has read in European textbooks and imperceptibly it becomes not even the replica of Europe, but its caricature. This class, said Fanon prophetically, is not capable of building industries. It is completely canalized into activities of the intermediary type. Its innermost vocation seems to be to keep in the running and to be part of the racket. The psychology of the national bourgeoisie is that of a businessman, not that of a captain of industry. History has proven Fanon right for the African elites remain parasites incapable of carrying out the bourgeois revolution.

For example, France has retained, in most of its former sub-Saharan African colonies, a position that is unmatched anywhere else in the Third World (de Lusignan, 1969). The monetary system of these countries is, in effect, based on the principle of free and absolute movement of capital at a fixed exchange rate (subject to change by 'common agreement') guaranteed by the metropolis. In return for this guarantee the local central banks are permitted to support African treasuries only within very narrow limits.

Furthermore, the main commercial banks operating in these countries are branches and subsidiaries of metropolitan banks, and can therefore always counter the monetary policy that the local central banks want to pursue, in the event that this policy is not attractive to them, by the simple expedient of transferring funds to or from their Paris headquarters. Examples are not in limited supply. Local banks in Franc Zone Africa (Mentan, 1985) have been known to make massive transfers of their capital to France to take advantage of higher interest rates. In these circumstances the country's monetary integration in the metropolitan finance economy is total, equivalent to that of a metropolitan province; the local central banks do not deserve the description as they are no more than issuing houses circulating a French Franc printed with an unusual design: there is only one central bank for the whole of the Franc zone: the Banque de France.

IMF membership makes no sense to these states. And IMF membership is something of a legal fiction since its interventions make no more sense as the metropolitan system is responsible for the monetary administration of these countries. To the extent that France is wide open to the worldwide financial system, this total liberalism has no boundaries. The theory of the market on which it is based is, in turn, a manifestation of the assumption that the only development 'possible' requires the open door. A malicious mind would note that the African countries in question belong to the group of least developed countries. Consequently, reasoning on the basis of the correlation to which the advocates of these economic theories are so partial, would show the opposite of their assumption as the widest open door is associated with the least satisfactory performances.

One may argue that the structures of the centers-peripheries imbalance are not based on monetary integration. But there can be no monetary solution to center-periphery imbalance. The forms of this monetary integration are an additional severe handicap to any attempt at autocentric national or regional development. All the African states that did hope to guide their development in this direction had to break out of the yoke of the Franc zone. If they have sometimes 'become bankrupt', and have even sustained the monetary illusion we are criticizing, the reasons have nothing to do with an inevitable failure of national monetary management.

The monetary management of African countries in the Franc zone is 'passive,' in the sense that the currency issue is adjusted to the needs of the system's reproduction without giving it any power to play any significant part in its qualitative evolution. It follows nineteenth century style financial orthodoxy, which has no match in other Third World countries, or in modern developed capitalism, including metropolitan France, again despite the assertions of the fashionable Reaganite/IMF economic theology. This systematically deflationary policy at local level does not prevent the automatic importation of possible inflation from the metropolis. The organic ties between the local banks and the old colonial trading monopolies, who own the industrial plants in most of the countries in question, provide a de facto privilege to the economic interests of the metropolis that is less obvious as well as difficult to quantify (Ake, 1981).

The inherent faults of this system are such that it seemed to be on the verge of explosion in the 1970s. Reasonable reform proposals were put forward to allow more substantial monetary and financial co-operation with local treasuries (for development purposes) and the expansion of productive activities, plus flexible controls over transfers. Moreover, the proposals in question were for the purpose of maintaining regional monetary unions, while taking into account the variety of situations inherited from unequal regional development; they therefore contradicted the argument currently advanced that the Franc Zone was a 'factor for unity' in Africa. The general drift the African economies have suffered since the end of the 1970s put a stop to these propositions. The Franc Zone in its most traditional form is again flying high, has regained some of the countries that had left and has attracted new members like Equatorial Guinea. This 'innovation' is part of the widespread compradorization under way. The description remains accurate for today's elite who have grown through civilian politics, military governments, business and the civil service. Thus, by the 1970s this rapacious African elite had laid the foundation for the continent's crisis through wasteful spending, clientelist social engineering and indebtedness (Sandbrook, 1976).

Africa's crisis

There are apparently as many explanations for why things went so wrong in postcolonial Africa as there are analysts (Rodney, 1974). Some have located the root of the problem mainly in the despoliations and dispossessions of the colonial era. Others have blamed the 'personalized' state, as it is sometimes known, of the Nkrumahs, Kenyattas, Mobutus, Ahidjos, and Senghors, and the kleptocratic habits of the politicians who succeeded them. The artificiality of Africa's borders doubtless played a role in impeding political development because of endemic conflicts. Alongside all these explanations, there is the colder fact that Africa entered the world economy at a moment when neither cheap labor nor mineral riches that were really all it could bring to the economic table sufficed given the corruption of most African regimes to lead it to sustainable economic development. Some development officials and African intellectuals, while acknowledging this, claim that the problem all along has been that the Western model of modernization that Western donors and bankers and African elites embraced was wholly inappropriate for Africa (Onimode, 1988).

However, there are some theoretical and logical explanations for the rise of economic crisis in Africa from the 1970s to the 1990s. Six factors will be considered here though they may not be exhaustive, namely: (1) faultering economic growth; (2) population explosion; (3) neglect of human capital development; (4) high income disparities; (5) failure of personal rule and attendant rise of kleptocracy as a form of government; and (6) pegged currencies that undermine decision-making on vital economic matters.

Africa's economic growth

Generally, sub-Saharan Africa had a poor track record of economic performance from the early 1960s to the late 1990s (Onimode, 1989a, 1989b). In the 1960s and early 1970s, it had a small but positive GDP annual growth rates averaging 1.9 percent. However, from the mid-1970s to mid-1990s, Africa encountered economic regression with negative growth rates in GDP occurring in most of the countries, especially in the sub-Saharan region. Only in the past three years of the last decade did some African countries start to catch up with other developing economies. In 1999, the continent had an average growth rate of -0.3 percent. Overall, Africa had a thirty-year average GDP growth rate of 0.15 percent since independence. This is an extremely small growth considering the length of years, population size, and the extraordinary global economic and technological transformations that took place during the years 1960–2000.

According to estimates from the U.S. Energy Information Administration of November 2000, sub-Saharan Africa has the world's fastest growing population (approximately 3 percent a year), and is expected to be home to over a billion people by 2025. In recent years, more carefully shaped economic policies in many sub-Saharan African countries have led to improved economic performance. During 1995–1998, real GDP growth averaged 4.25 percent a year, an increase from less than 1.5 percent a year during 1990–1994. However, inadequate levels of investment of both physical and human capital persist, as exceptionally high levels of risk and uncertainty remain at the core of Africa's lack of competitiveness. In fact, a recent World Bank-sponsored report from the Regional Program on Enterprise Development (RPED) concluded that current policies in many sub-Saharan African nations undermine attempts towards increases in productivity and levels of efficiency at international prices. Physicians for these ills were in abundance.

The IMF and World Bank have been empowered by the governments which control it (led by the United States, the United Kingdom, Japan, Germany, France, Canada, and Italy—the so-called Group of 7, which holds over 40 percent of the votes on the boards of the two multilateral agencies) with imposing economic austerity policies on the countries of the so-called 'Third World' or 'global South.' Once Southern countries build up large external debts, as most have, they cannot get credit or cash anywhere else and are forced to go to these international institutions and accept whatever conditions are demanded of them. None of the countries has emerged from their debt problems; indeed most countries now have much higher levels of debt than when they first accepted IMF/World Bank 'assistance.'

The IMF/World Bank conditionalities (or structural adjustment programs) force borrowing African countries to promote sweatshops, exports to rich countries, and high-return cash investment. The resulting increase in international commerce—corporate globalization—led to demands by corporations and investors for ways to lock in their privileges and protection against the perceived danger of governments seizing assets or imposing new regulations in the name of 'nationalization.' The WTO was the answer to those demands, an institution whose secret tribunals overrule national laws if they are found to violate the rights of corporations.

The World Bank is best known for financing big projects like dams, roads, and power plants, supposedly designed to assist in economic development, but which have often been associated with monumental environmental devastation and social dislocation. In recent years, about half of its lending has gone to programs indistinguishable from the IMF's austerity plans that 'reform' economic policies by suffocating the poor and inviting corporate exploitation.

Population growth

Africa, with 13 percent of the world's population, is projected to see 34 percent of the globe's population increase over the next fifty years. With 13 percent of the world's population, Africa has 69 percent of the world's HIV/AIDS cases. Still, the population of the African continent is expected to rise from 800 million now to 1.8 billion in 2050, because the fertility rate of 38 births per 1,000 people is still much higher than the mortality rate of 14 deaths per 1,000. Also, 43 percent of the continent's population is under age fifteen years. Africa now produces nearly 30 percent less food per person than in 1967 (see, e.g., World Bank, 1997a, 1997b; UNDP, 2000, 2001, 2002).

Population growth rates in sub-Saharan Africa have declined since 1975 but only a little. Overall, total population growth since independence averaged 2.96 percent per annum. Still, fertility rates remain high in Africa. The influences of population explosion can have many traumatic effects on developing economies. Consider this in terms of the law of large numbers. A high child dependency rate is a leading indicator of a rapidly growing population: productivity of active workforce has to be shared among a larger number of families. Accordingly, Africa's dependency ratio remains standstill at 0.9 since the early 1980s. An expanding population might also put pressure on public provisions such as education and healthcare by absorbing resources that could have been utilized for other investment purposes. Furthermore, rapid population growth has accelerated urbanization—the high cost of financing urban infrastructure and services absorb vital resources as well. Because of state sponsored discriminatory policies against the agricultural sector, the rural populations of many sub-

Saharan African countries were also forced to migrate to cities in search of better opportunities. This area is one of the many problems that these countries must address and have to contend with when planning for the future.

Human capital development

On the social welfare front, life expectancy of Africans showed a significant improvement from as low as forty years in the 1960s to fifty-one years in 1997. Infant and child mortality rates also seemed to have declined over the years. These demographic trends are the most fundamental welfare indicators that show in fact Africans are living longer. This is good news! Underlying these results are improvements in public health provisions. Nonetheless, as encouraging as these trends may look, other developing regions have also shown even better and faster improvements in these areas. Many people in Africa still do not have access to adequate health services, safe water, and proper nutrition. Furthermore, one of the leading health concerns devastating the continent is the rapid spread of HIV/AIDS (*Joint World Bank, UNESCO and UNAIDS Press Release*, October 18, 2002). This is the most tragic disease, smashing lives more than any weapons of mass destruction, spreading very fast in heterosexual societies. Meanwhile, Africa's school enrollment rate in the 1960s and 1970s, which showed good improvement after decades of colonial neglect, is also worth mentioning. Education has improved quite a bit. However, this improvement was not carried into the 1980s due to budgetary constraints imposed on African governments by the Bretton Woods institutions in the name of structural adjustment programs (World Bank, 1996).

High degree of income inequality

Why does income inequality exist in Africa? Two hypotheses are essential to explain this phenomenon. The first hypothesis deals with African governments' discriminatory practices against agriculture. It is commonly reported that disparities exist between urban and rural areas of Africa despite the fact that most African populations consist of large agrarian societies. An estimated two-thirds rely on farming. Yet, the agricultural sector remains the most discriminated sector than any of the other. Indiscriminate government policies have promoted import-substitution industrialization and manufacturing at the expense of this sector. Under controlled prices and heavy taxation, farmers would be unwilling to produce crops.

As the state (Rothchild and Chazan, 1988) overtaxed the productive sector in its quest for economic hegemony, which it considered necessary to gain unchallenged political dominance, it destroyed the productive base of the state and alienated its producers. Acquiring both political and economic hegemony only meant that the state had denied its people economic autonomy and, politicized the economic process. The state now determined access to wealth and resources and only those who could gain access to the state were economically successful. Thus, the struggle for access to the state intensified and all those who failed to gain access became disaffected. Those citizens who joined civil society in its counter-hegemonic struggle against the state came from the ranks of the disaffected and disenfranchised (Carew, 1993).

Consequently, the bulk of farmers are out of work while fewer industrial workers lead separate lifestyles. On the other hand, the second hypothesis has to do with African governments' failure to accumulate safety nets for their populations. As long as poor policies persist, these governments are neither able to create nor transfer any wealth for their populations. The high degree of income inequality that persisted over the years has hurt Africa's development progress. Why?

This income disparity has received no economic attention in Africa. Clearly, in other regions of the world if disparities exist it is among the lower, middle, and/or high-income populations. In Africa, however, there are no such things as lower or middle class families. One is either rich or poor, and that is the bottom line of disparity! There also exist disproportionate and ever-growing gender discriminations in many sub-Saharan African countries. There have been discriminatory practices against women despite their active participation in their national economies. They perform most of the hard work; yet they are rarely rewarded for it. Thus, income disparities and inequalities have magnified the issue of poverty in sub-Saharan Africa. As a result, economic growth and development was stalled over the years.

As African economies moved rapidly in the direction of more outward-oriented (global) policies, national labor markets had to increasingly become linked to a broader world market. Internal segmentation of the labor market, however, impeded this process, diminishing gains from international specialization, inhibiting the expansion of employment, and resulting in inequality in the distribution of income.

The labor market in Africa thus became more characterized by enormous segmentation, resulting in very high levels of unemployment and underemployment among the indigenous African population. Much of this segmentation was a legacy from structural underdevelopment carried over from the colonial days and reinforced by the structures of neocolonial dependency and economic extraversion.

The most important potential solutions to expanding employment and decreasing labor market segmentation and devastating income inequalities in Africa today involve the following initiatives:

- Increase the overall rate of economic growth so as to absorb more labor into the economy;
- Promote faster growth in more labor-intensive sectors of the economy, such as the service sector and small and medium-scale enterprises;
- Improve labor productivity through capital investment, technological innovation, and increased training and education; and
- Remove distortions in the labor market that inhibit employment expansion, such as incentives that encourage capital intensive investment, artificially established wage and benefit rates, and costly labor regulations enforced by the government.

Effects of personal rule and poor institutional qualities

The ramifying evil of terrorism is not just the killing of innocent people but also the intrusion of fear into everyday life, the violation of private purposes, the insecurity of public spaces and the endless coerciveness of precaution. The fundamental principle of terrorism, that is, the last resort of an underprivileged and discriminated peoples to over-turn and change dominant political structures may be accepted or rejected. But, it must be understood that politics involves repetition, and terrorists often conveniently forget that it sometimes takes much more than one attempt to democratically change the prevailing structures of governance. It is now *passé* to say that the repetitive and continued discrimination against the poor and dispossessed in Africa foster terrorist movements. What have to be recognized now are the limitations of terrorism. Terrorists and terrorism can never engender values of a liberal democracy, pluralism or human rights. Such values are the realm of democratic mainstream politics. Terrorists everywhere have to realize that true peace, justice, and equality are not achieved through the barrel of a gun.

One must also remember that negotiated agreements or peace processes that address the symptoms of violent conflict must include provisions for future processes towards institution-building and transformation if they are to be sustainable. If they are merely concerned with ending hostilities but do not address the core causes of the underlying conflict, they will only be of temporary value. Institutionalizing respect for human rights—through for example an independent judiciary, an independent human rights commission and the constitutional entrenchment and animated application of fundamental rights—ensures that such human rights values inform and shape, and are an integral part of, conflict transformation processes.

Political factors. One of the fundamental hindrances to Africa's development (Almond and Coleman, 1960) is the issue of governance. Most African states are not, in any real sense, capitalist states. Elsewhere, the state has played a crucial role in facilitating capitalist expansion. But, in postcolonial Africa one finds a form of neopatrimonialism—personal rule—that introduces a variety of economic irrationalities. Productive economic activities are impeded by the political instability, systemic corruption and maladminstration associated with personal rule. In extreme cases, a downward spiral of political-economic decline is set in motion that is difficult to halt and reverse.

Nevertheless, there is some progress made in countries such as Botswana, Gambia, Senegal, South Africa, and Namibia that forged democratic traditions from within. However, because of the lack of shared powers in political structures and absence of transparencies instituted in legal frameworks, many state officials in African countries have lived to serve their self-interests (instead of their populations). Such despotic and corrupt regimes frown at democratic transitions. Cases exist such as: Zimbabwe, Liberia, Sudan, Ethiopia, Eritrea, the former Zaire, and Somalia to mention just a few.

Who ought to be held accountable for the peoples of Africa more than their leaders? Obviously, dictators as well as individual citizens are to blame for this. It is unfortunate that individual citizens have lost their leaders' trust and have found many other ways of influencing government systems than holding the all-powerful state officials to be accountable for their actions. This phenomenon has led to client-based governments throughout the entire continent. And it became safe to understand as a matter of political instinct that assuming the position of leadership became politicized by favors and grants. Consequently, leadership lacked proper legitimacy (Bayart, 1986).

Administrative factors. The postcolonial bureaucracy (Lonsdale, 1986) was mainly determined by the colonial administrative structure. In fact, the new postcolonial regimes simply inherited the bureaucracy of the colonial governments. That this might not have been such a good idea is suggested by two points: first, the colonial bureaucracy was statist and overcentralized. In the colonial state, administration was almost indistinguishable from the government; it was in fact the government. The postcolonial state similarly encouraged an overcentralized and greatly expanded bureaucracy. Unlike the colonial bureaucracy it became inefficient and wasteful, precipitating in a majority of cases an institutional collapse. Second, since the colonial bureaucracy owed its allegiance to the imperial government, it did not seem to change its modus operandi in the postcolonial state. It continued to function like a government within a government; often circumventing orders from nationalist leaders, who in many cases were viewed economically and intellectually as their inferiors. The bureaucracy eventually joined the politicians in institutionalizing corruption. As the government lost the ability to pay salaries and give other institutional support, bureaucrats used their offices and positions to enrich themselves at the expense of the state. All this compounded the problem of the soft state, leading in most cases to its political collapse (Carew, 1993).

In sum, African Governments had inward-looking import substitution policies that focused on providing further opportunities for rewarding policies only important to urban groups while at the same time indiscriminately neglecting the majority of peasant-farmers that were not politically important to state officials. Agriculture, the very livelihood of the African population, still suffers from state discrimination. Furthermore, the growth of the state (Leys, 1976) relative to the private sector in order to maximize the opportunities for patronage, graft and reward (including the creation of public enterprises) was proven to be an economic disaster. In fact, state paratstatals (government enterprises) failed to meet the basic needs of the public. Instead, they imposed heavy financial and economic burdens on many African economies. These government-controlled economies discouraged private businesses and entrepreneurs from entering the market. In short, more emphasis was given to the appropriation of resources by the state, rather than on growth and creation of wealth for the benefit of the majority of the populations. Thus, the effects of personal rule and poor institutional qualities have greatly hindered Africa's development and growth far beyond what is commonly reported.

Poor policy decisions in export and foreign exchange matters

Since the end of World War II, some former European colonies in Africa, especially French-speaking ones, have been under direct economic control and indirect political control by the Western European countries. France and Britain are clear European examples. This neo-colonial control has its reflection in the total lack of industrialization in the region.

Since 1958, when the Treaty of Rome was signed by the Western European countries, their relations with African countries were very well defined. History played a critical role in molding those relations. The European Community (EC) vision was defined as 'a natural partnership' with Africa, which had specific aims such as:

- build up a secure supply of raw materials,
- build up a secure market for European manufactured goods, and
- with the help of the U.S. 'protect' the African nations against the danger of becoming influenced by the former USSR or People's Republic of China.

The former EC utilized two instruments for doing that: trade preferences and direct aid, the latter with economic and political strings attached. In July 1964 the system was structured in what since then have been known as the Lomé Conventions even when the first two conventions took place in Yaoundé (Cameroon) and not Lomé (Togo). By the 1980s it was clear that available empirical evidence had tended to show that bilateral aid from EC countries was allocated among developing countries much more on the basis of donor interests than on that of recipient country needs (Maizels and Nissanke, 1984).

By the 1980s two differing points of view about the Lomé Convention emerged:

- Western European point of view: The ACP states have limited themselves to traditional exports . . . they have failed to match the productivity and quality advances of Asian and Latin American competitors.
- ACP countries' point of view: Some elements of the Convention, in fact, Hinder the growth of African, Caribbean and Pacific countries' exports the safeguard clause tends to Inhibit growth in areas where they could Enjoy the greatest dynamic comparative Advantage and provides a powerful Disincentive to their industrial development.[7]

This 'special relation' seems to have helped in stopping African growth between 1960 and 1975 and transforming it in a dramatic decrease until the 1990s. A number of African countries such as Ethiopia, Sudan, Zaire, Uganda, and Somalia, to mention just a few, and especially all African members of the Franc Zone, suffered overvalued exchange rates for much of the 1970s since their monies were tied to major convertible currencies like the French Franc. As a result, the price of foreign currencies in these countries fluctuated with the performance of the major currencies such as the U.S. dollar, the British pound and French Franc when the latter's Bretton Woods system of fixed exchange rates fell apart. In fact, the system of pegged currency was a passive strategy. It might have worked fairly well, had inflation in those countries kept pace with corresponding convertible currency countries.

How did African governments respond? They started to ration foreign exchange. Unfortunately, administration costs of allocating foreign exchange imposed heavy burdens on many African states. Scarcity of qualified personnel to facilitate the rationing of currencies added to the already existing difficulties. As foreign exchange commanded higher premiums in parallel (black) markets, both these states and businesses tried to corner as much of this rent as they could. Meanwhile, private agents spent much of their time and energy securing licenses and attending parallel markets than improving their services and/or creating new markets for their products.

The passive exchange rate policy was a disaster. Why? The following reasons should suffice. This method resulted in failed economic systems that were unable to create prevailing incentives for earning or saving foreign exchange. When domestic currencies fail to keep pace with foreign exchange rates, the terms of trade for export crops deteriorated and their incentive to produce undermined. These African countries were thus unable to produce export crops and import consumer goods. Hyped exchange rates also led to low local currency prices of imports compared with prices of competing domestic goods. Imported cereal effectively replaced Africa's domestic crops such as barely and sorghum. Consequently, local terms of export trade deteriorated more when imported goods effectively substituted homegrown goods. Undoubtedly, African governments' poor policy decisions regarding export and exchange rate matters had immensely ruined the growth and development of the African economy. In other words, factors such as: drought, civil wars, brain-drain, international trade barriers, openness to foreign direct investment, lack of accountability and many others combined with those mentioned above and therefore contributed to Africa's poor economic performance since independence.

During this period, attempts were made to diagnose the African crisis. Solutions of all hues came up, some of which just ditched Africa further into catastrophe. The World Bank's diagnosis of the African crisis was published in 1981 in a document called the Berg Report.[8] The Report blamed the crisis on the policies of African governments. It accused these governments of having undermined the process of development by destroying incentives of agricultural producers to increase output and exports. Overvalued national currencies, neglect of peasant agriculture, heavily protected manufacturing industries and excessive state intervention were singled out as the 'bad' policies most responsible for the African crisis. The cure for Africa's woes recommended by the World Bank included the conventional substantial currency devaluations, dismantling industrial protection, price incentives for agricultural production and exports, and substitution of private for public enterprise in both industry as well as in the provision of social services.

The Berg Report (which was commissioned by the World Bank) was challenged by two analyses of the causes of the African crisis in 1981. Robert Bates's *Markets and States in Tropical Africa*, highlighted the perils of state intervention in underdeveloped countries.[9] Bates accused state officials in African countries of using the powerful instruments of economic control that they had inherited from colonial regimes to benefit urban elites and themselves by destroying incentives of farmers to increase agricultural output. These policies undermined the process of development and therefore Bates proposed the dismantling of state power and leaving the peasantry free to take advantage of market opportunities as a solution. This was similar to the solutions advocated by the World Bank in the Berg and subsequent reports on Africa.[10]

However, Bates's interpretation of the African crisis was both more pessimistic and dismissive of the efforts of African governments than that of the World Bank. The World Bank assumed that an important reason for the 'bad' policies was that African governments had failed to understand their negative effects and that the positive effects of 'good' policies generate widespread support and prolong their stay in power. The World Bank proposal sought not just to set market forces free from governmental constraints and regulations but also aimed to undermine the legitimacy of the social forces that were unredeemably committed to 'bad' policies as effective means in the reproduction of their own power and privilege.

The 'internalist' and 'state-minimalist' diagnoses of the World Bank and the pessimists did not go unchallenged. The greatest challenge came from the African governments themselves. In a document published in 1981 as the Lagos Plan of Action (but signed in 1980 at a meeting in Lagos) the Heads of State of the Organization of African Unity (OAU) traced the crisis to a series of external shocks including deteriorating terms of trade for primary products, growing protectionism of wealthy countries, soaring interest rates and growing debt service commitments. The Lagos Plan of Action opted for a solution based not on world-market mechanisms, but on the capacity of African states to mobilize national resources and foster greater mutual economic integration and cooperation (OAU, 1981). In its emphasis on collective self-reliance through the eventual creation of a continental common market, the Lagos Plan of Action sought a resolution away from dependency in favor of empowerment. These pious hopes never lasted long.

Following swiftly on the heels of the promulgation of the Lagos Plan of Action, and in the midst of a rapidly deteriorating economic situation, the Sahelian drought and famine struck with staggering virulence, peaking in 1983–1984. The following year, a new summit of the OAU was convened in Addis Ababa and it came up with a document, *Africa's Priority Program for Economic Recovery, 1986–1990* (APPER), which emphasized once again the role of external shocks in deepening the crisis and the need for greater self-reliance in order to overcome it. In sharp contrast to the Lagos Plan of Action, however, APPER openly acknowledged the responsibilities of African governments for the crisis, and the limitations of any independent actions undertaken by African states. It agreed to implement a variety of policy reforms in the Berg Report and called on the international community to ease the crushing burden of Africa's external debt, and to stabilize and increase the prices paid for their exports. The result was set out in the *United Nations Program of Action for African Economic Recovery and Development, 1986–1990* (UNPAAERD) (Sawyer, 1990, pp. 218–223).

Fantu Cheru (1989, pp. 15–16) characterizes UNPAAERD as 'simply a reincarnation of the Berg Report.' This characterization is largely accurate but glosses over revisions of their neo-utilitarian, state-minimalist prescriptions of the IMF and World Bank and emphasis on the role of institutions and 'good governance' (Bates, 1992; World Bank, 1992). By 1997, the World Bank had abandoned the minimalist view of the state as evidenced by its *World Development Report* for that year. Earlier concerns with the size of state apparatuses and the extent of public intervention in the economy were completely overshadowed by the call for effective bureaucracies and activist states in the implementation of structural adjustment programs and fight against corruption. The new imperatives, however, put even greater responsibility on the shoulders of African elites and governments both for the failure of their economies to recover and for the social disasters accompanying that failure. Hopes for Africa's greater integration into the world economy, the freeing of markets from governmental control and the wider opportunities for private enterprise—that is, African compliance with IMF and World Bank prescriptions—were followed in short order by ever more pessimistic assessments of the capabilities of African governments and elites to resolve the long-standing crisis.[11]

The cure from the Bretton Woods Institutions was as follows. The IMF and World Bank prescribe cut backs, 'liberalization' of the economy and resource extraction/export-oriented open markets. To be attractive to foreign investors various regulations and standards are reduced or removed. Factors such as the following then, lead to further misery for the African nations and keep them dependent on developed nations:

- Poor countries must export more in order to raise enough money to pay off their debts in a timely manner.
- Because there are so many nations being asked or forced into the global market place—before they are economically and socially stable and ready—and told to concentrate on similar cash crops and commodities as others, it is like a huge price war.
- The resources then become even cheaper from the poorer regions (which favors consumers in the West).
- Governments then need to increase exports (by further reducing costs, making the resources even cheaper, etc.) just to keep their currencies stable (which may not be sustainable, either) and earn foreign exchange with which to help pay off debts.
- Governments therefore must:
    - spend less
    - reduce consumption
    - remove or decrease financial regulations
    - and so on.
- Over time then:
    - the value of labor decreases
    - capital flows become more volatile
    - and we get into a spiraling race to the bottom

  - social unrest is often one result.
- These nations are then told to peg their currencies to the dollar. But keeping the exchange rate stable is costly due to measures such as increased interest rates, etc.
- Investors obviously concerned about their assets and interests can then pull out very easily if things get tough.
- In worst cases capital flight can lead to economic collapse like we have seen in the Asian/global financial crisis of 1997/1998/1999, Mexico, Brazil and many other places; of course, the blame by free trade economists is laid on emerging markets and their government's restrictive or inefficient policies, crony capitalism etc., which is a cruel irony.

All of this has rendered Africa enormously dependent on official development aid and humanitarian assistance. This assistance rose steadily from the 1970s to the early 1990s. By the 1980s, this aid accounted for between 10 and 20 percent of the gross national product (GNP) of many African states. In the 1990s, however, donors gradually lost confidence in the efficacy of a development model that has been tried in one form or another since the 1960s in Africa. And yet these models and economic assistance cannot be shown to have substantially improved the situation of ordinary Africans. These aid dependent budgets have steadily been scaled back, both in percentage terms of national budgets of donor countries as well as in percentage terms of GNP of these needy African countries whose dictators spend much time masking their crimes and ineptitude. And the African tragedy has inevitably stormed in to crown the pessimism about Africa's recovery.

African tragedy

Today conflicts are changing from border conflicts with neighboring states to, more often, conflicts within African countries themselves. The reasons are poverty, unemployment, religious radicalism and a lack of social cohesion. But these social tensions are no longer kept within national borders—they seem to cross all borders; growing numbers of refugees and immigrants intensify xenophobia and racism; a country's lack of political stability threatens international peace and safety everywhere. We now all share borders with Rwanda, Sierra Leone, Liberia, Democratic Republic of Congo, and Somalia.

Poverty has always been the biggest threat to each individual (Mbaku, 1994b). Unemployment has always been the biggest threat to any society. Social disintegration has always been the biggest threat to all development. And all these societal ills weaken African states and expose them to radical religious infections of all hues. Africa's tragic situation is evident in all areas of interaction with its external environment.

Trade imbalance

There is an absurdity surrounding international trade. In a globalized world, trade is supposed to increase prosperity and circulate wealth, but the rules that govern world trade have increasingly favored the rich to the detriment of the poor. There is equally an unquantifiable human cost of trade imbalance. In Africa and other ACP countries, about 128 million people could be salvaged from the bondage of poverty if their share of world exports is increased by one percent, and this will have a multiplier benefit on health and healthcare provision for which peoples of these regions of the world suffer greatly. It is sad to note that when developing countries export to rich country markets, they face tariff barriers that are four times higher than those encountered by rich countries. These barriers cost the developing countries twice as much as they get in aid. Policies usually formulated by the rich countries of the world cast grave suffering on the poor people of the world.

Again, while rich countries keep their markets closed, poor countries have been pressured by the Bretton Woods institutions to open their markets with devastating consequences. Many of the rules of the World Trade Organization (WTO), which border on investment, intellectual property and services more often than not, protect the interest of rich countries and powerful Transnational Companies (TNCs), while huge costs are imposed on developing countries. For example, a huge trade imbalance between Africa and the United States shocked President Moi of Kenya who urgently called for a redress. The President gave the example of Kenya, which he said exported to the U.S. goods worth only $99 million, but paid $298 million for American products in the year 2000.[12] There is thus much injustice in world trade, which calls for fundamental reforms to reverse the imbalance. To redress this imbalance in favor of underdeveloped countries like those in Africa, certain measures must be taken, namely:

- Essentially, the WTO needs to be democratized to give stronger voice to poor countries.

- The World Bank and IMF must stop the use of conditionalities attached to their programs to force poor countries to open their markets, irrespective of consequences on the people.
- The cycle of subsidized agricultural over-production and export dumping by rich countries should be stopped.
- Rules that force governments to implement policies of liberalization or privatization of basic services should be abrogated.

The debt burden

That Africa is severely wounded by a global economic contraction is obvious. What little recovery there has been on the continent remains extremely precarious. The reasons are many. But certainly the gravest is that little of substance has been done to ease the crushing burden of the continent's debt. Sub-Saharan Africa alone owes over $227 billion, $379 for every man, woman, and child on the continent. By itself, the full servicing of this debt amounts to 25 percent of sub-Saharan Africa's total annual export earnings.

Debt has become an unwieldy slow-killer of Africa's developmental efforts like some prehistoric monster. The amount and usurious interest rates have been vital contributory factors (see, e.g., Avramovic, 1988). These rates are more than three times higher than the rates experienced by developed countries in the same period. The ruthless over-exploitation of the Third World, intensified after the collapse of socialism in Eastern Europe, has meant an enormous transfer of wealth from these countries to the coffers of the big multinational companies and banks. This can be seen in the burden of the debt, which has reached such proportions that even before the G8 meeting in Birmingham (May 1998) there was some talk about debt relief initiatives for some of the poorest countries. In the end nothing was agreed upon about debt relief. The World Bank has also started a Highly Indebted Poor Countries (HIPC) program aimed at cutting the debt burden of 41 countries, which spend more than 20 percent of their export earnings in debt service payments-never mind about actual repayment of the debt.

All these plans are not born out of the good will and charitable intentions of the World Bank and IMF executives. There are three main reasons for this. First of all it is very unlikely that these countries are ever going to be able to pay their debts at all. Therefore the World Bank and the IMF have decided to recognize reality and make the Western governments pay back what is owed to the lending banks with taxpayers' money. In this way the banks never lose. The main aim of these debt relief initiatives is, on the one hand, to make sure the bankers get their money back and on the other to lift these highly indebted countries to a point where they are able to ask for more loans! Secondly, the amount of the debt that these highly indebted countries owe as a percentage of the total debt of former colonial countries is very small. And thirdly, these plans come with a lot of conditions attached. The countries involved have to put in practice the 'recommendations' (that is, orders) of the IMF.

The IMF's infamous structural adjustment programs (SAPs) have now been around for long enough for any observer to know what their consequences are. To give just one example, Zambia was a relatively developed country, with schools and hospitals, a fully functioning educational system and a modern infrastructure built mainly on the basis of the income from the copper mines. A decade of IMF and World Bank imposed structural adjustment managed to push life expectancy down from 54.4 years in 1991 to 42.6 years in 1997. Literacy rates are declining, and, as a direct result of the increase in hospital charges, there are now 203 infant deaths per 1,000 births compared to 125 in 1991. Access to clean water is declining and 98.1 percent of the population live on $2 a day or less. Debt represents 225 percent of the GDP. It is no surprise therefore that there have recently been food riots in Zambia—and in other African countries, like Zimbabwe and Tanzania.

The debt burden of the world's poorest countries represents 94 percent of their annual economic input. For the countries in line for the HIPC program this figure averages 125 percent. The percentage of the debt in relation to export earnings has reached unheard-of levels: Somalia 3,671 percent, Guinea-Bissau 3,509 percent, Sudan 2,131 percent, Mozambique 1,411 percent, Ethiopia 1,377 percent, Rwanda 1,374 percent, Burundi 1,131 percent. And the situation, far from improving, is actually worsening. In 1980 the total debt of underdeveloped countries was $600 billion. In 1990 it had gone up to $1.4 trillion and in 1997 the figure was a staggering $2.17 trillion. It is important to note that in the 1990–1997 period, when the total debt increased by $770 billion, these countries had actually paid $1.83 trillion just on debt servicing. An even more scandalous picture emerges if we compare debt-servicing payments with aid given to these countries: for every $1 they receive in aid, they pay back $11 dollars in debt servicing (World Bank, 1992, pp. 2–3).

The effects of this situation are evident. The situation in the whole of sub-Saharan Africa is a nightmare. According to *The Economist* (June 6, 1998), 'Nearly half the continent's 760m people are "profoundly poor,"' surviving, it is said by the African Development Bank, on less than $1 a day. Despite encouraging signs in some parts of the continent, average real GDP growth fell in 1997 to 3.7 percent from 5 percent the previous year. Africa's recovery is still fragile and as vulnerable as ever to commodity prices and bad weather. Globalization of world trade could push the continent's economy further towards the margins. According to the World Bank, Africa attracted just 1.5 percent of the world's foreign direct investment in 1996. The biggest recipient, getting 32 percent of the total, was Nigeria, which, apart from having a lot of oil, is not reforming its economy in the way that the World Bank says is essential for attracting foreign investment.

Ironically, according to the World Bank's *Global Economic Prospects and the Developing Countries, 1998/1999*, within Africa, South Africa and the largest oil exporters were hit hardest. If they are excluded, overall GDP growth for the rest of sub-Saharan Africa would be 3.8 percent. The countries of francophone West Africa, which use the CFA franc, maintained close to 5 percent growth in 1998. Despite the challenges of adjusting to a less favorable external environment over the next two years or so, notes the report, the longer term outlook for Africa offers the promise of 'significant improvement.' We are already several years into that period and the situation gets worse every day.

The most disturbing aspect is that these debts are odious and illegitimate. A huge chunk of the external debt of African countries is composed of debt contracted in questionable circumstances. These are the debts being paid for loans that went to projects destructive of people and of the environment, loans that went to propping up military and civilian dictatorships, and loans that were pocketed by corrupt officials and earned usurious interest rates. In Nigeria, as a case in point, two-thirds of her over $28 billion external debt was contracted between 1983 and 1998 when the military was in power. This holds true for most African countries, where the bulk of the countries' loans were given to despots, against any common sense and economic logic (Osakwe, 1989).

This increased impoverishment of the population in most of the African world has given rise to a strange industry called criminality, arms trafficking, drug pushing, black market and the 'informal economy.' In some cases the black market represents a bigger share of the economy than the official market and infiltrates all sections of the state apparatus. They try to protect their interests in the political arena through fundamentalist and 'populist' forces. These are powerful economic forces that in many cases have interests, which enter into conflict with those of World Bank/IMF global forces.

A vicious circle

In Africa, poverty and the degradation of the environmental resources are inextricably linked: poverty leads to unsustainable use of resources, which again leads to further poverty. Fifty years ago, there was four times more water for each African than there is today. Now there are acute water shortages for crops and for livestock, for industry and sanitation in the cities, and almost everywhere there is a lack of water for drinking.

Africa's forests are diminishing. Farmers burn trees to create more firewood and clear forests to create more farmland to feed their children. In the space of fifteen years, Africa has lost an eighth of its forests. The land is over-grazed and over-cultivated. At the current rate, crop yields will be halved within forty years. As it is, Africa's food production per head is falling. Four out of ten people in sub-Saharan Africa are not getting enough to eat. Forecasters say that in a few years, Africa will be able to feed less than half its population.

The degradation of the land leads many people to search for a better life in the cities. Before independence, only one in seven Africans was a city-dweller. Today over a third are. Some migrants find jobs and opportunities for themselves and their children in the cities, but others find sprawling slums, polluted air and a lack of clean water. Sanitation is poor and infectious diseases like cholera and dysentery are widespread (O'Connor, 1983, 1991).

The cost of instability

Africa has faced numerous political, economic and security challenges that have now turned it into the major peacekeeping ground of the world. Border disputes, ethnic divisions, religious strife, military dictatorships and a general absence of a democratic political culture (Almond and Verba, 1960) have been among the causes of instability in Africa. Grinding poverty, disease, civil strife and the refugee problem have been some of the consequences of this instability. Chinua Achebe's book, *Things Fall Apart*, is one of the most powerful ever to emerge from Africa, and its title sums up the grim situation, which has prevailed throughout the continent.

A quick audit of Africa's democratic balance sheet shows that, by 2002, many countries were quite literally in the red. The fragile peace in

Angola, violent civil war in Côte d'Ivoire, civil strife in Sierra Leone where the West African peacekeeping force, ECOMOG, had become a combatant instead of peacekeeper, Rwanda remains a sharply divided nation between the Hutu majority and the Tutsi minority, while Burundi totters on the brink of an ethnic war, and anarchy and on-going genocide in Kivu province of the Democratic Republic of Congo that has dragged a number of countries in the Great Lakes region into war.

In short, Africa continues to be plagued by problems associated with military intervention and rule, shaky processes of democratization, and ethno-political factionalism. Available evidence reveals that a significant proportion of African rulers of late have not been graduates of civilian universities, but those of African military academies and similar institutions abroad (such as Westpoint in the United States, Sandhurst in the United Kingdom, and St Cyr in France). In order to grasp the extent of military involvement in African politics, one needs only remember some of the coups that have taken place on the continent between 1985 and 1996. The following chronological inventory serves as a stark reminder:

- In the Sudan, the army took over on April 6, 1985. While President Gafar Nimeiry visited Cairo, General Abdurahman Muhammed Sewar Al Dahab used the opportunity to seize power. Nimeiry had ruled the country for 16 years before his bloodless overthrow.
- In Uganda, General Tito Okello overthrew President Milton Obote on August 27, 1985. Obote had returned to power in 1980, following his overthrow by military dictator Idi Amin in 1971.
- In Lesotho, Prime Minister Leabua Jonathan's government was overthrown by Major General Lekhanya on January 20, 1986, and King Moshoeshoe II was installed as ruler.
- On January 26, 1986, the National Resistance Army, led by current Ugandan President Yoweri Museveni, captured Kampala and seized power from Tito Okello who, as indicated above, had overthrown Milton Obote the previous year.
- In Burundi, Colonel Baptista Bagaza was overthrown in a military coup on September 3, 1987. He had been in power since 1976 and was in Canada at the time of the coup. Major Pierre Buyoya took over.
- On June 30, 1989, the civilian Sudanese Government of Sadek El Mahdi was overthrown in a military coup. A military junta led by General Omar Hassan El Bashir seized power. They are still ruling to this day.

- On November 6, 1990, King Moshoeshoe II of Lesotho was overthrown by the military and replaced by his son, King Letsie III.
- In Mali, President Moussa Traore was overthrown in a bloody coup on March 26, 1991. He had ruled the country since 1968.
- In Sierra Leone, President Joseph Momoh, who had been in power since 1985, was overthrown on April 30, 1992 by Captain Valentine Strasser.
- On July 23, 1994, President Dawda Jawara of the Gambia was overthrown by Lieutenant Yaya Jammeh.
- On August 15, 1995, President Miguel Trovoada of São Tomé and Princípe was overthrown in a military coup. However, he managed to resume his rule on August 21, 1995, after Angolan mediation.
- In the Comoros, on September 28, 1995, notorious mercenary Bob Denard led the overthrow of President Said Mohamed Djoar, taking him prisoner. Six days later, a French military intervention force captured the mercenaries and restored the deposed president.
- In Niger, General Ibrahim Bare Mainassara overthrew civilian President Mahamane Ousmane in January 1996.
- On July 25, 1996, Burundi's President Sylvestre Ntibantunganya, a Hutu, was toppled by the Tutsi-dominated army and replaced by former strong man Major Pierre Buyoya.Apart from these 'classic military coups', there were a number of other events which illustrated the non-democratic nature of politics on the continent during this period. For example,the assassination of President Samuel Doe of Liberia in 1990, following massive civil unrest.
- Hussein Habre's escape from Chad in 1990, following a long-running rebellion.
- The overthrow of President Siad Barre in Somalia as a result of civil war; and
- The overthrow of President Mengistu Haile Mariam of Ethiopia in 1991 as a result of civil war.

Such events illustrate the tenuous nature of attempts to establish democracy in African countries. Political stability is thus crucial if Africa is to break out of the tragedy. But Africa sees lasting division, both within and between countries. The process of decolonization, prompted largely by nationalist agitation in the colonies and by other external factors, among them United States pressure for opening up those captive markets to its trade, was designed to oversee and orchestrate an orderly transition to political independence. That was especially true in Africa.

The colonial powers, as if to fulfill their 'civilizing mission,' appeared committed to transplanting Western European type of democratic regimes in their former colonies, without regard to circumstances such as ethnic and tribal social organizations, a fact which might have necessitated the search for alternative regimes (Hayward and Kandeh, 1987). Already implicit in the decolonization process was the presumption that the nation-state was a given, and that all that was needed was to fit the state with a Western European type democratic constitution; a democratic form of government would follow naturally.

The facts show that the colonial state was not a nation-state. It was a colonial creature, invented without regard to geographic and ethnic boundaries and ruled by force. Colonial domination kept its disparate ethnic groupings together through coercion and manipulation. In presuming these diverse groups as part of a nation, the colonialist was implying the existence of a common bond, cherished by all the groups, a bond which tied them together. This conveyed an element of consent or approval not only about how they were governed but on whether they wished to remain part of the body politic. Of course, the above was not consistent with African socio-political reality.

It is obviously not easy to govern countries with artificial borders and deep ethnic divides, and many sub-Saharan countries are marred by instability and conflict. Ethnic conflicts persist within the old artificial frontiers. As part of the vicious circle, these countries have especially low investments. By the 1980s, there had been over 50 military coups in African states. And today, one in three of the world's refugees—some nine and a half million people—are in Africa, where another 16 million are 'displaced,' the result of war, genocidal attacks or other human rights abuse.[13]

HIV/AIDS pandemic

Barton Gellman in the *Washington Post* (Wednesday, July 5, 2000, p. A01) argued that the belated global response to AIDS in Africa was a way of shunning signs of the coming plague. This assertion was timely. In Africa, the predicament of the poor is exacerbated by the spread of HIV/AIDS. Nearly one in thirty Africans is HIV positive. The poorest communities are the most disrupted, closing the circle once again. For instance, South Africa, one of the laboratories where the International Monetary Fund has gleefully practiced its anti-social experiments, is in a state of economic disintegration. In Southern Africa, a substantial portion of the population is infected with the HIV virus. The AIDS crisis is having a devastating impact on developing countries, especially in Africa. Health care systems weakened by the impact of AIDS, along with conflict and poor management cannot cope with traditional illnesses. Malaria and tuberculosis continue to kill millions. In fact, malaria alone is estimated to reduce GDP growth rates by 0.5 per year on average in sub-Saharan Africa. Life expectancy in the region fell from 50 years in 1987 to 47 years in 1999; in the countries hardest hit by AIDS (such as Botswana, Zimbabwe, South Africa, and Lesotho) the average lifespan was cut short by more than ten years (Poverty Net, 2002). The following show the alarming impact of AIDS on African societies:

- AIDS is now the leading cause of death in sub-Saharan Africa.
- Today 26 million Africans are living with HIV/AIDS, over 70 percent of the world total.
- 4 million more Africans were infected in 1999.
- 90 percent of the AIDS global death toll occurs in Africa.
- Over the next 5 years, 20 million more Africans will die from HIV/AIDS.
- More than 15.6 million African children have lost both parents to the AIDS virus.
- By the end of the decade, 40 million children will be orphaned in Africa.
- AIDS does not only affect sexually active adults. Of the 13 million Africans who have already died from AIDS, a fourth were children.

As African nations lose adults in their prime working years, orphans have no alternative but to quit school and try to provide for themselves and their younger siblings. The economic, social and political aid for the children has disintegrated, adding to an already desperate situation brought by the HIV/AIDS pandemic. Battling the African HIV/AIDS tragedy has proven next to impossible for a variety of reasons, including national debt levels that have placed a fiscal stranglehold on the continent's economies; a trade imbalance that has seen African exports drop to historic lows; and decreasing foreign aid levels from some of the world's richest nations.

Famine

Between 1960 and 1980, most African countries grew poorer, and most Africans find themselves worse off today than they were at independence.

Some indicators, like educational enrollments and life expectancy, have stagnated. Again, the contrast with East Asia, where, for example, average life expectancy rose ten years between 1980 and 1994, could not be more striking. Even food security has become an issue in Africa, since the continent's ability to feed itself became more and more of an endemic crisis in many areas by the 1980s. In terms of real incomes, even factoring in the improvements in the economic situation of some parts of the continent in the mid-1990s, the decline is equally acute. And whatever gains in agricultural production have been achieved, they have been more than offset by the vast increase in population, so that less food is available per capita in 2002 than in 1968.

The famine facing Southern Africa alone is a mounting concern in the region, as statistics of the starving have risen to more than 6 million people in Malawi, Zambia, Mozambique, Lesotho, Zimbabwe, and Swaziland. The cost of containing food shortages caused by the combination of poor yields, flash floods, recurrent drought, and warped economic policies is astronomical. The World Food Program estimates that close to 13 million people in the region will need food aid by the end of the year (Dawu, 2002). Malawi incidentally is faced with famine after it was forced to sell maize to earn dollars for debt servicing. The explanation given by Ann Pettifor of the New Economics Foundation is quite plausible in that just three months before the food crisis hit, Malawi was encouraged by the World Bank 'to keep foreign exchange instead of storing grain.' Why? Foreign exchange is needed to repay debts. Creditors will not accept debt repayments in Malawian kwachas. Nor indeed will the creditors accept debt payments in bags of maize. Only 'greenbacks' or other hard currencies will do. This is a repeat process of breaking down subsistence and self-help economies and getting people dependent on money. As soon as the essential relationships of life are dependent on money, this transfers enormous power to the people who control the processes by which money is created and allocated such as the World Bank and the International Monetary Fund.

The most important thing to understand about money is that money is not wealth. Money has no intrinsic value. It is of no use in feeding, clothing, housing or meeting any other need. The only other thing that makes money valuable is that by social convention people accept it as a medium of exchange. They thereby become conditioned to give real wealth in return for money. Real wealth consists of these things important to human life like maize in Malawi.

The result of tying social relations to money is that Africa has become a continent that is staggering backward on almost every front—education, sanitation, infant mortality, and disease eradication—while the rest of the world has charged forward into the twenty-first century. There is therefore an urgent necessity to adopt new models of development. An important aspect of these is the total cessation of the logic of structural adjustment for African countries. The New Partnership for African Development (NEPAD) offers a germane model. Europe and other industrialized countries should allow NEPAD to work by not subjecting it to international conditionalities that will strangulate the initiative.

The core strategy of NEPAD is the establishment of a 'new framework of interaction with the rest of the world including the industrialized countries and multilateral organizations' as a means of putting Africa on a high growth path. The major goals being pursued by the New Economic Partnership for Africa's Development are as outlined below:

- To achieve and sustain an average gross domestic product (GDP) growth of above 7 percent per annum for the next 15 years;
- To ensure that the continent achieves that agreed international development goals (IDGs). The said goals are as follows:
  - To reduce the proportion of people living in extreme poverty by half between 1990 and 2015;
  - To enroll children of school age in primary schools by 2015;
  - To make progress towards gender equality and empowering women by eliminating gender disparities in the enrolment in primary and secondary education by 2005;
  - To reduce infant and child mortality ratios by two thirds between 1990 and 2015;
  - To maternal mortality ratios by three- quarters by 1990 and 2015;
  - To provide access for all who need productive health services by 2015;
  - To implement national strategies for sustainable development by 2005, so as to reverse the loss of environmental resources by 2015.

However, at face value NEPAD appears to be very attractive to the ordinary unsuspecting African who would be tempted to believe in this presumably wholly African plan designed to resolve Africa's perennial socio-economic and political problems. But, the challenges are multiple.

First, the challenges of NEPAD are the dialectics (contractions in) of distribution and ownership of political power, corruption, poverty, disease, vandalism and asset stripping, and commitment to resolution of political differences.

War, political and ethnic conflicts on the continent are predominantly a result of lopsided and often non-existent commitment to resolution of political differences. There is need for Africa to build capacity to manage all aspects of conflict. This capacity should focus on means necessary to strengthen existing institutions, especially in four key areas:

- Prevention, management and resolution of conflict;
- Peacemaking, peacekeeping and peace enforcement;
- Post-conflict reconciliation, rehabilitation and reconstruction, and;
- Combating the illicit proliferation of small arms, light weapons and landmines.

Second, NEPAD does not necessarily offer any alternative to the dominant neo-liberal development paradigm that places unquestioning faith in uncontrolled, private sector led rapid economic growth as the answer to the problem of rampant poverty, despite the evidence that this strategy in fact deepens poverty, increases unemployment, and widens inequality in the short and the medium term, while making national economies extremely vulnerable to speculative capital and 'market sentiment.'

Third, and finally, NEPAD is yet to engage with communities and civil society organizations (including the labor movement, youths and women's movements, religious communities, non-governmental organizations, etc.) concerning its process and content.

Summarily, reforms are going on worldwide now. But they have had the weakest effect in Africa. If you begin weak, have long periods of unproductive dictatorship, and are then hit by a systemic crisis, you wind up the poorest and weakest region in the global system and increasingly marginalized. Enfeebled governments must contend with local factions and rebellions that can flare up, burn fiercely, and spread to nearby countries. Africa is seeing such an effect, as the terrible genocide that took place in Rwanda has repercussions in Burundi, Tanzania, and Uganda, as well as in Zaire. The spread of ethnic violence and the flight of a massive number of refugees are two of the worst consequences of factional violence—ethnic or religious in nature.

All the efforts of development experts who have crisscrossed Africa during the past three decades, and all the initiatives from donor governments, from the United Nations, from various foundations and think tanks that have been put forward have not produced a model capable of lifting the majority of Africans out of the terrible poverty in which they find themselves. The failure of the World Bank's controversial Structural Adjustment Initiative in the 1980s spelled the end of the old development model. And the realization that humanitarian aid could both destabilize fragile societies, as in Somalia in 1992, or contribute to the prolongation of war, as happened over the last decade in Sudan, left those eager to help Africa in a quandary. Development seemed to have been a false dawn. So had humanitarianism. But the question concerning what to put in their place remained. The needs have not gone away. They are as pressing today as they were when the basic structures of development assistance were erected in the 1960s.

It is therefore commonplace to hear nowadays that all United Nations Member States have pledged to: eradicate extreme poverty and hunger; achieve universal primary education, promote gender equality and empower women, reduce child mortality, improve maternal health and combat HIV/AIDS, malaria and other diseases by 2015. Other goals are, to ensure environmental sustainability and develop a global partnership for development. Lofty as these goals seem, one poser is: will the rest of the world attain them without Africa?

All these platitudes are asserted in the midst of a deepening world economic crisis, in which the entire African continent is suffering the consequences of market economics that have shattered whatever once existed of its social infrastructures and reduced millions of people to conditions that defy description. The paradox is that rich in natural resources, but crippled by debt, poverty and poor governance, Africa is caught in a tragically endless circle of environmental degradation and poverty. These goals are therefore practically unrealizable for most African countries with the current external debt burden, huge sums of its assets looted and stashed in private accounts in overseas banks, trade imbalance that largely favors the north to the continued detriment of the south.

As the social, political and environmental situation deteriorates in many countries, one is forced to raise the question: can Africa ever break out of the circle? Looking at the plight of Africa since the first Berlin conference in 1884, it is only spiritually, emotionally, morally and ideologically logical for Europe and Africa to retrace their steps to where they first blundered.

Besides, we consider Germany, now reunified and economically strong, as strategic in Europe and the European Union. It is also fair that Europe's response to Africa will depend on what Germany thinks and feels.

The idea or call for another Berlin conference was first muted by President Olusegun Obasanjo of Nigeria on his visit to Germany shortly after he assumed office in 1999.

The issues raised above represent the immediate and remote development challenges staring Africa in the face. To move forward, the following recommendations are expected of Europe, Africa and the G8 countries and governments:

- Looking at the plight of Africa since the first Berlin conference in 1884, it is only spiritually, emotionally, morally and historically logical for Europe and Africa to retrace their steps to where they first goofed.
- Institutionalization of a fair international arbitration process to resolve the debt problem to discourage lax lenders and irresponsible borrowing for future lending.
- Investigation, tracing, tracking and repatriation of all illicit funds kept in private bank accounts abroad akin to the measure on terrorist bank accounts and assets to check impunity risks on financial crime. An international convention on the stolen wealth is the most viable solution to the problem of money laundering. The convention could ensure fairness, transparency and accountability with regards to due process of law.
- The G8 plan of action should not emasculate NEPAD through conditionalities.
- Overseas Development Assistance should be made available unconditionally to fight underdevelopment in Africa.

Conflict-torn societies like those in Africa are characterized by the traumatic impoverishment of economic, political and social relations between groups and individuals. Previously existing divisions within society are exacerbated, and new divisions are created. Violently divided societies are cursed by institutional breakdown: weak or non-existent political institutions; weak or non-existent civil society institutions; and limited government legitimacy and authority. Even should the ensuing violence cease, it becomes extremely difficult to re-create a sense of identity and belonging among communities that have experienced political, economic and socio-cultural breakdown. While it may be possible to impose a sense of order from outside, the sense of community has to grow from within. The tasks of rebuilding physical infrastructure, eradicating poverty and apathy, and revitalizing the environment are no less daunting. The destitute situation of the population engendered by the enfeebled state lends weight to its easy capture and manipulation by external forces, especially those of faith that promise a better eternal life after this. And, this is why radical Islamism with its attendant proneness to violence easily benefits from this permissive environment to capture the weak and/or failed African state.

African 'liberation terrorism'

Today, Africa in general has serious political and economic problems. Unemployment runs at about 30 percent or more (Kingdon and Knight, 2001). Military spending is rampant (World Bank, 1998, pp. 222–223). Several nations are holding significant numbers of refugees from neighboring nations. Xenophobia and anti-refugee sentiment are growing. It's not at all safe and it's hard to tell combatants from noncombatants with all the insurgencies, rebellions, militias, proxy and civil wars.

African terrorism revolves around state, ethnic, religious, and tribal animosities. Dictatorships are common, and frequently produce state-sponsored terrorism. Ethnic cleansing and genocide are common at the hands of militia groups. Religious battles go on between the major denominations and hundreds of tribal religions. To understand the mess that is Africa requires an understanding of anti-colonialism as a source of terrorism.

Anti-colonial (nationalistic) terrorism existed in Africa from 1945 to 1975. Those were the years of the Wars of Independence from Western powers. Some were long guerrilla wars, and others simply involved terrorism. The chief architect of African terrorism was Franz Fanon, author of *The Wretched of the Earth*. Born in Martinique, and trained in France to become a psychiatrist, Fanon joined the Algerian War for Independence in 1954. His model of urban terrorism was not only practiced in Africa, but Asia, the Middle East, and Latin America as well. His ideas are summarized as follows:

Franz Fanon, a psychiatrist, believed that colonialism, and indeed, all things Western were the source of mental illness in the world. He wrote that Western influence has a dehumanizing effect by destroying the local cultures. The Third World suffers from a massive identity complex. Achieving freedom (and mental health) requires carrying out acts of violence. Peaceful efforts at political change are useless. Terrorism is better than guerrilla warfare because it terrorizes Westerners and their lackeys into submission. Any foreigner in the Third World is an appropriate target for terrorism.

Apparently the most complicated spot in Africa is probably central Africa, which teeters on the brink of constant Hutu-Tutsi conflict, a clash between socio-ethnic classes left over from colonial days. The Democratic Republic of Congo is where most of this is occurring. There are many rebellious military factions, and an overriding issue in the region is the Rwandan massacre. In 1994, Hutu militias killed more than 500,000 Tutsis as well as moderate Hutus. Backed by the governments of Rwanda and Uganda, Tutsi rebels then turned their attention toward Zaire, which was itself supported by troops from Chad, Zimbabwe, Angola, and Namibia. The continent's leaders have tried to hold peace talks among rival factions in neutral Burundi, but the horrors of the Rwandan genocide loom large in everyone's memory. Proxy wars are common with one nation fighting another by using another nation's armed forces. France maintains a permanent peacekeeping presence in the Congo, and the United States provides a significant amount of economic aid to the Congo government. Burundi has also been fighting a seven-year civil war, and is involved with the Congo conflict to a large degree.

Ideological terrorism in the region can be traced to Zimbabwe, where demands for more democracy and the idea of people-power revolutions included insurrections by a number of courageous academics, high school teachers, priests, students, lawyers, judges, and citizens in what was called the Movement for Democratic Change (MDC). The Zimbabwe example set the stage for more-or-less violent coups, which occurred in Somalia, Sudan, Sierra Leone, and Côte d'Ivoire. Most 'people-power' revolutions occur after an existing government tries to rig its own re-election. White settler-farmers controlled the rural countryside in Zimbabwe at the time of white minority rule. With Zimbabwe as a glowing example, elections tend to be accompanied by a reign of terror, where activists are rounded up and gangs of thugs roam the countryside, demanding to see the appropriate political party cards.

Immediately south of the Congo is Zambia, Africa's most aid-dependent nation, where there is much international effort, mostly from the World Bank, to get the government there to institute reforms before neighboring rebels attack or revolution takes place. In Zambia, as in most troubled African nations, the goal is to get government to provide basic services that governments are supposed to bring, such as employment, food, health care, and education.

Immediately south and north of the Congo, respectively, are Angola and the Sudan, which have also been sites of international reform efforts, this time on the part of church-led organizations. Other interesting patterns of church-led international involvement can be found in Chad, Senegal, Eritrea, and Somalia. The church-led movements are mostly aimed at getting governments to stop the torture of dissidents and execution of political prisoners. Chad and Senegal are suffering from intra-state wars while Eritrea is at constant war with Ethiopia. Angola and the Sudan are also war-torn regions. Angola's civil war has been between the government and right-wing guerrillas. During the 1970s and 1980s, Angola received Soviet financial support and Cuban military advisors. UNITA rebels were backed by the CIA and South Africa. UNITA is now backed locally by smuggled diamonds sold to external arms dealers.

The two giants in this region, Nigeria and South Africa, continue to make progress toward democracy, despite political instability and more than their share of natural disasters. Botswana, Ghana, Mali, Malawi, Mozambique, Namibia, and Tanzania also are making progress. Mozambique, in particular, is enjoying an economic boom, and is the fastest growing economy in Africa.

Nigeria is Africa's most populous nation, and perhaps the one with the closest ties to the United States. There is a well-trained military and law enforcement establishment in Nigeria that is mostly restrained. However, seething problems in the form of rebel unrest pervade the Niger Delta region and secessionist demands exist in the southwest. School closures are common in the wake of bomb scares. There is an impending crisis in law since some northern provinces have declared that Islamic Sharia law should be applied to criminal law, and this has sparked some deadly clashes between Christians and Muslims. Nigeria is often thought of by terrorism experts as a bellwether for the region as a whole.

South Africa is only one of a few African countries experimenting with a constitution, as in the constitutional democracy that was supposed to completely replace the remnants of apartheid in 1996. However, South Africa has a terrible crime problem, and their criminal justice system does not seem able to cope with it. The prisons are overfilled and police brutality is rampant. The African National Congress (ANC), which leads the government, seems to be losing its coalition power over the issue of justice reform, as new types of crimes always seem to keep breaking out, such as 'taxi violence' and mob rapes. Election violence is also common, especially in neighboring Lesotho.

In Côte d'Ivoire, sub-Saharan Africa's third-largest economy, soldiers have been launching coups to bring about military dictatorships. Africa as a whole seems prone to the establishment of military dictatorships, ever since the example set in the 1960s by Ugandan 'President for Life' Field Marshall Idi Amin.

In Guinea-Bissau, the army launches regular mutinies. West African peacekeepers have been in place since 1991 when the Sierra Leone crisis developed. In Sierra Leone, a vicious civil war erupted between rebel forces and the government. Nigerian-led ECOMOG peacekeepers were replaced by U.N. troops in 2000, and these peacekeepers, mostly British, are struggling to reestablish order in the region. There has also been the presence of American military advisers.

Destructive civil wars persist in Sierra Leone and the border between Liberia and Guinea where noncombatants seem to bear the brunt of the conflict. In Sierra Leone, pro-government forces are fighting anti-government forces in a militia war, and some five hundred U.N. peacekeepers were sent in, all of whom were captured and taken prisoner. The most well-known rebel militia group in Sierra Leone is the Revolutionary United Front (RUF). Guinea and Liberia have been sucked into a tangled web of cross-border attacks.

Angola has perhaps the world's most well-known civil war. Its government has been fighting a rebel force known as the National Union for the Total Independence of Angola (UNITA) since 1975. A number of Angolan refugees have escaped into Zambia. UNITA is known to have engaged in indiscriminate killings and guerrilla attacks.

The Sudan has been in a seventeen-year civil war with rebel forces (the Sudan People's Liberation Army) as well as the Khartoum government both engaging in atrocities such as the bombing of civilian targets. Sudan's conflicts involve groups supporting the Islamic government in Khartoum on the one hand, and freedom fighters in the predominantly Christian south on the other. Civil war is ongoing, and only occasionally interrupted by famine. The United States provides diplomatic backing for the Sudanese People's Liberation Organization, and the CIA funnels arms to the rebels through Eritrea and Uganda.

The northernmost nations of Algeria, Egypt, Libya, Morocco, and Tunisia are closely aligned with Palestinian movements. Palestinian refugees number in the thousands in these countries. Anti-Israeli sentiment runs high, as does anti-U.S. sentiment. Military justice tends to prevail in this region. Protesters, journalists, and intellectuals tend to be suppressed in the name of Muslim fundamentalism. Women in northern Africa suffer severe forms of discrimination, and women's rights is one of the most contested areas of reform along with worker's rights.

Algeria is a special case since the government there (with military backing) annulled the 1992 elections when moderate Islamists were poised to win. Civil war between the secular government and Islamic militants has been the case ever since. Horrific massacres and assassinations are rampant. Recent amnesty for guerrillas was only partially successful, though the more moderate of the two groups fighting the government has laid down its arms. Meanwhile, the most virulent guerrilla group, the Armed Islamic Group or GIA, has been linked to plots against the United States. In addition, Algeria's historical fight for independence from colonialism serves as a template for violence and hate against just about everybody. For example, Mohammed Harbi, Algeria's most renowned intellectual and former leader of the FLN, or National Liberation Front, has made African liberation politics a seedbed of hatred against Islamists and Westerners alike.

Libya is run by Col. Moammar Gadhafi, who came to power in 1969 and was almost overthrown in 1971 by his own Revolutionary Council. There have been subsequent attempts to assassinate him since. He is vehemently opposed to corrupt Arab governments manipulated by Western powers and interests, and his agents have carried out disco bombings in Berlin that killed U.S. servicemen and the PANAM 707 bombing over Lockerbie, Scotland.

Somalia, located on the Horn of Africa, has been a country without a government since a multi-factional civil war erupted in 1991. Prior to that, it was an U.S. client state during the Cold War, offsetting the Soviet ally Ethiopia next door. The United States attempted to work with its fledgling transitional government, but only with disastrous results. Eighteen marines were killed in 1993 by warlords and their bodies dragged through the streets. Recently suspected as a harbor for terrorists, the United States has tried working with the Rahanwein Resistance Army, a clan-based faction opposed to Somalia's fledgling Transitional National Government or TNG (which has ties to al-Itihaad), and with Mohamed Saeed Hirsi, the leader of an Ethiopian-backed faction also opposed to the government. Hirsi is also known as Gen. Morgan, and his faction is based around the southern Somali port of Kismayo. The TNG is the closest thing to a national government, but they don't even control the capital, Mogadishu. The warlord with the closest ties to terrorist groups was General Mohamed Farah Aideed.

Ethiopia has been engaged in border wars over the 1908 frontiers drawn by then colonial power, Italy. Its main enemy is Eritrea, formerly a part of Ethiopia, which won its independence with U.S. support in 1993. Both Ethiopia and Eritrea are led by democratically elected U.S. allies, but the United States has been unsuccessful in mediating their border dispute. Ethiopia is run by a Christian-sympathetic government which considers Islamic fundamentalism a threat. In recent years, U.S. troops have been waging campaigns inside Somalia to quell unrest. Ethiopia and Somalia continue to squabble over the Ogaden region.

In a nutshell, fissiparous tendencies threatening the very existence of the post-colonial state were there at the dawn of independence. To combat these forces, the first generation leadership opted for the construction of a 'strong state.' This drive led to the conversion of the 'strong state' into a mode of production. This was not a novel practice. It was a practice whose genesis could be traced back to the colonial state. And the inheritance African elites gave this as a historical raison d'être for the creation of a strong or authoritarian state for the sake of continuity (Chabal and Daloz, 1999).

Authoritarianism has been demonstrated to be the main defining characteristic of the post-colonial state in Africa. Throughout the continent power is concentrated in the executive arm as personified by the President, with the power, authority and prestige of the representative organs of the people such as the legislature and the courts of law diminished accordingly. The authoritarian state is characterized by an oppressive legal system within which the law is used by the state to terrorize and coerce its citizens rather than to confer rights upon them. Under such circumstances, the law serves as a constraining rather than liberating instrument. The corollary to this concentration of power is the restriction or outright suppression of power centers outside state structures, such as social organizations and popular movements.

Thus, the independent African state bears a strong resemblance to its colonial predecessor. Indeed, the post-colonial state inherited almost all the latter's laws and institutions. The Societies Ordinance, which had been the lynchpin of colonial control and terror over civil society, was also adopted without any substantial amendments other than the removal of the more irritating and racist colonial, and therefore embarrassing, references such as that to 'the Governor' or 'Colonial Administrator.' The underlying philosophy of authoritarianism that had informed colonial law and practice of state terror was, therefore, retained largely intact.

Now, however, state authoritarianism is justified not only by the need to preserve order but also by what has come to be known as the ideology of so-called developmentalism. The state had to be strong, the argument goes, in order to bring development to the people. Popular organizations such as trade unions, cooperatives, political parties and local governments were proscribed and their members terrorized in the vaunted interests of development. This explains why a bill of rights has rarely, if at all, found its way into constitutional amendments. Multi-party competition has only engendered cosmetic changes on forms of state terror. The substance confers obligations to the state, not rights.

The state justified its dirigiste, welfarist economic and social policies through the ideology of developmentalism as well. In this period it was virtually impossible to organize independently outside state structures. Some non-state organizations existed. These were, however, mostly charitable, religious bodies involved in provision of social services such as education and health care. They were tolerated because they were almost invariably apolitical and therefore posed little threat to the existing power structure. But organizations that threatened the state's authoritarian policies were not immune to repressive crackdowns by the state. For example, the banning of the East African Muslim Welfare Society and the Ruvuma Development Association in the late 1960s illustrates this repression in Tanzania. This dirigiste system has produced misery, disaffection and a convenient anarchic environment for breeding anti-state terrorism as well as recruitment into activities of international terrorist cartels.

Notes

1. The concept 'tragedy' is from Colin Ley's: 'Confronting the African Tragedy', *New Left Review*, March-April 1994, pp. 33–47.
2. According to Michel Camdessus' interview in *Les Echos*, Friday April 25 and Saturday April 26, 1997.
3. Interview by Evangelos A. Calamitsis, *IMF Bulletin*, Vol. 26, No. 13, 14 July Evangelos A. Calamitsis, the IMF's Director for Africa, 1997.
4. 'Rhodes, Cecil John', *Microsoft Encarta: CD-ROM. Microsoft*, 1998. See also 'Boer War', *Microsoft Encarta: CD-ROM. Microsoft*, 1998.
5. For the debate, see Keynes, J. M. 'The German Transfer Problem' and 'Views on the Transfer Problem', in *Economic Journal*, March 1929, June 1929 and September 1929; Bertil Ohlin, 'The Reparations Problem', *Index*, Svenska Hendelsbanken, April 1928; Bertil Ohlin, 'Transfer Difficulties, Real and Imagined', *Economic Journal*, June 1929; and Bertil Ohlin (1935), *Inter-regional and International Trade*, Harvard University Press: Cambridge, MA.

6. United Nations, The state of international economic cooperation and effective ways and measures of revitalizing the economic growth and development of developing countries, January 30, 1990, p. 9.
7. African, Caribbean and Pacific members of the Lomé Convention. A grand total of 70 countries linked to 15 European Union members. For further discussions see Gilli, R. E. (1993), *The European Community and the Developing Countries*, Cambridge University Press: Cambridge.
8. World Bank (1981), *Accelerated Development in Sub-Saharan Africa: An Agenda for Action*, Washington, D.C.: World Bank.
9. Bates, R. H. (1981), *Markets and States in Tropical Africa: The Political Basis of Agricultural Policy*, University of California Press: Berkeley and Los Angeles. For the emergence of the 'new' political economy of Africa in the 1980s, see among others Lancaster, C. (1988), 'Political Economy and Policy Reform in sub-Saharan Africa', in Commins, S. (ed.), *Africa's Development Challenges and the World Bank*, Westview Press: Boulder, CO.
10. See especially World Bank (1984), *Toward Sustained Development in Sub-Saharan Africa: A Joint Program of Action*, Washington, D.C.: World Bank; and World Bank (1986), *Financing Adjustment with Growth in Sub-Saharan Africa: 1986–1990*, Washington, D.C.: World Bank.
11. See Bush, R. and Szeftel, M. (1999), 'Commentary: Bringing Imperialism Back In', *Review of African Political Economy*, No. 80, p. 168. Two cover stories of *The Economist* also provide a good measure of this kind of swing. Just three years after claiming in a cover story that 'Sub-Saharan Africa is in better shape than it has been in a generation', on the cover of its May 13–19, 2000 issue *The Economist* declared Africa to be 'The Hopeless Continent.' In excoriating Africa's 'poor crop of leaders', who by 'personalizing power' have 'undermined rather than boosted national institutions' and turned their countries into 'shell states', with the trappings of modernity but a hollow core, the magazine asked: 'Does Africa have some inherent character flaw that keeps it backward and incapable of development?' Noting the contrast between the two cover stories, Johannesburg's business magazine *Financial Mail* retorted: 'Do the editors of *The Economist* have a character flaw that makes them incapable of consistent judgment?': see 'The Hopeless Continent', *World Press Review*, October 2000, pp. 24–25.
12. IPS, June 18, 2002, London.
13. See *The Nation* (Nairobi), February 20, 2000.

References

Ake, C. (1981), *A Political Economy of Africa*, Longman: London.

Almond, G. and Coleman, J. (1960), *The Politics of Developing Areas*, Princeton University Press: Princeton, NJ.

Almond, G. and Verba, S. (1965), *The Civic Culture*, Little, Brown and Company: Boston, MA.

Arrighi, G. (2002), 'The African Crisis: World Systemic and Regional Aspects', *New Left Review*, Vol. 15 (May-June), pp. 5–36.

Asiwaju, A. I. (ed.) (1984), *Partitioned Africans: Ethnic Relations Across Africa's International Boundaries, 1884–1984*, University of Lagos Press: Lagos, Nigeria.

Barongo, Y. (ed.) (1983), *Political Science in Africa*, Zed Press: London.

Bates, R. H. (1981), *Markets and States in Tropical Africa: The Political Basis of Agricultural Policy*, University of California Press: Berkeley and Los Angeles.

Bates, R. H. (1992), *Beyond the Miracle of the Market: The Political Economy of Agrarian Development in Kenya*, Cambridge University Press: Cambridge.

Bayart, J.-F. (1986), 'Civil society in Africa', in Chabal, P. (ed.), *Political Domination in Africa*, Cambridge University Press: Cambridge.

Boyles, D. (1988), *Africa Lives*, Weidenfeld and Nicolson.

Brunschwig, H. (1971), '"Scramble" et "Course au Clocher"', *Journal of African History*, Vol. 12, No. 1, pp. 139–141.

Bush, R., and M. Szeftel (1999), 'Commentary: Bringing Imperialism Back In', *Review of African Political Economy*, Vol. 26, No. 80, pp. 165–169.

Carew, G. M. (1993), 'Development Theory and the Promise of Democracy: The Future of Postcolonial African States', *Africa Today*, Vol. 40, No. 4, pp. 31–53.

Chabal, P. (1992), *Power in Africa: An Essay in Interpretation*. St. Martin's Press: New York.

Chabal, P. and Daloz, J. P. (1999), *Africa Works: Disorder as Political Instrument*, James Currey: Oxford.

Chamberlain, M. E. (1999), *The Scramble for Africa*, 2nd edition, UCL Press: London.

Cheru, F. (1989), *The Silent Revolution in Africa: Debt, Development and Democracy*, Zed Press: London.

Cohen, R. and Middleton, J. (eds.) (1970), *From Tribe to Nation in Africa: Studies in Incorporation Processes*, Challenger Publishing Company: Scranton, PA.

Collier, P. (1991), 'Africa's External Economic Relations, 1960–1990', *African Affairs*, Vol. 90, No. 360, pp. 339–356.

Davidson, B. (1974), *Can Africa Survive? Arguments Against Growth Without Development*, Little, Brown and Company: Boston, MA and Toronto.

Davidson, B. (1990), 'Historical Questions and Comparisons, Attitudes to Africa's Crisis', *World and I*, Vol. 05 (August), p. 591.

Dawu, J. (2002), 'Iden Wetherell: Pulling No Punches', *World Press Review* (October), pp. 20–21.

De Lusignan, G. (1969), *French Speaking African since Independence*, Pall Mall: London.

Dumett, R. E. (1998), *El Dorado in West Africa: The Gold-Mining Frontier, African Labor, and Colonial Capitalism in the Gold Coast, 1875–1900*, Ohio University Press: Athens, OH.

Fabra, P. (1983), 'General Indebtedness Keeps Rates Up', *The Wall Street Journal*, December 15, p. 1.

Fanon, F. (1965), *The Wretched of the Earth*, McGibbon and Kee: New York.

Farah, M. A. (1994), *Global Insights: People and Cultures*, New York: Glencoe.

Flint, J. (1974), *Cecil Rhodes*, Little, Brown and Company: Boston, MA.

Gilli, R. E. (1993), *The European Community and the Developing Countries*, Cambridge University Press: Cambridge.

Hayward, F. and Kandeh, F. (eds.) (1987), *Elections in Independent Africa*, Westview Press: Boulder, CO.

Hochschild, A. (1998), *King Leopold's Gold: A Story of Greed, Terror and Heroism in Colonial Africa*, Macmillan: London.
Hodgkin, T. (1956), *Nationalism in Colonial Africa*, Frederick Muller: London.
Hopkins, A. G. (1993), 'Blundering and Plundering: The Scramble for Africa Relived', *Journal of African History*, Vol. 34, No. 3, pp. 439–494.
Horne, G. (1998), 'Imperialist Scramble for Africa', *Political Affairs*, Vol. 77, No. 6, pp. 21–24.
Kagan, D. (1995), *The Western Heritage*, Prentice-Hall: Upper Saddle River, NJ.
Kingdon, G. and Knight, J. (2001), 'What Have We Learnt About Unemployment from Microdatasets in South Africa', *Social Dynamics* (Cape Town), Vol. 27, No. 1, pp. 79–95.
Lancaster, C. (1988), Political Economy and Policy Reform in sub-Saharan Africa, in Commins, S. (ed.), *Africa's Development Challenges and the World Bank*, Westview Press: Boulder, CO.
Leys, C. (1976), 'The Overdeveloped Colonial State: A Reevaluation', *Review of African Political Economy*, Vol. 5 (Spring), pp. 39–48.
Lonsdale, J. (1986), 'Political Accountability in African History', in Chabal, P. (ed.), *Political Domination in Africa*, Cambridge University Press: Cambridge.
MacKenzie, J. M. (1983), *The Partition of Africa, 1880–1900 and European Imperialism in the Nineteenth Century*, Methuen: London.
Maizels, A. and Nissanke, M. (1984), 'Motivations for Aid to Developing Countries', *World Development*, Vol. 12, No. 9, pp. 879–900.
Marquard, L. (1969), *A Short History of South Africa*, Praeger: New York.
Mazrui, A. and Tidy, M. (eds.) (1984), *Nationalism and New States in Africa*, Heinemann: London.
Mbaku, J. M. (1994a), 'Military Coups as Rent-Seeking Behavior', *Journal of Political and Military Sociology* 22 (Winter), pp. 241–284.
Mbaku, J. M. (1994b), 'Africa After More Than Thirty Years of Independence: Still Poor and Deprived', *Journal of Third World Studies*, Vol. 11, No. 2, pp. 13–58.
Mentan, T. (1985), 'French Monetary Imperialism in Africa: Implications for Cameroon's Foreign Policy', Ph.D. dissertation, University of Nigeria, Nsukka, Nigeria.
Meslier, J. (1864), *Le testament de Jean Meslier*, Tome (Vol.) II, np: Amsterdam.
Nkrumah, K. (1964), *Consciencism*, Monthly Review Press: New York.
OAU (1981), *The Lagos Plan of Action for the Economic Development of Africa 1980–2000*, International Institute for Labor Studies: Geneva.
O'Connor, A. (1983), *The African City*, Hutchison: London.
O'Connor, A. (1991), *Poverty in Africa: A Geographical Perspective*, Belhaven: London.
Ohlin, B. (1929), 'Transfer Difficulties, Real and Imagined', *Economic Journal*, Vol.39, No.154 (June), pp. 172–182.
Ohlin, B. (1935), *Inter-regional and International Trade*, Harvard University Press: Cambridge, MA.
Onimode, B. (1982), *Imperialism and Underdevelopment in Nigeria*, Zed Press: London.
Onimode, B. (1988). *A Political Economy of the African Crisis*, Zed Press: London.
Onimode, B. (ed.) (1989a), *The IMF, the World Bank and the African Debt, vol. 2, The Social and Political Impact*, Zed Press: London.
Onimode, B. (ed.) (1989b), *The IMF, the World Bank and the African Debt, vol. 1, The Economic Impact*, Zed Press: London.

Osakwe, J. O. (1989), 'The Problems of Debt and Development in sub-Saharan Africa', Presidential Address, 1989 Annual Conference of the Nigerian Economic Society, Ibadan, Nigeria.

Popper, K. (1963), *Conjectures and Refutations: The Growth of Scientific Knowledge*, Routledge: London.

Pronk, T. (2000), 'What Chemicals are Used in Gold Minning? How Bad is Gold Mining for the Environment?
Retrieved from http://www.bio.ns.ca/schools/mine/carol_2c.html, March 5, 2000.

Pye, L. and Verba, S. (eds.) (1965), *Political Culture and Political Development*, Princeton University Press: Princeton, NJ.

Ripley, E. A., Redmann, R. E., Crowder, A. A. and Ariano, T. C. (1996), *Environmental Effects of Mining*, St. Lucie Press: Delray Beach, FL.

Rodney, W. (1974), *How Europe Underdeveloped Africa*, Howard University Press: Washington, D.C.

Rothchild, D. (1986), 'Hegemonial Exchanges: An Alternative Model for Managing Conflicts in Middle Africa', in Thompson, D. and Ronen, D. (eds.), *Ethnicity, Politics and Development*, Lynne Rienner: Boulder, CO.

Rothchild, D. and Chazan, N. (eds.) (1988), *The Precarious Balance: State and Society in Africa*, Westview Press: Boulder, CO.

Sandbrook, R. (1976), 'The Crisis in Political Development Theory', *Journal of Development Studies*, Vol. 12, No. 2, pp. 165–185.

Sawyer, A. (1990), 'The Politics of Adjustment Policy', in Adedeji, A., Rasheed, S. and Morrison, M. (eds.), *The Human Dimension of Africa's Persistent Economic Crisis: Selected Papers*, Hans Zell: London.

Senghor, L. (1964), *On African Socialism*, Praeger: New York.

Sklar, R. (1986), 'Democracy in Africa', in Chabal, P. (ed.), *Political Domination in Africa*, Cambridge University Press: Cambridge.

Sparks, D. (1990), *Namibia: Industrial Development and Independence*, UNIDO: Vienna.

Taussig, F. W. (1915), *Some Aspects of the Tariff Question*, Harvard University Press: Cambridge, MA.

UNDP (2000), *Human Development Report, 2000*, Oxford University Press: New York.

UNDP (2001), *Human Development Report, 2001*, Oxford University Press: New York.

UNDP (2002), *Human Development Report, 2002*, Oxford University Press: New York.

Wheatcroft, G. (1985), *The Randlords*, Atheneum: New York.

Wilhelm, G. and VanZyl, D. J. (1981), *The Story of South Africa*, Human and Rousseau: Cape Town.

World Bank (1981), *Accelerated Development in sub-Saharan Africa: An Agenda for Action*, World Bank: Washington, D.C.

World Bank (1984), *Toward Sustained Development in sub-Saharan Africa: A joint program of action*, World Bank: Washington, D.C.

World Bank (1986), *Financing Adjustment with Growth in sub-Saharan Africa. 1986–1990*, World Bank: Washington, D.C.

World Bank (1989), *Sub-Saharan Africa: From Crisis to Sustainable Growth—A Long-Term Perspective Study*, World Bank: Washington, D.C.

World Bank (1992), *Governance and Development*, World Bank: Washington, D.C.

World Bank (1996), *African Development Indicators, 1996*, World Bank: Washington, D.C.

World Bank (1997a), *World Development Report, 1997*, Oxford University Press: New York.

World Bank (1997b), *World Development Indicators, 1997*, World Bank: Washington, D.C.

World Bank (1998), *World Development Report, 1998*, Oxford University Press: New York.

5

State, Permissive Environment, and Mass Terrorism

The African continent has been a victim of mass terror for many years (Combs, 1997, p. 13). By mass terror here we mean terror by a state, where the regime coerces the opposition in the population, whether organized or unorganized, sometimes in an institutional manner. This typology of terror visited on the African either by the colonial or post-colonial state conveys the painful impression that Africans are ripe only for repression. Time has not erased the structured violence because of another 'axis of evil' in the world: poverty and ignorance; disease and environmental disorder; corruption and political oppression, all of which are forms of, and further lead to, terrorism.

Globalization whose concepts of development, hinged upon liberalism and competition, inevitably engender economic and social Darwinism—the survival of the fittest and the exclusion of the rest (Clapham, 1985). In fact, global forces are increasingly hegemonic. And, in the case of Africa with its longstanding history of problems and dilemmas, globalization as an ideology is distinctly shaping the arenas of policy and the directions and scope of state patterns of behavior. The law of survival of the fittest sentences weak African states perpetually to be deprived, drifting, and always abandoned to their fate by these rampaging forces of globalization through permissive borders, economic disorders, and international terrorist networks.

The intensifying effects of attendant population growth, environmental degradation and economic disequilibrium, both nationally and internationally, have put African states in a tragic situation. This tragedy is evidenced by the erosion of social structures, increases in inequalities (especially in the distribution of income and wealth), resurgence of ethnic and religious conflicts, and micronationalism. And, current trends and modalities of such conflicts reflect transnational linkages or networks heavily reliant on the smuggling of the state's natural resources in exchange for military hardware required for sustaining intra-state wars. Under these conditions, international terrorist cartels fit very fast into the vacuum within the linkages, creating disorder and epidemics rooted in poverty, ignorance, and oppression, in corruption and incompetence.

The problem of permissiveness

Whether in the twenty-first century or in mankind's history, the problem of the weak state is not new. However, the post-seventeenth century world and the post-Cold War world have introduced new concepts and objective conditions. These new concepts and objective conditions now serve as turning points, which shape the meaning and the effects of nation-state weakness and failure.

The first turning point was The Treaty of Westphalia (1648). This Treaty brought to a close the religious wars in Europe. It also marked the beginnings of the modern state, a territorial entity in which the governed and the governing form a compact of reciprocal rights and obligations.

These rights and obligations take the form of a social contract. The governed consent to follow the decrees of the rulers and to support state structures through the commitment of personal time, fiscal resources and energy. In *extremis*, they commit even their lives for the survival of the state. In return for these sacrifices by the governed the government guarantees individual security—basically freedom from fear, from want, from internal fiscal resources and external conflict, and a varying degree of latitude in their daily endeavors. This social contract, in whatever form it assumed, was reinforced in the 19th century by the concept of the '*volk*,' in which the governed identified themselves as the state rather than a mere party to an agreement. This psychological fusion of governed with governing and the institutions of governance are called nationalism.

The term 'nationalism' is generally used to describe two phenomena: (1) the attitude that the members of a nation have when they care about their national identity, and (2) the actions that the members of a nation take when seeking to achieve (or sustain) some form of political sovereignty.

The first phenomenon raises questions about the concept of nation (or national identity), which is often defined in terms of common origin, ethnicity, or cultural ties, and while an individual's membership in a nation is often regarded as involuntary, it is sometimes regarded as voluntary. The second phenomenon raises questions about the whether sovereignty must be understood as the acquisition of full statehood with complete authority for domestic and international affairs (Gellner, 1983).

These developments occurred at the same time that Europeans were exploring and then intensively colonizing America, Asia, and Africa. The European colonizers often had no regard for the political structures and historic arrangements of these colonized areas. In the twentieth century, from the 1930s to 1991, the great powers were engaged in ideological struggles that strengthened nationalism within opposing nations and gave rise to competition for influence in countries in what was viewed as a zero-sum game for world dominance (Wolf, 1982). That is, in a zero-sum game, the payoff to one player is the negative of that going to the other. These ideological struggles therefore emphasized the political-military arena, with the presumption that the best way to influence political leanings and gain diplomatic support was to provide military hardware and pledges of military support against external foes.

Of course, with the collapse of the Soviet Union in 1991, the zero-sum game ended. For the most part western interest in the southern hemisphere which was left awash in military hardware at the same time that it remained an economic backwater faded. Nevertheless, it is not the presence of large quantities of arms amassed during the Cold War era that leads to what is termed the weak or failed or failing state. Historically states 'fail' because they cannot prevent conquest by a rival state. This may be a situation that may in fact result from the absence of sufficient quantities of armaments. But in the context of the late 20th century, a weak or failed or failing state is one in which the rulers either break the underlying contract by neglecting or ignoring the fundamental freedoms due their people or, as illustrated most graphically in Rwanda in 1994, actually direct the state apparatus against and encourage one segment of the population to hunt down another segment.

In either of these contexts, opposition thrives (Crummey, 1986). Unrequited, it is reinforced by armaments either stolen or seized from stocks already within the country or smuggled from other sources and other previous conflicts. Most often the arms of choice are of the cheap, plentiful, easily transported and used, low maintenance type. They may be in the form of small arms, light weapons, and explosives. And the plentiful supply of such weapons, which continue to be churned out by fifty African nations today, is what has earned this class of weaponry the sobriquet of 'conventional weapons of mass destruction.'

From preceding statements, it immediately becomes apparent that arms do not weaken or cause states to fail. They do not necessarily even rise to the level of being the proximate catalyst. The root problem, exacerbated by the failure of even rudimentary nationalism to take hold in many artificially created countries, is the lack of responsibility among the governing group to fulfill the state's part of the social contract. In the case of weak or failed states in Africa, international terrorist organizations with Islamic ties, including *al Qaeda* and *Lebanes e Hizbollah*, have gained a presence in the continent and continue to exploit its permissive operating environment—porous borders, conflict, lax financial systems, and the wide availability of smuggled weapons—to expand and strengthen their networks. But without any doubt, it is the quest for power and availability of foreign arms supplier and trainer, which translates the landscape of struggle from the political to the military realm. The result has been that of creating the 'complex emergencies' that involve huge population shifts, long-term agricultural insufficiency and general economic collapse, and civil population decimation from poverty, disease, starvation, and direct conflict. Somalia, Angola, Congo, and Sierra Leone are typical cases.

Elusive borders and terrorism

There have been debates about the relationship of individual African states to transnational organizations or non-state actors. These actors may be violent or non-violent ones. However, views range from those who emphasize the degree to which states are manipulated by these organizations to serve their individual and collective interests to those who emphasize the degree to which states are autonomous actors who deal with international organizations as one interest group. There has also been debate about the degree to which these organizations could escape control by the state machineries; and there are many who are arguing that their ability to do this has increased considerably in recent decades with the so-called globalization.

In addition, there have long been debates about the relationship of so-called sovereign states to each other. Views range from those who emphasize the effective sovereignty (Krasner, 2001) of the various states to those who are cynical about the ability of so-called weak states to resist the pressures (and blandishments) of so-called strong states. This kind of debate is apparently archaic. For example, the most horrendous, reprehensible and unexpected attacks on the twin towers of the World Trade Center, the Pentagon and the reportedly abortive attempt on the White House stunned and traumatized the entire American nation and shook the peace loving countries of the world. These meticulously planned and executed attacks caused enormous destruction of men and material, which the Americans could never have imagined even in the wildest of their dreams. These attacks made it abundantly clear that no country, however powerful, is invulnerable to desperate and unpredictable terrorist onslaughts.

The Organization of African Unity (OAU) expressed 'to the Government and people of the United States the full solidarity and the deepest condolence of the OAU and the entire people of Africa over this tragedy which affected not only the people of the United States but humanity as a whole.' This statement was contained in the OAU communiqué of September 20, 2001. The prompt reaction of the OAU was based on the fact that Africa is now unfortunately the world's soft underbelly for global terrorism. Al Qaeda and other terrorist cells are active throughout East, Southern, and West Africa, not to mention North Africa. These terrorist organizations hide throughout Africa. They plan, finance, train for, and execute terrorist operations in many parts of the continent, not just from the Sudan and Somalia.

Terrorist organizations take advantage of Africa's porous borders, weak and corrupt law enforcement and security services, and nascent judicial institutions to move men, weapons, and money around the globe. They also take advantage of poor, disillusioned populations, often with religious or ethnic grievances, to recruit for their jihad against their targets. In fact, terrorist networks are exploiting Africa thoroughly. And in the process, they are directly threatening the national security of declared target groups such as the United States and Israel. For the ordinary African, 'Is it not only death and hardship?' (Seequeh, 1996, p. 9).

The omnipresence of 'swamps' for breeding terrorists explains why there was nearly universal condemnation of the September 11 attacks on the United States among sub-Saharan African governments. These African governments also pledged their support for the war against terrorism. In addition to bilateral cooperation with the United States and the global coalition, multilateral organizations such as the Organization for African Unity and the Southern African Development Community have committed themselves to fighting terrorism. The shock produced by the September 11 attacks and renewed international cooperation to combat global terrorism is producing a new readiness on the part of African leaders to address the problems of international terrorism. Africa's increased cooperation may help counter the persistent threat and use of terrorism as an instrument of violence and coercion against civilians. Most terrorist attacks in Africa stem from internal civil unrest and spillover from regional wars as African rebel movements and opposition groups employ terrorist tactics in pursuit of their political, social, or economic goals. Countries where insurgent groups have indiscriminately employed terrorist tactics and attacked civilians include Somalia, the Democratic Republic of the Congo, Liberia and Sierra Leone. Further, these groups are able to flourish in 'failed states' or those with weak governments that are unable to monitor the activities of terrorists and their supporters within their borders. Terrorists could be using the illicit trade in conflict diamonds both to launder money and to finance their operations.

These were not idle speculations. A report by Lansana Gberie published by *All Africa* (November 15, 2001), evaluated probable links between Sierra Leone's large Lebanese merchant community and global terrorist networks in the context of near-collapsed state institutions and the traditional corruption of Sierra Leone's diamond industry. The 28-page report, entitled 'War and Peace in Sierra Leone: Diamonds, Corruption and the Lebanese Connection,' was written after three extended trips to Sierra Leone and other West African countries in 2001 and 2002.

According to the report, various factions in Middle Eastern conflicts, including the Hezbollah and Amal (which was founded by a Sierra Leonean-born Lebanese Nabbi Berri), have in the past raised substantial funding from the Lebanese community in Sierra Leone through the diamond trade, and the report argues that although evidence of links between this Diaspora community and the al Qaeda terrorist network is 'anecdotal,' the allegations are supported by generations of dubious activities by some Lebanese diamond dealers and tangible proofs of contacts between some of them and Middle Eastern terrorists on the *U.S. Most Wanted List* in recent years. The report follows-up on allegations that al Qaeda may have gained millions of dollars from the Revolutionary United Front's (RUF) diamond trade. The author traces the involvement of two Lebanese diamond dealers with longstanding business and other interests in West Africa and the Congo, Aziz Nassour and Samih Ossailly.

In the wake of September 11, the threat of terrorism has given the problem of failed nation-states an immediacy and importance that transcends its previous humanitarian dimension. Since the early 1990s, wars in and among failed states have killed about eight million people, most of them civilians, and displaced another four million. The number of those impoverished, malnourished, and deprived of fundamental needs such as security, health care, and education has totaled in the hundreds of millions (Ravallion and Shaohua, 1996).

Although the phenomenon of state failure is not new, it has become much more relevant and worrying than ever before. In less interconnected eras, state weakness could be isolated and kept distant. Failure had fewer implications for peace and security. Now, these states pose dangers not only to themselves and their neighbors but also to peoples around the globe. Preventing states from failing, and resuscitating those that do fail are thus strategic and moral imperatives.

But weak or failed states are not homogeneous. The nature of state weakness or failure varies from place to place, sometimes dramatically. Failure and weakness can flow from a nation's geographical, physical, historical, and political circumstances, such as colonial errors and Cold War policy mistakes. More than structural or institutional weaknesses, human agency is also culpable, usually in a fatal way. Destructive decisions by individual leaders have almost always paved the way to state failure. President Mobutu Sese Seko's three-plus decades of kleptocratic rule sucked Zaire (now the Democratic Republic of Congo, or DRC) dry until he was deposed in 1997. In Sierra Leone, President Siaka Stevens (1967–1985) systematically plundered his tiny country and instrumentalized disorder. President Mohamed Siad Barre (1969–1991) did the same in Somalia. These rulers were personally greedy, but as predatory patrimonialists they also licensed and sponsored the avarice of others, thus preordaining the destruction of their states.

Today's weak and/or failed African states, such as Sierra Leone, and Somalia, are incapable of projecting power and asserting authority within their own borders, leaving their territories governmentally empty. This outcome is troubling to world order, especially to an international system that demands—indeed, counts on—a state's capacity to govern its space. Failed states have come to be feared as breeding grounds of instability, mass migration, and murder, as well as reservoirs and exporters of terror. The existence of these kinds of countries, and the instability that they harbor, not only threatens the lives and livelihoods of their own peoples, but endangers world peace.

The main problem with African international boundaries (Kaplan, 2000) is that the very notion of dividing territory with vertical lines was imposed on the continent just over a century ago by colonial mass terror.

The borders established [at the Berlin Conference] had little to do with geography or the lines that separated ethnic groups. The concept of linear boundaries did exist in Africa before partition, but it was merely one of a number of ways of dividing political space. In general, African pre-colonial polities were far more fluid than European states. In order to cope with the harsh natural environment, flexibility proved to be a far more effective method of political organization than fixed Western-style states. Where drought or disease struck one ethnic group, a state of any size was able to contract or even move itself wholesale. Political authority tended to follow trade routes, as with the Swahili in East Africa, and sovereignty was invested in people rather than land. The colonial division of Africa removed this flexibility and eventually led to the creation of almost 50 new African states, which were defined by fixed international boundaries. All such constructs are intrinsically artificial, but as the political map of Africa is relatively recent, those stresses and strains are bound to exert themselves in international relations.

Therefore, it is easy to understand why nearly every border in Africa has been disputed at some point in its history. Most of these claims date back to the colonial era, resulting from the uncertainty in the colonial administrative boundaries and lack of information about the continent's geography. In the early nineteenth century, it was hardly crucial where these lines fell exactly, since they usually passed through sparsely populated areas or mountainous ones that were largely unexplored and practically beyond colonial administrative control. Since most of these areas were under the domain of European colonialists as parceled out during the Berlin Conference, there was little reason to undertake precise border delineation on the continent. Upon independence, most of the emerging states in the region accepted the principle of *uti possedetis*, which provides that newly decolonized states should inherit the colonial administrative borders that they held at the time of independence. However, there was disagreement over what constituted evidence of such 'possession.' According to one view, only European legal documents could define borders (*uti possedetis juris*); but another view posited that lands actually held at the time of independence were the basis for continued possession (*uti possedetis facto*). For example, Ethiopia claimed large stretches of land beyond the borders that were stipulated in treaties, simply because it had the strongest claim to their 'control.'

For these reasons, borders in Africa have been disputed at one point or another, at times resulting in bloody armed confrontations (Zartman, 2001). The few boundaries that apparently never have been disputed often involve countries that were very unevenly matched in terms of standard measures of power at the time, such as population and military personnel and expenditures. In highly contentious border disputes, resolution has often taken decades, in some cases more than a century. Some territorial disputes were articulated only many years after independence, and after further exploration, as well as an initial period of state consolidation. The case of Somalia illustrates just why many of these disputes become violent and seemingly intractable, especially when it touches on ethnicity.

In other words, cartography is essential to grasping both the forces within Africa and the natural and political constraints, which continue to place this region at a disadvantage in the global order. This disadvantage also places the continent at the mercies of marauding transnational terrorists, drug-traffickers, smugglers, and all sorts of adventurers. Questions of what, why, and how plague and bedevil any discussions about issues of identity in Africa. But, as Mercer (1990, p. 4) rightly points out, identity 'only becomes an issue when it is in crisis, when something assumed to be fixed, coherent and stable is replaced by the expectancy of doubt and uncertainty.' The African continent is undergoing a crisis of identity. The concepts of nationhood, statehood and citizenship have undergone different interpretations in political discourse. Attempts have been made to answer such questions as: What is the nation in Africa? Where is the nation in Africa? What constitutes citizenship in Africa? Why was there genocide in Rwanda? Why has the Somali State collapsed? Is there anything like African identity? Or, has it any identifiable hallmarks?

Question of ethnicity and mass terror

Identity issues have historically been bloodletting in Africa (Nnoli, 1995, 1989). But, what is identity? Webster's dictionary states that identity is the distinguishing character or personality of an individual. Identity begins with our names, addresses, family groups, and cultural backgrounds, but how does it grow from there? Is identity how we see ourselves or how others see us? Is identity what we are or what we would like to be? Do we form our own identity or do others form it for us? Can identity be changed? Why is it important to express our identity?

These are not idle questions. The massacre of nearly one million Tutsi and moderate Hutus in Rwanda between April and June 1994 is instructive in any attempts to understand the phenomenon of mass terror. The Government of President Habyarimana had prepared the ground for such reckless carnage. 'The Manifesto of The Bahutu' published in *Kangura* (January 1991), referred to the Tutsi as 'foreigners.' They were identified as Rwanda's only source of ills and had to 'return home' if the country's problems were to be solved. This case leads us to one simple conclusion. And this conclusion is that an understanding of the nature of ethnicity, as well as of the origins and evolution of ethnic conflict, is essential for an understanding of ways to address and prevent such conflicts. Ethnicity, of course, is only one of the many ways in which people identify themselves: family, community, nation, class, occupation, gender, age and other group characteristics also form different layers of identity. People constantly change the focus of their identity, depending on where they are, what they are doing and whom they are with.

But ethnicity is distinct from other identifying characteristics in a number of ways. Ethnic diversity is a feature of virtually all societies. But how such diversity is perceived and the importance attached to it are constantly changing. The same ethnic markers—physical characteristics, cultural practices or religious beliefs—may be virtually ignored in one society, while they are considered extremely significant in another. The significance attached to ethnic differences rarely corresponded to objective differences. Collective memory of historical inter-ethnic relations is influenced by present circumstances and objectives.

Furthermore, ethnicity—perhaps more than other types of identity—has the potential to become totalizing, that is, to displace other loyalties and obligations and become the central basis of identity. At times, some segments of a society may choose to place primacy on ethnicity, so that people, whether of the same ethnic group or not, feel constrained to submerge their other identities and submit to the cultural traits of the dominant group. In such circumstances, ethnic conflict becomes likely: people's identities and alliances take on a single rather than a multiple focus. This new focus easily leads to a deepening and hardening of social divisions. Because of this capacity to claim primacy over other types of group loyalties, ethnicity can be a deeply emotional form of mobilization.

The ties that bind individuals belonging to different ethnic groups—those of place of residence, occupation, class or gender, for instance—lose their hold, allowing a demonization or dehumanization of those considered to be 'the other' that would not be possible if more flexible and holistic types of social identification were maintained. In extreme cases, other groups are characterized almost as if they were a different species, leading, in the worst instances, to a double standard of morality, atrocities and genocide as in Rwanda in 1994. Ethnicity becomes a powerful mobilizer when ethnic distinction is believed to be genetically given and unchangeable, and thus to necessitate eternal conflict. While it is important to recognize that this is how ethnic conflict is seen by many involved, ethnicity should not be reduced to eternal, genetically determined difference.

The weakness with this eternal view is that it fails to recognize the cognitive element of ethnic identity, which opens up possibilities for change. In this view, what groups consider to be their collective memory is often a function of their current social relations, social status and political aspirations. This has important policy implications: if collective memory is not lodged in some sort of 'objective' history, it is not immutable and is thus not a perpetual stumbling block to progress in ethnic relations.

Most of Africa is still basically a peasant society, confronted with sheer endless risks and insecurity, related to the climate, the exposure to the world economy, the political and military situation and killer diseases like malaria, and the AIDS pandemic. To survive in these rather adverse circumstances fall-back networks are of crucial importance and many African peasants (and urbanites!) have invested a lot of energy in broad and diverse social security networks. The basis for most of these networks is the extended family, nested in clans and further nested in ethnic groups. Decades of 'nation building' beyond ethnic loyalties have in most cases not resulted in a weakening of the ethnic loyalty. To the contrary, ethnic loyalties have strengthened in the recent decades of economic and political-military crisis situations. Africa's rapid urbanization did not result in a weakening of the ethnic ties either. To the contrary, urban migrants often maintain very strong links with their 'tribal background' and are often living among ethnic colleagues and organize their urban life often along ethnic lines. Many members of the urban elites all over Africa are nowadays part of 'cultural associations' (or '*associations des originaires*') fostering their links with a certain (rural) home area. The democratization and related freedom of association after 1989 mainly seems to have formed 'ethnic' unions, and parties, with urban elites playing major roles (Geschiere, 1997, pp. 3–4). Many 'break-away' religions (a remarkable 'growth sector' of African culture, and economy, both breaking away from the Christian and from the Islamic mainstream) are organized along ethnic lines, and have their services in 'local' languages.

In the political arena 'tribal' patronage is an important force and leading ethnic groups often need to balance their access to power by making and breaking political alliances with ethnic brokers from other ethnic groups. Democratization, which swept over Africa's political landscape after 1990, in many places resulted in the appearance or re-appearance of ethnic political parties (see Dietz and Foeken, 1994, for examples about Kenya and Cameroon, and Dietz and Foeken, 1999, for an analysis of Kenya).

Decentralization, en vogue in donor circles since the mid 1980s (see Wunch and Olowu, 1995), often resulted in the strengthening of ethnically-based local elites, at the expense of local minority groups. Autonomy then means exclusion for 'different' ethnic groups. The fate of the Peulh (or Fulani) in many West-African areas has become precarious, partly because of the localization of rules of access to resources, under the political patronage of sedentary groups which have long been oppressed by these same Peulh in former times, but who have now gained political dominance, based on their demographic strength and democratic elections (Azury, 1998). In the era of 'national unity,' just after independence, the centralized states corrected these tendencies of ethnic exclusivity, sometimes by waging a war against 'break-aways' (e.g., the bloody struggle in Katanga and Biafra). For more than thirty years the Organization of African Unity resisted the restructuring of Africa's political landscape. The OAU strongly favored the maintenance of the territorial organization of late colonial times, with the exception of some former trust areas of the League of Nations, and later the United Nations, which got a chance to vote for their new state (in Cameroon/Nigeria, Togo/Ghana), and with the exception of Somalia, Tanganyika/Zanzibar and Ethiopia/Eritrea which were united.

These historical examples demonstrate the centrality of ethnicity as a fundamental force in Africa. Every African belongs to one particular ethnic group or the other. Ethnicity refers to a subjective perception of common origins, historical memories, ties, and aspirations (Chazan, Lewis, Mortimer, Rothchild and Stedman, 1999, p. 108). Ethnicity focuses more on sentiments of origin and descent, rather than the geographical considerations of a nation (Thomson, 2000, p. 58).

The concept of ethnicity is a complex one. Ethnic consciousness on its own is not a problem. It becomes a problem when it is transformed into hostile prejudice directed against other people or groups. The consciousness of ethnicity is one of the consequences of colonialism. Colonialism established a new ethnic identity, which has become a permanent feature in Africa. Colonial ideology had dictated that Africans understood themselves essentially in ethnic terms. In describing the situation among the Ibo of Nigeria, Colson (1981, p. 29) observed:

> The Ibo communities may have felt some common identification as against communities of non-Ibo speakers, but this was probably minimal since they had no common name for themselves nor any tradition of a former unity. Ibo became a self-conscious unity only after they had been identified as such by foreigners who perceived common features of language and custom despite the manifest.

Colonialism brought about the emergence of 'ethnic groups' made up of different 'tribal' entities. For instance, an Ijebu man in Nigeria became to be called a 'Yoruba' man just as an Oyo man, despite the differences in dialects (Nnoli, 1978). Colonialism accomplished the arbitrary division of Africa into a series of artificial units. Some ethnic units however found themselves living on different sides of the colonial borders.

A simple look at ethnicity reveals a situation whereby members of a particular group mobilizes and aggregates their interests in competition with other groups, particularly for economic and/or political gains. As Osaghae notes, 'colonialism brought about the intensification of competition among ethnic and other groups for the scares resources and benefits of modernization. This competition not only made latent and dominant conflicts manifest, it also heightened existing ones and, in some cases, "created" new divisions' (Osaghae, 1994, p. 230). Thus, a closer look reveals the inherent danger in ethnic identity. Ethnicity can take the form of the domination of the state by one ethnic group to the exclusion of others. It can also take the form of competition between different ethnic groups for power and resources. Ethnicity provides the opportunity for conflicts over the distribution of power and resources. Ethnicity in some cases in Africa has turned out to have tragic consequences. War has stemmed out of ethnic ideologies, giving birth to programs of extermination. There are cases of ethnic cleansing, whereby a particular ethnic group sees another particular ethnic group as a threat and determines to remove them from a particular territory. This usually leads to war, especially since the other group will definitely put up resistance. A clear example of this is the conflict between Rwanda and Burundi. The two countries were under German rule between 1885 and 1918, before they were later entrusted to Belgium. Despite the fact that the Tutsi were in the minority, they constituted the ruling group. When Rwanda obtained independence in 1962, power shifted into the hands of the Hutu. The Hutu developed an ideology of politicized ethnicity in retaliation (De Waal, 2000, p. 45) for their earlier subjugation, exploitation and victimization. Burundi also became independent in 1962, but as a kingdom ruled by a chief. The chief was overthrown in 1966 by Tutsis from another group different from his own. After an uprising by the Hutus in 1972, the Tutsis killed them in large numbers. To date both countries are engaged in an endless war. This is a clear-cut case of ethnicity-generated genocide in Africa. One of the important factors to this war is that of citizenship. The Hutus consider themselves as the insiders (nationals) and the Tutsi are considered as outsiders both in Burundi and Rwanda (Oomen, 1997, p. 154). The Tutsi were believed to have migrated from Ethiopia about 400 years ago, thus, they had no right to citizenship and the Hutus want them to leave.

Even within the ethnic groups, there is usually no guarantee of bliss and conflict free relationships. All individuals in the ethnic group may not share the same ideology or subscribe to an ethnic cause. There are cases of serious conflicts among ethnic groups in Africa. A case in point is the perpetual conflict between the Ifes and Modakes, both members of the Yoruba ethnic group in Nigeria. These two groups have taken to killing themselves over the right of access to certain land borders between them.

However, this is not to conclude that the whole essence of ethnicity is negative. As Ake (1992) has argued, it is not clear that ethnicity by itself generates conflict or that it is inherently threatening. According to him, one may prefer one's kinsfolk or one's own community without being antagonistic to others. Deng also pointed out that 'it is never the mere differences of identity based on ethnic grounds that generate conflict, but the consequences of those differences in sharing power and the related distribution of resources and opportunities' (Cohen and Deng, 1998, p. 21). Ethnic differences do not always translate into open conflicts. Ethnic differences become charged when they are utilized for political and/or economic ends. The death toll of 2.5 million given by the International Rescue Committee in May 2001 concerning the struggle of entrepreneurs in Congo attests to the gruesome result of the war for looting rights in that devastated country.

Stateless societies?

Most of the central and southern regions of pre-colonial Africa have been described as stateless societies. These societies were considered stateless in the sense of not having formal state structures according to Europeans. It is not because they lacked political organization. In the few places where it was believed states existed, they were considered to be less defined. But there existed powerful kingdoms and empires with strong political organizations such as the Karnem-Bornu, Songhai, Oyo and Fulani empires. Africans interacted with themselves on the basis of economic and social activities. Africans went about their businesses and affairs without a consciousness of differences. This is not to say that pre-colonial Africa was without its problems. Inter-group and intra-group conflicts existed, but these involved groups, which were closely knit at the lower level and integrated under a powerful chieftain at the higher level (Osaghae, 1994, p. 228). One of the characteristics of these wars was the capturing of slaves. During wars in Africa, properties were destroyed, people were killed and many were taken as slaves. The number of slaves captured more often determined the level of conquests. These slaves were made to work on plantations and often as domestic hands. Slaves were sold to farmers who needed hands on their farms and plantations. Yet, this did not bring a gap or consciousness in the mind of the African. An African proverb says that the only difference between the birth of a slave and that of an heir is the circumstance.

Few scholars today would not regard the state of African societies and their political economies as regrettable and a serious embarrassment. After decades of costly struggle to rid themselves of the indignity of colonial domination, people in many African countries find themselves caught up in civil wars, brutal military or civilian dictatorships, economic degradation, helplessness and hopelessness. Even where there are semblances of parliamentary democracy, the requisite rule of law, freedom of the judiciary, the press, and association by individuals are often missing.

One may trace this African problem or dilemma as one may deem it, partially to the diversity of ethnic groups, many of which were forcibly and incongruously placed under common central governments by the Berlin Act of 1885. Most of these boundaries are not consistent with ethnic identities.

The picture, which emerges from this situation is a consistent logic of the 'Hobbesian jungle' in which life is 'solitary, poor, nasty, brutish, and short.' It is in such Hobbesian jungles that transnational terrorism finds both its sanctuary and recruits. That situation results from the exercise of unlimited powers by governments in the name of 'national unity;' hence the Lockean prescription of governments whose powers are constitutionally limited or the logic of John Locke's argument for constitutionally restrained governments as a means of preserving individual liberty might be the most suitable approach in this era of globalization.

Colonial determinants of Africa's weakness

Then came Western influence. The West began to take advantage of Africans even before the onset of colonialism. The Atlantic slave trade transported up to fifteen million people from Africa to work on the plantations of the Caribbean and the Americas, and more died in the process of capture, or during transit (Thomson, 2000, p. 16). The great 'scramble for Africa' saw the continent carved out and shared between the European powers. France favored North, West and Central Africa; Britain claimed great chunks of West, East, central and Southern Africa; Portugal took the territories of Angola, Mozambique and Guinea Bissau; Belgium got the Congo, Zaire and later Rwanda and Burundi; Italy established control in Libya, Eritrea, part of Somalia and briefly Ethiopia; Spain got north Morocco, the Spanish Sahara and Spanish Guinea; Germany gained areas in the south-west and the east, as well as the Cameroons and Togoland. Germany lost its territories due to its defeat in the First World War and the League of Nations distributed these territories among the other colonial powers.

European colonization of Africa followed a long history of contact between the two continents. Ancient Egyptian trade in the Mediterranean predates recorded history, and contact between Europe and other parts of North Africa dates back to the Greco-Roman period. Not until the 15th century, however, did the Portuguese establish trading posts on the sub-Saharan African shoreline. Although some early ports, such as Cape Town, became permanent settlements, the majority served as little more than entrepôts for the exchange of African and European goods. Over the next 400 years Europeans acquired slaves, gold, ivory, and later agricultural commodities from coastal traders and rulers, but—with the exception of South Africa and a handful of Portuguese holdings—made few attempts to settle or otherwise control the interior. By the second half of the 19th century, however, rapidly industrializing European economies needed reliable access to natural resources, new markets for their manufactured goods, and new sites for the investment of finance capital. The vast, mineral-rich African continent had the potential to offer all three.

Earlier European conquests of Asia and the New World had demonstrated the risks and costs of colonial occupation, leaving most late-nineteenth-century European rulers initially reluctant to attempt the same in Africa. It would certainly have been easier and cheaper to maintain established trade relations with the African merchants and rulers who, since the abolition of the transatlantic slave trade in 1807, had been transporting vast quantities of agricultural commodities—cocoa, peanuts, palm oil—to coastal towns such as Porto-Novo and Dakar. But African middlemen (and women) were not always amenable to the Europeans' terms of trade, and African rulers were in many cases preoccupied by internal power struggles and wars with neighboring states. Equally important, European powers viewed the quickening pace of their own neighbors' trade and exploratory expeditions in Africa—such as Richard Burton's voyages through East Africa, French expeditions up the river Niger, and Heinrich Barth's travels throughout central and northern Africa—as an indication that preemptive action was necessary, before a rival power established claims to valuable territory.

Thus, during the late nineteenth century 'scramble for Africa,' even leaders with little prior interest in colonization, such as German Chancellor Otto von Bismarck, staked claims to the continent. Meanwhile, Christian missionaries' calls for European intervention to end African slavery and 'barbaric' practices (such as human sacrifice in the kingdom of Dahomey) provided a moral rationale for European political and economic ambitions. These ambitions were officially legitimated and negotiated at the Berlin Conference of 1884–1885, when European leaders agreed to partition the African continent into neatly bordered 'spheres of influence.' Rapid conquest and treaty-making followed. By 1900, fewer than 30 years after the scramble had started, almost 90 percent of Africa was under European control.

Just as quickly, European powers were confronted with the basic problem of colonial occupation: how to rule effectively and cheaply over a foreign subject population? Although metropolitan governments clearly had to invest in the initial occupation, it was anticipated that colonial administrations would become self-sufficient. In other words, they were expected to establish a system of rule that would generate revenue but not revolt. European colonial powers struggled to find this ideal system for the next half century.

Colonialism brought about the establishment of rigid territorial and regional boundaries which cut across existing political, social, ethnic and religious borders (Chabal, 1992, p. 41). With colonialism came identity consciousness, which was manifested in the separation of the citizen from the subject. The colonial masters, seeking a good way to consolidate their powers and to make their task easier, came up with two solutions: direct and indirect rule. Direct rule connoted a single legal order defined by the 'civilized' laws of Europe. Although 'natives' would have to conform to European laws, only those 'civilized' would have access to European rights

(Mamdani, 1996, p. 16). Thus, 'civil society' then was one reserved for the 'civilized,' and from which the 'uncivilized' was excluded. The new colonial states were divided into colonies and protectorates. The Europeans settled in the colonies and the natives were restricted to the protectorates. Defending this arrangement, Lugard (1965, pp. 149–150) argued:

> On the one hand the policy does not impose any restriction on one race which is not applicable to the other. A European is as strictly prohibited from living in the native reservation, as a native is from living in the European quarter. On the other hand, since this feeling exists, it should in my opinion be made abundantly clear that what is aimed at is a segregation of social standards, and not a segregation of races. The Indian or the African gentleman who adopts the higher standard of civilization and desires to partake in such immunity from infection as segregation may convey, should be as free and welcome to live in the civilized reservation as the European, provided of course, that he does not bring with him a concourse of followers. The native peasants often share his hut with his goat, or sheep, or fowls. He loves to drum and dance at night, which deprives the European of sleep.

This was a clear show of racial segregation, though Lugard made an effort to deny this. It makes one want to ask: What were the Europeans doing in Africa in the first place? If the African drumming were a disturbance, why did they leave the tranquility of their homeland to come and be disturbed by the noise of the Africans? This chapter is therefore looking at these exploratory questions.

European concessionary companies

One of the earliest approaches to colonial rule in Africa was to delegate the task to one or more 'concessionary companies.' In German East Africa (present-day mainland Tanzania), French Equatorial Africa, and the Belgian King Leopold's Congo (later the Belgian Congo, present-day Democratic Republic of the Congo), for example, the metropolitan powers granted private companies large concessions of territory for economic activities such as mining, rubber-tapping, plantation agriculture, and railroad construction. The companies were typically also allowed to set up their own systems of taxation and labor recruitment. Although the concessionary system allowed European governments to occupy and exploit vast regions with a minimum of state financing and personnel, it proved untenable as a long-term solution. Especially in Central Africa, companies' use of forced labor and brutal discipline decimated regional populations, provoked public outrage in Europe, and often generated none of the anticipated profits. By the early twentieth century, most European governments were limiting the powers of the concessionary companies and establishing their own colonial administrations.

Direct rule

Most discussions of colonial rule distinguish between 'direct' and 'indirect rule.' Although the defining principles of the two forms of rule differed considerably, in practice direct rule administrations—most of which were in French colonies—incorporated elements of indirect rule, especially during the later colonial era.

Under direct rule, colonies were divided into districts administered by European appointees. In French West Africa, the chief district administrator, *the commandant de cercle*, was responsible for regional tax collection, labor and military recruitment, public works, education, local court cases, and the execution of dictates handed down from the colony's governor. Although Africans staffed the lower levels of the commandant's bureaucracy, most of the top officials were European. The commandant was also expected to maintain public order and discourage offensive or 'backward' local customs. Thus direct rule was seen as a means of 'civilizing' as well as controlling African populations.

Frequently, regional administrative borders cut through preexisting African polities and ethnic communities. In parts of French West Africa, these borders marked a deliberate policy to divide and weaken militarily powerful groups such as the Baule and the Fon, who for years had resisted foreign occupation. Another part of this policy, at least in the years during and after conquest, was a campaign to dethrone the 'great chiefs' of these and other African kingdoms and replace them with more malleable appointees. In general, these traditional authorities were viewed not only as political threats but as obstacles to the 'civilizing mission' of direct rule.

Direct rule encountered at least three practical problems. First, European governments lacked the personnel needed to administer their African colonies effectively. Although schools of colonial administration were well established in Europe by the early twentieth century, debilitating diseases and harsh climates discouraged officers from seeking posts in

Africa. European colonies often had fewer than one colonial officer for every 22,000 Africans, as was the case in Kenya in 1921. The Belgian Congo had a mere 2,384 officials for an African population of 9.4 million; French West Africa, with an African population of 15 million, employed only 3,660 French personnel.

Second, these administrators were responsible not only for large subject populations, but for vast territories. Travel over long distances was slow and arduous, and communication difficult. As a result, colonial governors had little contact with remote areas, where district administrators often proved incapable or uninterested in carrying out the dictates of their superiors.

Finally, colonial officials' limited knowledge of local languages and customs, combined with their often total lack of legitimacy, undermined their ability to recruit labor, collect taxes, or carry out other administrative duties effectively. In the end, both the 'great chiefs' and local village chiefs—both of which had greater legitimacy and more local-level contacts—proved indispensable to the project of colonial administration. For all these reasons, most European powers began to modify their approach to colonial rule in the early twentieth century.

Indirect rule

The alternative method, first adopted by the British, was to rule indirectly through 'traditional' African authorities. The logic of indirect rule was first articulated by F. J. D. Lugard, the high commissioner of the British protectorate of Northern Nigeria. Based on his observations of the Sokoto Caliphate and the kingdom of Buganda, Lugard recommended that colonial powers take advantage of existing African authority structures. In his book The Dual Mandate in British Tropical Africa, Lugard argued that Africans were better off ruled through their own 'traditional systems' and in accordance with the 'customary laws' of their own 'tribe.' Under indirect rule, 'tribal' authorities rather than European personnel would be given responsibility for regional administration and justice. Assumed to represent the highest of Africans' abilities, these kings and chiefs were expected to draw on customary laws to maintain obedience and public order, while also encouraging their subjects to appreciate modern European values.

Lugard emphasized the moral qualities of indirect rule, but it also offered—at least in theory—a number of practical advantages. Foremost, it promised to be cheap: African chiefs could raise the money for their own salaries from their own subjects. Indirect rule also appeared safer and more effective: by co-opting the chiefs' inherited legitimacy, European colonial powers hoped both to improve their ability to carry out routine functions, such as tax collection and labor recruitment, and to avoid large-scale revolts.

Above all, indirect rule assumed the sanctity of the tribe. In much of French West Africa, colonial administrations that had spent years trying to break down tribal authority structures ultimately sought to rehabilitate them. Besides locating and strengthening traditional authorities, colonial administrations endeavored to identify and delineate each tribe's homeland and customs. Often, they called on missionaries and anthropologists for assistance.

Indirect rule worked best in the regions where strong and highly organized states were already in place, like Northern Nigeria, and where the recognized authorities, like the Sokoto caliph, welcomed European collaboration. On the whole, however, erroneous assumptions about the nature of 'tribal' identity, authority, and customary law undermined the effectiveness and ultimately the sustainability of indirect rule.

Fundamental to the logic of indirect rule, for example, was the belief that Africa was comprised of hundreds of mutually exclusive, geographically distinct, and centrally ruled 'tribes.' In reality, African cultural identities were complex and dynamic. African polities also varied enormously in size and structure, from the hierarchical, multiethnic kingdoms of Kongo, Buganda, and Dahomey and the Sokoto Caliphate, to the loosely federated chieftaincies of the Haya people, to the village-based chiefdoms and councils of 'stateless' peoples such as the Baule in the Côte d'Ivoire, the Igbo of Nigeria, and the Nyamwezi of Tanzania. Nomadic groups, such as the Berbers and Tuaregs of West Africa, also confounded European efforts to assign Africans to 'tribal homelands.'

European colonial officials handled the ambiguities by imposing their own categories and by inventing tribal authority structures where none existed. In 1930 the British administration of Tanganyika (present-day Tanzania) issued the Native Administration Memorandum on Native Courts, which defined tribes as 'cultural units possessing a common language, a single social system, and an established customary law.' Assuming that German colonialism must have destroyed Tanganyika's tribal kingdoms, the British administration grouped disparate communities of Sukuma people under a centralized chief. In Libya the Italian administration randomly divided the Bedouins in 1929 and appointed them to tribes and subtribes. In Ruanda/Burundi—the Belgian government assigned Africans passes labeling them as either 'Hutu' or 'Tutsi,' thus creating a rigid distinction between previously contextual identities.

Identifying 'authentic' tribal authorities proved no less complicated. Where there was no obvious tribal ruler, colonial administrations summarily appointed one—typically a cooperative village 'big man.' Some nonhierarchical peoples, such as the Sagara of present-day Tanzania, were placed under the authority of a neighboring kingdom—in their case, the Zaramo—and expected to adopt its language and customs. In Kenya, Maasai religious leaders were appointed as chiefs, even though they had not previously held administrative responsibilities. In Senegal the French, despite concerns about the potential for mass Islamic resistance movements, reinforced the power of the marabouts (or holy men) of the Mourides brotherhood, largely because of their capacity to mobilize large numbers of young disciples for peanut farming.

Even where European colonial powers had no trouble identifying chiefs and kings, they were not always satisfied with them. In Dahomey, the French replaced three 'independent-minded' rulers within the first ten years of colonial rule. In Rhodesia (present-day Zimbabwe) in 1927, the British administration abolished hereditary rights of succession and assumed the power to appoint chiefs, thereby minimizing the chances of chiefly disobedience. Elsewhere, chiefs considered unsuitable were replaced with others deemed more authentic. In southern Upper Volta (present-day Burkina Faso), for example, the French replaced the Kong Jula they had originally appointed as canton chiefs with members of a local Zara clan (neither, in fact, had a long history of political domination in the region). Colonial administrators' ongoing efforts to find compliant local authorities meant that kings and chiefs enjoyed little job security.

However tenuous their employment, many African rulers were granted unprecedented powers by colonial administrations, often at the expense of preexisting judicial and advisory bodies. In precolonial Swaziland, for example, the king's power was checked by both the queen mother and a council composed of royal family members, village headmen, and commoners. Under British rule, women and commoners were excluded from the council, and the king's decisions were subject to approval only by the British administration. In many parts of Africa, chiefs were expected to allocate land and adjudicate local disputes, both responsibilities that had previously often belonged to lineage heads or village councils. Backing up chiefs' new powers was the implicit threat of military force, provided by colonial armies and police.

It soon became clear that this arrangement was susceptible to abuse. As George Padmore, the Caribbean Pan-Africanist observed in 1936 that the chief in Africa was the law, subject to only one higher authority, the white official stationed in his state as adviser. According to him no oriental despot ever had greater power than the black chiefs he saw as tyrants, thanks to the support, which they received from the white officials who quietly kept in the background (Hansberry, 1981). Some chiefs took advantage of their powers to collect additional taxes, recruit extra labor for their own plantations, and extract exorbitant tributes and services from their subjects. One German official in Tanganyika, for example, estimated that many chiefs were collecting seven times the required tax, and keeping the surplus. In the 1920s, the British and French attempted to prevent chiefs from taking excessive cuts from local revenue by giving them fixed salaries. In general, however, chiefs known to be corrupt who were otherwise cooperative were usually allowed to remain in office.

Not all chiefs abused their powers, of course, but most found their legitimacy tested by the duties of their office. Collecting taxes, requisitioning crops, recruiting youths for compulsory labor service and military service—only the most gifted leaders managed to carry out these tasks without provoking resentment, rebellion, or flight. In colonial Upper Volta, for example, tens of thousands of Mossi youths responded to their chiefs' efforts to recruit them for road and agricultural projects by fleeing south to the Gold Coast (present-day Ghana)

Finally, colonial administration's efforts to impose indirect rule were confounded by the ambiguities of so-called 'customary law.' Lugard and other administrators assumed each 'tribe' possessed a set of stable, universally understood laws. In fact, many African societies' laws were contested and often changing, and the era defined by Europeans as 'traditional Africa'—the nineteenth century—was a period of extraordinary upheaval. Shaka Zulu's conquests in southern Africa, the formation of the Sokoto Caliphate in West Africa, the rise of the trading empires of Msiri and Tippu Tip in East and Central Africa, and the holy wars of North Africa—all had altered the political landscapes as well as belief systems across the African continent.

Whether or not 'customary' laws were actually very old, most were not written down. As a result, colonial administrators consulted with chiefs, elders, missionaries, and anthropologists, all of whom described customs according to their own views and interests. Chiefs, for example, had an interest in strengthening their own authority to tax and fine subjects, while elders typically benefited from laws that allowed them control over youths and women. Missionaries often argued for the preservation for certain customs (as did anthropologists) but emphasized the injustices of those that interfered with their own evangelical objectives, such as arranged marriages.

Faced with a hodge-podge of often contradictory accounts, European officials codified those customary laws that seemed most likely to assure their own political, economic, and social objectives. Others they rejected entirely. In Rhodesia, for example, British commissioners were scandalized to learn that Ndebele women were allowed to marry whom they pleased. Assuming that the group's traditional laws must have been forgotten or swept away, the colonial commissioner brought in a copy of the Natal Native Code of 1891 (first applied in the Natal colony of present-day South Africa) to teach them how to behave like traditional Ndebele. Colonial administrations outlawed other customs that offended European sensibilities, such as slavery, but were often unable to enforce or uninterested in enforcing their own prohibitions.

Although the institution of customary law helped colonial officials win the cooperation of customary authorities, it did not prevent ongoing challenges to those authorities, especially at the local level. As the expansion of transportation systems and the market economy provided new opportunities for individual mobility and employment, formerly dependent members of rural communities—women and young men, in particular—often contested or simply disregarded the customary laws that dictated who they owed labor or who they could marry. Village chiefs and elders found it increasingly difficult to exert control over their own kin members. Especially after World War II, high rates of urban migration placed more and more Africans outside the jurisdiction of customary law, and into workplaces and social settings where they participated in growing nationalist movements. The stability that customary law was supposed to provide was fleeting at best.

Legacies

By the late 1940s, it was clear that colonial rule in Africa could only be sustained at an unduly high cost. As the European powers prepared for decolonization, Africans across much of the continent gained voting rights and increased representation in colonial legislatures in the 1950s. Faced with a new generation of African politicians, many of them schooled in socialist thought, chiefs and kings struggled to ensure themselves a role in the postcolonial power structure. Some, such as the kings of Swaziland and Morocco, did maintain real authority; but in more radical independent states, government leaders made a concerted effort to limit the powers of chiefs and other customary authorities.

Although scholars debate the extent to which contemporary Africa's political and economic woes can be 'blamed' on colonial rule, it is clear that rigid ethnic categories created during the colonial era have become one of the greatest obstacles to nation-building and regional stability in much of Africa. The fact that the postcolonial state has for many years been one of the only reliable channels of upward mobility in Africa has also undermined the stability and effectiveness of many governments. In addition, postcolonial African states have inherited their predecessors' ambivalence toward customary authorities. Modern African politicians look to village chiefs, spiritual leaders, clan heads, and other such authorities to support their development programs as well as their political campaigns, but cannot always depend on their loyalties. Finally, customary law remains a source of fierce debate, as African states continue to grapple with the problems of defining and legislating modern civil society.

However, the introduction of indirect rule during the colonial period entailed the 'invention of tradition' and thereby led to the production of a new social topography. Convinced that 'chiefs' could play a crucial role in the achievement of the colonial project, the British and other colonial powers tried to portray them as 'natural leaders of communal societies untroubled by a plurality of political ideologies, for whom consensus was an inherited state of mind rather than an ideological weapon of social conflict' (Lonsdale, 1989, p. 132). The new consensus was precarious as it depended on the ability of the ruler to satisfy demands that emanated from his society.

The system of indirect rule was inherited by the post-colonial state. However, the determination of the state to achieve its 'hegemonic project' prompted a modification of the relations that existed between the state and traditional authority. Evidence of this was the endeavor to convert the latter into a parasite of the state (*agent d'administration*). This was a cost-efficient method of imposing the domination of the state over civil society. Preoccupied with this goal, the governing class mistook indirect rule through traditional authority as practiced by the colonial powers as an indication of decision-making motivated solely by the will of one political leader. The subjects of the various chiefs seemingly acquiesced in this form of rule in the single-party state. However, the advent of multi-party politics and the quest for 'Jacobin democracy' has ushered in an era of dissent. The politicization of the role of the chief by the state has led to a breakdown of the consensus on the structured principle on which traditional authority was predicated. In most societies, the continuous identification of the chief with the state is having an analogous effect, the divestment of his power. And the emergence of 'moral pluralism,' that signals an end to the unchallenged hegemony of communal ideologies in these societies, is aiding and abetting this process. Insofar as it satisfies consumer preferences and adheres to the principle of supply and demand, it would not be questioned.

On the whole, the colonial state ostensibly sought to justify indirect rule as an efficient way of creating a Weberian state on a legal-rational basis. But indirect rule in the post-colonial state has contributed to the generation of the neo-patrimonial state that is the antithesis of the Weberian state.

Islamic counter-terrorist resistance

While the British were trying to spread the word of Christ, Berbers and Fulanis continued to preach the Islamic faith in West Africa. Already by 1809 all the Hausa states were under Muslim rule and Sokoto was established as the Caliphate for the region. In East Africa, Islam came from the East with the rule of the Omani sultanate; but many coastal people remained Muslim even though the power of the Sultanate began to give way to the British and Germans. It is estimated that nearly two thirds of Africa would have been converted to Islam had the European powers not embarked on the 'Scramble for Africa' in the 1880s.

Islam, compared to Christianity, had a great deal more to say about the precise nature of political rule and administration. In one sense, the order imposed by Islam impressed the Europeans—the British liked to work through Muslim leaders. On the other hand, Islam also endorsed the idea of sacred war, or jihad, a war launched against nonbelievers in order to spread the word of Islam, something the British saw as a threat to colonial control.

The Muslim brotherhoods also gained many new converts. European colonialists in many cases adopted Muslim law as a unifying administrative structure, rather than the indigenous and often competing tribal customs of their artificially demarcated colonies. Islam in Africa has to varying degrees incorporated tribal and pre-Islamic practices, and the Muslims of Africa have accepted claims of several self-proclaimed Mahdis. In the twentieth century, the Islamic religion has gained more converts in Africa than has Christianity, which continue to labor under the burden of identification with European imperialism (Hodgkin, 1963, pp. 91–97).

North Africa

During Muhammad's lifetime a group of Muslims escaped Meccan persecution (615) by fleeing to Ethiopia, where the Negus gave them protection. The spread of Islam in Africa began in the seventh and eighth centuries with the Umayyads, who brought the religion to the Middle East and to the littoral of North Africa. Along the coast of Africa Islam spread among the Berbers, who joined the Muslim community and almost immediately drove north across the Mediterranean into Europe. In Morocco, Muslims founded the city of Fés (808), which soon thereafter gave refuge to Andalusian Muslims fleeing an uprising in Côrdoba. On the east coast of Africa, where Arab mariners had for many years journeyed to trade, Arabs founded permanent colonies on the offshore islands, especially on Zanzibar, in the ninth and tenth centuries. From there Arab trade-routes into the interior of Africa helped the slow acceptance of Islam and led to the development of Swahili culture and language.

In the 1880s Mohammed Ahmed, the Mahdi (The Redeemed one) established himself as a Muslim leader, and set out to establish a new society in Sudan. The British were determined to crush him. When he died he became celebrated as a martyr in many parts of the Muslim world. In Central Sudan one of the Mahdi's disciples, Rabin ibn Fadl Allah, led a resistance against the French. On his death his son followed in his footsteps and fought the French for 15 years until he died in 1901. In Libya the Sanussi Brotherhood fought the Italians tenaciously for twenty years until 1932.

West Africa

Prior to the 19th century the greatest gains made by Islam were in the lands immediately south of the Sahara. The Islamization of West Africa began when the ancient kingdom of Ghana (c. 990) extended itself into the Sahara and the Islamic center at Sanhajah. Mansa Musa (1307–1332) of Mali was among the first to make Islam the state religion. By the sixteenth century, the empire of Mali and its successor-state, Songhaj, included several Saharan centers of trade and Muslim learning, such as Timbuktu. In the region of the East Sudan, Islamic penetration followed the route of the Nile.

By about 1366, Makurra, the more northerly of the two Christian kingdoms of the East Sudan, became Islamic. The other kingdom, Aloa, was captured (c. 1504) by the Muslims (Mazrui, 1967).

In the sixteenth century the Somali conqueror Ahmad Gran unsuccessfully attempted to convert Ethiopia to Islam. In the late eighteenth and early nineteenth centuries, Africa, like the rest of the Muslim world, was swept by a wave of religious reform. Militant reformers, such as the Fulani and the followers of Hajj Omar, greatly extended the area over which Islam held sway in West Africa. Usumanu dan Fodio (1809) founded the Sokoto caliphate, which was eventually incorporated under British rule into Nigeria (Palmer, 1943; Parrinder, 1960, pp. 12–15; Parrinder, 1959, pp. 130–141).

The Tukuloor Empire, located in what is now modern Mali and Burkina Faso, was founded in the 1860s by the hugely effective and militarily successful Al Haj Umar. His son Ahmadu came under growing pressure from the French in 1880s. He tried to negotiate with them in the face of growing disunity in the Empire. The French were keen to take advantage of this and very late in the day Ahmadu decided to launch a Holy War against them, calling on Muslims throughout the region; the response was weak and he was defeated by the French in 1890.

A far more successful and formidable enemy of the French was Samori Toure who kindled some of the glory of old Mali with his Mandinka Empire, defended by an army 30,000 strong. He kept this force very mobile, constantly surprising the French and had a tremendous sense of military tactics. He used the latest quick loading guns, which his blacksmiths knew how to mend. After his death, his son was defeated by the French in 1901.

Spirit mediums

A number of rebellions against European powers were inspired by spirit mediums. This tradition of fighting off bullets with magic potions and spells goes back hundreds of years. In the nineteenth century, these acts of resistance were common throughout Africa (Knight, 1994, pp. 155, 168–175).

Maji Maji

The hated regime of cotton growing provided the impetus for rebellion against German colonial rule in Tanganika. The leader of the Maji Maji movement was Kinjikitile Ngwale, a medium possessed with a snake spirit called Hongo. He encouraged his supporters to sprinkle their bodies with magic water, known as maji maji, which they believed would protect them from bullets.

His movement spread from his base in Ngarambe, some 200 miles south from Dar-es-Salaam. Five missionaries were murdered and German reinforcements were sent in. In the end, the magic water, which they thought would protect them from the German guns failed. Thousands were killed in battle. German revenge was terrible; a scorched earth policy wiped out whole villages and all their crops. It is estimated 250,000 died from famine.

Ambuya Nehanda

The Chimurenga wars 1896–1897 in Matabeleland and Shonaland (in modern Zimbabwe) were inspired by traditional prophets and priests or svikiro. They blamed the Europeans for all hardship: the hut tax, forced labour, drought, rinderpest. The most famous svikiro was Ambuya Nehanda. Some 8,000 Africans died in these wars. Four hundred and fifty Europeans were killed.

Christian dissent

John Chilembwe was an American trained missionary who returned to his native Nyasaland (now Malawi). He believed in a new African society based on Christian values but independent of Europeans. He attacked tax and recruitment, and led an armed insurrection against the British. He was executed in 1915. In Nigeria Garrick Braide called himself Elijah II and claimed the British were about to leave Nigeria because of the war—his prophesies contributed to a revolt in Kwale Ibo.

At the early stage of independence, numerous politically unskilled African leaders encountered elite, institutional, as well as state versus society challenges. Whilst considering the African elites responses to such demands, African scholars began to refer to African states as 'neo-patrimonial' in character. Most African leaders had particularly minimum political experience, weak institutional support, and a tenuous social base.

They had to create networks to unify control versus competitive elites, build effective, extensive public institutions to create a centralized state, and regularize a society represented by diverse interest groups. In the event, some African theorists contended that the post-independence leadership sought to develop weak authoritarian states.

These [African leaders] essentially rested on the use of power of the state in order to rectify a lack of power in other respects. Much of this enterprise was directed towards the domestic arena, and in the process strained to breaking point the relationships between African states and the societies, which they sought to govern (Clapham, 1985, p. 73). That is to say, the political elites had the power to coerce, hold sway, but did not have the ability to gain compliance. They could control their society, that is, limit dissent and remain in power by means of state terror. Yet, they could not promote economic development or adhere to the rule of law simply because the people did not believe in the legitimacy of the state.

Mamdani (1996, p. 11) best clarifies this notion by arguing that 'the state has turned into a weak Leviathan, suspended above society' rather than rooted in it. The guiding principle or 'idée-maîtresse' of these neo-patrimonial states was to construct durable social alliances and manage competitive pressures from different elite groups set for stabilizing their regimes. As Clapham (1985) formulates, 'leaders gained the power to decide which groups or interests they would incorporate into the political process, and which they would exclude. In the process, politics turned into a patronage operation, governed by the need for control on the part of the ruler, and the need for access to state benefits on the part of the subordinates' (Clapham, 1985, p. 59).

In its conception, the state left by colonial regimes was a legal rational state, constructed on Max Weber's model; providing law, order, regulation, and citizenship. It was seen as representing the public interests, organized around a constitution that set the rules of the game. Notwithstanding, in reality those elements were part of the facade of the state that was inherited from the colonial state. Jackson and Rosberg (1982a, p. 24) affirm that after independence most small ex-colonial state apparatuses sooner or later were transformed into far larger neopatrimonial-type administrations (also see Jackson and Rosberg, 1986, pp. 259–282). Hence, in most cases, the post-colonial rulers initiated a strategy enabling them to have diffuse, multiple roles to regulate power.

To that effect, post-colonial leaders developed a political strategy known as 'managerial strategy,' synthesizing two main components. Its first strategic feature consisted of limiting political 'inclusion.' The preeminent elite would bring into the political apparatus popular groups from their own ethnic clique they felt were reliable (Jackson, 1987; Jackson and Rosberg, 1986).

The second scheme, referred to as 'exclusion,' aimed at excluding any challenging elite group, or manipulating out any group by giving them limited benefits. Exclusion focused primarily on personal power.

Catherine Boone (1992, p. 130) holds that, 'these changes strengthened the African state as an institution of authoritarian rule, repression, and the extraction of rural surpluses via state-monopolized commercial circuits.' In the meantime, a familiar relationship between the ruler and the people was developed. Gradually, this neo-patrimonial apparatus created a government of persons, the state becoming an expansion of the rulers' household. An analogy can be made with the Mafia, although it was operated on a much larger scale for most African states. This system of governance focused on an individual's control, personal discretion receiving more importance than the effects of rules and laws.

The point is, there was little formal laws, it was literally 'work to rule.' The very core of a neo-patrimonial state was the ruler, while the state was seen as the source of power. 'States emerged as the sole viable mechanisms through which African leaders could maintain their power and seek their other goals. The preservation and if possible strengthening of the state became the overriding priority of the government' (Clapham, 1985, p. 57). A good specimen that has illustrated this type of governance is Mobutu Sese Seko's Zaire. Mobutu Sese Seko was able to use exceptional charismatic skills, as well as traditional values, such as a 'Leopard hat' drawn from the Congolese culture to reinforce his legitimacy. Mobutu Sese Seko created an image that the citizens from Zaire wanted to emulate.

The second major element of neopatrimonialism is the patron/client relationship also identified as patronage. The patron possesses more resources and is viewed as the dominant actor, the client being the subordinate. There is usually a reciprocal exchange of favors in this relationship, a form of loyalty that stabilizes the relationship. If the patron wants votes, the client will usually vote in accordance. This clientelism enabled personal prestige and security to be protected by any external forces. It created a pyramid that descends from central ruler to client to mass constituencies. Catherine Boone asserts that, 'Patronage politics provided an instrumental, material basis for consensus—a lowest common denominator for building ruling classes, working to divert political conflicts away from broader issues concerning the purposes of state power and toward short-run competition for access to state resources' (Boone, 1992, p. 134).

In order to consolidate his power, Mobutu Sese Seko along with other leaders had to create a web of networks essential for his survival. As a result, the neo-patrimonial patron-client relationship was diversified among the most important sectors of the state, the regime, and the government. Patronage occurred within ruling parties, military agencies, the central bank, legislature, provincial administration and intelligence services. Mobutu Sese Seko, as well as Haile Selassie of Ethiopia, and Felix Houphouet-Boigny of Côte d'Ivoire proved that once they had overcome the critical, unstable phase that often elapsed after three years, they usually overridden constitutional constraints, giving them free space to act as they wanted. Haile Selassie and Houphouet-Boigny went on to reign until natural death removed the latter from office.

Accordingly, it can be argued that neo-patrimonial rule consolidated and reinforced African political leaders political control, enabling them to privately appropriate state resources, while allowing them to govern for decades. On the other hand, As Chazan, Lewis, Mortimer, Rothchild and Stedman (1999, p. 268) contend, 'Patronage politics not only induced regime instability and undermined state autonomy, but in due course also reduced state capacities.' Clapham (1985) and Jackson and Rosberg (1982b) all agree that the patronage system that was opted by most African rulers had negative effects on African states economic development. Clapham (1985, p. 59) contends that this form of leadership do not encourage production, by giving incentives in the form of economic benefits or political participation to those who create wealth. Comparatively, this system was politically strong and stable, but it also perpetuated economic instability and stagnation (Lagos, 2001).

Failure of transition to democracy

There is widespread disillusionment over democratization in Africa (Bratton and van de Walle, 1997). Following the killing of pro-democracy demonstrators in Togo on February 11, 1992, in Madagascar on August 10, in Cameroon on May 26, 1990, and in Congo-Zaire on October 1991, it is understandable while the failure of democracy even to be in sight evokes so much anger and violence of despair. It goes as far as Afro-pessimism, which, however, is based on unrealistically high expectations and yardsticks. However, the fact is that in Africa very few clearly successful democratic transitions exist. Many of these processes are in the twilight zone, in the gray world between democracy and dictatorship. On the one hand, it can be seen that a democratic transition has in fact taken place in certain countries: the constitution has been democratized, and founding elections have been held and resulted in a change of government. But it is also clear that an interaction immediately comes into play in which political freedoms are temporarily restricted and then observed again, so that we generally see more or less free elections once the first legislative period expires. An open return to authoritarianism rarely occurs: no amendment to the constitution, no military coup. The gradual changes are enacted by the democratically elected government. A change of regime the other way round, from democracy to dictatorship, is difficult to capture.

On the other hand, there are cases in which authoritarian regimes were compelled to amend the constitution and hold elections under democratic conditions, but the old government remained in power because the opposition was split up. At the same time, exercise of power is not free from human rights violations. Classifying that as democracy appears to be impossible. Certain democratic progress was in fact achieved by constitutional reforms, but far from asserted in political practice. Transition has not been completed—neither in one direction nor the other. In constitutional terms, a democracy is in place, but no-one wants to call it that.

In both examples the transition process has come to a standstill and jelled into a type of 'hybrid' regime. This is located between dictatorship and democracy and fluctuates between the two poles, with basic human rights sometimes being observed and sometimes not. For the African context, I describe this kind of rule (a sub-type of the hybrid regime) as a 'neo-patrimonial multi-party system.'

The hybrid regime has in common with democracy the fact that its access to power and its legitimation is ensured by 'free' elections. Meanwhile, the remaining civil and political human rights are not always observed and not in the same way. Human rights violations are frequent, even if not in grave or systematic ways. The decisive criteria for identifying dictatorships is that no free elections take place in them and human rights are violated in continual and systematic form.

In contrast to many more pessimistic observers, I postulate that in the past decade in Africa considerable political changes accompanied the democratization movements. To be sure, these have not led to flourishing democracy. But in many African countries there is now better protection of fundamental human rights as well as political participation and civil rights.

Opposition groups now have quite different opportunities than those that were available to them up to the mid-1980s to make themselves heard and survive both politically and physically. This means that substantially better conditions are in place for all the political forces, which wish to deepen democracy in the sense of political and social participation.

The changes can be seen, if only very roughly, in the situation of political and civil rights in many African countries, as summarized in the annual Freedom House Index. According to the index the number of regimes classified as 'not-free' has declined markedly, almost halving. By contrast, the number of 'partly free' regimes and in particular those classified as 'free' has clearly increased.

The 'free' countries are Benin, Botswana, Cape Verde, Mali, Mauritius, Namibia, São Tomé and Principe, and South Africa. However, only five or six of these eight lands can be seen as young transition countries. Botswana and Mauritius have been regarded as democratic since the 1970s, and South Africa, without doubt a transition country, is a special case within Africa. So of the more than thirty attempts to democratize the political system since the beginning of the 1990s only five can be seen as successful. The rest are obviously, as described, in an ongoing transitional situation—or they have lapsed back into dictatorship.

Peculiarities of African transitions

Only a few political scientists dealing with African studies who have tackled research on transition have pointed out its special institutional conditions in Africa (Osaghae, 1995, pp. 183–197). These conditions mean that transitions there take place on the basis of neo-patrimonial regimes. A peculiarity of this kind of transition is that in most cases it is triggered by mass political protests or at least is accompanied by them.

In principle, four varieties of authoritarian regimes in Africa can be differentiated for the period before 1989/1990:

- Military oligarchies;
- Plebiscitary one-party systems;
- Competitive one-party systems; and
- Settler oligarchies.

Neo-patrimonialism

A precise definition of the term is not at hand. The simplest way to define neo-patrimonialism is to compare it with Max Weber's term 'patrimonialism.' He used it to describe a system of rule based on administrative and military personnel who were responsible only to the ruler. Neo-patrimonialism, which is a modern form of the traditional patrimonial form of rule, is a mixed system (Eisenstadt, 1973). Here, elements of patrimonial and rational-bureaucratic rule co-exist and are sometimes interwoven.

In a patrimonial system, all ruling relationships, both political and administrative, are personal relationships. There is no difference between the private and public spheres. By contrast, under a neo-patrimonial system the differentiation of private and public is recognized (at least formally), and therefore it can be referred to publicly. In practice, however, the private and public spheres often are not separated. That means two systems, the patrimonial system of personal relationships and the legal-rational one of the bureaucracy, exist side-by-side. De facto, however, that is not so because the patrimonial system penetrates the legal-rational one and deforms the logic of its functions.

Part of the patrimonial side of neo-patrimonialism is clientelism, which develops into extended networks of political clients. Political clientelism is about exchanging or arranging certain services and/or resources in return for political support, such as votes.

Unlike patrimonial-type clientelism, neo-patrimonialism focuses less on direct exchanges between patron and client and more on the 'arrangement' of services and resources. Most of the exchanges are not in the patron's own private possession, that is, they are not directly reciprocal. He transfers public goods and/or resources. Clientelism can be based on family relationships, but also exists without such links. It can be connected with traditional social relationships, but should be understood as a modern phenomenon.

Clientelism as a safeguard against insecurity

In the African context, it is significant that client relationships are comparatively unstable. Clientelism here is understood as a strategy to secure protection and achieve objectives in order to overcome ongoing insecurity in the social context, which exists due to unpredictable state institutions and politics. For its part, this strategy contributes directly to reproduction of this insecurity if largely general and competing recourse is made to the clientele strategy. It can be successful only if uncertainty over the behavior of state institutions continues.

With respect to business and development under such rule, one can say only that public office is used to accumulate private wealth by means of informal privatization. Political power is the basis of economic power. This means that income from rents is of central importance. The market is nullified or purposefully steered, sometimes by administrative instruments, sometimes by 'private,' informal means. Political office serves not only to secure rent income. Control over the steering of this income is of central importance for retaining political power. The result of the neo-patrimonializing of the state was finally the wrecking of its own structures. This was expressed from the beginning of the 1980s by various labels such as 'weak' or 'soft' state or 'lame Leviathan.'

In the background was the ongoing crisis of the African economies from the end of the 1970s, and in their wake the structural adjustment policy of the World Bank and IMF. The worsening conflicts over the remaining state services and resources, which were argued out ever less by legal means but increasingly via clienteles and corrupt practices, did the rest to weaken public institutions. The available clientele and the services and goods which were supposed to be distributed via administrative channels became ever more meager, and the output of state-maintained patronage ever smaller. Clientelism's input to integration for the authoritarian regimes became ever more selective and weaker. The implications are obvious: the elite not only ignored laws and decrees; bureaucratic and public norms and rules were openly and informally violated as a matter of almost daily routine.

Roots of neo-patrimonialism

The neo-patrimonializing of the state, however, was not first the result of the economic crisis in recent decades. Patrimonial systems characterized the pre-colonial world, and neo-patrimonial ruling practices the colonial era. The colonial state was not a modern rational state but a mixed structure of a rational and traditional one. British indirect rule defined the phenomenon and was also practiced in a very similar form in other colonies.

The rational state existed only as a core in the central administrations of the colonies' capitals. To deal with the native 'subjects' and secure its rule, the colonial administration used local authorities, meaning genuine or fictitious indigenous rulers. This realm of indirect rule remained the domain of patrimonial rule in which the local rulers confirmed by the colonial power could exercise their own power personally, arbitrarily, clientele-oriented and corruptly—within the limits set by the colonial state.

But the European administration also took an authoritarian, despotic and arbitrary line with the lowest level of the indigenous people. District officers and *commandants de cercle* had far-reaching powers and could scarcely be controlled by the central colonial administration.

The majority of the population in the colonies were mostly 'spared' direct contact with legal-rational administration until after the Second World War. Only later in the wake of decolonization was the bureaucracy expanded and staffed by local people. This, however, took place to an insufficient degree and only for a comparatively short period. A culture of legal-rational administration was able at best to develop in only rudimentary form. With independence, the patrimonial, clientele logic of rule spread to the remaining core of rational administrative bureaucracy.

Thus neo-patrimonialism means a form of rule for which a constitutive insecurity is dominant. State action is unpredictable for all actors other than the top patron, such as the president. Everyone strives by different means to make the uncertain system calculable for his private purposes. That means the state institutions can only fulfill in a limited way their universal mission in the sense of serving public well-being. And that in turn means they lack legitimacy and practical recognition among the people.

Instead, particularistic politics predominate. Thus, besides formal politics and the legal-rational institutions there is a second field of informal politics that seriously interferes with and harms the way the formal institutions function. Informal politics has reached such a dimension that one must speak of institutionalized informality.

The neo-patrimonial legacy

The transitions in Africa of the last ten years took place amid conditions of extreme institutional insecurity. A change of regime is always a situation of great uncertainty for all involved. The weak state does not suddenly become 'stronger' due to democratization. On the contrary, the democratically legitimized state inherits the institutional legacy of the neo-patrimonial state. The actors continue to have two institutionalized reference points: formal and informal politics and their respective institutions. New, transition-related uncertainty is added to the institutionalized insecurity of the old regime. At the same time, uncertainty is not confined to the old and new formal institutions; it also affects the old clientele networks because the change in power initially makes the established networks ineffective in their previous functions.

The old rulers and their friends will not support democracy. But the new 'friends of democracy' now in power also violate democratic principles often enough. Frequently, they were once part of the old regime and were merely pushed out of its clientele structure. Everyone was politically socialized in the neo-patrimonial system.

Generally speaking, the new 'friends of democracy' are confronted with a fundamental 'dilemma of candidature,' as Mainwaring, O'Donnell and Valenzuela called it in 1992. The first task is to institutionalize democracy, and the second is to retain power. In principle, it is not easy to reconcile the two. In view of the prevailing neo-patrimonial political culture, it proves to be an especially heavy burden.

Contradiction: Clientelism and rule of law

An interest in institutionalizing democracy demands that the democrats pursue a policy of reform that will strengthen all formal institutions of rule and give them practical legitimacy. That means that all interests of the rule of law must be supported. Thus, not only a proper judicial system must be set up but also a proper administration, one that enables politics that is oriented on public well-being, is universalistic and obeys rational-bureaucratic principles. To achieve that, clientele relationships, the state machinery and politics must be isolated from each other.

But because of the insecurity of neo-patrimonial conditions, interest in retaining power, which is linked directly to re-election, suggests not doing without the informal politics of the clientele networks in power. Interest in retaining power demands a strategic patronage policy, which opposes the reform tasks outlined above. So the political work of MPs and a new president faces a dilemma between reform (meaning institutionalizing democracy) and retaining power. The two are mutually exclusive or can be reconciled only with great political adroitness.

All these problems apply not only to state institutions but also to civil society and socio-political organizations such as NGOs and political parties. Informal, neo-patrimonial politics is also alive and well in these institutions. The parties, above all, with their diverse functions for democratic rule, manifest even more fragile bureaucratic structures than the state bureaucracy. This applies in a similar way to associations and NGOs and contributes to the organizational and political weakness of civil society vis-à-vis the government and state. Furthermore, the strong executive function of the African presidential system, which was not given up in the new democratic constitutions, enables the tradition of extra-formal politics to be continued. Weak institutionalizing of state organs and a strong executive president come together systematically to ensure the continued existence of the informal politics of patronage.

Fertile prospects for state weakness

Even if at times it may not appear so, the neo-patrimonial logic is by no means inescapable. Ongoing privatization since the 1990s and liberalization of business means that rent incomes are getting smaller and thus the opportunities for political patronage are becoming fewer (or are at least changing). With the increasing number of people losing the protection of patronage, the number of those in opposition who are standing up for proper, non-corrupt governance and articulating that in political parties and civil society organizations is also growing. The shrinking patronage resources of the authoritarian regime have already strengthened the ranks of the democracy movement, including by groups of entrepreneurs, some of whom finance the opposition and thereby have contributed to their organizational capability. By this means the existing democratic potential of civil society can equally be strengthened, such as by young politicians who are committed to liberal, rule-of-law standards. In addition, these forces, or at least those in countries dependent on external financing, can expect (conditional) international support.

Meanwhile, contrary tendencies should not be overlooked. Privatization and liberalization also involve the danger that state institutions and their legitimacy will be weakened further in the eyes of the people if they do not deliver expected social and economic benefits.

By the late 1980s, Africa's economic failures and political instability had pushed the continent into international receivership position. This receivership status or the syndrome of touting begging bowls around IMF and World Bank buildings in Washington, D.C. made the continent ripe for external co-optation and capture by the international financial institutions, most notably the IMF and the World Bank. Thus, virtually all African countries have embraced a new economic ideology, which represents at the same time a fundamental shift in economic policy making.

What is African identity?

Identity politics is frequently dismissed as an anachronistic survival from a time when kinship (blood relations), religion or local belonging formed the basis of politics. Against this view, it has been argued many times, always correctly, that although identity politics tends to be dressed in traditional garb, beneath the surface it is a product of modernity. The strong emotions associated with a tradition, a culture or a religion can never be mobilized unless people feel that it is under siege. To put it metaphorically: A fish knows nothing of water as long as it is surrounded by it, but the moment it is pulled out into the air, it develops an intense interest in the water and nostalgia for it. Indeed, it could be said that the fish discovers the water only the moment it is removed from it.

Viewed in this way, the collective emotions of identities politics depend on and reveal themselves to be deeply modern emotions associated with the sense of loss experienced in situations of rapid change. Ethnic nationalism, minority movements and politicized religion offer a larger share of the cake as well as a positive sense of self, and like it or not, these movements will remain influential in most parts of the world until something better comes along.

The construction of what Africa means must take account of the nature of popular historical memory, symbolic identification, and the codes and experiences of people if it is to perform its ideological function successfully. People can and do refuse to consent to a construction of their identity which does not resonate within the structures and layers of popular consciousness and knowledge. The dialectical tension between agency and determinations shapes the contours of identity. An African identity crisis cannot therefore be a simple conflict between modernity and tradition but between a highly dependent and dictatorial process of modernization and retraditionalizing rhetoric based on indigenous culture in which competing communicative structures offer different definitions and visions of the continent's community.

Since the collapse of the Soviet Union, followed closely by the information revolution, students of international politics have been trying to come to terms with the fact that existing analytical tools have left them totally unprepared. The dominant Cold War framework, realism, proved woefully inadequate to the task of understanding how a great power like the Soviet Union could suddenly reinterpret its own national security interests, shortly before dissolving into a myriad of unanticipated new national identities. These national identities became infectious, though difficult to define.

In fact, identity and consciousness are so recursive that it is often difficult to tell which comes before the other in the manner of causality (Osaghae, 1994, p. 233). Identity is the distinguishing character that makes a people. Consciousness on the other hand is the awakening to or awareness of the identity. It has to do with the individual realizing whom he is, where he came from, what is expected of him and how he is to relate to others. It signifies the way in which one is the same with some others who share the same position, and how he is different from those who do not. Identity defines the creation of the inclusive pronoun 'we' and the exclusivity of 'they.' In traditional societies the individual's identity was usually fixed and stable. Identity was a function of predefined social roles and a traditional system of myths, which provided orientation and religious sanctions that dictated one's place in the world and rigorously circumscribed the realm of thought and behavior. One was born and died as a member of one's clan and 'tribe,' a member of a fixed kinship system. Identity then was unproblematic and not subject to reflection or discussion. Individuals did not undergo identity crises, or give thought to the modification of their identity. The individual did not question his existence within his clan and/or 'tribe.' The individual was a hunter or gatherer, and a member of the 'tribe,' and that was that (Kellner, 1992). Identity became an issue in Africa as a result of contact with the Europeans. With colonialism, identity became more mobile, multiple, personal, self-reflective, subject to change and problematic. As a result of this contact, Africans have formed four levels of conflictual identities: racial identity, national identity, ethnic identity and individual identity.

Racial identity and random terrorism

The concept of race has its roots in biological classification. This classification of race placed emphasis on variations in the external physical characteristics of the peoples of the world. Racism, however, is an ideology and practice based on the assumed superiority of certain races over another. Race consciousness forms the social lens through which we assign value to experiences. It has to do with how the individual's role and place in the society are viewed. Race consciousness is not an objective condition in that the way you identify yourself as an individual who lives within the world political economic system affects the way you perceive, interpret and act upon issues in international relations. Science and technology developed consonant to such racial frameworks will only reinforce unequal social relationships and will not lead to greater social justice. But, racial thinking affects human judgments.

The problem of Africa started with race consciousness, what W.E.B DuBois called the problem of the color line (DuBois, 1903). Colonialism brought with it the concepts of 'we' and 'they.' Just like the consciousness of the naked state of Adam and Eve in the Garden of Eden after eating the 'forbidden fruit' (*Holy Bible*, NIV, 1987: Genesis 3), Africans were made to see themselves as 'black' people. Africans were made to believe that they were inferior to the Europeans. They were brainwashed to believing that the African culture and everything African is inferior to that of the European. This feeling is still plaguing Africa till today. Before the coming of the Europeans, blackness was taken for granted by Africans. Africans were later made to feel as if blackness is a curse and not the other way round. For instance, 'black' was identified with evil and debasement, while 'white' represents the good and pure. God is 'white' and the devil is 'black.' All that was African was considered dark and barbaric whereas 'whiteness' and 'white' culture represented the epitome of modernity—'the civilized world.' Africans were made to believe that their ancestors were savages living on trees, and the Europeans saw it has their duty to bring civilization to Africa. African cultural forms almost faded into obscurity and were replaced with European culture. Africans were dehumanized and humiliated to the point that the Europeans were treated like 'gods.' Take the case of the daily routine of the British district commissioner of Tunduru in southern Tangayinka as an example of the humiliation Africans suffered in the hands of the Europeans:

> D was in the habit of going for a walk every evening, wearing a hat. When, towards sunset, he came to the point of turning home, he would hang his hat on a convenient tree and proceed on his way hatless. The first African who passed that way after him and saw the hat was expected to bring it to D's house and hand it over to his servants, even if he was going in the opposite direction with a long journey ahead of him. If he ignored the hat, he would be haunted by the fear that D's intelligence system would catch up with him (Lumley, 1976, p. 55).

The worst example one can give of the humiliation suffered by the Africans in the hands of the Europeans is that of South Africa. South Africa, until recently suffered the worst insult of racial discrimination in Africa. South Africans were made to become strangers in their own land. A vigorous set of laws was passed to regulate the relations between the races. That is, mass terror was 'used as a means to reorganize economic space and control mobility within and between spaces. War (was then) understood as an effort to concentrate violence in manageable and exchangeable forms' (see 'Youth and Conflict in Kivu: Komona clair,' *Journal of Humanitarian Assistance*, July 21, 2000). There were the Population Regulation Act, the Prohibition of Mixed Marriages Act, the Immorality Act, the Reservation of Separate Amenities Act, and the Group Areas Act, which strictly segregated South Africa by race (Chazan et al., 1999, p. 471). To avoid miscegenation, the South African urban areas were separated into what was called locations. Following the passage of the 1902 Native Reserve Location Acts, in 1903, two locations were set up in the Cape; one in Ndabeni (Cape Town) and the other in New Brighton (Port Elizabeth). Two locations were also set up in Transvaal in the same year and in 1904, two were set up in Natal (Hindson, 1987, pp. 31–32).

The situation was worsened by the recommendation of the Stallard Commission of 1922. The Commission recommended that: 'the native shall only be allowed to enter urban areas, which are essentially the white man's creation, when he is willing to enter and to minister to the need of the white man, and should depart therefore when he ceases so to minister' (Posel, 1991, p. 40). By legislative fiat and administrative measures, the White autocracy steadily destroyed the property-owning classes among blacks. Beginning with the Natives Land Act of 1913, these measures were followed up by the Natives Land and Trust Act of 1935, the Asiatic Land Tenure Act of 1946, The Group Areas Act of 1951, the Bantu Authorities Act of the same year and a host of others that bankrupted the Black property-owning classes by restricting their rights to own property and engage in commerce. Policies were formulated which made certain forms of skilled work the exclusive preserve of Whites. State policy thus created a racial hierarchy graded by skin color, with Whites at the top and Africans at the bottom (Jordan, 1997).

In 1950, the Population Registration Act required that all South Africans be racially classified into one of three categories: white, black (African), or colored (of mixed decent). The colored category included major subgroups of Indians and Asians. Classification into these categories was based principally on appearance, social acceptance, and descent. A white person for example, was defined as 'in appearance obviously a white person or generally accepted as a white person.' A person could not be considered white if one of his or her parents were non-white. For a person to be considered 'obviously white,' 'his habits, education, and speech and deportment and demean or' had to be taken into account. A colored person is one that is neither black nor white. Non-compliance with the race laws was dealt with harshly. All blacks were required to carry 'pass books' containing fingerprints, photo and information on access to non-black areas. Hundreds were sent to jail daily by commissioners' courts for staying longer than seventy-two hours without the requisite permission to do so or for failing to produce their passbook on demand (Mamdani, 1996, p. 228).

In 1951, the Bantu Authorities Act established independent states known as 'homelands.' Each African was assigned to these states based on records of origin. The Africans became 'citizens' of the homeland, losing all involvement with the South African Parliament, which was the complete overlord of South Africa. Voting and every other political activity were restricted to the homelands. Between 1976 and 1981, four of these homelands were created, denationalizing nine million South Africans. Africans living in the homelands needed passports to enter South Africa. They thus, became aliens in their own country.

In 1953, the Public Safety Act and the Criminal Law Amendment Act were passed, which empowered the government to declare stringent states of emergency and increased penalties for protesting against or supporting the repeal of a law. The penalties included fines, imprisonment and whippings. In 1960, a large group of blacks in Sharpeville refused to carry their passes. The government's response was to declare a state of emergency, which lasted for 156 days. At least 69 people died and about 187 people were wounded.

The penalties imposed on political protest, even non-violent protest, were severe. During the states of emergency, which continued intermittently until 1989, a low-level police official could detain anyone without a hearing for up to six months. Thousands of individuals died in custody, frequently after gruesome acts of torture. Those who were tried, like Nelson Mandela, were sentenced to death, banished, or imprisoned for life.

Although South Africa's emancipation came in 1994, the scars left by apartheid are still fresh and it will definitely take a very long time to undo the damages that have been done to the dignity of the South Africans. Many black South Africans still have to struggle to make ends meet. Many cannot get good jobs because they do not have quality education. Many still live in shacks and shantytowns. The average black man in South Africa cannot live in the same house with the whites. A white man still cannot rent his house out to a black man, especially if they are to be living in the same compound. Many still work as domestic hands for the whites.

Another negative effect of colonialism is the deculturing of the French colonial area, which was made possible by the process of assimilation into French culture. The French totally substituted African culture with French culture. The colonized were made to see themselves as French men. Countries like Senegal and Côte d'Ivoire still see themselves as extensions of France. As Fanon (1963, p. 170) pointed out, 'Colonization is not satisfied merely with holding a people in its grip and emptying the native's brain of all form and content. By a kind of perverted logic, it turns to the past of oppressed people, and distorts, disfigures and destroys it.'

National identity and terror

In discussing the roles played by nationality, the nation-state, and identity in contemporary African culture, one needs to think beyond the nation. This is not to suggest that thought alone will carry one beyond the nation or that the nation is largely a thought or imagined thing. Rather, it is to suggest that the role of intellectual practices is to identify the current crisis of the African nation and, in identifying it, to provide part of the apparatus of recognition for postnational forms.

Franz Fanon's (1963, pp. 166–199) understanding of the troubled existence of identity in a colonial society is very useful here. He analyzes the psychology of colonialism and shows how under it nothing is left to chance. Colonialism does not only control the material resources of a country it subjugates but that it turns to the past of the oppressed people, distorts, disfigures and tries to destroy it. Fanon is, here alluding to that process of the devaluation of the African past in which it was, and still is, represented by apologetic scholars of colonialism as one long night of barbarism, static and therefore needful of European technology, forms of political governance and cultural organizations to pull it out of its supposed inertia.

This notion of 'African reality' is an artificially constructed 'truth.' Contained in it is the image of colonialism portraying the identity of Africans as marginally its *other*—an inferior race the colonizer had come to redeem and protect from self-destruction. If, for Fanon, the colonial period was less stable and incoherent because it was itself defined by the binary divisions of colonizer and colonized, black and white—signifiers whose coded meanings have continued to thrive into the period after direct colonial rule, the 'post-colonial' stage in the history of Africa is an 'after' period of deepening contradictory complexities, indeed, one of shifting identities.

Today, political power is now in the hands of a class of blacks who participate actively in the exploitation and pillaging of their own people. The political situation of increased gender and class inequalities after independence not only underpin this decisive rift developing between the leaders and the poor masses in Africa. It also compels analysts to pluralize their way of narrating the nation. This is a theoretical challenge, which will inevitably collide with models of national identity insisting on a single destiny for Africans themselves.

The usage of the controversial term 'post-colonial' to analyze the processes by which people or social 'subjects' occupy new positionalities in the period after direct colonial rule should therefore not be taken to mean that there has been a total break with the structures of colonialism. These structures (economic, political and cultural) are in the new context of today being contested by emergent power blocks albeit in a changed environment of more brutal forces of globalization, for instance radical Islamic fundamentalism. The latter has seriously weakened and undermined though not completely destroyed national economies, borders, politics and cultures. In other words, that local African political and cultural space upon which global forces play themselves out in terms of domination and its resistance is one in which new bases of power proclaiming new truths of the nation are created. In these local spaces defined by common national borders, identities multiply, are transformed and circulate in a political environment:

> made up not of one coherent 'public space,' nor is it determined by any single organizing principle. It is rather a plurality of spheres and arenas, each having its own separate logic yet nonetheless liable to be entangled with other logics when operating in certain specific contexts . . . Faced with this . . . the postcolonial 'subject' mobilizes not a single 'identity,' but several fluid identities which, by their very nature, must be constantly 'revised' in order to achieve maximum instrumentality and efficacy as and when required (Mbembe, 2001, p. 104; als see Mbembe, 1992; Adeeko, 2002).

One may therefore approach the concept of the state by looking at the formally recognized state entities as they exist in the United Nations and in the matrix of international diplomatic relations between 180-odd territorial entities in the world (e.g., see Dietz and Van der Wusten, 1991). One can also approach the concept of the state by looking at functions which are 'normally' provided by state agencies. And, as a corollary, one can then determine what agencies actually provide these services in current-day Africa. Basic questions to be answered are:

- Who provides safety and defense against enemy attacks?
- To whom should tax money be paid?
- Who restores peace and order after (violent) conflicts and who formulates norms for acceptable social behavior?
- Who determines the rules for access to and use of natural resources?
- Who takes care of construction and maintenance of physical infrastructure?
- Who assists in the improvement of production and trade?
- Who sets the rules for the functioning of the market and the currency?
- Who provides education and training?
- Who provides health care?

In current-day Africa the central state is only one of a multitude of actors playing these roles, and in many areas the relative importance of the central state agencies and its civil servants has dwindled. If we look at the political economy of many peasant households, beyond what is consumed by the micro-household, what is marketed (a lot in an informal market, sometimes in barter form) and what is paid to the central government as tax, fees and fines, a considerable part of products, labor and income is contributed to representatives of a local government, to representatives of the army or armed terrorist (guerrilla) forces, the police, political parties, movements, or unions, 'guardians' and other 'mafia-entrepreneurs,' to 'projects' (so-called voluntary contributions), to 'owners' of resources (e.g. forest guards, water pump attendants), to school boards, to a variety of health care providers and to religious/spiritual entrepreneurs.

In addition there are the never-ending contributions to clan elders, ethnic brokers, parents-in-law, members of the extended family and creditors. People are entwined in a chaotic network of pseudo-tributary payments, far beyond the obligations to the central state. Many people's lives have come to depend to a considerable degree upon the gifts and 'payments' of their network partners, including those relatives and friends who regularly remit money and goods from abroad. And many people try to maintain and enlarge such networks as an investment in future claims of contra-support.

Diminishing central state presence and importance means a growing advantage to both local and global agencies. Decentralization along ethnic lines means a strengthened role of ethnic leaders, and of a hierarchy of clan and sub-clan leaders, often intertwined with religious authority. Sometimes these form part of 'local government,' but often not. In many places it has also meant a larger payment of tribute to locally active 'forces of violence': official bearers of arms, like policemen, soldiers, wildlife and forestry guards, and unofficial usurpers, like members of guerrilla movements, children's 'armies' or gangs, dealers in gold, precious stones and arms, drug traffickers and what is loosely described as 'criminals,' related or not to the central state apparatus, which, according to some, shows signs of 'criminalization' (Bayart, Ellis and Hibou, 1999, p. xiv: 'a return to the heart of darkness,' which 'does not mean a return to 'tradition,' but rather to a noxious cocktail of commerce and violence').

One is tempted to call this a process of political (and economic) feudalization, with the use of (or the threat to use) arms as the most important method of access to resources, and violence-based rent as the redistributive mechanism. On the other hand, there is an anarchistic type of globalization going on. In part of Africa the people's network is full of international elements: foreign companies, development aid donors, foreign soldiers and mercenaries, representatives of UN agencies, all types of non-governmental agencies, Christian mission/church agencies and Islamic organizations. In quite a number of cases these can function in ways that are rather autonomous from any central government involvement, and new alliances have formed temporary co-operation in these zones of 'anarchistic recolonization' or 'crumbled globalization.' In other areas very few of these foreign actors dare to operate. These have become 'no-go-areas,' far from the eyes of the world and most of the times left alone to fend for themselves (southern Sudan, Liberia, Sierra Leone, Somalia are only a few of these types of areas).

Thus, the consciousness of nationhood is a legacy of colonialism in many African societies. African nation-states emerged as a result of boundaries created by the colonial masters. The present geopolitical structure of Africa is ascribed to the arbitrary partition of Africa among the European imperial powers at the Berlin Conference of 1884–1885 (Oommen, 1997, p. 178). Hence, the identity of being classified or referred to as a Nigerian or Kenyan or Ghanaian, as the case may be, began. National identity is thus a conscious orientation and loyalty to a nation-state. Individuals within the nation-state identify with the national symbols such as flags, anthems and ceremonies and share in its national values and ways of life.

The creation of these nation-states brought with it the concept of citizenship. At independence, the constitutions the colonial masters fashioned for African countries included provisions with regards to the acquisition of citizenship. An individual can become a citizen by virtue of birth or descent, by naturalization and by marriage. There is however an ambiguity in determining whom a citizen really is. Most African countries have laws on citizenship with ethnic undertones. Independence for African states in most cases did not bring about a nation-state, where every member is seen as part of the nation. Citizenship is mostly based on the virtue of kinship or community of origin of an individual's parents or even grandparents rather than by virtue of birth in the country. In other words, people who have been around for several generations' back are still considered as 'foreigners' and are issued 'resident permit'; their children born in the country are not regarded as citizens. Most of the constitutions do not define residency as a basis for citizenship within the countries. For instance in Nigeria, the presence of non-indigenes in other states within the country is not properly addressed. There is no clear indication of the status of Nigerians whose families have had cause to move from their states of origin to another for varying reasons. Do children that are now born in this new state of residence have any right of claim? Should they be referred to as 'foreigners' or are they entitled to the same treatment and rights as the indigenous people? Should emphasis be placed on residency as against blood and birth? Two dissenting members of the Constitutional Drafting Committee in 1976, Segun Osoba and Yusuf Bala Usman, observed that 'no matter how long a Nigerian has resided in a state of Nigeria of which none of his parents is an indigene, such a Nigerian cannot enjoy the right to participate fully in the public life of that state' (Osoba and Usman, 1976, p. 15). The 1999 Constitution still did not address this issue. This situation may erode the feeling of belonging to the nation-state and is more likely to impede integration and nation building. The trend is well summarized by General Obasanjo thus:

> A man from Gongola State (now Adamawa State) working for the Nigerian Railways in Abeokuta and whose children cannot secure places for schools in his place of work and where he pays his tax, just because he is not an indigene of the State where he works, will find it almost inconceivable to see himself as a Nigerian . . . The consequent

> internalization of this ill-feeling will undoubtedly be passed on to his children who are victims of these strangling acts by states and local governments in Ogun State, even though those children were born in Ogun State. The children will be further ensnared in the destructive throes of ethnicism if on being sent to Gongola State they obtain admission to schools without much ado and just because their father is an indigene of Gongola State (Obasanjo, 1989, p. 116).

General Obasanjo's sermon brings out a very different conception of identity that is incompatible with that of Nigerian Muslims who insist: 'We will be betraying the cause of Islam and the integrity of the Muslim umma if we fail to discharge our obligations as Muslims. These obligations entail, among other things, the establishment of Islam as a complete polity and the dismantling of all Western influences as they affect us' (Sulaiman, 1988, p. 17).

Thus, identity here is viewed in religious terms, not territorial ones. And, understandably, Imam Ayatollah Khomeini's injunction that Islam is a 'religion that provides guidance for conducting the affairs of state and a guide to the straight path, which is neither Eastern nor Western. It is a religion where worship is joined to politics and practical activity is a form of worship' convinces Nigerian Muslims of their 'birthright to dominate till eternity the political and economic privileges of this great country (Nigeria)' as published by the Nigerian *Punch* of April 24, 1988, p. 8. Religious identity now becomes paramount. According to this theocratic identity thinking, a non-Nigerian Muslim even qualifies for these 'political and economic privileges' of Nigeria than a Nigerian Christian. Thus, religion becomes the primary determinant in the definition of national identity.

Some African states issue identity cards to their 'citizens.' These identity cards are symbols of exclusion and sometimes a cunning way of identifying people by their ethnic affiliation. Rwanda and South Africa are typical examples of the havoc the identity card can wreak within a nation. In Rwanda, for instance, the identity card was the main practical way of differentiating between a Hutu and a Tutsi. This made it easier for discrimination and even extermination. According to the summary of a report in the *African Rights* (1994):

> Many Tutsis have been killed either because their ID card marked them out as a Tutsi or because they did not have their card with them at the time and were therefore unable to prove they were not a Tutsi and to

escape the relentless discrimination they suffered, over the years many Tutsi bribed local government officials to get their ID card changed to Hutu.

Other African country examples could be instructive here.

Sierra Leone the failing state

Sierra Leone represents a disturbing trend in West Africa—the failing state. The tiny West African nation of Sierra Leone has been involved in civil and cross-border conflict for almost a decade. The civil war in Liberia spilled over to neighboring Sierra Leone at the instigation of Liberian warlord Charles Taylor. Taylor's men have helped organize and support the Sierra Leone rebel group, the Revolutionary United Front (RUF). The RUF first emerged as a fighting organization struggling against the governing regime of Sierra Leone in 1991. Even the election in 1996 of Ahmad Tejan Kabbah as president failed to placate the RUF, which has had an extremely successful campaign during the winter of 1998–1999.

Armed with weapons from its neighboring Liberian supporters, the RUF has waged a vicious terror campaign. Reports from the Sierra Leone capital, Freetown, reveal continued use of child soldiers and now mass mutilations and pillaging. With news of increased atrocities committed not only by the RUF but also by government forces and the ECOMOG peace-keeping force, Sierra Leone's troubles seem to be intensifying.

Although Sierra Leone is one of the poorest nations in the world, the opposing forces have had no trouble finding means by which their weapons purchases could be financed. Small arms are plentiful in West Africa. Weapons from resolved conflicts in Afghanistan, Mali, South Africa, Mozambique, and Angola have all made their way to Sierra Leone. Much of the weaponry acquired by the RUF has been financed with diamonds from mines in RUF-controlled territories. The Sierra Leone government, on the other hand, employed the services of Executive Outcomes, a South African mercenary organization, to help support its forces. Out of money, the government now is forced to rely on the international community and more specifically the West African peacekeeping force, ECOMOG, led by Nigeria.

West Africa is one conflict-raged region of the world where the direct connection has been made between weapons and the perpetuation of conflicts that otherwise probably would have ended. Significantly, this connection has been made, not by outsiders but by the people of the region themselves through bartering arms for diamonds. Recognition of this lethal connection is embodied in the West African Moratorium. The Moratorium pledges all state signatories to halt the production, import, and export of small arms for a three-year period. The moratorium went into effect November 1, 1998 (see details of the moratorium below). Although Sierra Leone signed the moratorium, the proliferation of small arms into the country has not ended. The RUF and government forces continue to have access to an ample supply of the weaponry needed to wage the war. Absent a workable enforcement mechanism or at lest a verification regime, the signing of a piece of paper means nothing—most particularly for a failing state unable to exert its power or provide for individual security.

Somalia the failed state

Somalia's civil war has been raging since 1991 after the overthrow of dictator Mohammed Siad Barre. In November 1991, rival factions began fighting in the capital city, Mogadishu. As the southern part of the country faced anarchy, the Somali National Movement (SNM) declared an independent state of Somaliland in the north. Since May 1991 Somalia has not had a recognized government. Rival clans have competed for power for the last eight years, and with arms continuing to freely flow from Ethiopia and, more recently, from Eritrea, Somalia's civil war could last another decade.

Somalia is a prime example of a failed state. With no recognized government in place, Somalia swings back and forth between the perils of anarchy and military rule. When U.S. Marines arrived in Somalia in 1992 they faced well-armed rebel groups armed with—among other small arms models—American made M-16s. The force that pushed the United States out of Somalia was not armed with heavy conventional weapons, but with predominantly small arms and light weapons. Yet these proved sufficient to allow rival warring clans to completely decimate the nation's higher political institutions during this decade.

The sheer quantities of small arms in Somalia have been detrimental to the region as well. The unregulated passage of arms and explosives coupled with lax controls at the Kenyan border provided a conduit for the people and materials used in the bombings of the two U.S. embassies in Africa in 1998. As East Africa faces erupting conflicts between Ethiopia and Eritrea, and localized fighting continues in Kenyan and Uganda, the Somalis are taking advantage of this new pipeline for weapons and supplies.

Efforts to rid Somalia of weapons in the past, namely during the UN Peacekeeping operation in Somalia (UNOSOM), were unsuccessful; virtually no weapons have been removed from Somali society. As a result, the eruption of new conflicts can only increase the supply of weapons already in the country and continue to provide the international community with no clear cut measures by which Somalia can be redeemed from its total collapse at the nation-state level.

Small arms and light weapons are an entire class of weapons ignored too long by governments and policy makers. There is no universal treaty or international standard applicable to small arms. However, as the realization grows of the detrimental effects of small arms and light weapons on all aspects of individual, national and international security, policy makers have begun several initiatives that attempt to control small arms at the regional and international level.

So far this new concern for some form of coherent action on small arms has produced numerous international meetings and calls for action. To date, however, the majority of efforts have been relatively imprecise and ineffective because they attempt to cover too much ground. Furthermore, in some nations, the primacy of domestic gun ownership and gun use legislation has been championed over the creation of international standards. Three of the most substantial initiatives underway—and those that have the best chance at making (or that have already made) real progress in regulating small arms—have been initiated by the UN, the Organization of American States, and West Africa.

West African moratorium

As mentioned earlier, the entire West African region has been wracked by civil wars, rebel insurgencies, and above all the massive proliferation of small arms. To combat these problems, the heads of the sixteen member states of the Economic Community of West African States (ECOWAS) signed on October 31, 1998 a renewable three-year moratorium on the production, import, and export of light weapons. The Moratorium, absent enforcement provisions, took effect November 1, 1998. The historic West Africa enterprise was developed under the initiative of the President of Mali, Alpha Oumar Konare, in December 1996. After Mali successfully concluded a peace agreement within its own country, surplus weapons were burned in a symbolic 'Flame of Peace' ceremony.

Even as Mali destroyed additional excess weapons, the devastation caused by small arms in the rest of the West African region continued. Obviously more needed to be done. The West African States held meetings with the Wassenaar arms producing states to discuss the concept of an arms moratorium. Finally, 'The Oslo Platform for a Moratorium on Small Arms in West Africa' was issued in April 1998. This document, the result of a meeting of thirteen West African countries, twenty-three Wassenaar Arrangement arms exporting countries, UN organizations, NGOs, and observer nations, provided a formal framework for the moratorium effort. This framework includes the Program of Coordination and Assistance on Security and Development (PCASED)—an important linkage of development to security—and a secretariat to coordinate the development and implementation of the moratorium mechanism. The effectiveness of the small arms moratorium has yet to be determined. Sierra Leone and other West African countries continue to be plagued by violence and war. In the continued absence of enforcement provisions or penalties for violating the Moratorium, both supplying and buying countries and groups may well continue to traffic in arms.

Analysis of the constellation of challenges created by small arms and light weapons suggest two primary courses for action. The first is to gain control of the vast stocks of small arms and light weapons in the world. Initially, this requires a system of transparency in which quantities, types, and locations of weapons are publicly identified. Admittedly, this is a monumental task and, with over twenty significant conflicts still raging in the world, one that will remain incomplete for a number of years. In conjunction with this process, nations should develop processes by which their manufacture or purchase of new weapons is offset by the destruction—not the transfer—of old weapons. This will be equally difficult to achieve because weapons transfers mean money for the selling state whereas destruction costs money. However, a model—and similar rationale—might be found in the U.S. Cooperative Threat Reduction Program with Russia, which is aimed at increasing the security of both nations through U.S. funds to help Russia account for and safeguard nuclear weapons, fissile material, and nuclear know-how.

Second, the concept of sovereignty that grew out of Westphalia and is enshrined in the Charter of the United Nations must be modified. Slowly, all too slowly it may seem to some, this is being done. Interventions sanctioned by the UN Security Council have become relatively common in the last decade even if they have occurred generally after one or more rounds of civil war. This remains a very delicate diplomatic area, but until the world community decides that it can intervene before states fail, it will forever be forced into more costly reactions to events.

In short, the choice lies between rationally anticipating and preventing state failure and allowing irrational forces to isolate and dominate internal state dynamics. In the latter instance, a destructive and divisive climate of thought can permeate a society. And this is where danger should be most apparent, for in such a climate mass manipulation is easy, the appeal to violence in the name of 'duty' and hatred of an enemy is made, and the chaos of war ensues. From this point the cycle of killing spins on. The first dead demand further sacrifices from their compatriots, for at this point no price is too high to pay. Only the lack of new victims, exhaustion, or overwhelming force from outside can end the ensuing carnage.

The real question of identity

What is identity? This is a philosophical question (in my opinion). Since I'm not a philosopher, I will present my own view in simple terms. Identity is something someone identifies himself with as well as the psychological feeling of 'oneness' with the identified (my definition). When many individualities in the 20th century began raising the issue of Africa's 'identity crisis,' they felt that something, a certain basis they had identified themselves with, had disappeared from the continent and they had left alone facing the cold and alien unknown. Hence there are many artists and writers who have searched and are searching for their identity (Botha and Burger, 1989, pp. 21, 24; Botha and Van Aswegen, 1992; Tomaselli, 1990).

If one speaks about a national identity crisis, then, presumably, in a certain nation there appear certain groups of people, who no longer feel to belong to the nation in question. But again, I would not rush to accuse 'cosmopolitanism' for that, since cosmopolitans, indeed, do not feel any identity crisis, as they identify themselves with the entire world—the global village—(in this respect, they have solved their identity problem). Here, we shall take the example of Nigeria—the most populous African nation.

Since the end of the Cold War, religion and ethnicity have been major causes of domestic conflict, especially in Nigeria. While the primary causes of ethnic conflict are non-religious ethnic issues, the majority of ethnic conflicts involve religious issues. Religion causes ethnic conflicts when another group threatens the religious beliefs of an ethnic group or when religious laws are believed to call for conflictive action. Religion therefore becomes involved in ethnic conflicts that have secular causes through the use of religious institutions and legitimacy in the conflict. Occasionally, this involvement of religion can transform a secular conflict of ethnic, individual or national identity into a religious one.

The 1990s witnessed attempts by the leading donor agencies to force Africa towards 'cleaner' governments. 'Good governance' became the new catchword, and for the Dutch government even the yardstick for its restructured development assistance policy. There is a Weberian illusion of the state behind this image: of neutrality, social harmony, professionalism, transparency and rationality. However, African states are not at all Weberian. Where coordination and rational 'weighing' of claims is the donor's dream, chaos, often deliberately created, is the overriding practice. Where 'control' is the aim, a thriving parallel economy and underground polity is the rule. Acquiring governmental power is often a gateway to exclusive amassing of wealth by a happy few, as long as it lasts. For the excluded majority the government is there to avoid, and if chances present themselves (often in the form of donor-funded projects) it is regarded as wise to 'eat' as much and as fast as possible of the crumbs, which fall from the elite's table. Fluid boundaries between public means and private gains are the rule, and what you can't get by being smart, you get by being violent.

Getting access to government positions is a game with high stakes, not so much because the state funds as such are so rich, because we have seen they are not, but because access to state power gives access to land, mineral wealth and labor resources, and to arms and the armed forces, to assist in 'primitive accumulation' or outright theft. The political elites of independent African states basically came from four sources. In some areas, especially those with indirect rule during previous colonial times (e.g., Nigeria before military rule; Cameroon before 1982, but not Uganda) it was a historical extension of precolonial elites, often with an Islamic background.

In some areas the leaders were recruited from among groups, which had close links with the colonial conquerors, against formerly leading ethnic groups which had been fighting against colonial rule (Ghana's coastal groups versus the Ashanti are an interesting example). In many other areas the activities of Christian missions had created a 'social turn-around' in which former marginal social groups were the first recruits of these missions and where they became the first well-educated groups, active in the labor unions, in independence movements and in academic life. Tanzania's Nyerere, Zambia's Kaunda, Kenya's Arap Moi and Cameroon's Biya are all examples. Another important recruitment ground were the marginal areas, which had often fed the expanding armies in late colonial and early independence times, and which suddenly became important after military coups (Uganda under Idi Amin, Togo under Eyadéma are good examples).

Finally the leaders of revolutionary movements in case of violent anti-colonial and anti-dictatorship struggles, with their background of labor and people's movements, became important after the victory of their movements. These were often well-educated people, with foreign exposure, and a personal history of being imprisoned, tortured and/or exiled (examples abound in southern Africa, in the Great Lakes area and in the Horn). Most African states have gone through dramatic successions of these types of leadership profiles.

In considering these concepts and profiles, the most important element common to them all is the individual. Individuals make up the races, the nations and the ethnic group. Everything revolves around the individuals within a particular setting. The individual's identity is capable of being changed, reshaped and redefined, at times by mere religious affiliation. The individual is socially constructed through nationality, race, sex, gender, class, ethnicity, culture, or radicalized experiences. He has to struggle between conflicting identities based on his position in the society—as a member of a community, ethnic group, religion, as a child, as a parent, as a worker. The African individual has been greatly shaped by his contact with western civilization. Religion, western education, urbanization, western capitalism takes their toll on the individual. Colonialism invented an African 'torn between his "traditional" ethnic, religious, regional and "irrational" roots and his "modern" social, political, "rational" and economic attributes"' (Chabal, 1992, pp. 41–42). In fact, colonial westernization hybridized the African.

> These identities are in the wane. Territorial boundaries in Africa are not only elusive. They are deceptive as well. Africa's political maps create a conceptual barrier that prevents us from understanding the political crack-up occurring in the continent. In Nigeria, for example, Muslim fundamentalism and evangelical Christian militancy are on the ascendant. And northern Muslim anxiety over southern (Christian) control of the economy is intense. This explains the weakness in efforts to keep the country together.

This century, France and Britain will become more occupied with European politics than African troubles. In West Africa, Nigeria's shifting boundaries will shift again and again. They will shift to incorporate the Republic of Niger due to its Hausa links. They will also shift to incorporate the Republic of Benin due to its Yoruba link. And, why not Cameroon with its Hausa-Fulbe, Kanuri, and Ejagham links?

Part of this quandary is that although the population belts are horizontal, the borders erected by European colonialists are vertical. And they are thus at cross-purposes with both topography and demography. The population densities too increase as one travels southward away from the Sahara desert and toward the tropical abundance of the Atlantic littoral. And so is Islamic radicalism. And, likely so, the recruitment grounds for networked terrorism inspired by spiritual motivations.

Permissive environment, minerals, and terrorism

Africa has been dogged by border disputes both on land and, increasingly so, over maritime boundaries. The main problem with African international boundaries is that the very notion of dividing territory with lines was imposed on the continent just over a century ago. The concept of linear boundaries did exist in Africa before partition, but it was merely one of a number of ways of dividing political space. In general, African pre-colonial polities were far more fluid than European states. In order to cope with the harsh natural environment, flexibility proved to be a far more effective method of political organization than fixed Western-style states. Where drought or disease struck one ethnic group, a state of any size was able to contract or even move itself wholesale. Political authority tended to follow trade routes, as with the Swahili in East Africa, and sovereignty was invested in people rather than land. The colonial division of Africa removed this flexibility and eventually led to the creation of almost fifty new African states, which were defined by fixed international boundaries. All such constructs are intrinsically artificial, but as the political map of Africa is relatively recent, those stresses and strains are bound to exert themselves in international relations. The project of 'national unity' which many African states have tried to support after getting political independence has failed in many countries. Forces of globalization and of localization have undermined the central state's ability to continue playing a major role, while the economic crisis in many African countries and donor reluctance to continue support to 'bad governance' has weakened the financial ability of central states to do so. It seems that the crumbling of effective state power often takes the form of 'ethnic nationalism.' This would mean that not fifty but more than 1,000 territorial units would be the future form of the Africa of the twenty-first century. Ethnic nationality not only means that there will be more room for ethnic specificity in cultural symbolism (use of the ethnic language in local government, and in education; more emphasis on the historical cultural heritage of the particular ethnic groups; 'invention of tradition'), but also that claims on access to and use of resources will be ethnically organized (also see Mohamed Salih 1999). Inclusion and exclusion will then be organized along lines of 'ethnic belonging,' of 'autochthones' versus 'immigrants,' 'strangers' or 'outsiders' (Geschiere, 1997).

The problem is, though, that ethnicity in the past has always been very dynamic, with collective memories both full of strife and of collaboration and adoption. 'Historical areas' for specific ethnic groups do not exist. A reconstruction of ethnic-territorial 'roots' shows a chaos of competing claims. Depending on the period, and of the source of information, the maps of 'territorial heritage' look completely different. Geschiere (1997, p. 3) rightly stresses that African societies are extremely mobile, with 'constantly changing contours of local units . . . open and . . . inclusive tendencies (which) made it very hard to draw more or less fixed boundaries.'

If ethnic nationalism will become the rule, as trends show, both in rural areas and in urban areas exclusive ethnic zones respecting ethnic quarters will be the geographical form of this ethnic nationalism. Members of other ethnic groups or of minority groups will be regarded as intruders, with at best temporary rights of stay. The existing fluidity of social and spatial boundaries will then be frozen into social-spatial rigidities. Violent ethnic cleansing creates both a large internal homogeneity and empty 'no-go-areas' in between war-torn zones.

In these situations inter-ethnic friendships and marriages will be regarded as contemptuous. The ethnic 'level of scale' then becomes important as the determinant of togetherness. In a Kenyan context: is it enough to be Nilotic (a 'supra-ethnic identity,' against being Bantu or Cushitic?) or is ethnic nationality defined at a lower level, like being 'Kalenjin' (against being Luo, or Turkana, other subgroups of the Nilotes), or even lower, like being Pokot (and easily killing co-Kalenjin like the neighboring Marakwet), or lower still, like being 'Kassauria-Pokot' or 'Kapcheripkwo-Pokot'? The Somali story shows where this will lead to. It is a next step to create a hierarchy of 'ethnic purity,' where the myths of clan histories play a role as well, as many clans were in the past accepted as refugees, and a lot of inter-clan and inter-ethnic marriages took place in the past.

With stricter adherence to (sub-) ethnic identity the redistribution of assets, labor and products takes a more restricted form. In times of increasing insecurity this can easily increase the vulnerability of large groups, and spark off a downward spiral of competition for scarce resources, ruled by violence and destruction, as Homer-Dixon (1999) writes. Layered or even multi-ethnic identities will become more difficult to maintain then, as well as ethnic jumps to and fro, as is practiced in some communities (Schlee, 1989 on northern Kenya).

Most problematic will it be in amalgamated ethnic 'melting pots,' the metropoles, plantations and mining areas, which always attracted scores of people from a large variety of ethnic backgrounds, who often formed their own cultures and 'pidgin' languages. These former champions of 'national unity' will then become despised because of their 'lack of roots,' unless they reinvent their 'origins.' Quite a number of observers of African affairs after independence were convinced that the urban elites would be the first to forget about their ethnicity and would embrace the new nationalism, forged around the state, and even part of an 'Pan-African Nation.' Kaunda's 'one Zambia, one Nation' appeared to be easily founded on the urban population in this urban country.

Recently this same former President was challenged by the new, also urban-based rulers, that he 'was not even a Zambian' (being born in Malawi, and as such suddenly being regarded as a non-citizen, a 'stranger'). What happened to Kaunda, outcasting, might happen to many, and many urbanites nowadays invest in the symbolism of 'ethnic belonging' and in intra-ethnic networks of mutual support, which become 'identity markers.' Urban people who have not invested in a 'rural home' are nowadays ridiculed in countries as far apart as Ghana and Kenya, because 'they have no place to be buried,' 'no links with their forefathers,' 'no roots with their ancestry.' Even those tycoons who have invested (and acquired recourses) in a multitude of locations, nowadays make sure that they have a special bond with their 'home area.' And this bond with the 'home area' has become the bane of Africa—a derivative of conflicts. According to the Stockholm International Peace Research Institute (SIPRI),

> in 2001, there were 24 major armed conflicts in 22 locations in the world. Both the number of major armed conflicts and the number of conflict locations in 2001 were slightly lower than in 2000, when there were 25 major armed conflicts in 23 locations. Africa continued to be

> the region with the greatest number of conflicts. Worldwide, there were approximately equal numbers of contests for control of government and for territory.

SIPRI defines a major armed conflict as one, which results in '100 or more deaths' during the year. Interestingly, according to SIPRI,

> eleven of the 15 conflicts have lasted for 8 or more years. One of the reasons for their endurance is the inability of either side to prevail by force. In the vast majority of these conflicts, rebels used a guerrilla military strategy. They supported their military effort through the sale of minerals, timber and narcotics and through remittances from supporters abroad. However, very few groups tried to win the loyalty of the population through political, economic or social programs.

Many African countries continued to suffer from civil unrest and the consequences thereof during 2001. Countries affected by civil unrest during 2001 included Algeria, Angola, Burundi, Central African Republic, Chad, Comoros, Democratic Republic of Congo, Republic of Congo, Guinea, Liberia, Nigeria, Rwanda, Somalia, Sudan and Zimbabwe. Nevertheless, there were a number of bright spots. According to reports, the December 2000 peace treaty between Ethiopia and Eritrea is holding firm—the UN Mission in Ethiopia and Eritrea (UNMEE) remains in force. It would also appear that hostilities in Sierra Leone have (essentially) ceased, however, the UN Mission in Sierra Leone (UNAMSIL) remains in attendance. During January 2002, a formal peace accord was signed between the Chad government and the rebel Movement for Democracy and Justice in Chad (MDJT). The accord is sponsored by Libya, who has accepted responsibility for ensuring that the arrangement holds. Additionally, during March 2001, the Senegalese government and the main rebel group, the *Mouvement des Forces Démocratiques de Casamance* (MFDC) signed a peace accord.

These peace accords, numerous and optimistic as they appear, do not free the continent's mineral resources from being a curse to its people. Diamonds are among the most treasured symbols of love and affection in the West, and they are never more important than on Valentine's Day. But in some parts of West, Central, North and East Africa, they have become a source of violent conflict and unspeakable atrocities. Criminal gangs have taken control of many of the diamond mines in such countries as Sierra Leone, Angola, and Congo. They use the profits from diamond sales to terrorize civilians and further expand their influence. Nowhere has the effect of the illicit diamond trade been more graphic than in Sierra Leone. Sierra Leone is rich in diamonds, and yet it is among the poorest nations in the world. As early as 1991, the rebel group Revolutionary United Front (RUF), began taking control of many of Sierra Leone's diamond mines. The RUF is notorious for its use of amputations, murder, and rape in waging its campaign of terror. Images of infants missing limbs and disemboweled pregnant women have horrified and disgusted us. But now, sadly, we must add a new image to this pictorial: sequential explosions over the New York City skyline, the collapse of two massive skyscrapers, and the violent death of more than three thousand Americans.

However, global information is reaching the far corners of the continent nowadays and there are few places not feeling the impact of long-distance economic forces on a world scale, if only because of the arms trade. In a globalized world the 'backward' (re) construction of 'national' identities along (micro-) ethnic lines goes together with linking with the outside world. This is not possible without inter-ethnic brokers and traders. In the colonial past racial outsiders played such roles, like Indians ('Asians') in southern and eastern Africa; Arabs at the coast of the Indian Ocean, and Greeks and Lebanese in West Africa. After independence some 'African' groups started to play such roles as well (like the Kikuyu and the Somali in Kenya) or re-established (or better: increased) roles played in pre-colonial times (like the Hausa and some of the Peulh sections in West Africa). However, it is risky business. In crisis situations, the representatives of the 'globalized forces' often play the roles of brokers and 'traders.'

Natural resources and terrorism

Natural resources are being depleted with little gain to Africa's economies because resources are not treated as capital. The reason is that the present unsuitable system of national income accounting ordained by the global trading system is biased against natural resource-dependent economies. Yet, most of the World's gold and gem diamonds, cobalt, copper and chrome are produced in the African continent. And there is a growing body of evidence linking Osama bin Laden's terror network and conflict diamonds. This link has elevated the issue of conflict diamonds from one of humanitarian concern to one of national security concern. The link between the illicit diamond trade and terrorism makes sense. Diamonds provide terrorists an ideal way to conceal funds, move funds across borders, and to liquefy funds quickly. We do not yet know how many millions of dollars al Qaeda and other terrorist networks may have raised through the illicit diamond trade, but I suspect that this number is at least in the tens of millions. As if the deaths of thousands of innocent West Africans were not enough, new information linking conflict diamonds to Osama bin Laden necessitated a legislative response.

In 2001, negotiations between non-governmental organizations and the jewelry industry produced a bipartisan piece of legislation that would have prohibited the importation of diamonds into the United States from any country that did not have a diamond certification system. Under this system, diamonds entering the United States would have to be packaged in tamper-proof containers and be accompanied by an official certificate from the recognized government of the exporting country. When the Commerce, Justice, State appropriations bill passed the Senate 97 to 0 on September 13, 2001, it contained this consensus legislation. The House Ways and Means Committee objected to the conflict diamonds provision on jurisdictional grounds and demanded that it be stripped out. It was not until news of a possible link between conflict diamonds and terrorism surfaced that the Ways and Means Committee finally acted on conflict diamonds legislation.

Mineral resources are now linked to the suffering of thousands of Africans, and now perhaps to the deaths of thousands of Americans. To ease the suffering of the Africans, to protect the legitimate diamond trade that is the lifeblood of many African countries, and now for international security, an end must be put to conflict diamonds. As conflicts flare up in Côte d'Ivoire, Sierra Leone, Liberia, and Guinea with almost rhythmic regularity, one tends to ask oneself what should have been done, what must now be done, and what must be done differently in the future to transform the mineral curse into mineral salvation?

The fact that non-Africans profiteering from endemic conflicts in the continent enjoy Africa's wealth is relative. And this non-African profiteering warrants the raising of this question in order to understand why it happens that way. In a stretch of border covering 80 kilometers between South Africa and Mozambique there are almost 70 uncontrolled crossing points. The terrain and climate along this border make it difficult to patrol. It is through these routes that the illegal smuggling of goods, such as firearms, stolen cars and illegal immigrants, is occurring on a large scale. Africa's diamonds too follow the same routes (Van Bockstael, 2000).

According to Wax (2002, p. A01), workers at the Indian Ocean city's bustling port of Mombassa say drug lords can sneak 600 pounds of cocaine into the country by slipping a crisp \$100 bill into a policeman's pocket. Land mines, guns and fake passports can sail through the port for what dockworkers and police call in Swahili *kitu kidogo*—literally a 'little something,' but more commonly understood to mean a fat wad of cash.

'In Kenya, you can bomb the whole country for a \$50 bribe, and everyone knows it,' said Joseph Mutisya, 34, a laborer who works at the port. 'There's a lot of poverty here. People come from all over—Yemen, Somalia, the Middle East. They bring weapons. They bring whatever they want if they pay a bribe.' That kind of Wild West atmosphere, combined with desperate poverty, porous borders and increasingly pro-Palestinian feelings among the large Muslim population along Kenya's coast, has made this country an easy target for the kind of terrorist attacks that claimed sixteen lives in Mombasa on Thursday, November 28, 2002. The sixteen people—ten Kenyans, three Israelis and three suicide bombers—were killed at the Israeli-owned Paradise Hotel when a four-wheel-drive vehicle laden with explosives crashed into the hotel lobby at 8:30 a.m. Moments earlier, two missiles were fired at a Boeing 757 as it took off from Mombasa's airport bound for Tel Aviv. The missiles missed their target. Kenya was also the scene of a suicide attack four years ago, when a truck bomber hit the U.S. Embassy in Nairobi, the capital, killing more than 200 people. The same day, another truck bomb killed a dozen people at the U.S. embassy in Dar es Salaam, capital of neighboring Tanzania.

Investigation of the coordinated embassy bombings led to indictments against Osama bin Laden and members of his al Qaeda network, four of whom were convicted in U.S. courts. One, Mohammed Saddiq Odeh, allegedly set up a fishing business in Mombasa with al Qaeda money and handed a portion of his revenue over to the organization; another, Wadih el-Hage, reputed to have been Osama bin Laden's secretary, was accused of setting up al Qaeda's East Africa cell in Nairobi in 1994. In the wake of the 2002 attacks, suspicions again turned toward al Qaeda. Though a Palestinian group claimed responsibility for the attack, U.S. officials in Washington have said a likely suspect might be al-Ittihad al-Islamiya, a Somali Muslim group with links to al Qaeda and a record of activity throughout the Horn of Africa, including Mombasa.

Kenyan authorities continued to hold four Somalis and six Pakistanis in connection with the attacks. 'Kenya is a country frequented by people of so many backgrounds and nationalities coming in and out,' Sunkuli said. 'Kenya has been attacked before. Any place can be attacked, but we are looking at how these missiles were brought into the country and how the bombers got in.'

Not everyone who wants to enter Kenya worries about such formalities. Nairobi, one of Africa's largest and busiest cities, is a well-known haven for shady characters from other countries. Human rights groups report that leaders of Rwanda's 1994 genocide and fugitives from other African wars have frequently fled to Kenya, which ranks as one of the most corrupt nations in the world, according to the watchdog group Transparency International. 'The general complaint is that in Kenya you report something to the police and nothing happens, you end up having to pay a bribe,' said Ben Mwashoti, a Mombasa dockworker. 'Illegal documents, sugar, electronics and people sneaking in, all come through here because people have no money. They take bribes, and now we're all suffering because of it.'

There is no question that the failed system in Kenya has made it a real easy place for terrorist attacks. Like the coastline, the border between Kenya and Somalia is extremely porous, allowing goods and people to move easily back and forth. Intelligence agencies have blamed the Somali-based al-Ittihad for attacks in Somalia and Ethiopia and say it has been active in Kenya as well.

But many Kenyans say their country is simply too poor to root out terrorist groups. There are few jobs in the weak economy. Some of those who do find work as police or border guards are frequently unpaid because government workers, according to Transparency International (a corruption watchdog group), pocket salaries. Sometimes, Kenyans say, they have no way to feed their families other than by taking bribes. That kind of poverty makes intelligence officials wonder whether terrorist groups will find a willing labor pool in East Africa.

Kenya's population of thirty-one million is about 10 percent Muslim. Islamic militancy was seldom a concern until the 1998 U.S. embassy bombings, and today, many Kenyan Muslims say they share the anger felt by Muslims elsewhere, especially regarding the Arab-Israeli conflict. Some said the Septempter 11, 2001, attacks in the United States and the Embassy bombings made them feel that Israel's actions in the West Bank and Gaza Strip were the cause of the international terrorist violence.

At the Bawaryz Mosque in Mombasa, some of those attending afternoon prayers said that the Palestinian cause had become as important to them as the struggle against white-minority rule in South Africa once was. The mosque's leader preached peace, but many outside said anger at the United States and Israel was justified. They praised Osama bin Laden, calling him a defender of Islam.

'Kenyan Muslims have started to care about this, and we think it's a good cause,' said Garib Kassim, a businessman. 'No one should be surprised that this bombing happened here. We don't want people to die. But it will keep happening more and more here and around the world unless Israel leaves Palestine alone.'

Conflicts, refugees, and terrorism

According to Funk and Wagnalls New Encyclopedia, a refugee is a person who has fled or been expelled from his or her country of origin because of natural catastrophe, war or military occupation, or fear of religious, racial, or political persecution. Africa, with more than 600 different ethnic groups, has about one-third of the world's refugees, people uprooted by famine or by political liberation struggles and escaping racial and ethnic oppression and economic hardship. Caught in the turmoil that characterizes developing nations in the twentieth century, some African nations have refugees going both in and out of their country, something that exists nowhere else.

There are currently over 9,500,000 refugees in Africa. For example, *The World Almanac and Book of Facts*, *World Refugee Survey 1993* published by the U.S. Committee for Refugees gives some interesting facts. Here is a short list of how many refugees are, and where they can be found:

- *Congo-Zaire*: This country has by far the largest number of refugees in Africa. On November 21, 1996, the High Commissioner reported that over 1.4 million Rwandan Hutus were currently in this country. In addition there were about 500,000 Angolan, Sudanese and Burundi refugees in Zaire.
- *Malawi*: The country is inhabited by 700,000 refugees from Mozambique.
- *Sudan*: The 650,000 refugees in Sudan come from Eritrea, Ethiopia, and Chad.
- *Guinea*: There are about 600,000 refugees in Guinea. Most of them are from Liberia and Sierra Leone.
- *Tanzania*: This country hosts 500,000 refugees from Burundi and Mozambique.

These are only the five most significant African refugee host countries. Most other African countries also host refugees. The case of Burundi is very instructive. Fights between government forces and armed groups in the area of a refugee camp in Burundi (Mugano) in January 1996 resulted in the mass departure of 15,000 refugees from this camp (Rwandese) into neighboring Tanzania. Tanzania already hosts 700,000 Rwandese and Burundi refugees. In the same month, an additional 16,000 refugees from Burundi (mostly Rwandese but also some Burundi) were attempting to go into Tanzania. Since 1993 about 200,000 people from Burundi have left their country, due to violent political fights. It is estimated that at least 400,000 people inside Burundi have been forced out of their own place of origin and are dispersed somewhere in Burundi, now refugees within their home country.

The main problem with refugees is of course a political one. Unfortunately, African political systems have not yet achieved the degree of stability and justice people would hope for. The results of this are frequently wars and battles between different ethnic groups, which have some kind of access to the power structure in the different countries. It seems difficult, as can be seen by the present tensions and wars between Hutus and Tutsis in Zaire, Burundi and Rwanda, to influence the African politics from outside Africa. The reasons people have to flee their country are complex. Sometimes people leave because they do not have enough food or work to be able to survive. Mostly they leave because of fear of war. The developed world certainly plays a role in these wars, be it directly or indirectly:

- Many of the problems that appear today originally stem from when, in the nineteenth century, European statesmen divided Africa up into colonies without respecting the natives.
- Some countries, particularly England, France, Germany, and Austria make money by selling weapons all over the world, not caring about how and by whom these weapons are going to be used.
- If Western countries had put more political will-power into reducing poverty, lack of education and tension in Africa, they would have succeeded. They did not. And the attendant poverty, illiteracy and conflicts have paved the way for criminal gangs to infiltrate and create partnerships and alliances of a destructive nature among Africans. Specifically, the partnerships and alliances forged by al Qaeda give the organization two advantages: a global reach and a continuous flow of fresh recruits to supply the core business: acts of terror around the world. For instance, terrorist attacks against Israel interests in Kenya on Thursday, November 28, 2002, happened only days after a meeting of

lawyers in East Africa had warned that the region could become the hub of terrorism activities because of the poor handling of refugees.

The New York-based Lawyers Committee for Human Rights and the Stanley Foundation who organized the meeting, in Entebbe town of Uganda, discovered that a group called Al-Itihaad is recruiting and training Somali refugees and other sympathizers on terrorism activities in parts of Kenya, specifically at the Daadab camp located at the North Eastern province near Somalia. 'Somali refugees have begun to conduct religious training that is akin to Taliban-styled madrassa classes in refugee camps, allegedly in preparation for defending Islam and Somali nationhood,' said Monica Kathina Juma of the Centre for Refugees Studies. The training is based on the need to counter what Somali refugees see as the mechanizations for the United States to punish Somalis for their acts against the U.S.-led Operation Restore Hope against the late warlord Farah Aideed in 1993.

The lawyers said hands-off handling of refugees in East Africa and the fact that the Great Lakes region is characterized by failing states makes it a suitable soft spot for terrorist networks to operate. Lawyers recommended that refugees should not be confined to camps, but allowed to integrate with the people, a policy that has been adopted by West African countries.

In conclusion, admittedly, Africa has been dogged by border disputes both on land and, increasingly so, over maritime boundaries. Will the African Union act as a more cohesive agent than the OAU was? It is common knowledge that economic development in Africa is pitifully slow and geographically disjointed. The continent attracts less inward investment per head than anywhere else in the world, while most African states continue to trade more actively with their former colonial rulers than with their neighbors. There are many reasons for this, but cross-border political instability and boundary disputes are undoubtedly a major factor.

This was recognized by the Organization of African Unity (OAU) as the continent's most pressing problem, when it was founded in 1963. As its first act, the OAU chose to guarantee the territorial sovereignty of its member states, in an attempt to avert the disorder that a realignment of Africa's boundaries would surely have prompted. Four decades on, and for better or for worse, the continent's boundaries remain virtually unchanged. While the boundaries are the same, they remain obstacles to trade but not to conflict. One of the greatest challenges facing the new African Union (AU) will be to maintain the internal and external sovereignty of its member states. While the plans for a continental central bank and parliament may be welcomed, the real challenge for the new organization will be to bring stability to the most troubled of continents.

African governments nowadays show no evidence of ability to function, let alone to implement even marginal improvements. This inability sets the stage for an anarchic implosion of criminal violence. There are hordes of young men and women everywhere in Africa. They are rushing into the cities where they, wittingly or not, remake civilizations and redefine their identities in terms of religion and tribal ethnicity. These identities do not coincide with the borders of existing states.

The fundamental problem here is that whereas rural poverty is age-old and almost a normal part of the social fabric, urban poverty is socially very destabilizing. As Nigeria, Kenya, Egypt, Saudi Arabia, Algeria, and others have shown, Islamic extremism is the psychological defense mechanism of many urbanized peasants threatened with the loss of traditions in pseudo-modern cities. They see, but may not have access to water and electricity. They are assaulted by a physically unhealthy environment everyday. It is in these pseudo-modern cities that their values are under attack. Under these dehumanizing circumstances, Islam's militancy renders life very attractive to these downtrodden and dispossessed folks. In fact, it is the one religion that is prepared to fight anywhere, anytime. Indeed, a political era like this that is driven by environmental stress, increased cultural sensitivity, unregulated urbanization, and refugee migrations is one created for the spread and intensification of religious Messianism, especially of the radical Islamic variant.

Islam, of course, is now the world's fastest growing religion. These young men and women are like loose molecules in a very unsettling social fluid. And this fluid is surely on the verge of igniting. The spark could come from Islamic radicalism like in Mombassa or Kaduna. The most peaceful and viable approach to tempering Islamic extremism among such young men and women is that their Islamism should be hobbled by syncretism with animism or Christianity. This can make new converts less apt to become violently anti-Western extremists. It will also make for a weakened version of the Islamic faith.

Finally, and in sum, a sequence of Africa's political maps from 1850 until 2000 shows an extreme political fluidity. The instability of Africa's territorial system of political governance will also be a feature of the twenty-first century and there are signs of further crumbling of a state system that already counts more than fifty state units.

In the late nineteenth century, European powers claimed political suzerainty all over Africa, which was effectuated in the early part of the

20th Century and dwindled after the Second World War. Between 1952 and 1965 most African territories became 'independent' again and members of the United Nations. A few laggards still resisted or became 'special cases.' The Portuguese territories only became independent states after 1974. The Spanish Sahara is still an unsettled case, conquered by Morocco, but claimed by an independence movement, acknowledged by the Organization of African Unity and by the United Nations. Southern Rhodesia first needed a period of settler-declared 'unilateral' independence before it became really independent in 1980. South West Africa only became independent Namibia in 1990. South Africa, although formally independent since 1910, only got majority rule and 'real independence' in 1994.

Currently a few territories remain as colonial remnants: Ceuta, Melilla and the Canary Islands of Spain, the Azores and Madeira of Portugal, Réunion and Mayotte of France, Saint Helena and Tristan da Cunha of Great Britain, all together with less than 0.01 percent of Africa's territory and less than one million of Africa's 800 million inhabitants. All these territories are bearing their own hallmarks of elusive boundaries with which Africa will be saddled. The explosion of inter-ethnic violence and the violence that goes together with new territorial arrangements in current-day Africa will not easily come to an end. It does not seem likely that some kind of African Union will be able to play the role of 'third party,' preventing and intervening in conflicts. A form of federalization of Africa, with ethnic units as its basic building blocks (as Ethiopia, Nigeria and Kenya are currently attempting with more or less success) will probably be a future outcome, but only after ages of struggle.

To state this point of view from a general perspective, African states have been most prone to mass terrorism because of their weakness. That is to say, they have unstable political structures (governments, bureaucracies, security forces, party systems, and so on) as well as fragmented political cultures (Laqueur, 2000, p. 207). Weak states, indeed, take the form of unpopular and illegitimate authoritarian governments or permissive and quarrelsome 'democracies.'

In its wake it leads to an economic collapse and in some areas already to a demographic collapse (enforced by famine, the impact of AIDS and the disappearance of 'formal' health care). Europe and the USA seem to turn their back on Africa; Japan—currently its most important 'donor'—seems to hesitate. Many Africans look northward for their survival. A further deterioration of Africa's situation might well mean a flood of migrants towards Europe, the Middle East and North America. United Europe could try to avoid a catastrophe by forming a monetary unity with Africa, followed by open boundaries for capital and labor, and support for the federalization of the Eurafrican Union, backed by rapid deployment forces for military and humanitarian intervention, under joint European and African leadership. If not, United Europe might as well choose the ostrich as its symbol. And the permissive African environment will continue to be a breeding ground for transnational terrorism and a threat to world peace with the state in Africa playing the role of conveyor-belt.

In conclusion, the development of a polity can be explained by studying the emergence of national or continental identity. This polity should not only appear as the product of conscious elite actions but as the outcome of negotiations (or lack thereof) between opposing visions within elite groups at the national or continental movement stage and at subsequent key historical moments. Polities where effective broad-based negotiations on identity values and beliefs conducted among competing elites tend to enjoy a greater degree of medium to long term stability, while those emerging societies where negotiations were not conducted and only one identity vision was imposed tend to suffer from identity and political crises in the course of their political development. Morocco and Algeria present two opposing cases: the former, in which broad-based inter-elite negotiations led to a definition of national identity that became widely shared by the population at large, and the latter, where the lack of such negotiations and the violent outcome of the civil war led to the imposition of only one identity vision and to the subsequent identity crisis that has plagued the country since the early 1980s. This identity crisis plaguing Algeria gives rise to a terror-prone society.

References

Adeeko, A. (2002), 'Bound to Violence?: Achille Mbembe on the Postcolony', *West Africa Review*, Vol. 3, No. 2.

African Rights (1994), *Rwanda: Death, Despair and Defiance*, African Rights: London.

Ake, C. (1992), 'What is the Problem of Ethnicity in Africa?, Keynote address at the Conference on Ethnicity, Society, and Conflict, University of Natal, Pietermaritzburg, South Africa, September 14–16.

Bayart, J.-F., Ellis, S. and Hibou, B. (1999), *The Criminalization of the State in Africa*, James Currey: London.

Boone, C. (1992), *Merchant Capital and the Roots of State Power in Senegal, 1930–1985*, Cambridge University Press: New York.

Botha, M. P. and Burger, F. (1989), 'A Weathervane in Uncertain Winds', *Weekly Mail*, July 14–20, pp. 21, 24.

Botha, M. P. and Van Aswegen, A. (1992), *Images of South Africa: The Rise of the Alternative Film*, Human Sciences Research Council: Pretoria.

Bratton, M. and Van de Walle, N. (1997), *Democratic Experiments in Africa: Regime Transitions in Comparative Perspective*, Cambridge University Press: New York.

Chabal, P. (1992), *Power in Africa*, Macmillan: London.

Chazan, N., Lewis, P., Mortimer, R. A., Rothchild, D. and Stedman, S. J. (1999), *Politics and Society in Contemporary Africa*, 3rd Edition, Lynne Rienner: Boulder, CO.

Clapham, C. (1985), *Third World Politics: An Introduction*, Routledge: London.

Cohen, R. and Deng, F. (1998), *Masses in Flight: The Global Crisis of Internal Displacement*, Brookings Institution: Washington, D.C.

Colson, E. (1981), 'African Society at the Time of the Scramble', in Gann, L. H. and Duignan, P. (eds.), *Colonialism in Africa, 1870–1960*, vol. 1, Cambridge University Press: Cambridge.

Combs, C. C. (1997), *Terrorism in the Twenty-First Century*, Prentice–Hall: Upper Saddle River, NJ.

Crummey, D. (ed.) (1986), *Banditry, Rebellion and Social Protest in Africa*, J. Currey: London.

Daddieh, C. K. (1995), 'Structural Adjustment Programs and Regional Integration: Compatable or Mutually Exclusive?', in Mingesteab, K. and B. I. Logan (eds.), *Beyond Economic Liberalization in Africa: Structural Adjustment and the Alternatives*, Zed Books: London.

De Waal, A. (ed.) (2000), *Who Fights? Who Cares?*, Africa World Press: Trenton, NJ.

Dietz, T. and Foeken, D. (1994), 'Leidt Afrikaanse democratisering tot etnishe polarisatie?' (Does Democratization in Africa Lead to Ethnic Polirization?), *Geografie*, Vol. 3, No. 1, pp. 30–34.

Dietz, T. and Foeken, D. (1999), 'Of Ethnicity, Manipulation and Observation: The 1992 and 1997 Elections in Kenya', in Abbink J and Hesseling, G. (eds.), *Election Observation and Democratization in Africa*, Macmillan: Basingstoke, UK.

Dietz, T. and Houtkamp, J. (1995), 'Foreign Aid to Africa: A Geographical Analysis', *TESG*, Vol. 86, No. 3, pp. 278–295.

Dietz, T. and Houtkaump, J. (1998), 'Foreign Aid to Africa: The Rise and Fall of Structural Development Aid', in Grant, R. and Nijman, J. (eds.), *The Global Crisis in Foreign Aid*, Syracuse University Press: Syracuse, NY.

Dietz, T. and Van der Wusten, J. (1991), 'Eurafrika: een analyse van internationale vervlechtingen tussen Afrika en Europa' (Eurafrica: An Analysis of International Relations Between Africa and Europe), *Geografisch Tijdschrift*, Vol. 2, pp. 104–114.

DuBois, W. E. B. (1903), *The Souls of Black Folk*, Penguin Books: New York.

Eisenstadt, S. (1973), *Traditional Patrimonialism and Modern Neopatrimonialism*, Sage Research Papers in Social Sciences, Beverly Hills, CA: Sage.

Fanon, F. (1963), *The Wretched of the Earth*, Paladin: London.

Gellner, E. (1983), *Nations and Nationalism*, Cornell University Press: Ithaca, NY.

Geschiere, P. (1997), 'Elites Imagining "Their" Region: The Paradoxes of Nation-Building, Locality and Citizenship in Postcolonial Africa', Paper presented at the International Conference on Globalization and the Reproduction of Inequalities in the Periphery, São Paulo, Brazil, September 21–24.

Hansberry, W. L. (1981), *Africa and Africans as Seen by Classical Writers*, Viking Press: New York.

Hodgkin, T. (1963), 'Islam, History and Politics', *Journal of Modern African Studies*, Vol. 1, No. 1, pp. 91–97.
The Holy Bible, 1987 Edition, Zondervan Bible Publishers: Grand Rapids, MI.
Homer-Dixon, T. F. (1999), *Environment, Scarcity, and Violence*, Princeton University Press: Princeton, NJ.
Hindson, D. (1987), *Pass Controls and the Urban African Proletariat in South Africa*, Raven Press: Johannesburg.
Jackson, R. H. (1987), 'Quasi-States, Dual Regimes, and Neoclassical Theory: International Jurisprudence and the Third World', *International Organization*, Vol. 41, pp. 519–549.
Jackson, R. H. and Rosberg, C. (1982a), 'Why Africa's Weak States Persist: The Empirical and Juridical in Statehood', *World Politics*, Vol. 35, No. 1, pp. 1–24.
Jackson, R. H. and Rosberg, C. (1982b), *Personal Rule in Black Africa*, University of California Press: Berkeley and Los Angeles.
Jackson, R. H. and Rosberg, C. (1986), 'Why Africa's Weak States Persist: The Empirical and Juridical in Statehood', in Kohli, A. (ed.), *The State and Development in the Third World*, Princeton University Press: Princeton, NJ.
Jordan, Z. P. (1997), 'The National Question in Post-'94 South Africa', A discussion paper prepared for the 50th National Conference of the ANC, Cape Town.
Kaplan, R. D. (2000), 'The Lawless Frontier', *The Atlantic*, September.
Kellner, D. (1992), 'Popular Culture and the Construction of Postmodern Identity', in Lash, S. and Friedman, J. (eds.), *Modernity and Identity*, Basil Blackwell: London.
Knight, I. J. (1994), *Warrior Chiefs of Southern Africa*, Firebird Books: New York.
Krasner, S. (2001), 'Sovereignty', *Foreign Policy*, January/February, pp. 20–29.
Lagos, M. (2001), 'How People View Democracy: Between Stability and Crisis in Latin America', *Journal of Democracy*, Vol. 12, No. 1, pp. 137–145.
Laqueur, W. (1990), 'Futility of Terrorism', in Kegley, Charles W. (ed.), *International Terrorism: Characteristics, Causes, Controls*, St. Martin's Press: New York.
Lugard, F. D. (1965), *The Dual Mandate in British Tropical Africa*, Frank Cass: London.
Lumley, E. K. (1976), *Forgotten Mandate: A British District Officer in Tangayika*, Archon Books: London.
Mainwaring, S., O'Donnell, G. and Valenzuela, S. (eds.) (1992), *Issues in Democratic Consolidation: The New South American Democracies*, University of Notre Dame Press: Notre Dame, IN.
Mamdani, M. (1996), *Citizen and Subject: Contemporary Africa and the Legacy of Late Colonialism*, Princeton University Press: Princeton, NJ.
Mazrui, A. (1967), 'Islam, Political Leadership and Economic Radicalism in Africa', *Comparative Studies in Sociology and History*, Vol. 9, pp. 274–291.
Mbembe, A. (1992), 'Provisional Notes on the Postcolony', *Africa*, Vol. 62, No. 1, pp. 3–29.
Mbembe, A. (2001), *On the Postcolony*, University of California Press: Berkeley and Los Angeles.
Mercer, K. (1990), 'Welcome to the Jungle', in Rutherford, J. (ed.), *Identity: Community, Culture, Difference*, Lawrence and Wishart.
Mwale, S. (1998), 'An African Renaissance Must Have Cultural Roots', *The East African*, April 6–12, p. 23.
Nnoli, O. (1978), *Ethnic Politics in Nigeria*, Fourth Dimension: Enugu.
Nnoli, O. (1989), *Conflict Politics in Africa*, Vintage: Ibadan.
Nnoli, O. (1995), *Ethnicity and National Development in Nigeria*, Ashgate: Aldershot, UK.

Nyasani, J. M. (1997), *The African Psyche*, University of Nairobi and Theological Printing Press: Nairobi.

Obasanjo, O. (1989), *Constitution for National Integration and Development*, Friends Foundation Publishers: Lagos.

Oommen, T. K. (ed.) (1997), *Citizenship and National Identity: From Colonialism to Globalism*, Sage Publications: Beverly Hills, CA.

Osaghae, E. E. (1994), *Between State and Civil Society in Africa*, CODESERIA: Dakar, Senegal.

Osaghae, E. E. (1995), 'The Study of Political Transition in Africa', *Review of African Political Economy*, Vol. 22, No. 64, pp. 183–197.

Palmer, R. (1943), 'Islam in the Western Sudan and on the West Coast of Africa', in Arberry, A. J. (ed.), *Islam Today*, Faber & Faber: London.

Parrinder, G. (1959), 'Islam and West African Indigenous Religions', *Numen*, Vol. 6, pp. 130–141.

Parrinder, G. (1960), 'Islam in West Africa', *West African Review*, Vol. 31 (December), pp. 12–15.

Posel, D. (1991), *The Making of Apartheid, 1948–1961: Conflict and Compromise*, Clarendon Press: Oxford.

Rakiya, O. and de Waal, A. (1995), *African Rights: Rwanda, Death, Despair and Destruction*, African Rights: London.

Ravallion, M. and Shaohua, C. (1996), 'What Can New Survey Data Tell Us About Recent Changes in Living Standards in Developing and Transitional Economies?', Background paper to World Bank series on *Poverty Reduction and the World Bank: Progress and Challenges in the 1990s*, World Bank: Washington, D.C.

Salih, M. A. (1999), *Environment Politics and Liberation in Contemporary Africa*, Kluwer Academic Press: Dordrecht.

Schlee, G. (1989), *Identities on the Move: Clanship and Pastoralism in Northern Kenya*, Manchester University Press: Manchester.

Seequeh, S. (1996), 'Our Political Crisis: Revolutions or Holocaust?', *Heritage*, No. 5 (November), pp. 5–12.

Sulaiman, I. I. (1988), 'A Fresh Constitution Required', in Sulaiman, I. I. and Abdulkadir, S. (eds.), *On the Political Future of Nigeria*, Hudahuda: Zaria, Nigeria.

Thompson, A. (2000), *An Introduction to African Politics*, Routledge: London.

Tomaselli, K. G. (1990), 'Cultural Reconstruction in South African Cinema', in Blignaut, J. and Metz, C. (eds.), *Showdata Bulletin*, Vol. 5, Showdata: Johannesburg.

Wolf, R. (1982) *Europe and the People Without a History*, University of California Press: Berkeley and Los Angeles.

Wunsch, J. S. and Olowu, D. (1995), *The Failure of the Centralized State: Institutions and Self-governance in Africa*, ICS Press: San Diego, CA.

Zartman, I. W. (2001), 'Bordering on War (Boundaries Between African Nations)', *Foreign Policy*, May/June, pp. 66–67.

6

Weak African States, Islamic Theopolitics, and Terrorism

Africa is far from being immune to the illness of nation-state weakness and/or failure. For all their differences, successful states resemble each other because they have all found ways to function as polities; they have cohesive national identities and social compacts that bind them together. Weak and unsuccessful states like those in Africa, however, fail as polities for a wide variety of reasons. Some have been torn asunder by civil war, others by external aggression. Some have foundered on unresolved conflicts based on clan or ethnicity; drought and grinding poverty have claimed still more. All have potential for destabilizing their neighbors.

Prominent among these destabilizing characteristics is an infectious ideological vacuum, which terrorists seek to fill by exploiting radical political religion. Radical political religion is perhaps the least understood among the various ideologies, which, in the aftermath of the disintegration of the Soviet Union, are challenging the established order of nation-states. And yet, in the next several decades, the Islamist form of this phenomenon may well have a disproportionate impact on the transformation of global politics despite its humble Arab origin (Abu-Rabi, 1996, p. 370; Ahmed, 1992, p. 294).

The Islamic faith and Muslims have played a crucial role in the development of Africa, not only in North Africa and West Africa where it is still the dominant religion, but also in East Africa, where its dominance decreases as one moves south, and in Southern Africa, where it was introduced through slaves and political exiles and is most prominent today in the cities of Durban and Cape Town.

Theopolitics, Arabism, and Islamism

Until recently, the study of African states has focused almost exclusively on personalities and on the regime, especially on its non-democratic aspects. It has done so at the expense of accounting fully for the forces of skepticism, liberty, and creativity that struggle against repressive conformism and state hegemony. Strangely, there seems to be no scholarly awareness of the simple fact that however influential state repression appears in word and deed, however evident the trappings of state authority, people come into being, thrive, marry, raise families, think, laugh, and cry without regard to—indeed, sometimes in utter defiance of—the strictures of the state or state authority. This chapter examines how African peoples live and flourish while trying to shape their political and religious surroundings outside the formal structures of the state, through an established religion like Islam.

Media interest in Islam exploded following the attack on the United States on September 11, 2001. General Tommy Franks, former head of the U.S. Central Command, in an interview with the BBC in Ethiopia, following his tour of the Horn of Africa expressed concern over the situation in Somalia:

> 'We have known of links to al Qaeda [terrorist network] in and through Somalia for a considerable period of time.' He added that the U.S. 'will not take off the table the possibility of action against countries of concern . . . We are interested in states where there is a history of terrorist networks, training operations and that sort of thing,' he said. 'And so we are going to continue to keep our options open and continue to conduct dialogue with the frontline nations such as Eritrea, Djibouti, Kenya and Ethiopia' (BBC Focus On Africa, March 19, 2002).

Media interest and General Frank's tour raised two pertinent questions: (1) What is the relationship between the September 11 attackers and Somalia? (2) Is Islam linked to terrorism of the ilk of September 11? History can help us get answers to these questions (see, e.g., *Reuters*,

October 19, 2001; *Church and Society Magazine*, January-March, 2000, p. 33).

The Soviet withdrawal from Afghanistan took place in 1989. The infectious Islamic jihad against 'infidels' carried out by returning veterans from the war in Afghanistan spread particularly rapidly in Algeria, Egypt and the Sudan. In Algeria, tens of thousands of people died and several times this number were wounded, displaced from their homes or disappeared in the events that followed the cancellation of the 1992 elections. In one of its most gruesome episodes, 412 men, women, and children were hacked to death on the night of December 29, 1997 in three isolated villages in Algeria's Elizane region. Excerpts obtained from the *ENN Intelligence Report*, March 6, 1997, bear witness to these atrocities (http://www.emergency.com/algera97.html).

Algeria has been in a state of virtual civil war since early 1992, as economic stagnation and massive unemployment in the post-independence *bidonvilles* or shantytowns that ringed its cities provided fertile seed for radicalization. This was financed first by countries such as Saudi Arabia and later by largesse from Osama bin Laden and other radical private financiers. In the final years of the Afghan war, from 1986 to 1989, somewhere between 600 and 1000 battle hardened Algerian nationals returned home from the 'just war' (Shittier, 1987).

Only early and effective countermeasures from Tunisia, Libya, Egypt and other sub-Saharan African states managed to halt the spread of radical terror further afield. Despite these efforts, fifty-eight foreign tourists and four Egyptians were massacred in Luxor, Upper Egypt, in November 1997, garnering international attention and damaging that country's vital tourist industry. The subsequent bombing of two American embassies in Nairobi and Dar-es-Salaam on August 7, 1998—and evident but unsuccessful attempts to destroy others in Kampala (as well as Bangkok and Tirana)—reflected the extent to which Africa, despite its oft reported global strategic marginalization, had been drawn into a new chapter in an old story. The international character of this threat was reflected in the U.S. retaliatory cruise missile attack on a chemical factory in Khartoum, Sudan on August 20, 1998. Further north, the summer 1995 assassination attempt on Egyptian President Husni Mubarak in Addis Ababa, Ethiopia, blamed on *Al Ittihaad* members, had already increased the tension between Egypt, Sudan and Ethiopia. The ripple effects from that conflict would even add to the motivation for a wave of terrorist attacks in South Africa in the late-1990s.

Conflict and cooperation

Conflict and co-operation characterize inter-Arab relations (Burgat and Dowell, 1993). These conflictual and cooperative interactions have been sharpened by historical factors such as: (1) pan-Arab ideology; (2) stark realities of multiple Arab nation- states with competing interests; (3) competition for the role of regional Arab leadership; and, (4) various social, economic and personal factors. The creation of an Arab state system, League of Arab States, never helped matters (Fox, 1970).

The League of Arab States was founded in 1945, marking the tangible emergence of an Arab state system within the broader Middle East region.[1] Since then, the common Arab opposition to Israel has resulted in the formation of three all-Arab war coalitions (1948, 1967 and 1973). In 1950, the League formally forbade any Arab state to make a separate peace with Israel, with the threat of major sanctions in case of violation.[2] This fundamental tenet of collective Arab action remained in force for nearly 30 years, until Anwar Sadat's lone peace initiative with Israel.

Sadat's initiative was greeted by most Arab-Islamist states with disbelief, confusion and outright anger at his treachery. The price was Egypt's isolation and suspension from the Arab League. Isolation and suspension were only temporary because Egypt never denounced the peace initiative with Israel. And by the 1980s, Egypt bounced back to restore its standing at the center of the Arab world in her capacity as supplier of military equipment and manpower to Iraq in its eight-year war with Iran. Concurrently, Arab states, at the Fez Summit Conference in September 1982, collectively endorsed the idea of a political settlement with Israel.[3] The Fez resolutions stood in sharp contrast to the famous 'Four No's' of the Khartoum Arab Summit Conference of August 1967, illustrating the distance, which the tottering Arab position had traveled.[4]

The gradual evolution of Arab states' policies in favor of a contractual peace with Israel therefore gained the day. This *volte-face* was a derivative of fragmentation and inferiority vis-à-vis Israeli and American power, rather than from Arab cohesiveness or national interest. That is, the Arabs yielded to a peace settlement based on what for the Arab world was an unfavorable balance of power[5] due to the triumph of the West over the Soviet Union. The latter was the patron of radical Arab regimes and movements. The collapse of this secular radicalism came as an ironical incidental bonus to conservative pro-Arab monarchies and republics like Saudi Arabia. In addition, Arab military weakness and inferiority as evidenced by successive defeats in the 1948, 1967, and 1973 wars with Israel also stemmed from the reality of inter-Arab fragmentation.[6]

The founding myth of Arab solidarity had been repeatedly punctured beyond repair by a sequence of events: (1) the bloody, off-again, on-again Lebanese civil war between 1975–1990; (2) Egypt's abandonment of Arab ranks in favor of peace with Israel; (3) Syria's support for non-Arab Iran in its bitter eight year war with Iraq during the 1980s; (4) the all-too-obvious Arab inaction in the face of Israel's war against the PLO in Lebanon and Syria, in 1982; and (5) most traumatizing, Iraq's invasion and annexation of a fellow Arab state Kuwait, in August 1990, which led to the first full scale inter-Arab war in modern history.[7]

These policy shifts engendered by Arab weakness, inferiority and fragmentation manifested themselves in: (1) the large-scale Arab participation at the Madrid Peace Conference in 1991 and subsequent multilateral talks; (2) most Arab states' support for the Israeli-Palestinian and Israeli-Jordanian peace agreements between 1993–1995; (3) the lifting of the Gulf Arab states secondary and tertiary economic boycott of Israel; and (4) the establishment of some form of diplomatic relations with Israel by eight Arab League members (out of 21). In 1996, the Cairo Arab Summit Conference warned the new Netanyahu government in Israel of the consequences of any backsliding in the peace process as well as clearly endorsed the concept of a political settlement.[8]

Theopolitics and Islamic fundamentalism

The contradiction between the idealized pacifism of Islam, Arab Unity and the harsh realities of inter-Arab competition and rivalry, decline of Arabism as a functional ideology and the growing 'stateness' of most Arab states sounded the clarion call for the re-examination of Arabism and Islamism. It is therefore understandable why in the late 1980s and early 1990s, thousands of volunteers from across the Islamic world joined the anti-Communist jihad in Afghanistan. Since 1995, however, the rise of the Taliban movement brought with it a major resurgence of the jihad foreign legion. It also changed its complexion in several notable aspects (David, 2002).

Some 8,000 to 12,000 Muslims (many of them Tunisians, Algerians, Egyptians, Yemenis and Saudis) joined the jihadic foreign legion. These foreign combatants were better organized, and in many cases better equipped with heavier weaponry than their counterparts of the late 1980s and early 1990s. Operating at the center of a global network of radical Islamists, they were evidently ideologically more focused than their counterparts of the 1980s. Many of these young enthusiasts returned to radicalize Islamic movements in their home countries, and to establish a good platform for their sponsor.

However, there is an interesting connection between these groups, especially in recent years. These are their links to al Qaeda and the increasing role of the Egyptian and North-African Islamists connected with Osama bin Laden, whether in Afghanistan, or various other regions. Al Qaeda's perception of the global struggle, together with Osama bin Laden's *fatwah* of February 1998, gives them the legitimacy to commit criminal acts against the 'infidels'—despite a general religious ruling against indiscriminate criminal activity directed against non-Muslims.

The means of financing North African Islamists varies from direct transfer of cash by special couriers and a variety of legitimate bank accounts, to the financing of a wide range of associations, institutions for social and educational projects, hospitals, orphans and other humanitarian goals. Sometimes these humanitarian projects are legitimate, and used to further the popularity of the fundamentalist cause; in many cases, they are also used as a cover to raise and launder funds from the general population for terrorist activities (Weschler, 2001, p. 135; Emerson, 2000).

The money is transferred to the Arab or Muslim World by means both sophisticated and secret. But in most cases these are legitimate transactions through bank accounts in Europe, North America, and the Middle East. Some of the Islamic institutions in the West are used also to launder large sums of money transferred from different countries or wealthy individuals, primarily in Iran, Saudi Arabia, Kuwait and some other Gulf states. During the 1990s this transfer of money has gradually increased. Following the decision by the Gulf States to cease financing the PLO because of its position in the Gulf war, these states shifted their financial support to Islamic groups, organizations and projects. This led to the foundation of many kinds of institutions, cultural centers, publications, research institutes and welfare associations one of whose main goals was fund raising and money laundering. This was in addition to the use of these organizations for the spread of radical Islamist messages among Muslim populations in the West.

On the one hand, the Saudi government is the greatest financier of Muslim relief organizations in the world. But, on the other hand, by doing so it in certain areas directly assists publics that support Islamist terrorist groups, thus indirectly assisting these groups. There are numerous reports concerning one such official Saudi relief organization—the International Islamic Relief Organization (IIRO)—that it provides financial support to Wahhabi groups in the Middle East and Central Asia and North Africa.

As a flashback, since the end of the Cold War, the rise of Islamic consciousness as well as the concurrent rise of extremism and terror has been given almost unprecedented coverage in both the print and the electronic media. Edward W. Said (1997, pp. xi–xii) in the introduction to his book states that 'there has been an intense focus on Muslims and Islam in the American and Western media, most of it characterized by (a more) highly exaggerated stereotyping and belligerent hostility.' This would appear to stem from the many incidents of extremism and provocation that have occurred during the past two decades. Some of these include the bombing of the United States Marines barracks in 1983, in which 240 soldiers were killed, the bombing of the United States Embassy in Beirut, the taking of American hostages in Lebanon in the 1980s and a number of aircraft hijackings and bombings. The most notorious is the bombing of Pan Am Flight 103 over Lockerbie, Scotland in 1988.

These incidents were either traced to or were openly claimed by Islamic groups as the work of their 'warriors' and the cumulative effect of many such incidents has been the demonizing of Islam as a whole in the media and in the psyches of many citizens of non-Muslim countries, particularly in the United States and Western Europe. As Said (1997, p. 144) states, 'The media, the government, the geo-political strategists and . . . the academic experts on Islam are all in concert: Islam is a threat to Western civilization.'

Islamic fundamentalism as a concept

Religious militancy and terrorism pose a major problem to the contemporary world. The upsurge of militancy since the last three decades has been threatening to both those who govern the liberal democratic states within which terrorism is perpetrated, and the common people at large. The instruments of terror are varied and the motivations of militants diverse. Experts agree that militancy is the use of threat of violence, a method of combat or a strategy to achieve a certain goal, that its aim is to induce a state of fear in the victim, that it is ruthless and does not conform to humanitarian civil norms and that publicity is an essential factor in the terrorist strategy.

Militancy is a process comprising several phases; for others it is a strategy, for others still, a form of political and religious violence approximately insurrection, rebellion, anarchy or political-economic and religious protest or revolution. Militancy is also a major symptom of the dysfunction of a socio-political and cultural system afflicted by social immobilism, weak institutions or of political authority, a decline in religious values and resurgent radical neo-fascism or religious fundamentalism. In this context, terrorism is symptomatic of social disorganization associated with urbanization and political corruption. Militancy is undertaken by alienated, marginalized, predominantly frustrated people, who are pre-disposed towards violence.

Some militant activities begin and end in a single country. However, many transcend national borders. Thus militancy today has a uniquely transnational character that afflicts many countries and regions. In 1991, terrorists targeted the citizens and property across seventy-three countries in 533 separate attacks. Although militantism dates to antiquity it emerged as a significant international problem in the 1970s and 1980s in West Asia and North Africa. Militant terrorism is a tactic of the powerless against the powerful. It is not surprising that political, religious and ethnic movements perpetrate many acts of militancy. Those seeking independence and sovereign statehood like the Arab Palestinians and the Sahrwawis in Western Sahara typify the kind of independent aspirations that animate militant activity.

Guerrilla warfare normally associated with rural uprisings or protests is not a viable route to self-assertion in the urbanized areas of the industrialized world but militant tactics are. Frankly, militantism is not perceived to be a disease by all. A terrorist to one may be a liberator to another. Both government and counter-government movements claim to seek liberty, and both are labeled as terrorist or militant by the other. Seen from this aspect, terrorism by ideologically motivated fanatics, extremists, and militants at the periphery of society may not be different from the kind of militantism conducted by the state that they oppose. Militancy is seen as an end in itself or as a means to a given end. It has both tactical and strategic perspectives. It has a place among the means employed by extremist factions but what might loosely be termed Islamic militancy and terrorism emanating from the Middle East (where extreme violence is a part of political discourse) differ in their ideological inspiration and in their ultimate goals.

Their resort to terrorist methods often means that their goal is not seen as legitimate by the authorities, the public and the international community may express the aims of militants clearly or incoherently. Militancy and terrorism produce fear, and are intended to destroy public confidence in the authorities. It is, to some Western Observers, an abhorrent and unacceptable means of pursuing political and military ends. In general militancy or terrorism is interpreted as an illegitimate means of attempting to effect political change by the indiscriminate use of violence and force.

The wave of Islamic militancy (Kibble, 1995) that is currently sweeping the world and which is variedly referred to as radical Islamic Fundamentalism, Islamism, Islamic Resurgence and the world-wide Jihad movement has its remote origins in the Muslim Brotherhood movement in Egypt in the late 1920s. During the early years of its existence the Brotherhood advocated the revitalization of Islam as part of the anti-colonial movement among Egyptians. The Brotherhood soon spread to other parts of the Arab world where it acquired a more temporal and a less apolitical character as it became more deeply involved in the growing anti-colonial struggle that followed the end of the Second World War in 1945. As a result by the early 1950s the Brotherhood's welfare activities had become overshadowed by its commitment to mainly political objectives.

Two post-war developments that had a direct effect on the development of the radical Islamic Fundamentalist movement have been the Iranian revolution in the late 1970s and the Mujahideen resistance against the Soviet occupation of Afghanistan in the early 1980s. Both these events directly influenced the militant nature of the radical Fundamentalist movement. The current radical Islamic Fundamentalist movement has been described as essentially a struggle for the 'heart and soul of Islam.' Steven Emerson (1998a, pp. 16–26; 1998b, pp. 28–29) in his much publicized discussions on *The Worldwide Jihad Movement* writes that 'Fundamentalist Islamic terror represents one of the most lethal threats to the stability of Western Society.' It endeavors, he writes, to bring about the total subjugation of all non-believers or 'infidel' to the fundamental principles of Islam and the creation of a worldwide Islamic empire.

Radical Islamic fundamentalism should however not be confused with the broader Muslim fundamentalist movement that has been part of Islam since its inception in the seventh century. The vast majority of the world's more than one billion Muslims support neither violence nor terrorism to advance the belief and principles of Islam. Unlike their militant brethren their religious fervor is not directed at the forceful subjugation of the *infidel* but rather at the extension of Islam and its principles among both believers and non-believers through peaceful means. Nonetheless, the impression is often gained that although radical Islamic fundamentalism is a minority movement, it appears to have the tacit support of the international Islamic community as such, or at least then, a substantial part of that community.

Although the post-World War II struggle against colonialism, the revolution in Iran and the war in Afghanistan directly influenced the development of Islamic radicalism, it does not adequately explain the reasons for the radical Islamic fundamentalist movement's phenomenal growth over the last three decades. According to Abdulkader Tayob (1999), an Islamic scholar at the University of Cape Town, varying explanations have been advanced in an attempt to explain the current wave of Islamic resurgence. He states that the current wave of Islamic uprisings is symptomatic of the profound legitimacy crisis faced by Muslim countries. In response to the inability of secular ideologies to deliver on political and social promises, militant Islamic options have emerged. Consequently as the lower-class educated Muslims found the higher echelons of state power increasingly in the hands of small and often pro-Westernized cliques they turned to the ideology of Islamic resurgence as a way to challenge that political control. The current wave of Islamic resurgence within Muslim communities could also be viewed as a direct result of the religious dilemma posed by living in a world dominated by 'infidels.' From this point of view Islamic resurgence could be understood as part of a world-wide rejection of modernity (as represented primarily by the West) and seen as a last ditch defense of Allah. Finally, there are also those who have blamed the current wave of Islamic resurgence on modern concepts such as feminism and Marxism.

One of the most noticeable characteristic of the current wave of radical Islamic fundamentalism, is its vehement hostility towards the West or any doctrine, object or form that appears to have originated in the West. This hostility is directed primarily at the United States and Israel as well as Jews worldwide.

And even more noticeable if not perhaps the most noticeable characteristic of radical Islamic fundamentalism is its willingness to use violence and terrorism 'legitimate' means to achieve its aims and objectives. It is primarily this willingness to resort to extreme measures that has led contemporary Western governments to regard radical Islamic fundamentalism as the most potent threat against Western democracy and international stability since the end of the Cold War.

Radical Islamic fundamentalism in conjunction with the present day technological revolution, have devised an impressive international infrastructure that is backed by vast amounts of petrodollars. The logistics of this international infrastructure are geared towards international communication, fund-raising, the recruitment of volunteers and paramilitary training. In the development of this international infrastructure, the importance of the Internet, the swiftly expanding international computer-based information network is rapidly escalating.

From its sphere of influence in the Middle East and North Africa radical Islamic fundamentalism is steadily advancing throughout the African continent. Fears raised by this spread of Islamism is evidenced by screaming newspaper articles such as "Rising Muslim Power in Africa Causes Unrest in Nigeria and Elsewhere," which appeared in the *New York Times* (November 1, 2001), "Christian-Muslim Mix is Boiling Over in Africa (*Zenit*, October 20, 2001), and "Two Hundred Nigerian Christians Killed in Anti-American Riots" (*Compass Direct*, November 1, 2001. Present-day Sudan is already firmly enmeshed in its grip while the pro-western regimes of Egypt and Algeria appear to be its next immediate target. Many Western observers believe that should either Egypt or Algeria fall to the radical Muslim fundamentalist movement, this could have a domino effect on the rest of Africa. Should this come to pass, the world may eventually witness how one African country after another can succumb to the onslaught of radical Fundamentalism on the continent. Present indications points to the fact that South Africa with its apparently opulent socio-economic infrastructure, may not only play a significant role in such a development but it may be the ultimate target of the Islamic fundamentalist movement in Africa. In fact, fundamentalism as a concept, although popularly used in the context of describing Islamic extremism is, in fact, a term which originated to describe Christian doctrines which are based on a literal interpretation of the Bible. This can be traced back to late nineteenth century Protestant movements opposed to modern scientific theory and philosophy.

Islamic fundamentalism offers a radical reinterpretation of traditional Islamic concepts. And, its discourse on the subject of battle serves to mobilize believers, warn them against those identified as enemies, and encourage them to train, organize, and actively participate in the battle. Tactics differ as some fundamentalists tend to withdraw from society temporarily into isolationist separatism, while others actively engage in socio-political affairs to transform society. Both responses are forms of battle, whether they are seen as defensive action against attacking 'evil' forces or offensive campaigns to conquer enemies and transform the world.

The London-based *Economist* (October 20, 2001) estimates that a total of 500 people were killed in the two rounds of violence that occurred in northern Nigeria following the September 11 attacks in the United States. The *New York Times* (November 1, 2001) quotes a Western diplomat as saying that the death toll in the Nigerian riots may have been as high as 2,000 (also see *Reuters*, September 23, 2001; *Zenit*, September 13, 2001; *Compass Direct*, November 1, 2001).

Islamic fundamentalism can therefore be described as a doctrine that is based on a literal interpretation of the Qur'an. Islam is the religion of the Qur'an and it is therefore imperative that all Muslims, regardless of rite, sect or piety, believe in the inerrancy of the Qur'an as the revealed word of Allah, hence all Muslims may be classified as fundamentalists.

If most Muslims agree on the authenticity and inerrancy of the Qur'an, they do differ on its interpretation, a task traditionally reserved for learned jurists and theologians. Over the course of time, literal or rationalist theory emerged to accommodate changing conditions and the growth of human knowledge, hence the modernist view as previously described. In view of the emergence of the extremist view of fundamentalism, as expounded by contemporary Islamic leaders, it is curious to note that there are very few theoretical or theological theses or scholarly works that can be attributed to them. This lends credence to the argument by Marty and Appleby (1995, pp. 3–4) that 'As lay scholars of Islam, leaders of . . . fundamentalist movements are not theologians but social thinkers and political activists.' They have therefore been concerned with emphasizing segments of the Qur'an that serve their purposes (sometimes reduced to quoting of verses) rather than interpreting the text itself.

Though early in his career, the Prophet Muhammad recited verses that were kind to non-Muslims (see, e.g., Qur'an 2: 62; 2: 256), later in his life, his language changed. His last words commanding harm to non-Muslims are said to abrogate those verses commanding kindness. It is said that non-Muslims will be forgiven only if they turn to Islam and practice Islamic religious duties. No matter how Muslims try to explain away the above verses, terrorists use them so that to them the end justifies the means. Verses like these form the basis for one of the fundamental tenets of Islam: Jihad. Accordingly, Islam's ultimate goal is to enforce worldwide submission to the Qur'an at whatever cost. What we label as terrorists is simply a group of people who obey the Qur'an. Yet, what makes things more complicated is that Muslims in the world today are either ignorant of the teachings of the Qur'an, or they hide it (Chismar, 2001).

The emergence of Islamic extremism

When examining the differences between fundamentalism and extremism, as manifested in the terror tactics used by many extremist groups, it is well to note that, whilst fundamentalism is based on the basic tenets of the Qur'an, the extremists base much of their belief system on the content of the sharia or Islamic law. The sharia is based on the writings of the Prophet Muhammad and other Islamic jurists and is, in itself, an interpretation of the Qur'an.

Whilst the Qur'an espouses a common belief in the fundamentals (also known as the pillars) of Islam i.e. the pronouncement that there is no other God but Allah; that Muhammad is his messenger; prayer; fasting; almsgiving and the pilgrimage to Mecca, there are also six basic articles of faith which include belief in the Holy Books, angels, the Day of judgment and destiny. These, however, are not the points of emphasis in the jargon of contemporary Islamic movements, which instead focus on the necessity of establishing an Islamic government or authority to enforce the sharia law. In an article titled "Sharia and the Faith of Northern Christians" (*Church and Society Magazine*, January-March, 2000, pp. 17, 25), Emma Usman Shehu points out that Islamic law in Nigeria is a political weapon. This is confirmed by Bishop Mike Okonkwo, President of the Pentecostal Fellowship of Nigeria (*Compass Direct*, September 2000) who believes that sharia law is being employed to place other faiths in a noncompetitive position within Nigerian society.

Why has Islamic extremism become the most conspicuous force in current social and political trends in the Middle East? In answering this question two forces will be considered namely, the political situation and social/economic forces, which have contributed to its rise.

Political and social forces

The post-colonial period in the Middle East saw the rise of Arab nationalism together with the ideals of Pan-Arabism—that is, the notion of Arab brotherhood and solidarity within the community of Arab nations.

The diversity of the various Arab nations, together with their differing alliances, however, ensured that the much-vaunted Arab nationalism failed to produce any sort of cohesion in an era characterized by slogans of liberation, development and socialism. The vacuum left by the demise of Pan-Arabist nationalism was rapidly filled by the development of religion-based Islamism. A contributory factor was the failure of liberal regimes espousing the modernist view to make any real changes to the lives of most ordinary people and they were thus seen as elitist groups that were enriching only themselves. The Shah's rule in pre-revolutionary Iran is a case in point.

The defeat of the Arab forces and the failure to regain Palestine in the 1967 Six-Day War had also dealt a shattering blow to Arab nationalist/populist regimes led by Nasser's Egypt and sewed the first seeds of discontent which would sprout as Islamist (i.e., religion-based) extremism. The Cold War period also saw the West supporting the liberal or modernistic Arab states such as Saudi Arabia, Egypt and Algeria as a means of countering Soviet expansionism in the Middle East and to safeguard its interests in the oil-rich Arabian Peninsula. The volatile politics of the region, however, saw increasing competition for power and influence and the rising stature of Islamist groups as a counter to Western and Marxist influences in the region, a situation that, paradoxically, saw the West lend support to these groups as well.

As a result of this complex process of support and relationships, the mainstream Islamist forces were able to build a formidable international network extending through a broad range of religious, political, economic and welfare institutions. This would stand them in good stead when the time came to 'export' the Iranian revolution in the form of extremist actions and terror tactics (*Compass Direct*, September 2000).

Besides the social dislocation caused by the forces of rapid urbanization, the destruction of traditional institutions, social mobility and the expansion of education, the inability of the states to provide basic services to their citizens compounded the growing discontent with the existing social order. This left the area ripe for the revolution which was to come in Iran and which was the basis for the rise in Islamic extremism.

Extremism as a manifestation of Islamic fundamentalism

The main proponents of the extremist fundamentalist ideology are not religious leaders (known as Imams) but rather have risen from the ranks of the religious jurists (known as mullahs) who are proponents of the strict application of Islamic law or sharia. The basic tenets of their belief system hinge upon the necessity to establish a Muslim state governed by the sharia and administered by the mullahs as guardians thereof. They are mainly social and political activists who believe that it is only by means of the establishment of the Islamic state can Islamic law be enforced. They use the literal interpretation of the Qur'an and sharia selectively in order to justify their actions and to enforce their edicts. In Nigeria, the activities of these fanatics have placed peaceful coexistence of the country's various population groups at significant risk and threatened the sustainability of the nation-state (see, e.g., *Liberty*, March 2000).

They completely disregard the fact that the religious writings of Islam date back more than fourteen hundred years and regard the modernists who attempt to interpret those writings in the context of twentieth century human development as heretics and traitors to Islam and the teachings of Muhammad. Islamic fundamentalism had been gaining ground in many Muslim countries before the Iranian revolution in 1979. It was only with the ascendance of the Ayatollah Khomeini after the revolution that the extremism of the revolutionary mullahs made itself felt, firstly in Iran and later in other states mainly through other revolutionary leaders.

One of the main reasons for the spread of terrorism as a product of Islamic extremism is the concept of *niy'yah* or motive. The mullahs have declared that any action taken with a pure motive (i.e., the furtherance of the fundamentalist view) is acceptable in the eyes of Allah. In simple terms, the end justifies the means.

One of the tactics used by Khomeini and his adherents to mobilize support for the Islamic revolution is that of demonizing all non-adherents to the tenets of Islamic fundamentalism. This was achieved by inculcating the belief that anyone who is not a fundamentalist is an enemy of Allah and much of their venom was directed towards the United States, which has come to be characterized as the 'Great Satan.' World Jewry and particularly the state of Israel are also targets of this propaganda and this belief also explains the view that many Muslims themselves have to be 'redeemed' by coercion or force into subscribing to the fundamentalist view and practice. This basic view of two poles (believers and infidels), which have also been called 'The City of Faith' and 'The City of War' lead to the pronouncement that the only solution is the *jihad* or holy war and that all 'warriors' participating in the struggle for an Islamic world are heroes of the faith and will gain instant access to paradise (*Reuters*, November 6, 2001; *Compass Direct*, September 2000).

Who are these 'warriors' of the jihad? Many of them are young Muslims who have grown up in the numerous refugee camps of the Middle East and who have little, if any, education and no job. They have been harangued and indoctrinated by the mullah at the local mosque with hate-filled lectures against Jews and Americans and have been drawn into the world of the terrorist striking a blow for Allah against the hated infidels. This phenomenon of uneducated, rootless and anti-social youth being drawn into criminal activity is not peculiar to the Islamic fanatic but manifests itself in the urban gangs of the Cape Flats and the depressed urban jungles of many other countries and cities.

Islamic extremism and terrorism

No true Islamic State can currently be found anywhere in the world, less so in Africa. After the time of the Last Prophet and the Rightly-Guided Caliphs, the Islamic State declined in application until it was completely abandoned by Kamal Ataturk in 1924. Yet, both in the sources of Islam and in the hearts and minds of Muslims, it can never die. Therefore, we are simply bringing highlights and struggles raised by Muslims who insist on as well as fight against those who doubt or deny the validity of applying Islamic Law as universal law of the state in Africa.

Iran has been as good as Khomeini's word and has consistently and systematically supported the many militant and extremist groups which have sprung up in answer to Islamism's clarion call in many Middle Eastern countries. Groups such as Hezbollah in Iran, Hamas in Palestine and Al Jihad in Egypt have proliferated in many Muslim countries and are dedicated to achieving the 'true Islamic state.'

Besides the focus on Muslim countries, however, some of these groups have taken the fight to the West. Many terrorist attacks have been targeted at American installations in Middle East, European and African countries as well as within the United States itself, as evidenced by the bombing of the World Trade Center in New York in 1993. The motives for these attacks range from revenge for perceived American domination and influence to revenge for American support for Israel to punishment of the 'Great Satan.'

Europe, the United Kingdom, Japan, the Philippines and South Africa have all been the target of bombings, aircraft hijackings and hostage-taking and other forms of terror since the Iranian revolution and the success of the exporting of terror is evident from all these incidents. Besides Islamic terrorism, which is religion-based and has the aim of promoting Islamism as the only valid statehood, there are several other types of terrorism as defined by Taheri (1989, pp. 4–6). This is worth noting, as they will be relevant to the discussion on the threat to national security, which will be addressed later.

Terrorism aimed specifically at publicity seeking and focusing attention on particular causes or grievances has manifested itself since the 1960s and probably was seized upon when radical interest groups realized how much media attention religion-based terrorism was receiving. Guerrilla-style terror is usually aimed at the overthrowing of a dictatorial type of regime after the pattern of Cuba and Nicaragua. It is usually nationalistic in character and is confined to within the boundaries of the country concerned.

The urban criminal gangs which are becoming an increasingly perturbing force in many countries, often use terror tactics against rival gangs, the police and the authorities and usually have no specific motive other than power, prestige and profit. Vigilante groups can also be classified here although their motives may differ. A phenomenon which is on the rise in many religion-based and some nationalist-based extremist groups is the dabbling in crime, particularly the drug trade, to finance their activities due to other sources of support having dried up. An example is the Taliban in Afghanistan who were originally supported by the Soviet Union but who had to control the entire Afghan drug trade (chiefly hashish) as a source of funding.

There are two identified faces of the current wave of Islamic extremism sweeping the world. The first is the face of Islamism, which aims at establishing Islamic states around the world based on Islamic law and 'ruled' by the mullahs. There is no room for secularism or any sort of modernistic thought in such societies. It views modernization as 'westoxication.' The second face of Islamic extremism is that which has been exported to non-Muslim countries around the world. This variant is aimed at popularizing the Islamist cause, creating instability and fear in the hope of undermining the authority and legitimacy of non-Muslim governments or embarrassing/punishing countries for real or perceived 'crimes' against Islam. The United States, as the 'Great Satan' of fundamentalist Islam has been the victim of murderous acts of terror as the vehicle for manifesting such extremist views.

There is no doubt that Iran has been the main sponsor of such terrorism and has assisted extremist groups from around the world, many of them offshoots from its own Hezbollah group, with arms, finance and training at facilities situated within its borders. The notion of 'international terrorism' is thus real. O'Ballance (2000) explains that the Iranian connection is a network of embassies and diplomatic missions spread across the world, staffed with intelligence personnel who shelter terrorists, store their weaponry and monitor their prey, while diplomatic couriers carry explosives, arms and ammunition with impunity through national customs barriers (O'Ballance, 2000, p. vii).

That there have been dozens of terror attacks, hijackings and hostage dramas around the world is no longer in doubt. The colonial era, failed post-colonial attempts at state formation, and the creation of Israel engendered a series of Marxist and anti-Western transformations and movements throughout the Arab and Islamic world. The growth of these nationalist and revolutionary movements, along with their view that terrorism could be effective in reaching political goals, generated the first phase of modern international terrorism.

In the late 1960s Palestinian secular movements such as Al Fatah and the Popular Front for the Liberation of Palestine (PFLP) began to target civilians outside the immediate arena of conflict. Following Israel's 1967 defeat of Arab forces, Palestinian leaders realized that the Arab world was unable to militarily confront Israel. At the same time, lessons drawn from revolutionary movements in Latin America, North Africa, Southeast Asia as well as during the Jewish struggle against Britain in Palestine, saw the Palestinians move away from classic guerrilla, typically rural-based, warfare toward urban terrorism. Radical Palestinians took advantage of modern communication and transportation systems to internationalize their struggle. They launched a series of hijackings, kidnappings, bombings, and shootings.

These Palestinian groups became a model for numerous secular militants, and offered lessons for subsequent ethnic and religious movements. Palestinians created an extensive transnational extremist network—tied into which were various state sponsors such as the Soviet Union, certain Arab states, as well as traditional criminal organizations. By the end of the 1970s, the Palestinian secular network was a major channel for the spread of terrorist techniques worldwide.

Radical Palestinian groups

Popular Front for the Liberation of Palestine (PFLP): The PFLP, one of the original members of the PLO, is a Marxist-Leninist group founded in 1967 by George Habash. The group was against the 1993 Declaration of Principles and although it suspended its participation in the PLO, it held meetings with Arafat's Fatah party and PLO representatives in 1999 to discuss national unity. However, it continues to oppose negotiations with Israel. It committed numerous international terrorist attacks during the 1970s, and has allegedly been involved in attacks against Israel since the beginning of the second *intifadah* in September 2000. Syria has been a key source of safe haven and limited logistical support for the PFLP.

In fact, the PLO was founded in 1964 as a Palestinian nationalist umbrella organization committed to the creation of an independent Palestinian state. After the 1967 Arab-Israeli war, militia groups composing the PLO vied for control, with Al Fatah—led by Yasser Arafat—becoming dominant. Al Fatah joined the PLO in 1968 and won the leadership role in 1969. In 1969 Arafat assumed the position of PLO Executive Committee chairman, a position he still holds. Al Fatah essentially became the PLO, with other groups' influence on PLO actions increasingly marginalized. Al Fatah and other PLO components were pushed out of Jordan following clashes with Jordanian forces in 1970–1971. The Israeli invasion of Lebanon in 1982 led to the group's dispersal to several Middle Eastern countries, including Tunisia, Yemen, Algeria, Iraq, and others. The PLO maintains several military and intelligence wings that have carried out terrorist attacks, including Force 17 and the Western Sector. Two of its leaders, Abu Jihad and Abu Iyad, were assassinated. In the 1960s and the 1970s, Al Fatah offered training to a wide range of European, Middle Eastern, Asian, and African terrorist and insurgent groups and carried out numerous acts of international terrorism in Western Europe and the Middle East in the early-to-middle 1970s. Arafat signed the Declaration of Principles (DOP) with Israel in 1993—the Oslo Accords—and renounced terrorism and violence. The organization fragmented in the early 1980s, but remained the leading Palestinian political organization. Following the 1993 Oslo Accords, the PLO—read Al Fatah—leadership assumed control of the nascent Palestinian National Authority (PNA). Its various groups were:

- *Popular Front for the Liberation of Palestine-General Command (PFLP-GC)*: This group, led by Ahmed Jibril, split from the PFLP in

1968, wanting to focus more on terrorist than political action; violently opposed to the PLO and is closely tied to Syria and Iran. The PFLP-GC conducted multiple attacks in Europe and the Middle East during the 1970s and 1980s. Unique in that it conducted cross-border operations against Israel using unusual means, including hot-air balloons and motorized hang gliders. Currently focused on small-scale attacks in Israel, the West Bank, and Gaza Strip.

- *Abu Nidal Organization (ANO)*: Anti-Western and anti-Israel international terrorist organization led by Sabri al-Banna; left the PLO in 1974. Organizational structure composed of various functional committees, including political, military, and financial. The ANO has carried out terrorist attacks in 20 countries, killing or injuring almost 900 persons. Targets have included the United States, the United Kingdom, France, Israel, moderate Palestinians, the PLO, and various Arab countries. Major attacks included the Rome and Vienna airports in December 1985, the Neve Shalom synagogue in Istanbul and the Pan Am Flight 73 hijacking in Karachi in September 1986, and the City of Poros day-excursion ship attack in Greece in July 1988. Suspected of assassinating PLO deputy chief Abu Iyad and PLO security chief Abu Hul in Tunis in January 1991. ANO assassinated a Jordanian diplomat in Lebanon in January 1994. Has not attacked Western targets since the late 1980s. Al-Banna relocated to Iraq in December 1998, where the group maintains a presence. Financial problems and internal disorganization have reduced the group's capabilities; activities shut down in Libya and Egypt in 1999.

While these secular Palestinians dominated the scene during the 1970s, religious movements also grew. The failure of Arab nationalism in the 1967 war resulted in the strengthening of both progressive and extremist Islamic movements. In the Middle East, Islamic movements increasingly came into opposition with secular nationalism, providing an alternative source of social welfare and education in the vacuum left by the lack of government-led development—a key example is The Muslim Brotherhood. Islamic groups were supported by anti-nationalist conservative regimes, such as Saudi Arabia, to counter the expansion of nationalist ideology. Yet political Islam, more open to progressive change, was seen as a threat to conservative Arab regimes and thus support for more fundamentalist—and extremist—groups occurred to combat both nationalist and political Islamist movements.

The distinction between political and fundamentalist Islam is clear. Political Islam (Gilles, 2002), as opposed to fundamentalist or neo-fundamentalist Islam, posits a worldview that can deal with and selectively integrate modernity. In contrast, fundamentalist Islam calls for a return to an ontological form of Islam that rejects modernity; groups such as al Qaeda and the Egyptian Islamic Jihad are representative of fundamentalist Islam. Meanwhile, in Iran, a turn to revolutionary Shia Islam under the leadership of Ayatollah Khomeini further eroded the power and legitimacy of the U.S.-backed authoritarian Pahlevi regime, setting the stage for the Shah's downfall.

The year 1979 was a turning point in international terrorism. Throughout the Arab world (Juan, 1993) and the West, the Iranian Islamic revolution sparked fears of a wave of revolutionary Shia Islam. Meanwhile, the Soviet invasion of Afghanistan and the subsequent anti-Soviet *mujahedeen* war, lasting from 1979 to 1989, stimulated the rise and expansion of terrorist groups. Indeed, the growth of a post-jihad pool of well-trained, battle-hardened militants is a key trend in contemporary international terrorism and insurgency-related violence. Volunteers from various parts of the Islamic world fought in Afghanistan, supported by conservative countries such as Saudi Arabia. In Yemen, for instance, the Riyadh-backed Islamic Front was established to provide financial, logistical, and training support for Yemeni volunteers. So-called 'Arab-Afghans' have—and are—using their experience to support local insurgencies in North Africa, Kashmir, Chechnya, China, Bosnia, and the Philippines.

In the West, attention was focused on state sponsorship, specifically the Iranian-backed and Syrian-supported Hezbollah; state sponsors' use of secular Palestinian groups was also of concern. It is worth noting that unlike the 'secular' national, radical, anarchist terrorism sponsored by states such as Libya, Syria, Iraq, Cuba, North Korea, and behind the scenes by the former Soviet camp, most of the Islamic terrorist groups have never been sponsored by states. Many Egyptian organizations emerged from the Egyptian domestic landscape. Algerian groups likewise were not sponsored by foreign states. Hezbollah certainly can be viewed as an Iranian surrogate, but other movements, while open to state assistance, remain operationally and ideologically independent.

Hezbollah pioneered the use of suicide bombers in the Middle East, and was linked to the 1983 bombing and subsequent deaths of 241 U.S. marines in Beirut, Lebanon, as well as multiple kidnappings of U.S. and Western civilians and government officials. Hezbollah remains a key trainer of secular, Shia, and Sunni movements. As revealed during the investigation into the 1988 bombing of Pan Am Flight 103, Libyan intelligence officers were allegedly involved with the Palestinian Front for the Liberation of Palestine—General Command (PFLP-GC). Iraq and Syria were heavily involved in supporting various terrorist groups, with Baghdad using the Abu Nidal Organization on several occasions. State sponsors used terrorist groups to attack Israeli as well as Western interests, in addition to domestic and regional opponents.

Radical religious groups

Hezbollah: Radical Shia group formed in 1982 in Lebanon. Strongly anti-Western and anti-Israeli. Closely allied with, and often directed by, Iran but may have conducted operations that were not approved by Tehran. Known or suspected to have been involved in numerous anti-U.S. terrorist attacks, including the suicide truck bombing of the U.S. Embassy and U.S. Marine barracks in Beirut in October 1983 and the U.S. embassy annex in Beirut in September 1984. Elements of the group were responsible for the kidnapping and detention of U.S. and other Western hostages in Lebanon. The group also attacked the Israeli Embassy in Argentina in 1992 and is a suspect in the 1994 bombing of the Israeli cultural center in Buenos Aires. Operates in the Bekaa Valley, the southern suburbs of Beirut, and southern Lebanon. Has established cells in Europe, Africa, South America, North America, and Asia. Receives substantial amounts of financial, training, weapons, explosives, political, diplomatic, and organizational aid from Iran and Syria.

Egyptian Islamic Jihad (EIJ-Al-Jihad, Jihad Group, Islamic Jihad): Egyptian group active since the late 1970s. The EIJ is apparently split into two factions: one led by Ayman al-Zawahiri is a key leader in the Osama bin Laden (UBL) network—and the Vanguards of Conquest (Talaa' al-Fateh) led by Ahmad Husayn Agiza. Abbud al-Zumar, leader of the original Jihad, is imprisoned in Egypt and recently joined the group's jailed spiritual leader, Shaykh Umar Abd al-Rahman, in a call for a 'peaceful front.' The group's traditional goal is the overthrow of the Egyptian Government and creation of an Islamic state. Given its involvement with UBL, EIJ is likely increasingly willing to target U.S. interests. The group has threatened to strike the United States for its jailing of Shaykh al-

Rahman and the arrests of EIJ cadres in Albania, Azerbaijan, and the United Kingdom.

Palestinian Islamic Jihad (PIJ): The PIJ, emerging from radical Gazan Palestinians in the 1970s, is apparently a series of loosely affiliated factions rather than a cohesive group. The PIJ focus is the destruction of Israel and the creation of a Palestinian Islamic state. Due to Washington's support of Israel, the PIJ has threatened to strike American targets; the PIJ has not "specifically" conducted attacks against U.S. interests; Arab regimes deemed as un-Islamic are also threatened. The group has stated its willingness to hit American targets in Jordan. PIJ cadres reportedly receive funding from Tehran and logistical support from Syria.

Islamic Resistance Movement (HAMAS): Emerging from the Muslim Brotherhood during the first Palestinian *intifadah* in 1987, HAMAS has become the primary anti-Israeli religious opposition in the occupied territories. The group is mainly known for its use of suicide bombers and is loosely organized, with centers of strength in Gaza and certain areas in the West Bank. HAMAS, while condemning American policies favoring Israel, has not targeted the U.S. directly.

Al-Gamaat Al-Islamiyya (IG—the Islamic Group, al-Gama'at, Islamic Gama'at, Egyptian al-Gama'at al-Islamiyya, GI): The IG, begun in the 1970s, is the largest of the Egyptian militant groups. Its core goal is the overthrow of the Cairo regime and creation of an Islamic state. The IG appears to be a more loosely organized entity than the EIJ, and maintains a globally present external wing. IG leadership signed Osama Osama bin Laden's February 1998 anti-U.S. fatwa but has denied supporting UBL. Shaykh Umar Abd al-Rahman is al-Gama'at's spiritual leader, and thus the United States has been threatened with attack. From 1993 until the cease-fire, al-Gama'a launched attacks on tourists in Egypt, most notably the attack in November 1997 at Luxor that killed 58 foreign tourists. Also claimed responsibility for the attempt in June 1995 to assassinate Egyptian President Hosni Mubarak in Addis Ababa, Ethiopia. Has a worldwide presence, including Sudan, the United Kingdom, Afghanistan, Austria, and Yemen. The Egyptian Government believes that Iran, Osama bin Laden, and Afghan militant groups support the organization.

The disintegration of post-Cold War states, and the Cold War legacy of a world awash in advanced conventional weapons and know-how, has assisted the proliferation of terrorism worldwide. Vacuums of stability created by conflict and absence of governance (what U.S. Secretary of Defense Donald Rumsfeld calls 'ungoverned spaces') in areas such as the Balkans, Afghanistan, Colombia, and certain African countries offer ready made areas for terrorist training and recruitment activity, while smuggling and drug trafficking routes are often exploited by terrorists to support operations worldwide. With the increasing ease of transnational transportation and communication, the continued willingness of states such as Iran and Iraq to provide support, and dehumanizing ideologies that enable mass casualty attacks, the lethal potential of terrorist violence has reached new heights.

The region of Afghanistan—it is not a country in the conventional sense—has, particularly since the 1989 Soviet withdrawal, emerged as a terrorist training ground. Pakistan, struggling to balance its needs for political-economic reform with a domestic religious agenda, provides assistance to terrorist groups both in Afghanistan and Kashmir while acting as a further transit area between the Middle East and South Asia.

Since their emergence in 1994, the Pakistani-supported Taliban militia in Afghanistan has assumed several characteristics traditionally associated with state-sponsors of terrorism, providing logistical support, travel documentation, and training facilities. Although radical groups such as the Egyptian Islamic Jihad, Osama bin Laden's al Qaeda, and Kashmiri militants were in Afghanistan prior to the Taliban, the spread of Taliban control has seen Afghan-based terrorism evolve into a relatively coordinated, widespread activity focused on sustaining and developing terrorist capabilities. Since the mid-1990s, Pakistani-backed terrorist groups fighting in Kashmir have increasingly used training camps inside Taliban-controlled areas. At the same time, members of these groups, as well as thousands of youths from Pakistan's Northwest Frontier Province (NWFP), have fought with the Taliban against opposition forces. This activity has seen the rise of extremism in parts of Pakistan neighboring Afghanistan, further complicating the ability of Islamabad to exert control over militants. Moreover, the intermixing of Pakistani movements with the Taliban and their Arab-Afghan allies has seen ties between these groups strengthen. Since 1989 the increasing willingness of religious extremists to strike targets outside immediate country or regional areas underscores the global nature of contemporary terrorism. The groups constitute a scattered network of killers.

Militant Islamic terrorism: rise of al Qaeda

The Soviet withdrawal from Afghanistan took place in 1989. The infectious Islamic jihad against 'infidels' carried by returning veterans from the war in Afghanistan spread particularly rapidly in Algeria, Egypt and the Sudan.

Al Qaeda (The Base): Established by Osama bin Laden (UBL) circa 1990, al Qaeda aims to coordinate a transnational mujahideen network; stated goal is to 'reestablish the Muslim State' throughout the world via the overthrow of corrupt regimes in the Islamic world and the removal of foreign presence—primarily American and Israeli—from the Middle East. UBL has issued three anti-U.S. *fatwas* encouraging Muslims to take up arms against Washington's 'imperialism.' Al Qaeda provides financial, manpower, transportation, and training support to extremists worldwide. In February 1998 Osama bin Laden issued a statement under the banner of 'The World Islamic Front for Jihad Against The Jews and Crusaders,' saying it was the duty of all Muslims to kill U.S. citizens, civilian or military, and their allies. The militant group allegedly orchestrated the bombings of the U.S. Embassies in Nairobi, Kenya and Dar Es Salaam, Tanzania, on August 7, 1998. Claims that it was involved in the 1993 killing of U.S. servicemen in Somalia and the December 1992 bombings against U.S. troops in Aden, Yemen. Al Qaeda serves as the core of a loose umbrella organization that includes members of many Sunni Islamic extremist groups, including factions of the Egyptian Islamic Jihad (EIJ), the Gama'at al-Islamiyya (IG), and the Harakat ul-Mujahidin (HUM). The group is a prime suspect in the September 11 attacks as well as the USS Cole bombing.

Armed Islamic Group (GIA): Having initiated terrorist activities in 1992 following Algiers refusal to accept a democratically elected Islamist government, the GIA has conducted multiple mass killings of civilians and assassinations of Algerian leaders. While present in areas such as Yemen, the GIA reportedly does not target the U.S. directly. However, it is possible that GIA splinter movements or personnel may become involved in anti-U.S. action.

Aden-Abyan Islamic Army (AAIA): The Aden-Abyan Islamic Army is allegedly affiliated to the Yemeni Islamic Jihad and has been implicated in acts of violence with the stated goal to 'hoist the banner of al-Jihad, and fight secularism in Yemen and the Arab countries.' Aden-Abyan Islamic Army leader Zein al-Abideen al-Mehdar was executed for participating in the December 1998 kidnapping of sixteen Western tourists. Four of the hostages were killed and another thirteen hostages were freed when Yemeni security forces attacked the place where the hostages were being held. In March 1999 the group warned the United States and British ambassadors in Yemen to leave immediately.

Harakat ul-Mujahidin (HUM): Formerly part of the Harakat al-Ansar (HUA), the Pakistani-based HUM operates primarily in Kashmir. Long-time leader of the group, Fazlur Rehman Khalil, in mid-February stepped down; the popular Kashmiri commander and second-in-command, Farooq Kashmiri, assumed the reigns. Khalil, who has been linked to Osama bin Laden and signed his fatwa in February 1998 calling for attacks on U.S. and Western interests, assumed the position of HUM Secretary General. The HUM is linked to the militant group al-Faran that kidnapped five Western tourists in Kashmir in July 1995; one was killed in August 1995 and the other four reportedly were killed in December of the same year. Supporters are mostly Pakistanis and Kashmiris and also include Afghans and Arab veterans of the Afghan war. The HUM trains its militants in Afghanistan and Pakistan.

Jaish-e-Mohammed (Army of Mohammed): The Pakistan-based Jaish-e-Mohammed (JEM) has greatly expanded since Maulana Masood Azhar, a former ultra-fundamentalist Harakat ul-Ansar (HUA) leader, formed the group in February 2000. The group's aim is to unite Kashmir with Pakistan. It is politically aligned with the radical, pro-Taliban, political party, Jamiat-i Ulema-i Islam (JUI-F). The JEM maintains training camps in Afghanistan. Most of the JEM's cadre and material resources have been drawn from the militant groups Harakat ul-Jihad al-Islami (HUJI) and the Harakat ul-Mujahedin (HUM). The JEM has close ties to Afghan Arabs and the Taliban. Osama bin Laden is suspected of giving funding to the JEM. Group by this name claimed responsibility for the USS Cole attack.

Lashkar-e-Tayyiba (LT) (Army of the Righteous): The LT is the armed wing of the Pakistan-based religious organization, Markaz-ud-Dawa-wal-Irshad (MDI)—pa Sunni anti-U.S. missionary organization formed in 1989. One of the three largest and best-trained groups fighting in Kashmir against India, it is not connected to a political party. The LT leader is MDI chief, Professor Hafiz Mohammed Saeed. Almost all LT cadres are foreigners—

mostly Pakistanis from seminaries across the country and Afghan veterans of the Afghan wars. The LT trains its militants in mobile training camps across Pakistan-administered Kashmir and Afghanistan.

'Talibanization' of Nigeria?

One does not usually associate Nigeria with Islamic violence, or even just Islam. But in fact approximately 50 percent of the population is Muslim, 40 percent Christian, and various indigenous religions make up the remaining 10 percent. Religious violence (Falola, 1998) flared up when the Muslim dominated northern states such as Kaduna planned to introduce Islamic sharia law. More than 300 people are said to have died in just one week at the end of February, 2000, and as many as 1000 lives have been lost due to religious and ethnic unrest since May 1999 when democracy was restored. Apparently when it is a question of religion, many Nigerians very easily show their animal nature. It is in this context that attempts and effective imposition of Sharia on the inhabitants of the Northern states of Nigeria has been carried out with impunity. The spread of Islam in Nigeria dates back to the eleventh century when it first appeared in Borno in the northeast of the country. Later Islam emerged in Hausaland in the northwest and its influence was evident in Kano and Katsina. Islam was for quite some time the religion of the court and commerce, and was spread peacefully by Muslim clerics and traders. Increasingly, trans-Saharan trade came to be conducted by Muslims (Willis, 1977). In the second half of the eighteenth century a Muslim revival took place in western Africa, in which Fulani cattle-driving people, who had settled and adopted Islam, played a central role. In northern Nigeria, the Fulani scholar Uthman dan Fodio launched a jihad in 1804 that lasted for six years, aiming to revive and purify Islam, to eliminate syncretist beliefs and rituals, to remove all innovations contrary to the Koran and sharia, and to encourage less devout Muslims to return to orthodox and pure Islam. However, this religious revolution also had a political element concerning state formation and state conflict. It united the Hausa states under sharia law. In 1812 the Hausa dynasties became part of the Islamic State or Caliphate of Sokoto. The Sokoto Caliphate ended with partition in 1903 when the British incorporated it into the colony of Nigeria and the Sultan's power was transferred to the High Commissioner. However, many aspects of the caliphate structure, including the Islamic legal system, were retained and brought forward into the colonial period.

A new impetus to the spread of Islam was provided by Ahmadu Bello, the Premier of the Northern Region after Nigerian independence in 1960, with his Islamization program that led to the conversion of over 100,000 people in the provinces of Zaria and Niger. The military coup in 1966, which claimed the lives of many politicians including Ahmadu Bello, brought his Islamization program to an abrupt end but the 1970s saw continued government policy favoring the dominance of Islam. History has shown that Islamization was easier under military dictatorship and Islam spread quickly under Ibrahim Babangida (1985–1993).

Religious tensions between evangelical Christians and Islamic groups have long existed, but the anticipated extension of sharia law in a number of northern states has caused increased religious tension since December 1999. For example, in Ilorin, Kwara State, fourteen churches were burnt to the ground by suspected Islamic fundamentalists. News of the introduction of sharia law on January 1, 2000 in Zamfara State led to widespread violence in February/March 2000 in which property was destroyed and more than 1,000 people were killed. A second state, Kano State, adopted Islamic law in June 2001 and in 2002, a further ten northern states followed suit.

Though the Nigerian central government has openly recognized the incompatibility of sharia law with the federal constitution of the nation, President Olusegun Obasanjo has avoided intervening in decisions taken by states that apply Islamic law, merely calling for moderation. As an outspoken born-again Christian, he knows that vigorous condemnation of strict Islamic law will only inflame passions further and at the same time he fears that the spread of sharia law will increase religious tension and undermine Nigerian unity.

The growth of radical Islam has effects far wider than draconian punishments for offences such as adultery. Nigeria is about equally divided between Christians and Muslims, with a small number of animists. If radical Islam is left unchecked, it will continue to provoke widespread inter-religious conflict that, combined with endemic ethnic strife, may fragment the country. This could make the giant of sub-Saharan Africa—a major oil exporter to the United States and a new, struggling democracy-into a haven for Islamism, linked to foreign extremist terrorist groups of the ilk of al Qaeda.

As in much of Africa, family law in Nigeria has long drawn on sharia, the body of Islamic law and precedent. But the versions of sharia introduced in the last two years are closer to those imposed by the Taliban in Afghanistan or the Wahhabis in Saudi Arabia. Since 1999, Zamfara state has sexually segregated buses, taxis, and many public places, banned alcohol, enforced a dress code on women, and closed non-Muslim schools. Its *hizbah* (religious enforcers) mete out immediate, harsh punishments for 'un-Islamic' activities such as questioning Islamic teaching or women's wearing of pants.

In some states Muslims are subject to sharia even if they prefer civil courts that have protections under Nigeria's bill of rights. Non-Muslims are barred from being judges, prosecutors, and lawyers in the courts to which they may be subject. Sharia state governments have destroyed dozens of churches as religious irritants. The new laws are not subject to democratic control. Since proponents of the new code say that it is divinely ordained, no constitution or election is allowed to challenge it. Sharia therefore, supercedes the Nigerian constitution, and Zamfara's legislative assembly suspended two democratically elected Muslim members because they did not fully support the new laws.

The new laws have precipitated riots throughout the country. February 2000 saw the worst violence since Nigeria's civil war some 30 years ago. In Kaduna City, whole neighborhoods were destroyed. Police conservatively estimate that 600 people died; human rights groups say as many as 3,000. Perhaps 6,000 have been killed in the last two years in religion-related violence nationwide. After September 11, some Islamist violence took on a distinctly anti-American tone. In the cities of Jos and Kano, hundreds died in riots in September and October, with Muslims observed waving Osama bin Laden posters and Christians waving American flags. Osama bin Laden remains a hero in much of the north.

While no evidence has surfaced of al Qaeda operations in Nigeria, the extremism from which it draws support is spreading rapidly, and is encouraged by radical Islamic groups and foreign regimes. Sudan, which has already supplied Chechnya's criminal code, is running training programs for Nigeria's sharia judges. The Nigerian federal government's response has been ambivalent.

Nigeria is further proof, if any were needed, that radical Islam is not created or driven by opposition to U.S. policy on Israel. It is an aggressive, worldwide ideological movement with its sights set on Africa and Asia as much as the Middle East. The situation in Nigeria also provides an additional reason for the United States to drop its 30-year practice of downplaying demands for human rights and democracy in Muslim societies. The United States could urge Nigeria to oppose extremist sharia vigorously and help it to do so. Even hardheaded realists should see the importance of aiding the country to reform its troubled legal system nationwide and provide education that includes modern knowledge and promotes freedom as an alternative to Islamist schools. Otherwise Nigeria's fledgling democracy, regional power, and U.S. ally are bound to face further religious violence. As Nigerian novelist and Nobel laureate Wole Soyinka laments, 'The roof is already burning over our head—the prelude to civil war.'

Islamism in South Africa

Although South Africa is geographically far removed from the center of radical Islamic Fundamentalist development in the Middle East, North Africa and Asia religiously and politically the country's small but influential Muslim community has close ties to the rest of the Islamic world including the militant Islamic Fundamentalist movement. To understand any phenomenon, Muslims have to look to the Qur'an, and the Sunnah of the beloved Prophet (*Sallallahu 'Alaihi wa Sallam*), and the *seerah* (history) of the Prophet (*Sallallahu 'Alaihi wa Sallam*), the *sahaba* (his companions) and the s*aleheen* (pious). The Qur'an teaches us about our common humanity, that we are all descendants of Sayyidina Adam (peace be upon him) who was created from clay. It also teaches us racial equality. Two verses of the Qur'an suffice to illustrate this. Allah (*Subhanahu wa Ta'ala*) says:

> O people! Be careful of your duty to your Lord who created you from a single soul and from it created its mate and from these two spread abroad a multitude of men and women. Be careful of your duty toward Allah in Whom you claim (your rights) of one another, and toward the wombs (that bore you). Lo! Allah has been a Watcher over you' (Qur'an 4: 1).
>
> O mankind! Lo! We have created you male and female, and have made you nations and tribes that you may know one another. Lo! The noblest of you, in the sight of Allah is the best in conduct. Lo! Allah is Knower, Aware (Qur'an 43: 13).

In Islam, an Arab is not superior to a non-Arab. Every Muslim is a brother of another Muslim. Nobody has superiority over another except by piety and good action. This is what might have marveled and attracted Malcolm X when he went to Mecca.

And Al-Hajj Malik Sabbaz, Malcolm X, observed that there were tens of thousands of pilgrims, from all over the world. They were all colors from blue-eyed blondes to black-skinned Africans. But they were all participating in the same ritual, displaying a spirit of unity and brotherhood that his experiences in America had led him to believe it could never exist between the white and the non-white.

During eleven days in the Muslim world he ate from the same plate, drank from the same glass, and slept in the same bed (or on the same rug)—while praying to the same God—with fellow Muslims, whose eyes were the bluest of the blue, whose hair was the blondest of the blond, and whose skin was the whitest of white. And in the words and in the actions and in the deeds of the 'white' Muslims, he felt the same sincerity he felt among black African Muslims of Nigeria, Sudan and Ghana.

The abhorrent system of apartheid

So one can understand how abhorrent apartheid must have been to Malcolm X and indeed to all Muslims, a society where blacks were at the bottom, the 'colored' were in the middle and the whites at the top, where people were segregated and discriminated on the basis of race, where there were separate schools for blacks and whites, separate beaches for blacks and whites, separate libraries for blacks and whites, and so on. Where state violence was the order of the day and where Africans were shot down on the smallest of pretext, as if they were of no consequence. First, the Muslim countries and countries of Africa, Asia and South America ostracized South Africa. After immense pressure from them, the Western world had to reluctantly follow suit. South Africa was so much ostracized in the international community that it had only two friends left, the state of Israel, and Mrs. Margaret Thatcher, former British Prime Minister. It had no way out but to remove apartheid laws, release political detainees, lift the ban on political organizations and allow exiles to return home.

Sensing that its economic interests would henceforth be better served by Mr. Nelson Mandela as leader, the western world through its media, transformed him overnight from a 'terrorist' to a 'saint,' comparable to Mahatma Gandhi, pointing to just as they had transformed Mzee Jomo Kenyatta, the first President of Kenya 'from a leader to darkness and death,' to 'a visionary with fierce determination.' The support that Muslims across the world gave to the people of South Africa has not been lost on them. And support and vigilance has been enhanced. To give only one example, when Mr. Nelson Mandela visits Muslim countries, he receives twenty-one gun salutes.

Historical origins and spread of Islam in South Africa

Historically, Islam was first introduced into South Africa by people of Malay descent during the seventeenth and eighteenth century as well as through the immigration of Indian laborers during the nineteenth century. It is therefore thus not surprising that approximately 95 percent of all Muslims in South Africa belong to the Indian and colored communities. Although there are currently virtually no statistics available n the subject of how many people support the radical Islamic Fundamentalist movement in South Africa there are nonetheless growing indications that radical Islamic Fundamentalism is a growing force in the country and that members of the African (Black) communities are increasingly being targets for conversion to Islam by Muslim organizations in the Western Cape, Gauteng and KwaZulu-Natal such as the Islamic Propagation Center International (IPCI) in Durban. Conversion by Blacks to Islam is however not without its problems. Essa Al-Seppe a prominent black Muslim leader and chairman of the Muslim Youth Movement (MYM) in South Africa occasionally complained that he, his family, and his colleagues, all of whom are of African descent, are increasingly being subjected to racial remarks by Muslims of non-African descent, but in particular by Muslims from the Indian community. Hanan Ashrawi, the Palestinian Spokeswomen, who visited South Africa towards the end of 1994, told an audience in Johannesburg that South African Muslims were the most extreme racists that she had ever come across.

Since the Islamic revolution in Iran and the war in Afghanistan a number of militant but clandestine Muslim organizations have emerged in South Africa (Abdulkader, 1995). Most of these organizations had their origins in the 1980s and were part of the wider anti-apartheid struggle. One of the earliest Islamic Fundamentalist leaders in South Africa was Abdullah Haroun (also spelled Haron). Until his death in police detention in 1969 Haroun, who became the Imam of Stegman Road Mosque in Cape Town in 1955, was instrumental in the development of the Muslim anti-apartheid movement in South Africa. This helped to provide the foundation from which the radical Islamic Fundamentalist organizations of the 1980s such as Qibla and Al-Jihad developed.

Most of the militant Islamic fundamentalist organizations that formed part of the anti-apartheid struggle have turned their attention to the promotion of radical Islamic ideals since the political changes of the early 1990s. None of the militant Muslim Fundamentalist organizations currently in existence in South Africa have as yet openly committed themselves to policies favoring the suicide-bombings and terrorism that has become the hallmark of their radical brethren elsewhere in the world. At the same time, there are increasing signs that Islamic militancy may be growing in this country and that this is fuelled by developments in the Middle East as well as developments inside South Africa such as the country's escalating crime rate and the new ANC-led Government's inability to address the situation.

There are allegedly about six organizations with distinct militant Islamic aims and objectives operating in South Africa. The best known is Qibla. Lesser-known groupings are Al-Jihad, the Mujlisul Ulama of South Africa (MUSA), the Jihad Movement of South Africa and the Islamic Unity Convention (IUC). The IUC has been included here because of the militant statements made by some of its leader as well as the fact that the organization's national leadership has been taken over by Qibla. Achmad Cassim, the chairman of Qibla, was elected chairman of the IUC in 1995.

Although claims have been made that both the radical Middle Eastern Hamas and Hizballah organizations have a presence inside South Africa there are no clear evidence to confirm this. It is of course possible, as claimed by intelligence sources, that Hamas and Hizballah, may be operating under assumed names. This is a common practice in the Middle East where factions of the same organization often assume different names to protect them from detection and infiltration by the intelligence community. On the whole however, with the exception of Qibla and Al-jihad, very little is currently known about any of the organizations or the leadership that constitute the militant Islamic Fundamentalist movement in South Africa.

Al-Jihad

Al-Jihad was apparently established by Sharkey Gamieldien and Ismail Joubert in 1967. The aim of the organization was to participate in the Arab war against Israel. Al-Jihad however failed in these objectives and has yet to become a significant organization for the promotion of militant Islamic

Fundamentalism in South Africa. What remained of the initial organization came to center largely around the person of Ismail Joubert who, apparently is still trying to promote Al-Jihad as a major South African fundamentalist organization outside the country. Presumably the main reason for this is to procure funds from some of the oil rich Arab Muslim countries. Saudi Arabia, Iran and Libya in particular are known to annually giving large sums of money to Muslim organizations around the world for the promotion of Islam.

At the time of the Iranian revolution in 1979, Joubert proclaimed Al-Jihad to be the first and only Shi'ite Fundamentalist movement in South Africa loyal to the Ayatollah Khomeni and Iran. A massive portrait of the Ayatollah graces the entrance to the Al-Jihad center in Guguletu. Throughout the 1980s Joubert campaigned for the recognition of Al-Jihad as the only Shi'ite grouping in South Africa. However, the launching of Qibla and Hizballah in the 1980s effectively deprived him and Al-Jihad of that honor.

In 1983 Joubert, in an attempt to broaden Al-Jihad's support base aligned the organization with the newly formed United Democratic Front (UDF). As a result of this Joubert later claimed that Al-Jihad had been part of the armed struggle led by the ANC's military wing Umkhonto We Sizwe (MK) and as such to have been involved in the building of a radical anti-Apartheid Muslim infrastructure in the Black townships. Beyond this little is however currently known about Al-Jihad. The organization now appears to be largely inactive.

Qibla

Al-Jihad's main rival is Qibla, a radical Shi'ite Fundamentalist organization that was formed in Cape Town in 1980. Qibla was apparently created with the specific intention to promote the Iranian revolution and to propagate its strict Islamic principles among Muslims in South Africa. Qibla is led by Achmad Cassim who openly propagates the transformation of South Africa into a revolutionary Muslim state.

As pointed out earlier, before the political changes of February 2, 1990, Qibla played an active a role in the violence and public unrest that formed part of the anti-apartheid struggle in South Africa. Unlike Al-Jihad, Qibla however closely aligned itself with the organizations of the anti-Charterists movement such as the Pan-Africanist Congress (PAC) and the Azanian Peoples Organization (AZAPO). The PAC in particular was instrumental in arranging for the military training of Qibla cadres in Muslim countries such as Libya, Iran and Sudan.

In November 1990 it was reported that the PAC was in the process of reviving its long-standing but recently dormant ties with Iran and that the organization's acting President Clarence Makwetu and Western Cape organizer Barney Desai had visited Teheran for this purpose. According to Alexander the PAC's links with Iran goes back to the Iranian revolution in 1979 when the South African embassy in Tehran was handed to the PAC for its personal use. Relations between the PAC and Iran however soured during the Iran-Iraq war when the PAC and Qibla apparently took financial aid from both the Iranians and the Iraqis. The Iranians who did not like this suspended its support to the PAC and Qibla. However, since the end of the Gulf War and due to the growing support for Iran among Muslim Fundamentalists in South Africa, not to mention Iran's renewed interest in South Africa, relations between the PAC and Iran have returned to near normal.

On a different level Qibla's association with militant Black Consciousness organizations such as the PAC and AZAPO has also brought it in close contact with radical Black Pan-Africanist and pro-Islamic organizations in the United States such as the Nation of Islam. Qibla's activities have been highlighted by the following: (1) support for Saddam Hussein during the Gulf War, which included an offer to send a Muslim force of some 10,000 men to help Iraq in its war against the United States and its allies; (2) willingness to support the Palestine Liberation Organization (PLO) in a world-wide terror campaign should it be requested to do so; (3) demonstrations against the U.S. and Israeli embassies and Consular Offices in South Africa since 1986; (4) the infiltration of non-radical Muslim umbrella organizations such as the mass based Islamic Unity Convention (IUC); (5) the alleged invasion of the home of Mr. Dullah Omar, the Minister of Justice and Intelligence on March 14, 1996; and (6) the organization's alleged involvement in the execution of Rashaad Staggie, a leader of the Salt River-based Hard Living gang, on August 4, 1996.

Qibla members are seen as outspoken supporters of the Islamic Jihad. It views itself as the true protectors of orthodox Islamic values in a decaying Western orientated society and world. Muslims, they argue, owe it to their faith to oppose any corrupt and ineffective state. The movement's long-term goal is to assist pro-Islamic Fundamentalist countries in their attempts to establishment an Islamic republic in South Africa based on the principles of the Sharia and the teachings of the Qur'an. Like most, if not all radical Islamic fundamentalist organizations, Qibla looks to Iran for its spiritual and political guidance.

As part of the radical Left opposition Qibla rejects the present ANC government because it believes that it is committed to the transformation rather than the total destruction of apartheid and the redistribution of land and wealth. According to Qibla the ANC government is controlled and dictated to by Western capitalist interests. It believes that because of the extent to which Whites have exploited the 'Azanian masses' nothing less than a full blown Islamic revolution under the control of Qibla is required to bring about the just redistribution of land and wealth.

Although Qibla has made numerous attempts to extend its influence, its power-base remains to be in the Western Cape. Its head office is at Athlone. The current size of the organization's membership is not known and can only be speculated on. In the late 1980s Qibla allegedly had a membership of about 2000. Although Qibla was founded as a mass movement it never attain this goal. Most South African Muslim regards the organization and its ideals as too radical. In an attempt to increase its membership Qibla established the Shaheed Imam Haroon (SIHF) and the Mustadafin Foundations (MF) in the late 1980s. This endeavor however did not produced the required increase in membership numbers that was expected. As a result Qibla remained largely a minority base organization until the formation of the mass base Islamic Unity Convention (IUC) in early 1994.

In September 1994 Qibla was at the center of protest action against the moderate Muslim Judicial Council (MJC) when a small of group of its supporters demonstrated against Nazeen Mohamed, the President of the MJC when he visited parliament in Cape Town. It was apparently also involved in the planning of a Southern Africa Strategic Conference for Islamic Work. This conference which took place in Cape Town in April 1995, examined ways and means of promoting Islam in South and Southern Africa. Delegates from Iran, Iraq and Jordan were invited to attend the meeting.

Hizballah

The alleged Hizballah movement in South Africa is a splinter movement of the Islamic Liberation Movement of Azania (ILMA), which was established by Cassim Christianson and Muhammed Shabazz Cloete in the mid-1980s. The emphasis here is on allegedly because the accuracy of these and other facts pertaining to the possible presence of Hizballah in South Africa could not be established. Christianson, who is former member of the PAC and Qibla and Cloete who is a former representative of the PAC in Iran broke away from Qibla in about 1984–1985 to form a branch of Hizballah in South Africa.

The alleged establishment of Hizballah in South Africa apparently followed a more or lesser a similar path to that of the parent movement in Lebanon where a theologian was sent from Qum in Iran to develop the organization there. Sheikh Aftab Haider Kazani, a Pakistani Imam, was apparently sent from Qum to South Africa in the 1980s to promote Shi'ism in this country. With the Western Cape being the emerging center for Islamic Fundamentalism and Fundamentalist groupings at the time, Kazani set up an office at Rylands. From here he acquainted himself with the sentiments and needs of the local community as well as the leadership of local organizations, which he steadily began to influence with his teachings.

His activities in the Western Cape were not without their problems and opposition however. Ismail Joubert and Tatamkulu-Afrika of Al-Jihad as well as Cassim of Qibla strongly opposed Kazani's teachings and activities on the grounds that he was promoting Shi'ism at the cost of their organizations and their membership. Like Qibla and Al Jihad Kazani drew most of his supporters from the Colored and African communities around Cape Town.

In spite of the opposition that he encountered Kazani succeeded in developing a small but relatively successful Hizballah organization with close ties to Iran and the parent organization in Lebanon. It has been claimed that Kazani's success in the Western Cape was partly responsible for Qibla's declining support in the region during the late 1980s. Several Qibla members apparently left the organization during this period to join the ranks of Hizballah.

Membership figures for Hizballah are not available. Rumor has it that Hizballah has had a substantial growth in membership since the early 1990s and that it is receiving strong support from militant elements in the PAC and possibly AZAPO. Hizballah apparently also has a limited support base in Eldorado Park, Bosmont and Kathlehong in Gauteng where it has several branches consisting of dissident members of the PAC and AZAPO.

Many dissatisfied PAC youths apparently joined Hizballah after the failed attempt in April 1995 to replace the old guard leadership under Clarence Makwetu with a younger and more dynamic leadership. Since to be armed is an essential part of Hizballah's militant philosophy training in combat shooting is allegedly regularly done at a shooting range in Mitchell's Plain and on a farm near Paarl.

Hizballah apparently also propagates the believe that in the long run the new South African government will become even more anti-Islamic then the previous apartheid regime. Like Qibla Hizballah promote and supports the establishment of a full-blown Islamic republic in South Africa.

Apart from religious programmes and community work, which includes food distribution among the poor and the unemployed, Hizballah also observed religious occasions such as Eid. This has helped to provide it with a valuable foothold in some of the disadvantaged communities of the Western Cape and elsewhere. Hizballah currently produces a local newsletter called *Al-Hujjat*. It is however primarily distributed amongst the intelligentsia in the Muslim community.

Horn of Africa

Muslim Arab traders and settlers began pushing south from Egypt into northern Sudan in the seventh century. They settled into the area and began intermarrying with the local population The Muslim traders who came to the region were generally wealthy, and marrying into their families carried with it a great deal of prestige. Over time Islam and the Arabic language also became firmly established in the north. However, Islam spread quite slowly into the interior of the Sudan, only reaching the western and central regions around the fifteenth century. In the nineteenth century, Sudan fell under the colonial domination of Egypt and Britain. It gained independence in 1954. Today about two-thirds of Sudan's population of 29 million are Muslim. Another 30 percent, most of them southerners, practice indigenous religions or Christianity.

Islam reached the rest of the Horn of Africa from across the Red Sea. The Prophet Mohammed himself encouraged a band of persecuted Muslims to flee Arabia to Ethiopia and to seek protection from Ethiopia's Christian king. By the middle of the ninth century, Arab traders and artisans had settled in trading centers along the coast of what is now Eritrea, Dijbouti and Somalia. In the eleventh, twelfth and thirteenth centuries, two Arabian sheiks speeded the conversion of Somalia when they married into local families, giving rise to two of the largest clan-families in Somali today, the Darood and the Isaaq.

From the south of the Horn, Islam spread north and west from the Somali coast, reaching what is now southern Ethiopia in the ninth century. Muslim holy men and the Sufi brotherhoods helped set the mystical tone of Islam in the region. Within a few centuries, there were numerous Islam-dominated states in the region, principally governed by Hadiya-Sidama-speaking ethnic groups. These states lost power in the sixteenth century with the rise to power of the Oromo, an ethnic group that practiced the indigenous religions of the area. Muslims were faced with the choice of leaving the region or submitting to the Oromo regimes, including their religious practices. For the next two centuries, the Muslim populations, unable to practice Islam openly, were cut off from each other. An eighteenth-century wave of Islamicization from Somalia and Harar, a Muslim city in Ethiopia, reconnected these lowland communities. Muslims live throughout Ethiopia, but large concentrations can be found in Bale, Harerge and Welo. Meanwhile the highland Amhara and Tigrayan peoples have remained Christian.

Ethiopia was the only African state not to be colonized in the nineteenth century, and until its monarchy was overthrown in 1974, very few non-Christians held high positions in government or the military. However, Italy ruled Eritrea from 1889 until it surrendered the province to Britain in 1941. In 1952, an Eritrean government federated with Ethiopia replaced the British military administration. Eritrea rebelled against Ethiopia a few years later, finally gaining independence in 1993.

Somalia's about 7 million people are almost entirely Muslim today. The overwhelming majority are ethnic Somalis who speak the Somali language and trace their ancestry to the same ancestor, Samaale. They are divided into six large clan-families, four of them pastoral and two agricultural Each clan-family is divided into primary lineages, which are in turn divided into secondary and sometimes tertiary lineages. Related lineages within a clan form alliances to pay and receive blood compensation for each other in the case of homicide.

Somalia was divided between Britain and Italy during the colonial period. The two parts were reunited with independence in 1960, but in the early 1990s Somalia collapsed into civil war. The northern part of Somalia formerly controlled by the British has once again established itself as an autonomous territory, while the rest of Somalia remains without a formal government. With the disintegration of the central state, the lineage system has become the country's main form of social and economic organization.

Muslims make up an estimated 40 percent of Ethiopia's population of about 64 million (Ofcansky, 1993). Neighboring Eritrea, with a population of 4 million, is about evenly divided between Christians and Muslims. Tiny Djibouti, with only 638,000 people, is mostly Muslim. Nearly all the Muslims in the Horn are Sunni, but they belong to hundreds of different ethnic groups and they speak many different languages. As they adopted Islam, they did not necessarily shed their attachment to the traditions and beliefs of their earlier religion. In much of the region, indigenous customs remain an important part of religious and cultural practice. Ethiopia, in particular, saw no Arab immigration. Its Muslim peoples do not speak Arabic and never adopted Arab culture.

Legal practices and institutions

The disconnected nature of the Muslim communities in the Horn is evident in their application of sharia. The practice of sharia varies throughout the region, with some groups applying classical Islamic law across the board while others use a blend of Islamic and customary codes. Some, like the Beja in Sudan and Djibouti, have abandoned many of their local customs, in order to adhere to Islamic family law. Others accept sharia in the abstract but continue to practice their own customs. This is particularly noticeable in decisions about marriage partners and inheritance. Finally, certain groups known to be very devout Muslims, such as the Harari, a group of about 30,000 who live in the Ethiopia city of Harar, continue to practice traditions which are contrary to Islamic law, not even claiming to accept sharia when it conflicts with their own customs.

Under Emperor Haille Selassie, Ethiopian Muslims could bring matters of personal and family law before Islamic courts. Many did and probably continue to do so. However, others deal with such matters in terms of customary law. Ethiopia's 1995 constitution allows for decisions regarding marital and family issues to be decided according to prevailing local religious or customary laws, so long as all parties involved consent. Additionally, Ethiopia's court system includes sharia courts operating at all levels of jurisprudence in cases that involve marriages which occurred under Islamic law or where all involved parties are Muslim. These courts also address concerns involving inheritance disputes (Ofcansky, 1991, p. 123).

Sudan's imposition of sharia as state law in 1983 is a major factor in the current civil war between the north and south. Sharia was always the basis for personal status law in the north; the post-1983 reforms extended its reach to civil courts. Since President Mar Haas Ahead al-Basher came to power in 1989, the Sudanese government has embarked on a wholesale project of Islamizing the entire legal code (Fleuhr-Lobban, 1993).

At independence, Somalia had four distinct legal traditions: English common law, Italian law, share and Somali customary law. In 1973, President Said Bare introduced a unified civil code that sharply curtailed both sharia and Somali customary law. However, both legal codes have made a comeback since the central government disintegrated. Clan or lineage councils administer Somali customary law or here in the areas they control. The councils consist of all the adult males in the group (Metz, 1992). Since 1997, religious leaders have also set up local courts in the capital and a few other cities that pass judgments according to sharia. Wealthy contributors from the Gulf fund the sharia courts. The militiamen who enforce their rulings are devout Muslims who do not smoke, drink or chew the local stimulant, a narcotic leaf called *qat* (Murray, 2000).

Links with transnational terrorism

Very little is known about al Qaeda's and Osama bin Laden's links to the Horn of Africa, especially Somalia and Sudan, but they are well-established and extensive. The international action in November, 2001, against the al-Barakaat telecommunications company, the main financial institution used by Somalis abroad to transfer funds to Somalia, the allegations against the al-Shamal Islamic Bank in Khartoum and the lists of terrorist organizations published by the US, suggest that Washington views the Horn of Africa as al Qaeda's second theater of operations after Central Asia. The reason is that al Qaeda draws its recruits from locations as Afghanistan, Albania, Algeria, Azerbaijan, Bangladesh, Bosnia, Canada, Chechnya, Ecuador, Egypt, Eritrea, Ethiopia, Jordan, Kenya, Kosovo, Lebanon, Libya, Malaysia, Mauritania, Pakistan, Philippines, Qatar, Saudi Arabia, Somalia, Sudan, Tajikistan, Tanzania, Tunisia, Uganda, United Kingdom, United States, Uruguay, Uzbekistan, Yemen.

But the last few years have seen a relative decline in radical Islamism, especially its internationalist and terrorist groups. Al-Ittihaad, a radical Islamist movement active in southern Somalia and the Ogaden region of Ethiopia (Péninou, 2000, 1998), has less influence in the south of Somalia than it had five years ago, and the Islamic National Front in Sudan has split into two factions, the most moderate firmly ensconced in power. But it is by no means certain that the United States is appreciating the complexity of the situation on its merits. Over the last 10 years the main feature has been the steadily growing influence of warlords in Somalia, to some extent in Sudan and to a lesser degree in Ethiopia, with shifting alliances that have little to do with ideology.

After September 11, there are two potential winners in the new order, Sudan and Ethiopia, and two probable losers, Somalia and Eritrea. In Sudan, now an oil-producing country, President Omar al-Bashir seems set to emulate the success of his Pakistani counterpart. Over a year ago he agreed to the opening of an American anti-terrorist bureau in Khartoum, consolidated his break with the Islamist leader Hassan al-Turabi and managed to persuade some northern rebels to give up their armed struggle against his regime.

Even before the September attacks, the United States had realized the futility of its previous policy and reached the stage of trying to normalize its relationship with the Sudanese government. The European countries, for once all in agreement, enthusiastically backed this. In exchange for a few symbolic measures, President al-Bashir managed to keep the process going. On September 29, the UN Security Council lifted sanctions imposed on Sudan since 1996. Any chances of serious negotiations starting in the next few months to resolve the war in southern Sudan or bring the secular elements in the armed opposition (the NDA) over to the government side evaporated.

Not long after Somalia's central government imploded in 1991, emissaries of Osama bin Laden began slipping into this ragged border town more or less at will. Not even U.S. intelligence had heard of al Qaeda when the organization first sent agents to train local militiamen in this remote corner of Somalia that, by the mid-1990s, was being ruled by militant Islamic fundamentalists. But the fundamentalists are nowhere to be seen nowadays. Defeated by troops from neighboring Ethiopia in 1997, the remnants of al-Ittihad al-Islami melted into the local population after President Bush included the group on a list of terrorist organizations following the 11 September attacks on New York and the Pentagon.

Lawlessness has defined Somalia for more than a decade, and is now bringing it new attention of a sort. After years of being ignored by the West, this country of six million people, wrapped around the Horn of Africa, is routinely scanned by U.S. spy satellites and high-altitude American and French surveillance flights. German frigates cruise the coast. All are watching to see whether members of Osama bin Laden's al Qaeda network, escaping pressure across the seas in South Asia, turn up again in Somalia.

If any did, the United States 'will take appropriate action,' Secretary of State Colin L. Powell told a congressional committee on February 6, 2002. Off the Indian Ocean coast just south of Somalia, a flotilla of 3,000 U.S. Marines and sailors conducting 'intensive ground and air maneuvers' in a joint exercise with Kenyan forces underscores the point. The United States has not sent its military into Somalia. The only known insertion since September 11, 2001, was a handful of U.S. officials in civilian clothes, who met with warlords in the country's violent south in early December 2001, several weeks after Bush shut down a Somali money-transfer and telecommunications company accused of funneling profits to al Qaeda. The visit sparked a stream of media reports speculating that Somalia would be the next venue in the war on terrorism. But after a flurry of initial preparations, military options were limited to intensive surveillance.

The policy reflects the unanimous advice of Somalia experts to whom the U.S. government has turned since the early 1990s, when a U.S.-led intervention ended in the fiasco dramatized in the motion picture 'Black Hawk Down.' On October 3, 1993, a firefight left eighteen American soldiers dead and U.S. foreign policy deeply scarred. For Somalis, disinformation is a parlor game and they love to give out bad information on people they would like to see hit. Yet ignoring Somalia has its own risks, as the rise of al-Ittihad illustrates. The movement first emerged in Somalia from Islamic study groups and followers of the Muslim Brotherhood, an Egyptian group founded in the 1920s to encourage 'political Islam' and a return to governments based on the Koran. The brotherhood is now Egypt's main opposition group.

When Somalia's central government collapsed in 1991, al-Ittihad at first behaved like other factions, arming a militia to hold territory. After being beaten back in northern Somalia and the southern port of Mecca, the group had its greatest success in Gedo region, where the borders of Somalia, Kenya and Ethiopia converge. The group set up a local administration that residents and aid workers recall as significantly more secure and less corrupt than that of the warlords who preceded it. Scolding women for not covering their faces, its soldiers also enforced a stricter view of Islam than had been customary in Somalia.

To outsiders, however, the training camps were most worrisome. According to testimony at the trial of those suspected of blowing-up U.S. embassies in Kenya and Tanzania, Osama bin Laden routinely dispatched agents to Somalia while living in nearby Sudan between 1991 and 1996. Mohammad Atef, a senior al Qaeda military commander who was killed in Afghanistan during Operation 'Enduring Freedom,' made several trips, as did at least two of the men convicted in the 1998 embassy bombings.

Several traveled from Nairobi, the Kenyan capital, in the small planes that carry *khat*, a mildly narcotic plant, to Mandera in Kenya's northeast corner. From there, crossing into Somalia was, and is, as simple as climbing into a covered pickup that shuttles passengers across the border unchallenged, or avoiding the official crossing altogether.

The Somali group earned the label 'international terrorists' by carrying out bombings and assassination attempts in neighboring Ethiopia, whose rulers are Orthodox Christians. The attacks were aimed at destabilizing Ethiopia's central government and supporting a rebellion among the ethnic Somali Muslims who populate Ethiopia's Ogaden region. The Ethiopian government immediately offered to mount its own campaign against al-Ittihaad. Striking back, Ethiopian forces in 1996 and 1997 swept across the border and crushed al-Ittihad as a military force, reportedly killing several Arabs who fought alongside the Somalis. Ethiopia then established itself as the new power in this corner of Somalia, offering training and arms to factions and warlords who helped crush the militants.

There could be no better illustration of the ambiguity of the international war against terrorism. The benefits for the Ethiopian government were clear. A war against the Somalis was popular and never entailed any great military risks. It was a domestic policy gift to a government with a better image abroad than at home. It actually reinforced Ethiopia's policy over the last ten years of keeping Somalia broken up into four or five clan-based micro-states.

If the United States decides to intervene in this way through governments in the region, it will be surprised to find itself in the same camp as Hussein Muhammad Aidid, its sworn enemy in 1993. This leading Somali warlord, previously allied with al-Ittihaad, now sides with the Ethiopians. Like them he is opposed to the transitional government set up after the Arta conference, backed by the UN international agencies, even if the UN itself does not officially recognize it.

There is every chance that Afeworki's Eritrea, previously a bastion of the fight against militant Islamism in the region, will be further marginalized. One of the three factions in the tiny Eritrean Jihad is supported by al Qaeda, but it is a small and not very active group and has been further marginalized in the traditional opposition to the regime (the Alliance), itself less important since the emergence of strong internal opposition. So when Eritrea recently found itself on a U.S. list of twenty-five Muslim states subject to visa restrictions, its reaction was bitter. With the country's economy in a desperate state, despite an excellent harvest thanks to heavy rainfall, the government's authoritarianism means that Eritrea is not at the moment in a position to benefit from America's largesse in her recruitment of allies for the War On Terror. In sum, al Qaeda opposed the involvement of the United States armed forces in the Gulf War in 1991 and in Operation Restore Hope in Somalia in 1992 and 1993, which were viewed by al Qaeda as pretextual preparations for an American occupation of Islamic countries.

North Africa

In the late 1980s, misguided economic policies, bureaucratic mismanagement, political corruption, and cultural alienation combined to create a popular demand for change in Egypt, Algeria, Morocco, and Tunisia. It seemed for a time that a new and more open politics would transform the region. Instead, authoritarian states mobilized to repress the populist opposition led by radicalized and politicized Islamist movements.

Islamic radicalism in North Africa has three faces—a religious one which seeks through personal piety, prayer, and preaching to make society more 'just'; a reformist one which calls for legitimate political action using democratic, electoral means to change state and society from within; and an extremist face, which believes that only violent confrontation and destruction of the state can establish a new Islamic world order. Algeria, Tunisia, Morocco, Libya, and Egypt tend to regard the latter two as equally dangerous to regional and regime stability. Their concerns about regional security, if radical Islamists were to gain power, grew in 1991 when an Islamist political party—the Islamic Salvation Front (FIS)-scored a major election victory and appeared to be on the verge of gaining power in Algeria.

Over the subsequent four years, Algeria's neighbors watched in growing horror while the military-dominated Algerian government canceled elections, outlawed the FIS, and the country slipped into the chaos of urban terrorism and civil war. Determined not to repeat Algiers' mistake in allowing an Islamist party access to the political process, Tunis, Rabat, and Cairo sought to eliminate the opportunities for radical Islamist politicians to force a confrontation with the government, legally or illegally. Even Libya's Muamar Qadhafi, a long-time sponsor of Islamic 'liberation' movements, was not immune from Islamist-inspired opposition riots in several towns. Their answer was similar to that of the Algerian government-exclusion from the political process and containment through intimidation and force.

Islamists and theopolitics: Algerian quest for electoral justice

Islamic radicals and the then Algerian military-controlled government were on a collision course since the government canceled the second round of elections in early 1992. The first round of elections in December 1991 had been called by then President Chadli Bendjedid as an experiment in multiparty democracy. It culminated in a clear-cut victory for the FIS. The military forced Bendjedid to resign, canceled the results of the December election, and formed a five-man collective body to govern in Bendjedid's place. The cancellation, provoked out of fear of a second Islamist victory, triggered escalating violence. Islamic radicals began targeting foreign workers, as well as women, intellectuals, and government bureaucrats. The government declared a State of Emergency in February 1992 enhancing the powers of the security forces and in January 1994 appointed Liamine Zeroual president. In more than four years of virtual civil war, at least 50,000 civilians, militants, and military personnel have been killed. Neither the government nor the radical Islamists has been able to attract broad support among the Algerian population or deal a knockout blow to the other.

The goal of the Algerian military is to eliminate the Islamic radicals, introduce economic reform, and use dialogue with non-violent Islamists to marginalize the FIS and other opposition parties. Zeroual was elected President in what the regime describes as a large turnout in elections held in November 1995. This enhanced the regime's legitimacy and reinforced the generals' commitment to their strategy of eradication of the insurgents. Zeroual also offered to open dialogue with some Islamists-not the FIS-but there probably will be no concessions to the Islamists to broker peace, and the violence will likely continue. The larger than anticipated turn-out in the election, the militants' inability to disrupt them, and the oppositions' failure to sway the voters has strengthened the government's hand. However, that the large turnout and favorable vote is less an endorsement of government policies than a sign of general public weariness with militant-government violence. While the United States has few assets in Algeria, U.S. facilities have been attacked twice by Islamic militants and American citizens are at risk from terrorist attacks. U.S. forces could be in danger while evacuating U.S. and other foreign nationals from Algeria should the conflict widen.

Haunted by Algeria

Political leaders in Cairo, Rabat, and Tunis have watched the Algerian situation deteriorate into virtual civil war. Each government has Islamist parties, which are seeking entry into the political process by becoming legitimate parties, running candidates in elections, and holding government office. And, each has evolved a similar strategy to deny the Islamists legitimacy. They endeavor to be seen as supporting Islam by sponsoring non-violent, local religious institutions, most of which are on a government dole. These governments also rely on some degree of intimidation or outright repression. The measures range from social and economic ostracism to arrest, interrogation, exile, and, in Algeria, execution of suspected members of radical Islamist groups.

Egyptian Muslim Brotherhood

President Mubarak's most serious political challenge comes from the Muslim Brotherhood, the oldest and most mainstream Islamist organization in the Middle East. Brotherhood members have won control of many of Egypt's professional and trade associations and held seats in Parliament by running on legal parties' tickets. In order to protect its property and standing in Egypt, the increasingly popular organization has not openly challenged government restrictions on its activities.

The Brotherhood's threat to Mubarak is long-term. Smaller, violent groups pose the greatest danger to Egypt's immediate security. The Gamaat al-Islamiya and groups falling under the Islamic Jihad umbrella have been responsible for most terrorism in Egypt, from Anwar Sadat's assassination in 1981 to recent attacks on foreign tourists. For all the publicity their operations have garnered, however, the militant Islamist factions have not won the hearts or minds of the Egyptian people, who resent the danger and loss of economic well being caused by the violence.

Mubarak uses several methods to deal with his Islamist critics and opponents. He allows traditional Islamic clerics and scholars a wide role in interpreting Egyptian law and restricting press, media, the arts, academic scholarship, and even personal relationships. Cairo is also belatedly trying to establish social welfare programs to rival the Brotherhood's humanitarian activities. Cairo's efforts this summer to reassert a leadership role among the Arab states following the election of a right-wing government in Israel are also intended to boost the regime's Islamic legitimacy. In June, Cairo hosted the first Pan-Arab summit since 1990 to try to create a common Arab strategy to deal with the Israeli government's opposition to continuing the peace process.

However, Mubarak also regards the Brotherhood as being in league with radical Islamists and shows no interest in opening the political system to even non-violent members of the Brotherhood or in tolerating the adoption of more fundamentalist Islamic practices or sympathizers, especially in the military services. Cairo has banned political parties based on religion, conducted security sweeps before elections, changed elective municipal offices to appointive ones, and uses military rather than civilian courts to try suspects. Many Brotherhood politicians were arrested before last fall's election, including Sayf al-Banna, son of the organization's founder and a prominent leader in the movement. This happened despite the Brotherhood's acceptance of government restrictions on its political activities.

Morocco

Morocco's King Hassan relies on a unique factor to bolster his claims to political legitimacy and contain Islamist critics: his status as a descendant of the Prophet Muhammad and Commander of the Faithful. The King is seen at home as a strong leader. Radical Islam does not yet pose a serious threat to his rule, but poor economic growth, bleak job prospects, high unemployment, and a high birth rate could provide a receptive climate for the growth of radical Islamist movements. Added to this volatile mix is the King's apparent ill health and a son (and successor) perceived by many Moroccans as weak. Morocco could become vulnerable to an Islamist challenge from either its non-violent Islamist party—the Justice and Charity group—or the more extremist Islamic Youth Movement.

Tunisia

Tunisia's economic growth, high levels of education, and improved living standards coupled with coercive security measures against real and suspected Islamists have kept Islamist politics quiescent. To the Tunisian leadership, the chronic unrest in Algeria only shows the folly of allowing elections. Many Tunisians are reluctant to support a cause which seems to threaten their well-being. The principal Islamist opposition movement, An-Nahda, has been silenced at home and the activities of its exiled leader, Rashid Ghannouchi, curtailed.

Since the beginning of the contemporary wave of terrorism on July 22, 1968, the international counter-terrorist community has never seen an organization like al Qaeda. On that day, the Popular Front for the Liberation of Palestine hijacked a Tel Aviv-bound El Al flight to Algiers in the first aircraft hijacking by a Palestinian group. International efforts have been made to target al Qaeda after the simultaneous suicide bombing of two U.S. embassies in eastern Africa in October 1998 failed. Despite firing 75 cruise missiles into Afghanistan and then arresting its members worldwide, the bombing of USS Cole in October 2000 and the multiple bombing of U.S. targets inside continental U.S. in September 2001 could not be prevented.

This demonstrates the difficulties the U.S.-led coalition against terrorism are facing in the fight against its first target—al Qaeda and its leader Osama bin Laden. Al Qaeda's unusual capacity to withstand sustained human losses and material wastage is attributed to its unique structure and ideology.

Five characteristics enhance both al Qaeda's survivability and force multiplication. Al Qaeda is neither one single group nor a coalition of two dozen large, medium and small groups. It is a conglomerate of groups spread throughout the world, operating as a network. Its affiliates include the Egyptian Islamic Jehad (EIJ), Al Gammaya-al Islamia (IG: Islamic Group of Egypt), the Armed Islamic Group of Algeria (GIA), the Islamic Party of Turkestan (IPT: Islamic Movement of Uzbekistan), the Jaish-e-Mohammed of Kashmir (JM: Army of Mohommad), and the Abu Sayyaf Group of the Philippines (ASG). The constituent groups of the network have their own command, control and communication structures. But whenever there is the need, these groups interact or merge, ideologically, financially and operationally.

Al Qaeda provides leadership at both the international and national levels. Although Osama has identified the U.S. as its prime enemy, he is an internationalist. As such Osama is likely to target not only Western targets, but also regimes that identify with the West, from Israel to the Philippines. However, the leaders of the other groups that work with Osama also have crucial domestic agendas. For instance, while deputising for Osama, the Emir-General of al Qaeda, Dr. Ayman al-Zawahiri, also leads the EIJ in Egypt. Al Qaeda's broad ideological disposition advocates pan-Islam and not pan-Arabism. As a result, Osama's ideology cuts across divisions and appeals to both West Asian and non-West Asian groups, including Asian Islamic groups. His thinking in this direction was greatly influenced both by Abdullah Azzam, his Palestinian mentor, and by Hasan Turabi, the spiritual leader of Sudan.

However, Islamists in the Arab states of North Africa are having little success in gaining political power. This is due to repressive security measures and popular despair over the violence on both sides, especially in Algeria and Egypt. Islamists in Algeria lost the presidential election held in November 1995, and the Muslim Brotherhood in Egypt bowed to government tactics of arrests and a ban on political opposition activity in the recent elections. The governments of Egypt, Tunisia, Algeria, and Morocco have probably reached a plateau in their use of intimidation tactics against Islamist critics. They seem to lack the imagination or will to try new, less dire strategies for dealing with opponents. As long as coercion seems to work, they will have little incentive to reform their authoritarian regimes in North Africa.

The more violent Islamic radical movements in Egypt are apparently losing momentum. The increasing risk is that they will carry their struggle abroad. For example, Egyptian diplomats in Europe and South Asia have been the targets of terrorist attacks, and Algerian extremists have been responsible for terrorism in France. Except for Egypt, which receives nearly $2 billion in U.S. aid each year, the United States has little economic investment and minimal military or diplomatic commitments in the region. Governmental use of repression poses a longer-term challenge to U.S. interests, however, as it opposes a key traditional pillar of U.S. foreign policy: the global promotion of democracy and human rights.

In other words, efforts have not been made to solve problems posed by the low capacity and/or low political will of Arab state institutions in North Africa to provide all citizens with minimum levels of security and well-being. The humiliation which these states have suffered from Israeli military strikes and their shared feeling of loss of Arabic civilization to westernization is at the base of their frustrations.

One can write off the terrorist attacks of September 11 as the crazed act of a fanatical gang hell-bent on causing mayhem at any cost. Or one may also try to understand the attacks' root causes by taking a closer look at the world whose fragile ecology of power they upset. In this vein, the attacks can be interpreted as a symptom of increasingly bitter polarization between haves and have-nots. The danger for America is that its overwhelming power is feeding resentment—in the same countries that also feel they are missing out on the spoils of economic progress.

Many of the terrorist attacks carried out by North African Arabs instruct us that an asymmetric threat from terrorists has grown out of the incredible quantitative difference of force and of riches between North and South. Terrorist strikes were viewed as a balance of terror—and of anger, of desperation. People commit suicide attacks because they have nothing to lose and because they want to cause as much damage to the enemy as they can. It is a culture of defeat. This is perhaps the feeling of humiliation in the radical Arab states in North Africa—it is not just poverty, it is the defeat, it is feeling inferior to Israel and its allies.

It must be stated, however, that North African Islamists have been effective in their coordination and networking They, particularly in the US and Germany, have been able to follow through with their stated goals, and currently pose an effective terrorist challenge to the state Islamists, even without state backing, have coordinated terrorism transnationally in pursuit of pre-determined goals. Criminal activity by Algerian Islamists in Canada and the UK to finance terrorism in a second country, while retaining command and control in a third country, indicates a sophisticated level of networking.

Islamist terrorists have therefore adopted the network form, with disparate actors coming together to commit a terrorist act. The GIA bombings in France in the early 1990s were carried out by a networked organization with its command and control center in London, safe-housing in Belgium and targets in France. Likewise the American Jihad group of Shaykh Omar Abdurrahman was composed of members from disparate backgrounds, as is the al Qaeda group of Osama bin Laden, which was responsible for bombing the US embassies in East Africa in 1998, and the group arrested by police in January 2001 in Germany, Italy and the UK who it is alleged were plotting to blow up Strasbourg Cathedral.

Islamists have successfully demonstrated that geographical dispersion provides the security that a rigid hierarchy does not. Hamas constitutes yet another example of the network format, compared with, for instance, the hierarchical format of Arafat's al-Fatah. Hamas has separated its political and military wings, and its leadership is divided between Gaza and (until their exclusion) Jordan and now Syria. Yet, some of its political direction and most of its fund-raising has been carried out in the US whilst its publications are partly produced in the UK. (*Filistin al Muslima*, the main Hamas newspaper is published in London, as is *Palestine Times*, the editorial line of which is pro-Hamas.)

Armed Islamic Group

The Armed Islamic Group (known by its French acronym, GIA) is a radical offshoot of Algeria's main Islamist opposition. Since the North African country plunged into a bloody civil war in 1992, the group has been linked to terrorist attacks in Europe and to the massacres of tens of thousands of civilians in Algeria. In the past few years, many GIA members have joined other splinter Islamist groups or have been jailed or killed in government crackdowns.

Out of a bitter struggle for control of Algeria between Islamists and the country's authoritarian leadership. After winning independence from France in 1962, the country was governed by a socialist party called the National Liberation Front (FLN). Following a series of youth riots in the late 1980s, the FLN allowed the country's first multiparty elections. When a party of moderate and radical Islamists called the Islamic Salvation Front (FIS) won a round of parliamentary elections in 1991, the FLN nullified the victory and banned the FIS. The resultant public outcry turned violent, and the paramilitary wing of the FIS began targeting security forces. The GIA emerged as one of several radical FIS splinter factions that have continued to fight against Algeria's FLN-supported, military-dominated regimes, from the government that ruled the country until 1999 to the current, more conciliatory leadership.

The GIA aims to overthrow the secular Algerian regime and replace it with an Islamic state. Beyond that, however, the GIA has not articulated precise political goals, and GIA cells are said to operate independently. Most recent GIA attacks are thought to be either acts of retribution, assaults on wayward members, or simple banditry.

The GIA's massacres of civilians reached their height in the mid-1990s. Other GIA targets have included Algerian journalists, intellectuals, and secular schools. More recently, the GIA was thought to be behind two bombings in Algiers in August 2001.

The GIA is also accused of killing more than one hundred foreigners, mostly Europeans, since 1993. The group has a particular disdain for

France, the country's former colonial ruler and a major supporter of Algeria's military-backed regime. In 1994, GIA members hijacked an Air France flight, and in late 1999, a French court convicted several GIA members for a series of bombings in France in 1995.

Some GIA leaders may have had contact with Osama bin Laden while fighting in the 1979–1989 Afghan war against the Soviet Union. Osama bin Laden's al Qaeda terrorist network also includes some Algerians. The extent of the connection between the GIA and al Qaeda is unclear, experts say, but it is probably limited. The GIA operates principally in Algeria, and its objectives are more local than al Qaeda's ambitions for a global holy war.

Osama bin Laden and Egyptian terrorist groups

Recently the United States and Britain closed a number of diplomatic missions in Africa due to 'concrete information' that Osama bin Laden's network is planning another attack. The evidence that an attack may be in the works is said to include intercepted phone conversations in which bin Laden's operatives discussed the transferal of explosives and personnel. In addition, several embassies have also reportedly been under observation by unknown elements.

Osama bin Laden's televised interview on Qatar's al-Jazeera satellite would also seem to fit the pattern. In the past Osama bin Laden has been particularly outspoken just before attempting a terrorist operation. The timing of these events is interesting, in that Osama bin Laden's network has recently suffered a series of severe setbacks. With his back to the wall, Osama bin Laden may be more motivated than ever to perpetrate an attack.

Returnees from Albania

On April 18, 1999, one of the largest anti-terrorism trials in recent memory wound to a close in Egypt. The trial involved 107 Islamic fundamentalists, 63 of whom were tried in absentia. Most of the accused belonged to the Egyptian al-Jihad group, while the most notorious had ties to Osama bin Laden's al Qaeda organization. Among the suspects was one of the leaders of the Gama'a al-Islamiyah. The court sentenced several senior members of the Jihad group—including the organization's leader, Ayman Al-Zawahiri—to death or to life imprisonment. Al-Zawahiri, who was convicted in absentia, is a close associate of Osama bin Laden and one of the founders of the 'Islamic Front for Jihad against the Crusaders and the Jews.'

The proceedings came to be called the 'trial of the Albanian returnees,' due to the fact that twenty of the accused were extradited from Albania in July of 1998 in the wake of a foiled attack on an American installation in Tirana. A number of the others were arrested in various countries during 1998. The trial, which lasted from February to April 1999, revealed a wealth of details about the Egyptian Jihad—the group's structure, membership, policies and operational capabilities, as well as its connections with Osama bin Laden. The trial was a milestone in the worldwide fight against fundamentalist terrorism in general, over and above its importance to the Egyptian campaign against the al Jihad group.

The Egyptian Jihad Group carried out attacks against Egyptian officials. Among the group's targets are: the Chairman of Parliament (1990) and the Ministry of Interior (1993). In 1995 the Jihad orchestrated attacks outside of Egypt against the Egyptian attaché in Switzerland and the Egyptian embassy in Pakistan, resulting in the deaths of fifteen people. There have been sea changes in the declared policy of the al-Jihad group. In addition to its bitter ideological conflict with the 'heretical' Egyptian government, the organization began calling for attacks against American and Israeli targets. In the eyes of the Jihad group, these countries are the vanguard of a worldwide campaign to destroy Islam and its believers, with the help of the current Egyptian government.

This change was the result of, among other things, the Egyptian al-Jihad's joining the coalition of Islamic fundamentalist terrorist organizations led by the Afghan Veterans. The collaboration between the Egyptian organizations and al Qaeda played a key role in the formation of Osama bin Laden's 'Islamic Front for Jihad against the Jews and the Crusaders.'

Al-Jihad goes abroad?

The first hints of the Jihad's change in policy vis-à-vis attacks outside of Egypt were seen in a foiled attack against an American installation in Albania in June 1998. Members of al-Jihad were also involved in the bombing of the American embassies in Nairobi and Dar-es-Salaam, which killed 224 people and wounded nearly 2,000.

The interrogation of several of the perpetrators of that attack led to the arrest of other members of Osama bin Laden's network in Germany and in

England. The details revealed by the investigation—together with the lessons learned from the Egyptian group's involvement in the terrorist attacks in New York in 1993—led to an increased cooperation between the United States and Egypt in the fight against the 'International Islamic Front.'

Egypt, through the good offices of the Americans, gained the cooperation of a number of other countries, among them: Albania, Azerbaijan, Bulgaria, South Africa, Equador, Saudi Arabia, Kuwait and the United Arab Emirates. This cooperation resulted in the extradition of members of the Jihad Group and Osama bin Laden's network to Egypt.

Thus, the Egyptian groups' involvement in terror outside of Egypt brought about a severe backlash—a worldwide cooperative effort that dealt a significant blow to Osama bin Laden's coalition. Yet another setback to Osama bin Laden was the public declaration of a unilateral cessation of terrorism against the Egyptian government by the exiled leaders of the Gama'a al-Islamiya, Egypt's largest terrorist group. This declaration resulted in a massive release of Gama'a operatives from Egyptian prisons. From the time of the founding of the International Islamic Front in February 1998, Osama bin Laden had assigned the Gama'a al Islamiyya a central operational position in the religious-military hierarchy of the organization.

In sum, despite the considerable achievements of the Egyptian and American counter-terrorism efforts, it must be remembered that the fight against Islamic fundamentalist terror is long and involved, replete with attacks and counter-attacks. Although the fundamentalists have suffered some serious setbacks, it's safe to assume that the last shot has not been fired. The militant declarations of al-Zawahiri in the wake of his conviction in absentia in Cairo, as well as Osama bin Laden's ceaseless threats only strengthen this conviction.

The American precautions are an indication of the seriousness with which they view the threat. This, together with the recent threats made by Osama bin Laden and his Egyptian colleagues, and the loss of prestige suffered by the Islamic Front, would seem to portend a concentrated effort on the part of Osama bin Laden's network to execute another round of attacks in the near future.

Deadly terrorist activities

The Jihad group specializes in armed attacks against high-level Egyptian Government officials. The original Jihad was responsible for the assassination in 1981 of President Anwar Sadat. Unlike al-Gama'at al-Islamiyya, which mainly targets mid- and lower-level security personnel, Coptic Christians, and Western tourists, al-Jihad appears to concentrate primarily on high-level, high-profile Egyptian Government officials, including cabinet ministers. It claimed responsibility for the attempted assassinations of Interior Minister Hassan Al-Alfi in August 1993 and prime minister Atef Sedky in November 1993.

In view of the grave threat posed by the Jihad factions to the Egyptian regime, and due to the large number of terrorist attacks for which they were responsible, the Egyptian security forces have given top priority to their war on the organization. During the tenure of former Egyptian Minister of Interior General Zaki Badr, some 8,000 Jihad activists were imprisoned. However, the organization's infrastructure was not destroyed, and when General Abd al-Halim Moussa took office as Interior Minister, the Jihad groups actually stepped up their activities. In response, General Moussa declared in October 1990 that the security forces had committed themselves to the complete elimination of the Jihad organization in Egypt, as well as that of other organizations acting to undermine governmental stability.

In June 1992, after activists of the Islamic Jihad in Egypt murdered Faraj Fodah, an author who had openly supported Israeli-Egyptian peace, a 'hit list' was revealed that had been prepared by organization activists and which included the names of tens of Egyptians to be killed by the Islamic Jihad, including the Interior Minister, General Moussa; the journalist Anis Mansour; and others. Since 1993 the group has not conducted an attack inside Egypt. However there have been repeated threats to retaliate against the United States, for its incarceration of Sheikh Umar Abd al-Rahman and, eventually, for the arrests of its members in Albania, Azerbaijan, and the United Kingdom. The deadly activities in other mineral-rich African countries are multiple, especially in South Africa.

Egypt confronts terrorism

The anti-fundamentalism of the secular Egyptian regimes has often been very brutal. Egypt has waged a bitter campaign of state violence, mass arrests, and financial crackdowns against Jamaat al-Islamiyya, Egyptian Islamic Jihad, and other Islamist groups during much of the 1990s. Experts say the government has largely succeeded in stopping them from carrying out terrorist attacks inside Egypt. But human rights groups say that Egyptian President Hosni Mubarak's regime has often used torture as part of its crackdown and sometimes has taken family members of Islamist leaders hostage.

The rise to power of Anwar al Sadat following the death of Gamal Abdul Nasser in 1970 ushered in a new social and political era in Egypt (Al-Sayyid, 1993, p. 228). Sadat's rule was characterized by the demilitarization of the state in favor of the bourgeoisie and the opening of Egypt to capitalism, and to the West through *infitah* (the open door) (Metz, 1991, p. xxi). His signing of the historic Camp David Accords in September 1978 and the Egyptian-Israeli Peace Treaty in March 1979, coupled with increasing repression of domestic opposition, ultimately led to Sadat's October 1981 assassination by a Muslim extremist group (*Al Jihad: Holy War*) opposed to peace with Israel.

Hosni Mubarak assumed the presidency of Egypt in 1981. And, on his accession to power, Mubarak immediately demonstrated a commitment to gradualism aimed at modifying and preserving the best elements of his predecessors' accomplishments. He has also had to balance the demands of Islamists with his plans to promote a secular Egyptian state for reasons of political survival. Since Sadat's assassination in 1981, Mubarak has been engaged in an on-again-off-again war with Muslim extremist groups, partly as a result of the regime's inability to solve many of Egypt's horrendous economic, political and social problems. Along with the Muslim Brotherhood and mainstream pro-government clergy, the Islamic opposition in Egypt includes two more militant strands: underground groups known as Jamaat, and local associations known as Jamiyat (Rubin, 1990). The Jamaat believe that the Brotherhood has sold out to the secular system, that state and society have become un-Islamic, and that Muslims must rise in a jihad that will produce a new Islamic state (McCormick, 1995, p. 433).

Unable to confront the Egyptian State legally and/or militarily, some Egyptian groups seek to undermine the viability of the Egyptian State through the use of terrorism. The problem has been so bad since 1981 (although it has been especially bad since 1992), that President Mubarak has maintained a state of emergency during his entire term (McCormick, 1995, p. 421). Mubarak's policy options have been limited by Egypt's severe economic and social problems, by the need to contain the Islamic opposition, and by Egypt's position at the hub of the Arab world (McCormick 1995, p. 421; Palmer, Leila and Yassin 1988, p. 10).

The Mubarak regime has responded to this problem with force, in effect, attempting to eliminate the growing terrorist threat by inflicting destructions upon the perpetrators of terrorism (Trapp, Palmer and Smith, 1994, p. 1). The punitive responses to terrorism adopted by the Mubarak regime have operated on three levels: (1) the legal level; (2) the military level; and (3) the non-military level. Legal counter-terrorist measures focus on the enactment of tough anti-terrorist laws, the arresting of criminals and the carrying out of sentences (i.e., hanging, life sentences and the like). Military measures include such repressive tactics as security sweeps of towns, raids of suspected terrorists hiding places, and the demolition of houses belonging to suspected terrorists. Finally, Egypt has utilized non-military measures, including the implementation of curfew and travel restrictions, purges of 'radical' elements in the military, bureaucracy, and schools, as well as the deportation of suspected terrorists out of Egypt.

A pattern of terror and counter-terror has persisted in Egypt at least since the days of Nasser, but especially since the death of Sadat in 1981. The most recent, and some (Murphy, 1994, p. 78) say worst, upsurge in Egypt's terror-counter-terror (since 1992) dynamic has led some observers (Neier, 1996, p. 691; Al-Sayyid, 1993, pp. 239–242; Reed, 1993, pp. 94–96) to question the utility of repressive counter-terrorist responses as a strategy for deterring terrorism.

In other words: (1) do punitive measures (i.e., 'iron fist' strategies) reduce terrorism, or simply contribute to increased levels of terrorism?; and (2) what is the cause of fundamentalist terrorism in Egypt? The first question is an interesting one to ask because, from the standpoint of 'official' policy, there exists a difference of opinion as to which is the best counter-terrorist strategy: a repressive strategy, a passive strategy, or an accommodative policy?

The United States, Egypt, and Israel have generally followed more repressive strategies while Western European states, conversely, have advocated the more passive approaches (they argue simply that violence begets more violence). Israeli, U.S. and Egyptian officials respond to the increasing criticism of their more repressive policies by arguing that passive and accommodative approaches merely encourage terrorism. The second question is interesting on its face: if the cause(s) of terrorism can be found, then logically, solutions to terrorism can be addressed and the problem ameliorated.

According to Reed (1993, p. 99), published lists of those accused of terrorism show that militancy appeals to young disadvantaged men-tradesmen, food vendors, schoolteachers, students, the unemployed. Such men find themselves in a terrible position in today's Egypt. Important to note however, is that the largest and most important Islamic organization, the Muslim Brotherhood, long ago renounced violence, and thus seeks to peacefully transform Egyptian society through education, social programs and the political process (Lief, 1993, p. 42). However, because these more militant groups have been operating in Egypt for so long (at least since the defeat in the 1967 war with Israel), they are doing so much damage to Egypt's economic base, tourism. During 1992–1993, attacks on tourists left 290 people dead, 670 wounded, and made a major dent in one of Egypt's main foreign capital and jobs (Hedges, 1994a, sec. F, p. xx3), and because the problem seems to be rising, the militant groups garner most of the domestic and international media attention.

However, an analytical definition of terrorism and Egypt's counter-terrorism is essential. To avoid the intellectual bog that surrounds the political and emotional debate about what is or is not terrorism, it is necessary to conceptualize the term in such a way that allows for empirical observation and analysis. There is little consensus, however, in the literature dealing with terrorism on what does or does not constitute terrorism or terrorist acts (Schmid and Jongman, 1988; Thackrah, 1987; Crenshaw, 1992). In fact, Walter Laqueur (1986) has pointed out that 109 different definitions of the term were advanced between 1936 and 1985, with more appearing since 1986. Furthermore, efforts in the academic world to come to some consensus on a definition have proven problematic. In practice, scholars and politicians have used for example, the terms 'terrorism' and 'terrorists' alike as labels to tar their enemies. The cliché 'one man's terrorist is another man's freedom fighter' is a notorious reflection of this fruitless game of semantics. As Richard Baxter (1974, p. 5), professor of law at Harvard University and judge on the International Court of Justice, once remarked, 'we have cause to regret that a legal concept of "terrorism" was ever inflicted upon us. The term is imprecise; it is ambiguous; and above all, it serves no operative legal purpose.'

Most definitions of terrorism, according to Crenshaw (1992, p. 1), however, divided on other points, agree that it is a form of political violence. A compilation of just some of the various definitions is provided as follows: terrorism is often seen as the use of force (Gurr, 1970; Schmid and Jongman, 1988; Anand, 1993; Crenshaw, 1992) against random or symbolic victims (Hanle, 1989; Thackrah, 1987) to produce terror or fear (Anand, 1984; Schmid and Jongman, 1988). The objectives are seen as political in nature (Gurr 1986; Miller, 1988; Mickolous, 1983), although some scholars do not see the political condition as a necessary one (Hanle, 1989). In contrast to those who see terrorism as the use of force, some argue that the threat of force is a sufficient condition for a terrorist act (Wardlaw, 1982; Wilkinson, 1987). Some include elements of the outcome in their definition of terrorism (fear) which they posit leads to a behavior change (Schmid and Jongman, 1988). A compelling argument is also made that intent defines terrorist action irrespective of the outcome (Merari, 1981).

Because we shall conceptualize the term in such a way that allows for empirical observation and analysis, the Trapp (1994) and Trapp, Palmer, and Smith (1994) definitions of terrorism are followed. Terrorism is here defined as the 'range of politically motivated violent acts bracketed by riots and violent political protest on one side and guerrilla warfare on the other' (Trapp, 1994, p. 6). Included within this range are the following: assassinations, kidnappings, explosive bombings, incendiary bombings, letter bombings, hostage seizures, and armed attacks involving rifles, pistols, grenades, bazookas, mortars, and other precision munitions. Following this line of reasoning then, I conceptualize terrorism as the use or threat of anxiety-inducing violence 'for political purposes by groups or individuals' (Mickolous, 1983, p. 21), particularly against innocent people.

The study of counter-terrorism is comprised of two bodies of scholarly work: one is a more broadly focused mixture which addresses a veritable laundry list of dimensions: from the causes of terrorism, to the media's impact on terrorism, to the most effective method of dealing with these terrorists (Alona, 1978; Reich, 1990; Murphy, 1989; Livingstone, 1982). The other body of work on counter-terrorism is comprised of a small group of narrowly focused works examining specific aspects of governmental behavior rather than the policy or the concept as a whole (Enders and Sandler, 1993; Cauley and Sandler, 1988; Olson, 1989; Trapp, 1994). According to Trapp (1994, pp. 13–14), there is still some confusion about which types of counter-terrorist strategies most effectively eliminate terrorism. He elaborates:

> [First] because of the search for answers, our understanding of terrorism is far from complete and as a body of knowledge, the literature of terrorism is best characterized as a compilation of different viewpoints . . . Second, despite the advancement of numerous theories of . . . counter-terrorism . . . few scholars have gathered data on terrorism or counter-terrorism by which these theories and models are to be tested . . . This is particularly true of counter-terrorism theories

that have been supported with anecdotal facts, not systematically generated empirical data.

Trapp (1994, p. 9) adds that the disagreements over how governments should respond to terrorism, which stem from differences in opinion about what causes terrorism, also contribute to the confusion. Three strategies of counter-terrorism currently dominate the terrorist literature: a theory of repressive counter-terrorism, an accommodative theory, and a theory advocating a more passive strategy. These 'abstract' theories are important because they serve as the foundation for governmental policy, particularly the policies of Egypt, Israel, the United States, and Western Europe.

Some argue that repressive strategies are the best way of combating terrorism because these tactics deny the terrorists the political benefits they seek to gain from committing terrorism in the first place. Routine retaliations are fully discounted by the terrorists and have little effect on the rate of terrorist activity. Thomas Schelling (1978, p. 74). However, the Egyptian counter-terrorist policy falls within this policy subset retaliations. This policy is based on the premise that terrorism is a rational, utility-maximizing behavior strategy designed by political extremists who seek to maximize political objectives by undermining the political fabric of the country (the 'political causes' theory of terrorism). Hence, instead of rewarding terrorists through passivity or accommodation, advocates of this approach (Netanyahu, 1986; Laqueur, 1986; Lichbach, 1987) argue that governments must be firm and, if necessary, respond with force and repression. Proponents of this strategy (Sandler, 1983; Atkinson, 1987; Lichbach, 1987) argue that because the motives of the terrorists are deliberate, rational, and ideological, governments should avoid actions that reward them. This viewpoint is representative of the 'political causes' theory of terrorism that regards terrorism simply as a rational and deliberate political strategy employed by political extremists who want to change the present structure of the international system.

Others argue that accommodative and passive strategies are the most efficacious strategies for dealing with terrorism. Accommodative strategies revolve around the notion that terrorism is not simply a rational decision, but rather a reaction to miserable economic, political, and social conditions. That is, the terrorists are conceived of as turning to terrorism out of desperation. Finally, some argue that pro-active measures, whether repressive or accommodative, are ineffective because they serve to legitimize or reward the terrorists. Those advocating this approach (Long,

1990; Chomsky and Hermann, 1988) argue that governments should follow a passive strategy consisting of defensive measures designed to prevent the occurrence of terrorism (Trapp, 1994, p. 12).

Both policies are oriented around the argument that the causes of terrorism are not primarily political, but cultural, economic, and social as well. This 'root causes' theory is based on the assumption that terrorism is largely the product of grievances arising from the heightened awareness of rapidly deteriorating cultural, social and economic conditions. Furthermore, the logic of granting concessions and accommodation is that these measures 'cure' the causes of terrorism, because these measures reputedly ameliorate the motivations for terrorism (Trapp, 1994, p. 55).

Despite some confusion about which is the most effective strategy, counter-terrorism as a concept is easily defined. Following Trapp (1994, p. 152) and Trapp, Palmer and Smith (1994), I define counter-terrorism 'as an identifiable government action undertaken in response to an act of terrorism or a string of terrorist events.' That is, counter-terrorism is conceived of as a proactive strategy that consists of repressive measures designed to compel the sponsors of terrorism to end their activities.

Egypt's counter-terrorism strategies

Since the 1979 signing of the Egyptian-Israeli Peace Accords, and the subsequent assassination of President Anwar Sadat, Egypt has been ensconced in an on-again, off-again action-reaction terrorist-counter-terrorist cycle. Furthermore, since the spring of 1992, Egypt has experienced the worst and longest upsurge in Islamic terrorism since 1981. Since 1992, the Islamic Group and Islamic Jihad (the most prominent of Egypt's Islamic terrorist organizations) have been engaged in a bloody campaign against the Mubarak government (Hedges, 1992a, sec. L, p. L6).

Two basic questions usually guide this line of research: (a) what are the roots of these conflicts whereby some groups experience intense political violence while others do not; and (b) what are the patterns of internal conflict? (Miller, 1988, p. 72). The targets for their bullets and bombs have shifted from Muslim opinion leaders who frown on fundamentalism and Christian Coptics, to foreign tourists, police officers, and government officials (Nelan, 1993, pp. 28–29). For example, Abdel Rahman, a spiritual guide to the militant Islamic Jihad, condemned Egypt as a tyrannical state that 'won't last' (Hedges, 1992b, sec. A, p. A1; 1993a, sec. A, p. A4). Militant groups, in effect, have vowed to continue their campaign to destabilize Egypt's economy and public life. According to Chris Hedges,

'Islamic Group has said that it will kill [Hosni] Mubarak in its drive to establish a theocracy in Egypt, along the lines of Iran' (Hedges, 1993b, sec. A, p. A3). No matter whom they shoot at, their long-term goals remain constant: to topple the secular government of Hosni Mubarak and install a purely Islamic state that would turn against Western influence, end corruption, and impose strict Islamic law (Hedges, 1993c, sec. A1, p. A6).

The Mubarak regime's reaction or counter-terrorist strategy is two-pronged. On one level, the Egyptian government has adopted a repressive strategy designed to deny the terrorists the political benefits that they seek to gain. Or, as Brig General Baheddine Ibrahim stated in 1993, 'either there is a state or there is not. We will fight them until we crush them. We have no other choice' (Hedges, 1994b, sec. A, p. A3). This more repressive strategy thus seeks to meet force with force, and in the process drive the costs of terrorism to such high levels that terrorism will cease or at least decrease to tolerable levels (i.e., the 'iron fist' approach). The question is: what is tolerable and what costs are inflicted on the Mubarak regime in the process of wiping out the terrorists?

The elements of Egypt's more repressive prong are legal security measures, military, and non-military in nature. Examples of each include the following measures:

- *Legal security measures*: In November 1993, the government created a series of tougher anti-terrorist laws in which membership in a militant terrorist organization has been rendered a crime punishable by death. The fourteen men executed by hanging in June and July of 1993, and the dozens more thus far in 1994 after military trials, are examples of this iron fist method of punishing violent Islamic militants (Hedges, 1994c, sec. A, p. A3). The powers of security forces were also broadened under the 1981 emergency decree, which included the right to detain people without trial. Since the early 1980s, literally thousands of suspected militants were rounded up and tossed into prison, where human rights groups reported that they were routinely tortured during their 'preventive detention.'
- *Military*: The use of military forces to destroy or damage the facilities or supplies of a target group became commonplace. It included: security sweeps of cities, raids on buildings suspected of harboring terrorists, the leveling of their homes, shoot-outs with terrorists, and the occupation and control of areas/buildings suspected of harboring terrorists. For example, on March 12, 1993, police lobbed tear gas

grenades into a mosque in Aswan and killed seven people and wounded fifteen others as they tried to escape the fumes (Reed, 1993, p. 103).

- *Non-military*: The non-military component of the Egyptian repressive counter-terrorism 'prong' includes imposing general curfew and travel restrictions, purging governmental institutions and public schools of suspected militants, deporting suspected militants from Egypt, closing schools, and disconnecting telephone services. Examples include the July 1993 request for the extradition of Sheik Abdel Rahman, who was ailing in an Upstate New York prison hospital (Lief, 1993, p. 42); the attempt to sever links between Egyptian fundamentalists and their growing network of financiers and supporters in the United States, Pakistan, Saudi Arabia and Sudan (Nelan, 1993, p. 28); and the attempt by the Mubarak government to purge the military of terrorists who have infiltrated it—an alarming development considering the degree to which the regime relies on the military for stability, order, and support. In August 1993, 53 suspected militants went on trial for allegedly infiltrating the army and committing acts of terrorism. Three of them were found guilty and hung (Bartholet, Berger and Liu 1993, p. 41).

The second prong is a more accommodative strategy which aims to 'win the hearts and minds' of its populace. Hence, the regime is well aware that it must reach out with carrots as well as sticks. This involves the tacit acknowledgment that the perception of state neglect and corruption, in part, has contributed to growing economic misery and crime, especially in southern and upper Egypt, both strongholds of terrorist groups and breeding grounds for would be terrorists. Besides promising to improve economic conditions, the Mubarak regime also began to challenge the militant groups' claim of conformity to religious values (particularly Islamic ones) by increasing discussions of 'moderate' Islamic values on state controlled television and radio; it commenced courting cooperative Muslim clerics to preach against terrorism; it also conducts a propaganda campaign on the state run television oriented around a daily broadcast called 'No to Terrorism,' which features street interviews with Egyptians who condemn the terrorist violence and praise the police and the Mubarak regime (Hedges, 1993c, sec. A1, p. A6). What are possible explanations why Egypt's iron fist counter-terrorist policy has thus far not achieved its objective of 'eliminating' or containing the spread of domestic terrorism?

The possible explanations are as follows. First of all, Egypt's iron fist counter-terrorist policy seems to be more a response to the symptoms rather than to the underlying causes of Egypt's terrorism problem. As previously shown, legal and military actions have not reduced the level of terrorism in Egypt. In fact, in recent years, terrorism has greatly expanded, not diminished. Thus, as Trapp (1994, pp. 181–182) put it, Egypt's repressive, 'iron fist' counter-terrorist policy has failed 'to deliver the knock-out blow . . . [Egyptian] leaders argue it has provided.' As in Israel, repression alone cannot end the campaign of terrorism in Egypt. It is quite clear that the success of the Islamic fundamentalist movement in Egypt, in part, has been due to its ability to channel public discontent with the economy into support for an Islamic regime (Reed, 1993, p. 97; Kepel, 1985, p. 235). That is, poverty and unemployment are potentially problematic because they promote resentment among the poor and by the educated middle classes who are being turned away from public employment (and who thus become poor), and which then are exploited by the Islamic opposition (McCormick, 1995, p. 437; Reed, 1993, pp. 103–104).

According to the World Bank (1994, p. 162), in terms of Egypt's economy, the 1980s and early 1990s could be described as a lost decade and a half. The rate of economic growth (GNP per capita growth) dropped from 7.4 percent in 1981 to 1.8 in 1992. Furthermore, the new decade commenced with the significant fall of Egypt from the World Bank's group of lower middle-income countries to its group of lower income countries. World Bank statistics also indicated a rise in the rate of inflation (from 11.5 percent in 1981 to 21.3 percent by 1989) during this period, as well as a drop of ten percent in the real income of industrial workers, their share of the value added declining from 54 percent in 1970 to 35 percent in 1989 (World Bank, 1994, p. 174). Also of critical importance is the alleged 'growing gap between rich and poor and the deteriorating economic conditions of low income groups' (Murphy, 1994, p. 79). In addition, terrorist attacks on tourists have put a severe strain on tourism, thereby constraining the prospects of a $2 billion to $4 billion a year industry (Hedges, 1994a, sec. F, p. xx3; Reed, 1993, p. 96). Finally, according to World Bank projections, despite government efforts to bring population growth down to 2.4 percent, one million babies are born each year. Egypt's population is now estimated at 57 million but expected to double within the next twenty years (Palmer, Leila and Yassin, 1988, p. 1). The current zero to one percent economic growth rate is not enough to keep the already low $700 annual per capita income from decreasing even further.

Because of the severe nature of these problems and the limited capacity of the Egyptian bureaucracy to solve them (see especially Palmer, Leila and Yassin, 1988), solutions to these, and other, problems seem limited.

However, as those who advocate 'root causes' theory believe, attempts to 'eliminate' these problems must be immediately undertaken. In particular, efforts must be made to lower inflation, raise incomes, expand economy and economic opportunity, especially for those who are young, educated and without prospects. Many fear that if these problems are not addressed a broadening of the radical Islamic movement's support, particularly among those already openly alienated from the present system, will result.

Mubarak's dilemma, of course, is that he needs to improve the performance of the economy quickly or the militants will continue to gain new recruits. However, curtailing rising inflation, unemployment, and falling wages will require massive reform of the bureaucracy and privatization of the economy (i.e., the elimination of price supports, the rationalization of its currency, the elimination of pieces of the bloated bureaucracy and the like). These reforms—the shock therapy advocated by the United States and the IMF—would likely continue to exacerbate the already existing problems in the short term, thereby turning more against the regime. Hence, Mubarak is in a bind; if he reforms too rapidly he risks causing even greater hardship among Egypt's population and driving inflation even higher, which could trigger a new wave of riots, terrorism, and the like. Yet, the economy needs to be reformed. The question is, how should Mubarak proceed: slowly and gradually, or rapidly and massively? Given the extent of the problems, the ramifications of shock therapy, and Mubarak's legendary low-key, cautious, and conciliatory nature, it is more than likely that gradual reform will continue to be the choice. In sum, a perpetuation of the massive social and economic problems has created a critical mass of individuals willing to engage in terrorism against the Mubarak regime.

A second observation is that, despite the punitive measures, the Islamic militants have shown that they have the organization and determination to wage a protracted campaign against the state. Despite the fact that the more militant Islamic movement lacks a charismatic leader (Murphy, 1994; Reed, 1993), the Islamic tide in Egypt (as of 1997) is clearly still rising. The militants are capitalizing on the country's economic problems: its listless dependence on outside funding from mostly unidentified sources inside and outside Egypt (possibly in Iran and the Sudan), as well as the perception that the Mubarak regime is corrupt, insensitive, arrogant, and repressive (Murphy, 1994). While dangerous, the militants are fragmented by organizational problems, ideological, personality and tactical differences, and are beginning to alienate the Egyptian population with their militancy, due to the deaths of large numbers of innocent civilians and the loss of billions of dollars in tourist revenue (Murphy, 1994; Reed, 1993; McCormick, 1995, p. 394).

Third, both domestic and international criticism of the more repressive aspects of Egypt's counter-terrorist policy has weakened its ability to continue to pursue its policy with the same force and vigor. Criticism from groups that monitor human rights like Middle East Watch and Amnesty International initially prompted international criticism of much of Egypt's policy—from the UN and from the U.S. State Department. The nearly $3 billion in yearly aid that Egypt receives from the United States is in jeopardy, some say, because of America's inward, post-Cold War orientation and because of the supposed abuses being committed by the Mubarak regime against its population. These claims may be highly exaggerated given Egypt's pivotal position in America's overall security planning in the Middle East. Domestically, criticism from human rights groups such as the Egyptian Organization for Human Rights, the Muslim Brotherhood, and some of the less violent Islamic groups has also had the effect of somewhat limiting and constraining the regime's counter-terrorist policy (Neier, 1996, p. 691).

Fourth, it is also likely that the ferocity and frequency of the more repressive aspects of Egypt's counter-terrorist strategy has had the unwitting effect of precipitating new and more frequent terrorism. The government's harsh security crackdown (including the use of military courts for civilians, the use of torture, and the public execution of militants), has generated some resentment as well as fear, especially from many residing in Cairo's slums and poverty-ridden Upper Egypt (Murphy, 1994). However, in the absence of public opinion polling and a more probing press, it is difficult to accurately gauge Egyptian public opinion on this matter of iron fist repression.

Lastly, it is even clear that the scope of Egypt's counter-terrorist policy has had the unintended effect of even further radicalizing an already radicalized and militant Islamic movement. Through public accounts of human rights abuses including torture, coupled with the violent nature of security sweeps of towns in Upper Egypt as well as the willingness of the security forces to use deadly force, demolish homes, and arrest massive numbers of suspected terrorists, has served to reinforce the hatred of Egyptian security measures and the present Mubarak regime. In sum, short of dialog between the government and its radical Islamic opponents—an option that neither side seems seriously interested in at the moment—it is difficult to envision a complete cessation of the current problem.

Summarily, this exemplary preliminary analysis of Egypt's iron fist counter-terrorist policy indicates that the policy has not, up to 2004, reduced terrorism. The future needs to focus on the more accommodative aspects of Egypt's current policy in order to evaluate and compare it to the more punitive aspects of the policy. Furthermore, a more elaborate model of what precisely is the driving force of terrorism in Egypt needs to be delineated and tackled. Finally, future analyses of counter-terrorism in Egypt need to explore other factors. The role of intensity of news coverage on mass perceptions of terrorism and the counter-terrorist policy; the relationship between intensity of terrorism and intensity of the counter-terrorist reaction; and, levels of cohesion and conflict within the Islamic movement must be explored.

Notes

1. Porath, Y. (1986), *In Search of Arab Unity, 1930–1945*, Frank Cass: London.
2. Maddy-Weitzman, B. (1993), *The Crystallization of the Arab State System, 1945–1954*, Syracuse University Pres: Syracuse, NY, pp. 133–135.
3 Dishon, D. and Maddy-Weitzman, B. (1984), 'Inter-Arab Relations', *Middle East Contemporary Survey, 1981–1982*, Vol. 6, Holmes and Meier: New York, pp. 253–258.
4. For more information on the evolution of the inter-Arab-Arab-Israeli nexus, see Sela, A. (1998), *The Decline of the Arab-Israeli Conflict*, SUNY Press: Albany, NY.
5. Ajami, F. (1998), *The Dream Palace of the Arabs*, Pantheon Books: New York, pp. 253–312.
6. Ajami, F. (1981), *The Arab Predicament*, Cambridge University Press: Cambridge.
7. Maddy-Weitzman, B. (1993), 'Continuity and Change in the Inter-Arab System', in Barzilai, G., Klieman, A. and Shidlo, G. (eds.), *The Gulf Crisis and its Global Aftermath*, Routledge: London.
8. Maddy-Weitzman, B. (1997), 'Inter-Arab Relations', *Middle East Contemporary Survey*, Vol. 20, Westview Press: Boulder, CO, pp. 77–78.

References

Abbink, J. (1999), 'Ethiopian Islam and the Challenge of Diversity', *ISIM Newsletter*, No. 4 (December), p. 24.

Abu-Rabi, Ibrahim M. (1996), *Intellectual Origins of Islamic Resurgence in the Modern Arab World*, SUNY Press: Albany, NY.

Ahmed, Akbar S. (1992), *Postmodernism and Islam: Predicament and Promise*, Routledge: New York.

Ajami, F. (1981), *The Arab Predicament*, Cambridge University Press: Cambridge.

Ajami, F. (1994), 'The Battle for Egypt's Soul', *U.S. News and World Report*, June 27, pp. 42–45.

Ajami, F. (1998), *The Dream Palace of the Arabs*, Pantheon Books: New York.

Alexander, Y. (ed.) (1994), *Middle East Terrorism: Current Threats and Future Prospects*, G. K. Hall: New York.

Al-Sayyid, M. (1993), 'A Civil Society in Egypt?', *Middle East Journal*, Vol. 47, No. 2, pp. 228–242.

Anand, P. (1993), *Foundation of Rational Choice Under Risk*, Oxford University Press: Oxford.

Atkinson, A. B. (1987), *The Economics of Inequality*, Clarendon Press: Oxford.

Bartholet, J., Berger, C. and Liu, M. (1993), 'A Wave of Terror All Their Own', *Newsweek*, August 30, pp. 41–42.

Baxter, R. (1974), *Recent Codification of the Law of State Responsible for Injuries to Aliens*, Oceana Publishers: New York.

Blechman, B. (1972), *Strategic Forces: Issues for the Mid-Seventies*, Brookings Institution: Washington, D.C.

Bremer, P. (1989), 'Continuing the Fight Against Terrorism', *Terrorism*, Vol. 12, No. 2, pp. 81–87.

Brophy-Baermann, B. and Conybeare, J. (1994), 'Retaliating Against Terrorism: Rational Expectations and the Optimality of Rules Versus Discretion', *American Journal of Political Science*, Vol. 38, No. 1, pp. 196–210.

Bukay, D. (2002), *Total Terrorism in the Name of Allah*: *The Emergence of the New Islamic Fundamentalists*, Shaarei Tikva, Israel: Ariel Center for Policy Research.

Burgat, F. and Dowell, W. (1993), *The Islamic Movement in North Africa*, Center for Middle Eastern Studies, University of Texas at Austin: Austin, TX.

Cauley, J. and Sandler, T. (1988), 'Fighting WW II: A Suggested Strategy', *Terrorism*, Vol. 11, No. 1, pp. 181–195.

Chismar, J. (2001), "Nation Under Different Gods?', *Religion Today*, September 19.

Chomsky, N. and Hermann, E. (1988), *The Culture of Terrorism*, South End Press: Boston.

Cole, J. R. (1993), *Colonialism and Revolution in the Middle East: Social and Cultural Origins of Egypt's Urabi Movement*, Princeton University Press: Princeton, NJ.

Crenshaw, M. (1990), 'The Logic of Terrorism', in Reich, W. (ed.), *Origins of Terrorism: Psychologies, Ideologies, Theologies, States of Mind*, Cambridge University Press.

Crenshaw, M. (1992), 'Current Research on Terrorism: The Academic Perspective', *Studies in Conflict and Terrorism*, Vol. 15, No. 1, pp. 1–11.

Davies, T. R. (1977), 'Feedback Processes and International Terrorism', Ph.D. Dissertation, Florida State University, Tallahassee, FL.

Dessouki, A. H. (1992), 'Egypt's Response to the Persian Gulf Crisis', *Current History*, Vol. 91, No. 561, pp. 34–37.

Dishon, D. and Maddy-Weitzman, B. (1984), 'Inter-Arab Relations', *Middle East Contemporary Survey, 1981–1982*, Vol. 6, Holmes and Meir: New York, pp. 253–258.

Emerson, S. (1998a), 'Inside the Osama bin Laden Investigation', *Journal of Counterterrorism & Security International*, Vol. 5 (Fall), pp. 16–26.

Emerson, S. (1998b), 'Osama bin Laden's Special Operations Man', *Journal of Counterterrorism & Security International*, Vol. 5 (Fall), pp. 28–29.

Enders, W. and Sandler, T. (1993), 'The Effectiveness of Antiterrorism Policies: A Vector-Autoregression-Intervention Analysis', *American Political Science Review*, Vol. 87, No. 4 (December), pp. 829-845.

Esack, F. (1996), 'Taking on the State: PAGAD and Islamic Radicalism', *Indicator SA*, Vol. 13, No. 4 (Spring).

Evans, A. and Murphy, J. F. (1978), *Legal Aspects of International Terrorism*, Lexington Books: Lexington, MA.

Falola, T. (1998), *Violence in Nigeria: The Crisis of Religious Politics and Secular Ideologies*, University of Rochester Press: Rochester, NY.

Fluehr–Lobban, C. (1993), 'Personal Status Law in Sudan', in Bowen, D. L. and Early, E. (eds.), *Everyday Life in the Middle East*, Indiana University Press: Bloomington, IN.

Fox, J. G. (1970), *The Arab's Dilemma: Islamism or Nationalism*, Air War College: Maxwell AFB, AL.

Gilles, K. (2002), *Jihad: the Trail of Political Islam* (trans. by Anthony Roberts), Harvard University Press: Cambridge, MA.

Gurr, T. R. (1970), *Why Men Rebel*, Princeton University Press: Princeton, NJ.

Hanle, D. (1989), *Terrorism: The Newest Face of Warfare*, Pergamon Press: New York.

Hedges, C. (1992a), 'Domestic Problems Hurt Rising Stature of Egypt', *New York Times*, July 12, p. L6.

Hedges, C. (1992b), 'As Islamic Militants Thunder, Egypt Grows More Nervous', *New York Times*, November 12, p. A1.

Hedges, C. (1993a), 'Fury of Islam Dims Expatriate Sparkle on the Nile', *New York Times*, March 31, p. A4.

Hedges, C. (1993b), 'Everywhere in Saudi Arabia, Islam is Watching', *New York Times*, January 6, p. A4.

Hedges, C. (1993c), 'Egypt's War with the Militants: Both Sides Harden Positions', *New York Times*, April 1, p. A6.

Hedges, C. (1994a), 'Egyptian Tourism Faces New Drop Amid Attacks', *New York Times*, January 2, p. xx3.

Hedges, C. (1994b), 'Egypt Loses Ground to Militants and Fear', *New York Times*, February 1994, p. A3.

Hedges, C. (1994c), 'Egypt Begins Crackdown on Strongest Opposition Group', *New York Times*, June 19, p. A3.

Hewitt, C. (1992), 'The Costs of Terrorism: A Cross-National Study of Six Countries', *Studies in Conflict and Terrorism*, Vol. 15, No. 1, pp. 169–179.

Ibrahim, Youssef (1993), 'Egyptian Militants Blamed in Attack on Security Chief', *New York Times*, August 19, pp. A1, A10.

Karawan, I. (1994), 'Sadat and the Egyptian-Israeli Peace Revisited', *International Journal of Middle East Studies*, Vol. 26, No. 2, pp. 249–266.

Kennedy, M. (1986), 'The Root Causes of Terrorism', *The Humanist*, Vol. 46, No. 5, pp. 5–9.

Kepel, G. (1985), *The Prophet and the Pharaoh: Muslim Extremism in Egypt*, Al Saqi Books: London.

Kibble, D. G. (1995), 'Understanding Islamic Fundamentalism', *Military Review* (September-October), pp. 40–45.

Kibble, D. G. (1998), 'Islamic Fundamentalism: A Transitory Threat?' *Strategic Review*, Vol. 26, No. 2, pp. 11–18.

Laquer, W. (1986), 'Reflections on Terrorism', *Foreign Affairs*, Vol. 64, No. 2, pp. 86–104.

Lichbach, M. (1987), 'Deterrence or Escalation?: The Puzzle of Aggregate Studies of Repression and Dissent', *Journal of Conflict Resolution*, Vol. 31, No. 2, pp. 266–297.

Lief, L. (1993), 'The Battle of Egypt', *U.S. News and World Report*, July 19, pp. 42–44.

Livingstone, N. (1982), *The War Against Terrorism*, Lexington Books: Lexington, MA.

Long, D. (1990), *The Anatomy of Terrorism*, The Free Press: New York.

Maddy-Weiztman, B. (1993a), 'Continuity and Change in the Inter-Arab System', in Barzilai, G. Klieman, A. and Shidlo, G. (eds.), *The Gulf Crisis and its Global Aftermath*, Routledge: London.

Maddy-Weitzman, B. (1993b), *The Crystallization of the Arab State System, 1945–1954*, Syracuse University Press: Syracuse, NY.

Maddy-Weitzman, B. (1997), 'Inter-Arab Relations', *Middle East Contemporary Survey*, Vol. 20, pp. 77–78.

Marty, M. E. and Appleby, R. S. (eds.) (1995), *Fundamentalism Comprehended*, University of Chicago Press: Chicago.

McCormick, J. (1995), *Comparative Politics in Transition*, Wadsworth Publishing Company: Belmont, CA.

McKinlay, R. and Mughan, A. (1984), *Aid and Arms to the Third World: An Analysis*, F. Pinter: London.

Meari, A. (1981), *The Soviet Bloc and World Terrorism*, Tel Aviv University Press: Tel Aviv, Israel.

Metz, H. C. (ed.) (1991), *Egypt: A Country Study*, U.S. Government Printing Office: Washington, D.C.

Metz, H. C. (ed.) (1992), *Somalia: A Country Study*, U.S. Government Printing Office: Washington, D.C.

Mickolous, E. (1978), 'An Events Data Base for Studying Transnational Terrorism', in Hever, R. J. (ed.), *Quantitative Approaches Political Intelligence: The CIA Experience*, Westview Press: Boulder, CO.

Mickolous, E. (1983), 'Tracking the Growth and Prevalence of International Terrorism', in Montana, P. and Roukis, G. (eds.), *Managing Terrorism: A Strategy for the Corporate Executive*, Greenwood Publishing Group: Westport, CT.

Miller, R. (1988), 'The Literature of Terrorism', *Terrorism*, Vol. 11, No. 3, pp. 63–87.

Murphy, C. (1994), 'Egypt: An Uneasy Portent of Change?', *Current History*, Vol. 93, No. 580, pp. 78–83.

Murphy, J. (1989), *State Support of International Terrorism: Legal, Political, and Economic Dimensions*, Westview Press: Boulder, CO.

Murray, K. (2000), 'Sharia is the Only Rule of Law in Somalia', *Reuters News Service*, October 13.

Napoli, J. (1994), 'New Film's Popularity Gives Mubarak Government a Victory', *The Washington Report on the Middle East*, Vol. 1, No. 6, pp. 50, 81.

Neier, A. (1996), 'Watching Rights', *The Nation*, Vol. 256, No. 20, p. 691.

Nelan, B. (1993), 'Bombs in the Name of Allah', *Time*, August 30, pp. 28–30.

Netanyahu, B. (1996), *Terrorism: How the West Can Win*, Farrar, Strauss, Giroux: New York.

Norval, M. (1999), *Triumph of Disorder: Islamic Fundamentalism, the New Face of War*, McKenna Publishing Group: Indian Wells, CA.

O'Ballance, E. (1989), *Terrorism in the 1980s*, London: Arms and Armour Press.
O'Ballance, E. (1997), *Islamic Fundamentalist Terrorism 1979–95: The Iranian Connection*, London: Macmillan.
O'Ballance, E. (2000), *Sudan, Civil War and Terrorism, 1956–99*, St. Martin's Press: New York.
Ofcansky, T. P. (ed.) (1991), *Ethiopia: A Country Study*, U.S. Printing Office: Washington, D.C.
Olson, W. J. (1989), 'Low Intensity Conflict: The Challenge to the National Interest', *Terrorism*, Vol. 12, No. 2, pp. 75–80.
Oots, K. (1986), *A Political Organization Approach to Transnational Terrorism*, Greenwood Publishing Group: New York.
Palmer, M. (1973), *The Dilemmas of Political Development: An Introduction to the Politics of the Developing Areas*, F. E. Peacock Publishers: Itasca, IL.
Palmer, M., Al-Hegelah, A., Abdelrahman, M. B., Leila, A. and Yassin, E. S. (1989), 'Bureaucratic Innovation and Economic Development in the Middle East: A Study of Egypt, Saudi Arabia and the Sudan', *Journal of Asian and African Studies*, Vol. 24, No. 1–2, pp. 13–17.
Palmer, M., Leila, A. and Yassin, E. S. (1988), *The Egyptian Bureaucracy*, Syracuse University Press: Syracuse, NY.
Péninou, J.-L. (1998), 'Ethiopia-Eritrea: Background to the Conflict', *Le Monde Diplomatique* (English edition), July.
Péninou, J.-L. (2000), 'Ethiopia Invades Eritrea', *Le Monde Diplomatique* (English edition), July.
Poe, S. C. (1994), 'Human Rights and U.S. Economic Aid During the Reagan Years', *Social Science Quarterly*, Vol. 75 (September), pp. 495–512.
Porath, Y. (1986), *In Search of Arab Unity, 1930–1945*, Frank Cass: London.
Reed, S. (1993), 'The Battle for Egypt', *Foreign Affairs*, Vol. 72, No. 4, pp. 94–107.
Reed, S. and Gauch, S. (1993), 'Could Egypt be the Next Iran?', *International Business*, Vol. 3327, No. 4, pp. 48–50.
Reich, W. (ed.) (1990), *Origins of Terrorism: Psychologies, Ideologies, States of Mind*, Cambridge University Press: Cambridge.
Richmond, B. (2001), 'Don't Hit the Snooze Button', Retrieved from http://www.foryourglory.org, February 10, 2004.
Rubin, B. (1990), *Islamic Fundamentalism in Egyptian Politics*, St. Martin's Press: New York.
Said, E. W. (1997), *Covering Islam: How the Media and Experts Determine How We See the World*, Vintage Books: London.
Sandler, T. (1983), *The Theory and Situations of Internal Politics*, Westview Press: Boulder, CO.
Schelling, T. (1978), *Micromotives & Macrobehavior*, W. W. Norton: New York.
Schmid, A. and Jongman, A. (1988), *Political Terrorism: A New Guide to Actors, Authors, Concepts, Data Bases, Theories*, and Literature, Transaction Books: New York.
Sela, A. (1998), *The Decline of the Arab-Israeli Conflict*, SUNY Press: Albany, NY.
Shehu, E. U. (2000), 'Sharia and the Faith of Northern Christians', *Church and Society Magazine*, January-March, pp. 17, 25.
Shittier, Ch. H. (1987), *The Just War in Certain Religious Traditions: Christianity, Judaism, Islam, and Buddhism*, Library of Congress: Washington, D.C.

Sidahmed, A. S. and Ehteshami, A. (eds.) (1996), *Islamic Fundamentalism*, Westview Press: Boulder, CO.

Slann, M. and Schechterman, B. (eds.) *(1987), Multidimensional Terrorism*, Lynne Rienner: Boulder, CO.

Taheri, A. (1989), *Holy Terror: The Inside Story of Islamic Terrorism*, Sphere Books Limited: London.

Taylor, C. (ed.) (1980), *Indicator Systems for Political, Economic and Social Analysis*, Oelgeschlager, Gunn and Hain: Cambridge, MA.

Tayob, A. (1995), 'Islamic Resurgence in South Africa', *The Muslim Youth Movement*, University of Cape Town Press: Cape Town.

Tayob, A. (1999), *Islam in South Africa: Mosques, Imams, and Sermons*, University of Florida Press: Gainesville.

Thackrah, J. (1987), *Encyclopedia of Terrorism and Political Violence*, Routledge and Kegan: New York.

Tinaz, N. (1996), 'The Nation of Islam: Historical Evolution and Transformation of the Movement', *Journal of Muslim Minority Affairs*, Vol. 16, No. 2, pp. 193–209.

Trapp, F. J. (1994), 'Does a Repressive Counterterrorist Strategy Reduce Terrorism?: An Empirical Study of Israel's Iron Fist Strategy for the Period 1968 to 1987', Ph.D. Dissertation, Florida State University, Tallahassee, FL.

Trapp, F. J., Palmer, M. and Smith, D. L. (1994), 'Punitive Responses and the Deterrence of Terrorism: An Empirical Analysis of the Effectiveness of Israel's Counterterrorism Strategy', paper presented at the 1994 annual meeting of the American Political Science Association, New York City, NY.

Wardlaw, G. (1982), *Political Terrorism: Theory, Tactics, and Counter-Measures*, Cambridge University Press: Cambridge.

Wiemann, G. and Brosius, H.-B. (1989), 'The Predictability of International Terrorism: A Time Series Analysis', *Terrorism*, Vol. 12, No. 2, pp. 491–502.

Weschler, W. (2001), 'Strangling the Hydra: Targeting al Qaeda's Finances', in Hoge, J. F., Jr. and Rose, G. (eds.), *How Did This Happen? Terrorism and the New War*, Public Affairs: New York.

Wilkonson, P. (1987), *Terrorism and the Liberal State*, Macmillan: London.

Willis, J. R. (1977), *Studies on the History of Islam in West Africa*, 3 volumes, London: Frank Cass.

World Bank (1994), *World Development Report, 1994*, World Bank: Washington, D.C.

Wright, R. (1985), *Sacred Rage: The Crusade of Modern Islam*, Simon & Schuster: New York.

7

Conclusion

Transnational terrorism in Africa is nurtured and sustained by the interaction of a lack of economic perspectives, social deprivation, a loss of cultural identity, political repression and a dysfunctional state. In other words, poverty and ignorance, disease and environmental disorder, corruption and political oppression provide fertile ground for breeding terrorist networks. Indeed, they constitute another 'axis of evil' angering and frustrating people all over the continent. These elements are not in short supply in Africa. But socio-economic grievances alone do not justify or adequately explain transnational terrorism in general and the rampaging Islamic terrorist cartels around the continent in particular and in the world in general.

Sub-Saharan Africa is showing many factors, which led to the rise of international terrorism in the Middle East, North Africa and Central Asia. However, the emergence of a genuinely African type of international terrorism is rather improbable. This is unthinkable, at least for the foreseeable future. The main terrorist threat in Africa arises from the incapability of African states to control their territory and to protect potential targets of terrorist assaults due to the statist nature of African regimes.

Statist tradition

The state system in Africa is apparently an updated heir of the French state of the eighteenth century. It is centralized, unitary, regulatory, intrusive, and mercantilist. It was the French state system that served as the model for Africa in its early formative years of the 1960s, not the U.S. model with its emphasis on individual freedom and laissez-faire. If we know the workings of the French system of capitalism and the state's strong role in the economy, we have a solid basis for understanding how the African state systems operated before their implosion in the 1990s.

A strong central state might have been necessary in Africa not just for historical and cultural reasons but for very practical ones. The region had long lacked the organization, infrastructure, and the web of associational life that Alexis de Tocqueville recognized as necessary to democracy and commerce. It is also a land of huge distances, empty spaces, underdeveloped transportation grids, and sometimes unruly territories as well as unruly ruling classes. In such conditions, and in the absence of a strong private sector or associational life, the African state was obliged to step into the vacuum. To the extent these conditions remain the same today, the state is still obliged to play a strong role.

Countries have large state sectors and mercantilist economies not necessarily because their decision-makers are irrational or misguided, but because they are responding to a logic and sociopolitical context quite different from that of more advanced capitalist systems. In Africa, a powerful state was seen by its rulers as a necessity to fill the void because of the lack of associational life, the poor infrastructure, the persistent fear of chaos and instability, and the historical absence of a strong private sector. The state, according to this logic, had to be not only strong but also centralized, unitary (little division of powers), frequently authoritarian, and often corporatist, in the sense of creating official, government-run unions and other groups in the absence of genuine, grassroots pluralism.

Paradoxically, the desire for a strong state was born out of weakness, not strength. If Africa had strong democracies and strong private sectors capable of stimulating development, it could dispense with its strong, mercantilist state. But it does not, and so the state must step in. Similarly with the state's reach: if Africa really had effective institutions at the grassroots level, it would not need such powerful, centralized, and often authoritarian governments.

The same logic applies to employment. A strong private sector would solve Africa's perennial problems of unemployment and underemployment, which often reaches 40 to 60 percent of the population. Such high unemployment levels are a formula for chaos, food riots, vandalism, and revolution as we have seen at times in the urban ghettos of the United States. So the answer to this unemployment problem is to put as many persons as possible on the public payroll: friends, cronies, family members, followers, clientele, and even political foes (a public salary is a way of neutralizing opposition). The result is bloated and inefficient bureaucracies that are responding to a clear, political logic even if economic rationality suffers.

If private sector employment were readily available, then state downsizing would be both painless and easy. But industry, manufacturing, and private capitalism are still in their infancy in much of Africa. Until these private sectors are larger and stronger, Africa will be reluctant to downsize. The risks politically are too large, especially now that the region is dominated by elected 'democracies.' That explains why state downsizing and privatization are so rapid or precipitous that they are not calibrated to the growth of private sectors capable of filling the region's historic institutional and associational voids, and staving off the fear of chaos, instability, and ungovernability still present in the continent.

The statist tradition has suffered horrendous attacks. African states have ceased to enjoy any monopolistic control or to have the capacity to establish and promote actions in the basic areas of national sovereignty. First of all, communications are no longer the best example of political control of society in Africa. Even radio and television have also escaped state control, thus the communication revolution has reduced the African State to a pygmy.

Secondly, technological development and commercialization of its products depend more on the private sector than on the state. This affects investment capabilities, particularly in technological development designed for war. Transnational terrorist networks may even avail themselves of these technologies than most African states. Thirdly, financial transactions flow around the world and generate regional and global crises with little capacity for intervention by the state. Money laundering is a shouting example in the hands of terrorist cartels involved in 'blood diamond' transactions.

Fourthly, African states reinsure investments, but their ability to control decisions about where to invest and from where to get investments is minimal, if not negligible. The structural adjustment programs totally exclude African states from any such decision-making. Thus the state is reduced to an impotent spectator in any development project in the country. Fifthly, international migration and the ability of the state to control the movement of people has diminished. This loss of the power to control migration partially explains why members of terrorist cells criss-cross the African continent and operate with impunity.

Finally, international trade has exposed Africa to use and abuse by marauding terrorist gangs. Drug-trafficking, trade in small arms, trafficking in gold and diamonds, and money laundering offer opportunities for terrorist cartels to penetrate and operate in Africa. These basic areas of statist politics and other terrorist attractions account for the weakness of African states. And these weaknesses thus render the state prone to capture and abuse by forces like transnational terrorist cartels.

Characteristics of state weakness

The state has been the most prominent feature of the international political system, since the Treaty of Westphalia in 1648. In Africa, the colonial state has persisted for so long that it is easy to take the permanence of its role in the organization of society for granted. Lately, however, there is a growing body of evidence dealing with the erosion of the power of the sovereign state in post-colonial Africa. Usually, this centers around the impact of what is generally referred to as 'globalization', and the emergence of major transnational economic and financial actors able to shift their operations almost at will and answerable to no one nation's political masters. This erosion of state power has signified the removal of several instruments of economic sovereignty from the control of the state, accounting for the weakness and/ or even collapse of the state itself.

Hannah Arendt wrote in her book, *On Violence* (1970), that the Third World was not a reality. To her, it is an ideology. This presentation contends that the nationalist and populist policies of the past explain the recent developments in contemporary Africa. Populist policies and Third World discourse were at their apex during the 1960 and 1970 decades, and are the key variables for any explanation pertaining to the technological and cultural backwardness of modern day Africa. These variables include the enormous foreign debt, the recurrent devaluation of the national currencies, creeping consumer prices, a closed economy, an educational system and academic staff confined within their petty boundaries, and rampant corruption at all levels. All these factors had by 1980, taken their toll on the vast majority of the middle class and the poor in Africa. While the period between 1982 and 1986 were critical years that served as the turning point away from those years of populist policies and African discourse, the consequences of the 1960 and 1970 decades have proven its resilience.

Businesses and businessmen, with few exceptions were heavily dependent on the state enterprises as they profited in the short term under a protected market. On the other hand, in a competitive world market since Africa's market reforms, they have paid a costly price. This proved true because state-run monopolies, public services and a vast majority of enterprises did not invest in new technology and a modern communication system. Nor did the state encourage an efficient petroleum industry. State owned industries produced and sold with total disregard for productivity and quality. A similar situation existed in the state-run agricultural sector where several million peasants produced cash crops under government supervision. The government at fixed prices purchased their produce with little regard for cost, quality and productivity. The banking system, configured by the state, funded such industrial plants and services and agricultural projects.

This set of relations built around production and distribution had their counterpart in labor relations and amongst agricultural and rural workers linked to the Marketing Boards and hence, the African governments. As the corporate state expanded, the number of bureaucrats and workers increased accordingly. Tax money was freely spent, and since enough was available due to abundant foreign credit backed up by oil and other natural resources, many states tended to equate social benefits with privileges granted by government officials, mainly the President, his cabinet members and state governors.

Changes in Africa began several decades ago, albeit the grip that the government had on social life remained substantial until the mid 1980's when state power began to seriously weaken and erode. Population growth by the mid sixties had become such that the state-directed sectors of the economy were incapable of integrating newcomers. As urban industrialization paced ahead, the gap between workers and peasants widened. Highly skilled workers' unions began to act independently. State-controlled workers organizations, in order to assert their roles in the new economy, began to negotiate directly with private companies as workers accepted the link between income and productivity. Non-strategic workers unions gradually saw both salary and negotiating power diminish as the era of trade unionism dwindled away. The trend that differentiated workers' interests as it divided them occurred at a time when the Trade Union's old timers lost their punch or passed away.

Taxes increased affecting labor and white-collar workers. Inflation became endemic. Public services proved ineffective. Most of what has been described thus far relates to the end of the trade unions' monopoly over power, and as such had a synergetic effect. Political parties and movements changed as they shifted from confrontational and class struggle tactics toward an electoral, institutional, open and inclusive political strategy. Left wing groups broke apart from their traditional central and bureaucratic political parties, particularly after 1968, and created informal organizations linking their political activities to urban squatters, peasants and independent workers. Significantly, these independent groups formed coalitions on specific issues with progressive sectors, which set the basis for what currently occurs nowadays among state and national political factions and fractions.

As the liberalization of international communism gained momentum, formal parties reorganized under various coalitions. Communists and socialist intellectuals began to participate in a manner in factions, particularly in strategic committees related to financial issues. Moreover, groups inside the Churches developed into important political movements, which converged with many radical groups.

The state lost foothold in Africa, yet retained its strength with 99.9 percent of the vote in the areas where illiteracy was rampant. As Africans pressed for political reforms, the international context changed, directing the government to loosen restraints and promote electoral reforms such as providing new seats in Assemblies for minorities that took into account proportional representation based on votes. Traditional and new political parties profited and soon increased their seats at National and at the municipal level.

As already alluded to above, internal mutations were directly correlated to changing world contexts. The early 1980s currency devaluations and the 1986 oil crisis are examples. Devastating effects crippled the protracted nationalist policies, propelling government policies toward an open economy. Africa made a late and hasty entrance into an open world economy. Drastic reforms were undertaken without provisions in the form of acting regulatory boards as those of the European Union. State property and state-run businesses were privatized in haste and through an essentially ungoverned process. In less than a decade, hundreds of insolvent industries and state institutions were injudiciously closed, while the most profitable ones were sold to businessmen. By mid 1990s, most economic and social sectors were unregulated and existed in a state of free for all.

The whole process ripped apart traditional pacts and arrangements beneficial to the 'parties-in power,' its ruling groups and its favored social classes. Workers and private business disrupted the relationship between the president, his party and society. As the social configuration became transformed, workers, industrial groups and government clienteles shifted alliances within and without the ruling parties producing much disruption and crises among factions.

African states, with their feeble institutional system of justice and political limitations on the courts of law and their administration, brought out the worst of capitalism in an already gravely corrupt system. State enterprises such as the telephone system and banking sectors were sold, disregarding the buyers' financial credentials. Moreover, small and medium-sized businesses went bankrupt; the poorly trained working force was left jobless. All this occurred in states whose basic weaknesses already are the outrageous disparity in income and education, and unequal access to the rule of law.

Another related issue, basic to any understanding of why and how the whole set of arrangements changed, was the end of the Cold War which was marked symbolically by the fall of the Berlin Wall on November 9, 1989. Worldwide diplomacy as of then, operated on a multilateral basis and U.S. diplomacy was obliged to interact with the European Union, China, Japan, the Middle East, and others. In this international political climate, Africa was unable to play a basic role as an intermediate power group.

It thus became fashionable, even de rigueur, to call for state downsizing and privatization as the formula for economic growth. The need for open and free markets and for the state to get out of the way of constructive entrepreneurial activity is certainly clear to most of us. Along with democracy and free trade, open markets constitute one of the three policy ingredients in the celebrated 'Washington consensus.' These policies were:

- Fiscal discipline;
- A redirection of public expenditure priorities toward fields offering both high economic returns and the potential to improve income distribution, such as primary health care, primary education, and infrastructure;
- Tax reform (to lower marginal rates and broaden the tax base);
- Interest rate liberalization;
- A competitive exchange rate;
- Trade liberalization;
- Liberalization of inflows of foreign direct investment
- Privatization;
- Deregulation (to abolish barriers to entry and exit); and
- Secure property rights.

Since then, the phrase 'Washington Consensus' has become a lightning rod for dissatisfaction amongst anti-globalization protestors, skeptical African politicians and officials, trade negotiators, and numerous others. While the economic logic of state downsizing is evident, there is also an often forgotten political logic in maintaining a state system of a certain size and responsiveness.

Just as there are distinct forms of capitalism, there are also distinct types of states, and of state-society and state-economy relations. Often the economic logic of reducing the state's size runs contrary to the political logic both of creating needed infrastructure and of maintaining necessary patronage functions. It is frequently infrastructure—roads, highways, electricity, water, education—that determines the area in which business will invest. And only an effective government can provide that. Unfortunately, the African state's patronage functions were not kept in balance with its more limited economic roles and the economies were destabilized.

Networked terrorism as beneficiary

Historically, terrorism is an age-old stratagem. The simple reason is that both war and terrorism create new uncertainties that confound ordinary human calculations and may even deter global commitments. Of late, terrorism has gained renewed international attention. Terrorist attacks are now acknowledged as reflecting a watershed in international concern with networked or transnational terrorism. But, these tragic attacks never occurred as isolated events. Nor do these events reflect a sudden threat. In fact, it is simply a symbolic reaffirmation of a violent trend that had been evident for several years. Where terror had previously been an uncomfortable adjunct to anarchism, liberation wars, counter-insurgency campaigns and the battlefields of the Cold War, the events of September 11, 2001, took terrorism to a global level.

The resurgence of global terror during the 1990s has its roots in the development of a covert alliance to counter and reverse Soviet expansion in Central-South Asia, Afghanistan in particular. The Soviet experience in Afghanistan is its own version of the American experiences in Vietnam. The bitter Soviet experience has today spawned a number of offshoots, coalescing around new global targets such as the United States of America, Israel and those perceived to be their close allies.

There is no insinuation here of attributing a single causal motive to the recent scourge of viral networked terrorism. The aim has been rather to point to the interconnected nature of these events and their pluri-causal nature. It is in this vein that this work examined the extent to which these developments have provided a new impetus to the violent pursuit of radical objectives that feed upon latent and deep divisions along cultural and religious grounds within African states.

Terrorism is, among other things, the weapon used by the weak against the strong. It has been universally condemned and, under the relevant international agreements, all countries have committed themselves to combating and cooperating effectively against terrorism. They have undertaken not to permit their territories to be used by terrorist organizations. But, condemnation and denial of use of territory are no solutions to networked terrorist cells today. Why? The break up of the largest terrorist cartels in Afghanistan did not end networked terrorism; rather the surviving participants dispersed over a wide area, forming smaller groups, which gradually learned how to interact with each other in spreading international insecurity. The bombing of Israeli-run Paradise Hotel in Kenya in November 2002 demonstrates amply how terrorist networks can benefit from state weakness.

The issue of weakness of African states and their proneness to capture by international terrorist networks appears to have been widely viewed as an extension of radical Islamism with its jihadic tendencies. This situation is awkward for Africa and is usually only dealt with in unavoidable circumstances. However, given the networked terrorist and criminal activities throughout the continent and beyond, it poses a real threat to the security of several African states. Put in less diplomatic terms, the governments of some African states either turn a blind eye to the activities of the terrorist networks on their soil or in the worst case actively support these networks with training and logistics.

The impact on Africa of the terrorist attacks on the U.S. and Israeli targets and the U.S. reaction and increasingly active local Islamist organizations is likely to be continued sporadic outbursts of protest and occasional violence. The relatively porous nature of national borders of African states and the weakness of the African governments in detecting terrorists, means that the continent may well serve as either a transit point or a sanctuary for transnational terrorists. However, the African governments have a narrow path to tread in protecting the continent from terrorist activity and ensuring the states are not used by terrorist networks as a sanctuary, and preventing the spillover of radicalism from Islamist organizations to moderate African Muslims who advocate political pluralism and human rights.

Whether out of conviction or opportunism, the Islamists shaped their political discourse to match that of their vanquished rivals. Islamic rhetoric became an instrument of mobilization, serving as a cover for nationalist and anti-imperialist objectives. But it also had a social component, and included denunciations of the injustices, corruption, and tyranny that characterized the reigning oligarchies. Political Islam thus became one of the few outlets for protest and action. Ayatollah Khomeini's pronouncements, minus their theological references, were virtually indistinguishable from statements from Third World leaders such as the late Egyptian President Gamal Abdel Nasser. The leader of the Iranian revolution thus came to occupy that part of the political spectrum that the Shah of Iran bequeathed to him after having overseen the destruction of the democratic opposition parties of both the left and the right.

Although demagogic in nature, the Islamists' political and social program gained more favor with the public than their religious message, which was primarily reactionary, misogynistic and morally repressive. This is the sole explanation for the Islamists' success following, and not before, their transformation into militant nationalists. They undoubtedly benefited from wide-ranging assistance (especially financial) from states that claimed Islamic roots, such as Saudi Arabia and the Gulf states, which sought to strengthen their own bases after the fall of regimes hostile to their interests. It later became clear that this support was not reciprocal, since these governments did not realize that political Islam, as a brand-new phenomenon, was not necessarily sympathetic to their interests.

Faced with this threat, the Arab regimes tried to neutralize the Islamists, either by pursuing them with extraordinary brutality or by integrating them within state institutions, retaining the ability to co-opt them. The Islamists were successfully co-opted in countries such as Lebanon, Jordan, Kuwait and Yemen, where they have representation in parliament, and in some cases in government. By contrast, the Islamists suffered appalling massacres in Syria and ruthless repression in Tunisia and Iraq. In Algeria, those who seek to stamp out the Islamists have only succeeded in prolonging a particularly bloody conflict.

It would be wrong to conclude that clashes between the established regimes and the Islamists pit supporters of secularism against its opponents. Some states opposed to political Islam have constitutions and legislation that conform to the teachings of the sacred texts. Other states fight so passionately to become more Islamic than their opponents that they have come to resemble them. Saudi Arabia and Egypt are both examples of this phenomenon. With rare exceptions, their governments have at times colluded with the Islamists in the fight against even more fearsome rivals.

The case of Israel is virtually identical. Successive Israeli governments discreetly supported the Muslim Brotherhood in the Occupied Territories while the Brotherhood was exclusively attacking Yasser Arafat's Palestine Liberation Organization (PLO), which it viewed as a gang of nationalists and Marxists, all traitors to Islam. The Israeli leadership realized its short-sightedness during the first intifada, begun in 1987, when the Brotherhood gave birth to Hamas, dedicated to the liberation of Palestine through armed struggle and terrorism.

The Soviet retreat from Afghanistan, the Gulf war and the collapse of the Soviet empire changed the picture radically and brought about a new sort of Islamism, which grew in the mountains of Afghanistan. The mujahedin did not see themselves as mere back-up troops for the United States; they believed, along with Osama bin Laden and his future supporters, that they had liberated Islamic land through valor, sacrifice and, in many cases, martyrdom. Their disappointment in the aftermath of victory was commensurate with their self-styled role. They had no jobs or resources, nor did they receive gratitude, compensation or inclusion in any future plans for the country.

The United States, grateful nonetheless, did exert discreet pressure on reluctant governments, urging them to repatriate fighters who would go on to devote themselves to violence in Algeria, Kashmir, Palestine, Lebanon, Egypt, then Bosnia and Chechnya. When Egypt repeatedly refused to welcome back Sheikh Omar Abdel Rahman, who was implicated in President Sadat's assassination, the US granted him a visa in 1990, followed by permanent resident status. In 1993 the sheikh masterminded the first attack on the World Trade Center and was given a life sentence.

The 1990–1991 Gulf war sparked demonstrations and protests throughout the Arab and Muslim worlds, not out of sympathy with Saddam Hussein as some claimed, but in protest at Washington's bias and double standards. Indignant nationalist and Islamist media asked why only Iraq faced sanctions for its invasion of Kuwait when Israel had occupied Arab territories for decades with impunity. And in the wake of the Gulf war, why did the US set up bases in several Gulf countries, most notably in the holy land of Saudi Arabia, if not to protect various unpopular and/or unstable regimes? The world's sole superpower became the favorite target of Islamists of all persuasions, including those who went on to adopt the Osama bin Laden label.

Is this a case of knee-jerk anti-Americanism? Hostility toward U.S. foreign policy is not an intrinsically Arab or Muslim phenomenon, as some observers imply; in fact, there is now worldwide resentment in Africa, Latin America, Asia and Europe, within Muslim and non-Muslim communities alike. But anti-American sentiment is not irreversible; indeed, the United States has been highly popular among Arab peoples at various points in recent history. President Wilson's calls for the emancipation of all colonized peoples following the First World War established this popularity. In 1945 President Roosevelt, together with Saudi Arabia's King Ibn Saud, sought to resolve the Palestinian problem with the cooperation of the Arab states; after the Second World War the United States was thought to be opposed to British and French colonialism. And during the 1956 Suez crisis, President Eisenhower called on the United Kingdom, France and Israel to end their military action against Egypt and withdraw their troops forthwith. At such moments, an Osama bin Laden would have had no grounds for existence.

Is transnational terrorist activity inextricably linked to Islam? Terrorism is actually a worldwide scourge that has reared its ugly head under diverse conditions and in countries as dissimilar as Germany, Japan, Italy, Argentina and Greece. Before it assumed its recent Islamic form, it was successively or simultaneously Palestinian, Israeli, Egyptian, Yemeni. It was also endemic, occasional, individual, nationalist or governmental in nature, and it primarily targeted local populations.

Founded by Osama bin Laden at the end of the anti-Soviet war in Afghanistan, the al Qaeda brand of terrorism is an entirely new historical phenomenon, quite different in its make-up. Targeting U.S. interests almost exclusively, it is transnational in its recruitment and identity since it claims to act on behalf of the *umma*, the Muslim nation, which is spread over five continents. This is a global phenomenon insofar as al Qaeda operates on a worldwide scale in more than 50 countries and makes use of practices and technology made possible by globalization.

Often influenced by Western culture, al Qaeda's members are recruited among the middle classes and work in small semi-autonomous cells even when inspired by directives from the 'center.' This nebulous organization is not the direct tool of any state; for financial and logistical support, it relies on private collaborators, charitable associations and wealthy backers. Unlike the previous generation of terrorists, who acted on behalf of organizations that also (simultaneously) engaged in non-violent political activities, Osama bin Laden's disciples apparently do not have any structured popular support. They are in some ways marginalized, yet they claim to speak and act on behalf of some one billion Muslims of all religious persuasions.

What value can be ascribed to the fatwas of Osama bin Laden and his jihad-hungry cohorts, whose religious authority is dubious, if not non-existent? Branded a heretic and repudiated by Islamists and Muslim leaders alike, Osama bin Laden appears to have earned the indulgence and sympathy of many people, both Muslim and non-Muslim. As U.S. Secretary of State Colin Powell pursued a Middle East peace mission fraught with difficulties, anti-Israel and anti-U.S. demonstrations in some Muslim countries were increasingly heating up. Protests, often characterized by clashes with police, became daily occurrences in some Middle Eastern and Asian cities and there were reports that volunteers were signing up to fight alongside the Palestinians against Israel. Some demonstrators were invoking the name of Osama bin Laden saying: 'Beloved bin Laden, strike Tel Aviv!' The Sudanese demonstrators also yelled 'Down with USA!' and expressed support for a boycott of American products because of Washington's support for Israel. Many of the protests across the Muslim world have turned violent, especially where demonstrators have tried to force their way closer to U.S. or United Nations missions.

This is not as paradoxical as it may seem. In their quest for justice and recognition, the victims of globalization also see themselves as suffering at the hands of arrogant U.S. hegemony. Even though they show little tolerance for overbearing theologians or al Qaeda's unspeakable methods, these people have proven receptive to Osama bin Laden's political message (Murdoch, 2001). Having chosen to ignore this reality, those waging the Enduring Freedom military campaign lent credence to the notion of a religious war.

Osama bin Laden, an individual political entrepreneur, can be isolated and 'disowned' more easily than can an Islamic state. Should immediate U.S. military action also encompass Iraq and Hezbollah, the repercussions for Pakistan and other Islamic and Arab states is incalculable. Such a broad range of attacks will appear to much of the Arab and Islamic world to be precisely what the Bush administration says it is not: the beginning of a campaign against all Arab and Islamic actors who stand outside the U.S. sphere. And this initial perception could tar all subsequent components of the prospective campaign against terrorism, including non-military ones.

Although war is an intentional goal-driven act, chaos is its constant companion. In war, unintended consequences abound. These subtract from (and can overwhelm) what is gained through war. As the scope of military action broadens, the inadvertent repercussions of that action also grow in magnitude, extent, and unpredictability. A recurrent example of inadvertent effects is the accidental killing of non-combatants. Although unintended, collateral casualties are an entirely predictable outcome of military action, especially when that action involves the aerial bombardment of political, infrastructure, military-industrial, and other dual use targets.

Africa's anti-terrorist legal framework

In President Bush's address to the African Growth and Opportunity Act Forum, on January 15, 2003, he declared:

> Every nation that seeks peace faces a common enemy today in global terror. The recent attacks in Mombassa remind us that Africa is on the front lines of the war against terror. All our citizens know the awful price of terror, and we will not rest until we have defeated terrorism in all its forms.

This was Bush. But, what did Africans do? In the Algiers Convention in 1999, OAU leaders accepted the need to promote human and moral values based on tolerance and the rejection of all forms of terrorism. A glaring omission in the Convention, however, is the exclusion of any reference to enforcement mechanisms in the event of a 'material breach' by a State Party not acting in accordance with the provisions of the Convention, or of effective monitoring mechanisms by the OAU to measure the compliance of State Parties to their legal commitments. The only provision here is a limp requirement (in Article 2) to notify the Secretary General of the OAU of all the legislative measures that State Parties have taken and the penalties imposed on terrorist acts within one year of ratification of, or accession to, the Convention.

Article 22 of the Algiers Convention effectively requires African States to comply with the general principles of international law, in particular the principles of international humanitarian law, as well as the African Charter on Human and Peoples' Rights. Inevitably human rights and the protection of peoples' rights are interpreted as constraining or limiting the fight against terrorism. The opposite is, of course, much closer to the truth since it is exactly the active provision and the rigorous protection of these rights and liberties that drain the oxygen for terrorists and their sympathizers.

The United Nations Security Council at its 4385th meeting on September 28th, 2001, adopted Resolution 1373 in accordance with the terms of Chapter VII of the Charter of the United Nations. All States (not just United Nation members) are bound in terms of international law to implement its operative provisions. Resolution 1373 reaffirmed Resolutions 1269 (1999) and 1368 (2001) as well as the principle established by the UN General Assembly (Resolution 2625 (XXV) 1970), namely that every State has the duty to refrain from organizing, instigating, assisting or participating in terrorist acts in another State or acquiescing in organizing activities within its territory directed towards the commission of such acts.

According to Resolution 1373, any act of international terrorism constitutes a threat to international peace and security. It requires all States to take certain action concerning terrorism and established a committee (the Counter-Terrorism Committee) of the Security Council to monitor implementation of the operative provisions of the Resolution. All States were required to report to the committee no later than 90 days from date of adoption (i.e., by December 27, 2001). By this date 117 of the 189 UN Member States had provided national reports on the steps they had taken to implement the Resolution and by April 15, 2002, 143 reports had been received and the Committee was following up with those countries that had not reported.

UNSC Resolution 1373 contains 18 sub-paragraphs, which constitute operative paragraphs 1-3. The principal features of Resolution 1373 are the criminalization of the financing and other acts of support of terrorism, the freezing of accounts, the introduction of effective border controls and other measures to accelerate the exchange of operational information. In many ways UNSC Resolution 1373 sought to fast-track elements borrowed from the Convention for the Suppression of the Financing of Terrorism, which now became binding on all states, without the cumbersome process of signatures, ratification and reservations.

At the initiative of the President of Senegal, Abdoulaye Wade, a Conference of African Heads of State and Governments was held in Dakar on October 17, 2001. The result was the Dakar Declaration against Terrorism expressing the concerns raised by the development of terrorism was adopted. According to this declaration, terrorism constitutes a blow to fundamental human rights, democracy and peace. The Summit expressed the wish to strengthen co-operation between States and the fight against terrorism in all its varieties and the Declaration provided for discussions and proposals concerning the formulation and adoption of an additional protocol to the Algiers Convention in accordance with the provisions of

Article 21 of that Convention. Senegal would subsequently proffer such a draft Protocol to the General Secretariat of the OAU in April 2002 at a time that the thrust of that document had been overtaken by the initiative of the Secretariat to work towards the development of an Action Plan and possibly an additional Protocol.

Shortly after the Dakar meeting, the Central Organ of the OAU Mechanism for Conflict Prevention, Management and Resolution held its 5th Extraordinary Session in New York City and issued a Communiqué (Communiqué issued by the Central Organ of the OAU Mechanism for Conflict Prevention, Management and Resolution at its 5th Extra-Ordinary Session at Ministerial Level on November 11, 2001 in New York City). The Central Organ inter alia:

- Welcomed the adoption of United Nations Security Council Resolution 1373 as well as the Dakar Declaration and requested member States to ensure their effective follow-up and implementation.
- Urged member States to sign and ratify the existing International Conventions relating to terrorism and called upon State Parties to those Conventions to fully and effectively implement their provisions.
- It further urged OAU Member States to sign and ratify the Algiers Convention so as to ensure its early entry into force and stressed that terrorism, as a universal phenomenon constitutes a serious violation of human rights.
- Specifically welcomed the proposal made in Dakar to prepare a Draft Additional Protocol to the Algiers Convention in conformity with Article 21 of that Convention.

On April 10, 2002, the International Convention for the Suppression and the Financing of Terrorism (1999) entered into force having received more than the required 22 ratifications. The Convention was adopted by the United Nations General Assembly in New York on December 9, 1999 and was opened for signature on January 10, 2000. As of April 2, 2002, 132 States had signed it and 26 States had completed the ratification process and become State Parties.

The Convention criminalizes the act of providing or collecting funds with the intention or knowledge that those funds will be used to carry out a terrorist attack, according to particular definitions, which are found in nine previously adopted anti-terrorist conventions, listed in an annex to the Convention. It adds substantial strength and enforcement opportunities to the network of interlocking Conventions on various aspects of terrorism created by the international community over the last thirty years. The Convention recognizes that financing is at the heart of terrorist activity and calls for efforts to identify, detect and freeze or seize any funds used or allocated for the purpose of committing a terrorist act. It also asks that States consider establishing mechanisms to use such funds to compensate victims or their families. Ironically, nobody took any pains to delineate the type of terrorism to fall under such sanctions.

For instance, al Qaeda has more the character of a network than an organization. The sinews that hold this network together internationally are not typical military command, control, and logistical arrangements. This is a network of influence, contacts, and comrades. Common training, shared wartime experience, and adherence to Osama bin Laden's perverse interpretations of Islam are the pivotal integrative elements. Some operatives, resources, and general directions flow from the center, but initiative is highly decentralized and much of the network's support is procured locally. In a sense, the existence of the network itself, i.e. the web of worldwide contacts that it embodies is the most important support that its individual cells receive. This type of formation cannot be easily decapitated or destroyed by one devastating blow to the center. Instead, measures of infiltration, detection, disruption, and interdiction must occur continuously in many localities. These measures, mostly involving intelligence gathering and law enforcement must be coordinated globally.

Challenges of transnational terrorism today

Imbalances in economic development between North and South directly fuel the fires of anti-Americanism and terrorism in Africa. They create a reservoir of young people without jobs who are willing to vent their spleen on targets selected by religious fanatics. Pluralist triumphalism about exporting Western liberal polity and economy to end all inequalities does not stand ground on serious scrutiny in the face of mounting challenges. These challenges are posed by weapons of mass destruction which can very easily slip into the hands of killers, mobsters and assassins.

Chemo-bio terrorist challenges

In the past, there has been very little overlap among the expert communities on terrorism, nuclear nonproliferation, and chemical and biological weapons. Within the chem-bio community, the focus has been almost exclusively on the problems of arms control and military preparedness. Within the nuclear nonproliferation community, the focus has been locked singularly on the nuclear problem, with a shifting interest in recent years from weapons to materials. Within the community of experts on terrorism, there has been at best a very limited interest in the problem of mass destruction terrorism. Moreover, what little attention it has been given, this topic has typically treated the chem-bio problem as merely a lesser-included aspect of the nuclear one. It is time to begin to break down these barriers among communities, to test the assumptions that have defined the scope of this work, and to try to arrive at fresh insights of policy relevance.

As debates on terrorism in Africa have begun to unfold after the attacks at the Paradise Hotel in Mombasa, World Trade Center, Tokyo subway system, Oklahoma City, U.S. Embassies in Kenya and Tanzania and Khobar Towers, four factors have emerged that should be kept in mind as researchers continue with their dialogue today. First, there is a very striking propensity to hysteria. The discussion of loose nukes, new terrorists, militia movements, and the like has fueled expectations of mass destructions just around the next corner. How many times has the public heard terrorism pundits speak ominously of the massive wave of casualties certain to be inflicted upon society sooner or later? A little investigation reveals that such predictions are a staple of the public commentary on terrorism, which suggests that any researcher should be wary of them. But one cannot easily dismiss these pundits as modern day Chicken Littles, with their cry that the sky is falling. Instead, perhaps it should be remembered that the Boy Who Cried Wolf cried so often that no one was prepared when the wolf finally stood at the door.

Second, there is a fascination with the technical, which fuels the hysteria. The technical possibilities associated with uncontrolled fissile materials, the biotechnology revolution, and the Internet are truly terrible. But, fears of technical possibilities must be squared with the historical record—those acts of violence in which mass casualties were a primary goal are a very tiny proportion of the total set of terrorist acts. We must concern ourselves not just with the ability of terrorists to inflict mass casualties, but their will to do so as well.

This fascination with the technical points to motivations driving terrorists. It is also a topic that is at once elusive and fundamental to this work. I find it useful to distinguish between two basic sets of terrorists in terms of their motivations. One group is motivated primarily by the desire to extract a political concession from the state, and thus carefully calibrates the level of violence so as to attract attention to its cause without delegitimizing that cause in the eyes of perceived constituents and without invoking a strong counter reaction by the state. The other group is motivated by a desire to punish, coerce, collapse, and destroy, whether for purposes political, practical, or spiritual, and disregards the thresholds of pain and tolerance in the attacked societies—or specifically calculates them in order to exceed them. Of course, this type of motivation calls into question the very definition of terrorism, which is typically understood as being about generating fear to reap its political benefits.

The third factor is the difficulty of conducting and facilitating a public policy dialogue that helps rather than hurts. Terrorists, after all, pay attention to what the terrorism experts say and write. Advertising vulnerabilities isn't smart. But many of the most interested terrorists already have access to just about all of the technical information they could want. Ignorance of this topic lodges not so much among terrorists as among the public policy community. That ignorance is dangerous. It may inflame passions in the wake of some future event in a way that leads to draconian governmental responses that harm civil liberties, and, why not, personal security. It is incumbent upon any policy research community to frame the issues in ways that inform the choices that impact on the technical and political readiness of African as well as world communities for mass casualty terrorism.

The fourth factor is the assumption that because the problem of mass casualty terrorism seems to be new, we must be starting from scratch in policy. This is simply wrong. African states have been concerned with terrorism for many years, including to a limited but nonetheless important degree the problem of mass casualty terrorism. Old approaches were revamped by the recent Counterterrorism Act and Nunn-Lugar II. It must be asked today how present policy approaches can be amended and refined in light of recent progress in meeting new challenges and new experiences and understandings of the problem of transnational terrorism. How to sustain the political commitment to the policy agenda in such a way that recent initiatives are fully implemented must be considered. To be sure, a mass casualty terrorist event would provide the incentive to such full implementation. But that is a high-priced motivator. One should also understand that managing the consequences of such an attack involves a great deal more than simply cleaning up the mess—government's response will be widely watched as a measure of its capacity to respond efficiently and compassionately while also protecting African values and institutions, all while securing a just and definitive closure to the event.

To illustrate concerning the dispersion of energy, during preparations for operations in Afghanistan the United States patched together a threadbare and uneven consensus among the region's states. It certainly was not the kind of arrangement that helped these states peacefully work through their concerns and differences in the aftermath of a significant change in Afghanistan. In several cases consensus was forged through arm-twisting and promises of renewed access to military goods and assistance. These measures won acquiescence to U.S. military operations, but they did not contribute to stability in the aftermath of the overthrow of the Taliban.

Evidently, the expansion of war aims adversely affected the achievement of those goals that are most essential-destroying al Qaeda cells globally. Trying to achieve more, less was accomplished. The capacity to adapt and respond effectively to unforeseen developments both during and after a campaign diminished as the scope of that campaign was expanded to Iraq. This is partly because expansion taxes capabilities; it draws down reserves; and partly because expansion exacerbates the fog and friction of war. It also raises questions such as: which is that Islamic state to be attacked next by America? Such a question demands a special effort today aimed at building some bridges among specialist communities in research; to give better academic focus to the problem so that policy can be motivated by more than just fear; and to help calibrate the roles of weak African states and the international community in meeting the challenges of transnational mass terrorism.

The accelerating pace of political, technological, social and economic change in today's world, conventionally ascribed to the phenomenon of globalization is essentially changing the character of threats to national and international security. Uneven distribution of wealth and depletion of natural resources magnify the brutality and expand the scope of armed conflicts around the globe while the somewhat 'looser' nature of the globalizing post-bipolar world increases the risks arising from the proliferation of weapons of mass destruction or epidemics of infectious terror attacks. Violent conflict and economic hardship boost largely uncontrolled migration threatening social and political stability both in advanced and developing countries. Local security challenges can spread rapidly to acquire a regional or global reach. The international community is becoming increasingly concerned with 'human security' no longer acquiescing to discretionary rule within a country's borders. Hence, many types of security threats, such as civil wars, ethnic conflict or authoritarianism, now emerge as 'new global' challenges.

At the same time, the 'old global' security challenges, such as indiscriminate massive trade in arms, money laundering, drug trafficking and international terrorism, have grown out of previous proportion and also acquired global dimensions. Along with newly emerged threats, they are now being magnified by border transparency and the internationalization of finance.

The info-terrorist challenges in Africa today

These may best be represented in question form such as:

- How can weak African states and their national security establishments respond to the informational attacks of terrorists, when the terrorists hide behind a veil of digital anonymity?
- How much of information terrorism is a military concern and how much is within the jurisdiction of the continent's law enforcement agencies?
- How can we better discern what is a political crime, and what is a 'common' crime (e.g. motivated by greed) in the info-sphere?
- How can the national security establishment balance defending the National Information Infrastructure while being sensitive to civil 'cyber-liberties' and rights to privacy?
- How can a centralized, geographically focused national security establishment respond effectively to a digitally networked international enemy?

Indeed, information warfare, loosely defined, is targeting the information and information systems that comprise and support civilian and military infrastructures of an adversary. Information warfare runs deeper than attacks on tanks and troops: an information warfare campaign can target and disrupt the information and networks that support crucial day-to-day workings of civilian, commercial, and military systems, e.g., air traffic control, power grids, stock markets, international financial transactions, logistics controls, etc.

Information terrorism is an important subset of information warfare—perhaps more challenging to confront and respond to, because of the difficulty of determining the political agenda or sponsors of the perpetrators. Political terrorism is the systematic use of actual or threatened physical violence in the pursuit of a political objective, to create a general climate of public fear and destabilize a society, and thus influence the population or government policy. In a legal sense, information terrorism can be the intentional abuse of a digital information system, network, or component toward an end that supports or facilitates a terrorist campaign or action. In this case, the system abuse would not necessarily result in direct violence against humans, although it may still incite fear. Information terrorism is the nexus between criminal information system fraud or abuse, and the physical violence of terrorism.

Information technology offers new opportunities to terrorists. A terrorist organization can reap low-risk, highly visible payoffs by attacking information systems. In an effort to attract the attention of the public, political terrorists perpetrate their acts with the media at the forefront of their strategy: this strategy calculus is based on the assumption that access to the communication structure is directly related to power (Schmid and DeGraaf, 1982). Believers in this assumption might target digital information systems in pursuit of political goals.

As technology becomes more cost-effective to terrorists—that is, its availability and potential for disruptive effects rise while its financial and other costs go down—terrorists will become more technologically oriented in tactics and strategies. In 1977, terrorist expert Robert Kupperman, then Chief Scientist of the U.S. Arms Control and Disarmament Agency, recognized that increasing societal reliance upon technology changes the nature of the threat posed by terrorists:

> Commercial aircraft, natural gas pipelines, the electric power grid, offshore oil rigs, and computers storing government and corporate records are examples of sabotage-prone targets whose destruction would have derivative effects of far higher intensity than their primary losses would suggest . . . Thirty years ago terrorists could not have obtained extraordinary leverage. Today, however, the foci of communications, production, and distribution are relatively small in number and highly vulnerable (Kupperman, 1989, p. 26).

The criminal and subversive connotations of the term 'terrorist' have resulted in many acts of computer abuse being labeled 'information terrorism.' These acts have ranged from using personal information for extortion, to hacking into a network, to physical and/or electronic destruction of a digital information system. This is too simplistic a taxonomy for such a complex phenomenon.

Labeling every malicious use of a computer system as 'terrorism' serves only to exacerbate confusion and even panic among users and the general public, and frequently hinders prosecution and prevention by blurring the motivations behind the crime. Furthermore, political crimes have vastly different implications for national security and defense policy, than other 'common' crimes. Terrorism is a political crime: an attack on the legitimacy of a specific government, ideology, or policy. Hacking into a system to erase files out of sheer ego, or stealing information with the sole intent to blackmail, is nothing more than simple theft, fraud, or extortion, and certainly is not an attack upon the general legitimacy of the government. Policy and methodology to counter crime depends a great deal upon criminal motivations: thus, clearer and more concise definitions of 'information terrorism' are needed if it is to be addressed by national security policy. Attacks on the legitimacy of a government or its policies are not 'common' criminal acts. The quasi-criminal, quasi-military nature of terrorism blurs the distinction between crime and warfare. Distinctions between law enforcement and military duties become equally blurred (Hundley and Anderson, 1996), and can be clarified only through coherent policy dictating those duties, based upon a clear view of the nature of the enemy.

This claim derives from the notion that in political crimes, as opposed to crimes for ego or greed, the perpetrator and the beneficiary are usually not the same person, with more tenuous connections, and the intended long-term gains from the crime are usually abstract. Viewing this from a law enforcement perspective, it places primacy on the motivations of the act. However, viewed from a military perspective, it is the act itself, which merits focus. The reason is that it is the act itself, which wreaks the damage and poses the threat to national security. This is one of many facets in the argument surrounding the degree to which counterterrorism should be approached from a military vis-à-vis law enforcement perspective.

The National Information Infrastructure (NII), and Global Information Infrastructure (GII) support financial, commercial and military information transfers for consumers, businesses, and countries. Considering the presence of computers in modern society, it is not surprising that terrorists have occasionally targeted computer systems in the past. A 'PLO' virus was developed at Hebrew University in Israel; in Japan, groups have attacked the computerized control systems for commuter trains, paralyzing major cities for hours; the Italian Red Brigade's manifesto specified the destruction of computer systems and installations as an objective for 'striking at the heart of the state' (Fites, Johnson and Kratz, 1993, p. 63). More recently, Sinn Fein supporters working out of the University of Texas, Austin, posted sensitive details about British army intelligence installations, military bases, and police stations in Northern Ireland on the Internet (CNN, 1996). Terrorism is a rapidly evolving and responsive phenomenon. Terrorist technology and tactics are sensitive to their target political cultures, and have progressed at a rate commensurate with dominant military, commercial, and social technologies.

In a third-wave (Toffler, 1980) society, there are two general methods in which a terrorist might employ an information terrorist attack: (1) when information technology is a target, and/or (2) when IT is the tool of a larger operation. The first method implies a terrorist would target an information system for sabotage, either electronic or physical, thus destroying or disrupting the information system itself and any information infrastructure (e.g., power, communications) dependent upon the targeted technology. The second method implies a terrorist would manipulate and exploit an information system, altering or stealing data, or forcing the system to perform a function for which it was not meant such as spoofing air traffic control. It is possible that the IRA were specifically targeting the Square Mile of London on a weekend to minimize casualties but maximize damage to a financial center of Western Europe. African countries have always faced a dilemma in combating anti-regime terrorism, while balancing civil liberty with civil security. Combating information terrorism encounters these common dilemmas as well as problems specific to the global character of information technology.

Technology and terrorism

The steady increase in the destructive capacity of small terrorist groups and individuals is driven largely by three technological advances: more powerful weapons, the dramatic progress in communications and information processing, and more abundant opportunities to divert non-weapon technologies to destructive uses.

Consider first the advances in weapons technology. Over the last century, progress in materials engineering, the chemistry of explosives, and miniaturization of electronics has brought steady improvement in all key weapons characteristics, including accuracy, disruptive and destructive power, range, portability, ruggedness, ease-of-use, and affordability. Improvements in light weapons are particularly relevant to trends in terrorism and violence by small groups, where the devices of choice include rocket-propelled grenade launchers, machine guns, light mortars, land mines, and cheap assault rifles such as the famed AK-47. The effects of improvements in these weapons are particularly noticeable in developing countries. A few decades ago, a small band of terrorists or insurgents attacking a rural village might have used bolt-action rifles, which take precious time to reload. Today, cheap assault rifles multiply the possible casualties resulting from such an attack. As technological change makes it easier to kill, societies are more likely to become locked into perpetual cycles of attack and counterattack that render any normal trajectory of political and economic development impossible.

Meanwhile, new communications technologies—from satellite phones to the Internet—allow violent groups to marshal resources and coordinate activities around the planet. Transnational terrorist organizations can use the Internet to share information on weapons and recruiting tactics, arrange surreptitious fund transfers across borders, and plan attacks. These new technologies can also dramatically enhance the reach and power of age-old procedures. Take the ancient *hawala* system of moving money between countries, widely used in Middle Eastern and Asian societies. The system, which relies on brokers linked together by clan-based networks of trust, has become faster and more effective through the use of the Internet.

Information-processing technologies have also boosted the power of terrorists by allowing them to hide or encrypt their messages. The power of a modern laptop computer today is comparable to the computational power available in the entire U.S. Defense Department in the mid-1960s. Terrorists can use this power to run widely available state-of-the-art encryption software. Sometimes less advanced computer technologies are just as effective. For instance, individuals can use a method called steganography (hidden writing) to embed messages into digital photographs or music clips. Posted on publicly available Web sites, the photos or clips are downloaded by collaborators as necessary. At latest count, 140 easy-to-use steganography tools are available on the Internet. Many other off-the-shelf technologies—such as 'spread-spectrum' radios that randomly switch their broadcasting and receiving signals—allow terrorists to obscure their messages and make themselves invisible.

The Web also provides access to critical information. The September 11 terrorists could have found there all the details they needed about the floor plans and design characteristics of the World Trade Center and about how demolition experts use progressive collapse to destroy large buildings. The Web also makes available sets of instructions—or 'technical ingenuity'—needed to combine readily available materials in destructive ways. Practically anything an extremist wants to know about kidnapping, bomb making, and assassination is now available online. One somewhat facetious example: It is possible to convert everyday materials into potentially destructive devices like the 'potato cannon.' With a barrel and combustion chamber fashioned from common plastic pipe, and with propane as an explosive propellant, a well-made cannon can hurl a homely spud hundreds of meters—or throw chaff onto electrical substations. A quick search of the Web reveals dozens of sites giving instructions on how to make one.

Finally, modern, high-tech societies are filled with supercharged devices packed with energy, combustibles, and poisons, giving terrorists ample opportunities to divert such non-weapon technologies to destructive ends. To cause horrendous damage, all terrorists must do is figure out how to release this power and let it run wild or, as they did on September 11, take control of this power and retarget it. Indeed, the assaults on New York City and the Pentagon were not low-tech affairs, as is often argued. True, the terrorists used simple box cutters to hijack the planes, but the box cutters were no more than the 'keys' that allowed the terrorists to convert a high-tech means of transport into a high-tech weapon of mass destruction. Once the hijackers had used these keys to access and turn on their weapon, they were able to deliver a kiloton of explosive power into the World Trade Center with deadly accuracy.

Which way?

Instances of turmoil are the local and particular manifestations of a common crisis of individual and group identity in the context of deepening social inequality and fragmentation in Africa. The combined effects of weakened state administrative and policy apparatuses, the current cessation of bipolar ideological competition and the accelerating and unaccountable processes known as globalization have called into question some of the more fundamental and familiar premises upon which our lives and our sense of security are based. Prominent among these is the nation-state project. Globalization and the expansion of economic scale have implications not only for state capacity and legitimacy, but also for society at large as various groups and individuals seek to redefine themselves in a rapidly changing domestic and individual environment. It is scarcely surprising when, in such circumstances, other certainties suddenly become negotiable.

What could possibly replace or supplement the weak and/or failing state in Africa? It must be evident that one of the essential weaknesses of the nation-state project on the African continent was the massive increase in political scale, which it implied. Abstract ideas of statehood were expected to do service in place of a moral universe of values based on assumptions about kinship and shared origins, in which the sacred and profane were inextricably linked. This, rather than the artificial boundaries per se, lies at the heart of the problem. It certainly seems evident that such feelings of belonging as most African peoples have, remain rooted in their local communities with their familiar bases of kinship and allegiance. No parallel community has yet been created at national level.

Faced with this situation, many citizens have sought solutions to the problem of personal security outside the state arena. Of the survival strategies adopted by Africans in their confrontation with the harsh realities of their condition, one of the more common is 'avoiding the state.' This strategy has obvious implications for the viability of the state project, politically as well as economically. It also brings us to consider whether the Western belief of creating room for and strengthening African civil society will have the expected consequences: that this will help to promote the consolidation of democratic structures that reinforce and legitimize the modern state. This is a matter for debate, and the argument about the future of the state in Africa has to take cognizance of the emergence of different and particularistic forms of civil society in Africa, sometimes as alternatives to, and sometimes as adjuncts of the state and its owners.

The term 'civil society' has only recently been extended in the literature on Africa to include ethnic associations, which, with other associations of similar type, have important political functions beyond the surveillance of state agencies. In the Western political science canon, the concept 'civil society' has generally implied the opening of opportunities for individual freedom. But one should be careful not to misapply Western political constructs to African circumstances. In Western history, the public realm has been shared between the state, other political organizations and civil society, all of which were assumed to have some concern for individual liberty, which simply is not the African historical experience. The pre-colonial African state rarely felt the need to justify its existence in terms of meeting the needs of individuals. Nor did the colonial state often include the security and welfare needs of ordinary Africans in its considerations. As Peter Ekeh has argued, this heritage has been passed on to the post-colonial state and, as a consequence, the ordinary individual has sought to attain his security and welfare needs in ways and idioms different from those with which we are familiar in Western political thought (Ekeh, 1992, pp. 187–192; Lock, 1999, pp. 20–31). As has been suggested above, the principal structures with which the individual has sought alliance are kinship organizations, which have expanded and developed along a path quite distinct from the European experience.

The avenues of escape open to African publics are not likely to recommend themselves to those who earn their living in the wealthier parts of the economy. Certainly, there will be interaction between the formal and informal, in economics as in politics, and in certain circumstances various parties may seek to benefit from a condition of 'controlled chaos,' what is becoming known as the political economy of disorder. Nevertheless, a modicum of order and predictability are demanded by those who seek to hold on to the limp reins of state power, and those who seek to take advantage of their claims to sovereign status in order to exploit such parts of the national resource base as may be secured.

The reduction in global ideological conflict has reduced the political and military incentives for outside powers to intervene on the continent; and contrary to some expectations, an Africa omitted from the calculations of external rivals has not become a more peaceful place. That local disputes are now less globalized, means that outside powers have less influence on the conduct, termination and outcome of these conflicts. Local rivalries and antagonisms are given freer rein, being more remote from world centers of power and insignificant in terms of the global system. African states can no longer rely on outside assistance to end local wars that are no threat to vital foreign interests.

External non-state actors have stepped into the void left by the international community, sometimes as proxies, sometimes as independent agents, able by virtue of their wealth and command of expertise to influence events to their local and often short-term advantage. It is for all the world as if Africa has returned to the 1880s, and the age of the chartered companies, marking out their enclaves in an otherwise disorderly environment. Today's chartered companies or non-state actors in Africa are apparently networked terrorism.

Most scholars are relative newcomers to the topic of mass terrorism and transnational non-state actors. Over the last couple of years, and especially after the U.S. Embassy attacks in Africa, many scholars have worked into the topic. They have approached it from the particular perspective of terrorist use of chemical and biological weapons. There is no better example than this topic of how much work any community of scholars, analysts, and policy makers have to do to catch up with a world changing more rapidly than the current concept (globalization) of it.

Terrorism thrives on myths. Many deceptive and dangerous delusions have been in the air since September 11. These include the myths that:

(1) terrorists can not really be freedom fighters struggling to establish their own state and peaceful relations with their neighbors; (2) Islam, a faith that fostered peace and a great civilization in the past, cannot be held responsible for providing a spawning ground for terror today; (3) terrorism is not the last resort of the poor, the dispossessed, and the desperate peoples of the Middle East; (4) Arab states with stable governments and viable economies can control the rising tide of Islamic militancy within their borders; and (5) the nations of the West, especially the United States, are not to blame for the authoritarian, corrupt, and backward status of the states of the Middle East. We need to dispel the myths and look reality in the eye. And the best and lasting solution to terrorism can only come through the application of the careful hand of justice rather than the clumsy fist of a crusade. We need a global coalition for freedom and justice and not merely a global alliance against terrorism.

What should therefore be done to lessen the risk of networked or complex terrorism in Africa? Today's Africa provides highly favorable conditions for terrorist recruitment and activity. There is hyperinflation, high unemployment, massive foreign debt, widespread poverty, drug overlords, proliferation of arms, and government corruption. The numbers of those frustrated by these conditions are constantly on the increase, and so is their awareness of the life-style of the better-off and the vulnerability of the better-off. Among the better-off themselves are bored young people looking for the kicks that violence can provide, and thus for causes that legitimize violence. These are not in short supply. A wide variety of people feel starved for attention, and one surefire way of attracting instantaneous worldwide attention through television is to slaughter a considerable number of human beings, in a spectacular fashion, in the name of a cause.

The causes themselves that may or hardly constitute the sole motivation of the terrorists are not irrelevant. The cause legitimizes the act of terror in the terrorist's own eyes and in those of others belonging to his nation, faith, or culture. Certain cultures and subcultures, homes of frustrated causes, are destined breeding grounds for terrorism. The Islamic culture is the most notable example. That culture's view of its own rightful position in the world is profoundly at variance with the actual order of the contemporary world. It is God's will that the House of Islam should triumph over the House of War (the non-Moslem world), and not just by spiritual means. 'Islam Means Victory' is a slogan of the Iranian fundamentalists in the Gulf War. To strike a blow against the House of War is meritorious; consequently, there is widespread support for activities condemned in the West as terrorist. Israel is one main target for these activities, but the activities would not be likely to cease even if Israel came to an end. The Great Satan in the eyes of Ayatollah Khomeini—and the millions for whom he speaks—is not Israel but the United States. The defeat of Israel would, in those eyes, be no more than a portent of the impending defeat of the Great Satan. What the West calls terrorism should then be multiplied rather than abandoned.

The wellsprings of terrorism are widespread and deep. The interaction between modern communications systems and archaic fanaticism (and other sources of resentment and ambition) is likely to continue to stimulate terrorist activity. In these conditions, talk about extirpating terrorism—and unilateral exploits backing such talk—are likely to be counterproductive. They present terrorists with a 'victory,' merely by the fact of being able to continue their activity. Similarly, solemn promises never to negotiate with terrorists can play into the hands of terrorists. Terrorists holding hostages can force a democratic government to negotiate. If the democratic government then pretends that no negotiation took place, this helps the credibility of the terrorists, not that of the democratic government. It is not possible to extirpate terrorism from the face of the globe. But it should be possible to reduce the incidence and effectiveness of terrorism, through coordinated international action, of which Africa is an integral element in the anti-terrorist struggle.

In order to prosecute the war against terrorism in Africa successfully one must recognize the fact that those who subscribe to militant Islam would like to conflate the fight for change in their parts of the world with the use of political violence to accomplish their goals. Manipulating Islamic texts on social justice and banking heavily on the need to resort to jihadic means to settle scores with the ruling elites of their societies, these system challengers of the Muslim African states could be influenced by forces in the Middle East. Yet, because the African Muslim states are not homogeneous and their conditions are not identical, it would be dangerous and unwise to come up with one prescription.

However, one should point out the fact that the cannon fodder for any terrorist acts are most likely going to be young Africans who are terribly indoctrinated about the poor state of Islam and Muslims in the world and the need to correct such inequities in the world system. Although most African states, including predominantly Muslim countries, have majorities of young people, the chances for successful recruitment of sizable African armies for these purveyors of terrorism are limited. This is largely due to the degree of Western cultural penetration in most of the sub-Saharan African states and the growing fascination with creature comforts even when they do not have any means to realize their dreams of owning things for the West. Yet, this source of strength on our part could turn against us if the potential sources of dissatisfaction are not addressed through an effective and meaningful aid program. Indeed, one irony of this war against global terrorism is the fact that what we failed to do for African development during the Cold War must now be done with deliberate speed if we are to curb the forces of terrorism and lay the foundations for a strong African link in the chain against global terrorism.

This idea of strengthening the African link in the chain against global terrorism deserves our attention for four important reasons. First, Africa is the weakest political territory to penetrate international terrorists. The weakness of Africa lies in two factors. One is the weak nature of the African state, and the other is the corrupt manner of the African political class. A combination of these two factors makes this vast continent an explosive Pandora's box. The United States has worldwide interests and Africa is a major part of that global strategic chain. For this and other related reasons it certainly makes political sense for U.S. policy makers to pay greater attention to Africa. The United States may often times play political Gulliver to the African Lilliputs; but in a world that is increasingly becoming dangerous and deadly, it would be politically prudent to strengthen materially and strategically the weakest links to your chain of self protection. Greater USAID involvement in the development process in Africa could make a big difference.

Secondly, the U.S. government must come to the realization that the war on global terrorism can only be won first in the minds and hearts of the African Muslims and then in the global battlefields. Here is where the democratic hand of the United States becomes a potential source of strength in the war against the terrorists. By supporting and strengthening the second wave of democratization in the African continent, U.S. leaders at all levels of government could make African governments, not only materially effective in dealing with the knotty problems of economic and social development, but they could also help in the planting of the seeds of democratic governance in many parts of Africa. As in the Middle East, where the Cold War policies of the United States helped maintain many an autocratic regime, in many African states where Muslims live either as minorities or majorities, systems of government have not always been democratic. For this and other related reasons it makes good political sense for the U.S. government to invest heavily in the democratic enterprise. Indeed, in the war against terrorism, the democratic card pays bigger dividends.

The third factor in this war against terrorism is for the U.S. government to initiate a dialogue between African Muslims and the American people. By drawing upon its own cultural and moral resources in the formulation and development of programs linking Americans and Africans, especially Muslim Africans, the United States could help set the stage for 'detalibization' of many African *madrassas* (Qura'nic schools). This is particularly so since in places like northern Nigeria the spirit of militant Islam has occasionally over the last thirty years taken the lives of thousands of people in interreligious strife and violence. This state of affairs has developed in that part of the African continent, largely because the lower classes (the *talakwawa*) have found in militant Islam avenues of self-expression. This is to say, these lower classes have vented their rage and anger through destructive actions against state and private property. Their emotional fragility and their vulnerability to the sloganeering of 'pie in the sky' rhetoric of Islamic militants, could ignite the firs of sectarianism and inter-religious warfare.

By supporting scholars of Islam who show evidence of reform and modernization, the United States could help the advancement of such points of view through exchanges between American Muslim centers of learning and the African Muslim centers of learning. This is one way of nipping in the bud any attempts at subversion and recruitment of African Muslim youth. The U.S. government can only inoculate these young people from the promises and offers of the likes of Osama bin Laden when the bread and butter issues are addressed in their home countries. This is as true in Northern Nigeria, as in other parts of Western and Eastern Africa.

The fourth factor in this war on global terrorism in Africa lies in the curriculum development of the African states. Even though African school textbooks have not generally fostered any sense of religious bigotry, there is still the greater need to encourage the cultivation of tolerance in the school system. Here the interfaith experiences of many urban areas of the United States must begin to be shared abroad. American missionaries abroad who have not taken pain to indulge in the art of inter-religious dialogue at home before their pointing abroad may have to explore this unfamiliar territory in their own interest and in the long-term interest of their church and state. Similarly, the U.S. government must begin to study carefully how the American Muslim communities and their non-governmental organizations could contribute positively to the prosecution of this war against global terrorism through the dissemination of correct and reliable information about the American experience and the Muslims stake in it. By encouraging such acts of patriotism among American

Muslims, the U.S. authorities can make their Muslim minorities equal partners in the promotion of the American experiment abroad. There is so little to lose and so much to gain.

The fifth and last factor in this war could be the rigorous implementation of the following measures: (1) police infiltration of terrorist cartels in order to secure the arrest of its members; (2) reduction of prison sentences for repentant terrorists who supply vital information about the plans, activities and hideouts for terrorists; (3) police concentration on limited and manageable terrorist targets such as airports, border crossings and harbors; (4) adequate domestic and international legislation permitting the monitoring of suspected phone and internet communications networks; (5) cooperation among nations in intelligence sharing concerning terrorist suspects; and (6) control of arms and drug trafficking.

References

Arendt, H. (1970), *On Violence*, Harvest, Harcourt Brace & Company: New York.

Ekeh, P. P. (1992), 'The Constitution of Civil Society in African History and Politics', in Caron, B., Gboyega, A. and Osaghae, E. E. (eds.), *Proceedings of the Symposium on Democratic Transition in Africa*, Center for Research, Documentation and University Exchange: Ibadan, Nigeria.

Fites, P., Johnson, P. and Kratz, M. (1992), *The Computer Virus Crisis*, Van Nostrand Reinhold: New York.

Hundley, R. and Anderson, R. (1996), 'Security in Cyberspace: An Emerging Challenge for Society', Retrieved April 5, 1996 from http://www.rand.org/publications/RRR/RRR.fall95.cyber/wild.html.

Kupperman, R. (1989), 'Facing Tomorrow's Terrorist Incident Today', in Wardlaw, G. (ed.), *Political Terrorism*, Cambridge University Press: Cambridge.

Lock, P. (1999), 'Africa, Military Downsizing and the Growth in the Security Industry', in Cilliers, J. and Mason, P. (eds.), *Peace, Profit or Plunder? The Privatization of Security in War-torn African Societies*, Institute for Security Studies: Pretoria.

Murdock, L. (2001), ''Bin Laden "Funded Christian Haters"', *Sydney Morning Herald*, September 28.

Schmid, A. P. and DeGraaf, J. F. A. (1982), *Violence as Communication: Insurgent Terrorism and the Western News Media*, Sage: Beverly Hills, CA.

Toffler, A. (1980), *The Third Wave*, William Morrow and Company, Inc.: New York.

Index

Printed in the United States
by Baker & Taylor Publisher Services